C000295783

QUALITATIVE SECONDARY RESEARCH

Sara Miller McCune founded SAGE Publishing in 1965 to support the dissemination of usable knowledge and educate a global community. SAGE publishes more than 1000 journals and over 800 new books each year, spanning a wide range of subject areas. Our growing selection of library products includes archives, data, case studies and video. SAGE remains majority owned by our founder and after her lifetime will become owned by a charitable trust that secures the company's continued independence.

Los Angeles | London | New Delhi | Singapore | Washington DC | Melbourne

QUALITATIVE SECONDARY RESEARCH

A Step-By-Step Guide

CLAIRE LARGAN
THERESA MORRIS

Los Angeles | London | New Delhi
Singapore | Washington DC | Melbourne

Los Angeles | London | New Delhi
Singapore | Washington DC | Melbourne

SAGE Publications Ltd
1 Oliver's Yard
55 City Road
London EC1Y 1SP

SAGE Publications Inc.
2455 Teller Road
Thousand Oaks, California 91320

SAGE Publications India Pvt Ltd
B 1/I 1 Mohan Cooperative Industrial Area
Mathura Road
New Delhi 110 044

SAGE Publications Asia-Pacific Pte Ltd
3 Church Street
#10-04 Samsung Hub
Singapore 049483

Editor: Jai Seaman
Editorial assistant: Charlotte Bush
Production editor: Rachel Burrows
Copyeditor: Jill Birch
Proofreader: Brian McDowell
Marketing manager: Susheel Gokarakonda
Cover design: Sheila Tong
Typeset by: C&M Digitals (P) Ltd, Chennai, India
Printed and bound by CPI Group (UK) Ltd,
Croydon, CR0 4YY

© Claire Largan and Theresa M. Morris 2019

First published 2019

Apart from any fair dealing for the purposes of research or
private study, or criticism or review, as permitted under the
Copyright, Designs and Patents Act, 1988, this publication
may be reproduced, stored or transmitted in any form, or by
any means, only with the prior permission in writing of the
publishers, or in the case of reprographic reproduction, in
accordance with the terms of licences issued by the Copyright
Licensing Agency. Enquiries concerning reproduction outside
those terms should be sent to the publishers.

Library of Congress Control Number: 2018958139

British Library Cataloguing in Publication data

A catalogue record for this book is available from
the British Library

ISBN 978-1-5264-1097-9
ISBN 978-1-5264-1098-6 (pbk)

At SAGE we take sustainability seriously. Most of our products are printed in the UK using responsibly sourced
papers and boards. When we print overseas we ensure sustainable papers are used as measured by the PREPS
grading system. We undertake an annual audit to monitor our sustainability.

CONTENTS

List of Figures and Tables   ix
About the Authors   xiv

Introduction   1

1   Introducing Qualitative Secondary Research   13
What is qualitative secondary research?   14
Considering the benefits of qualitative secondary research   16
What types of data can I use?   18
Classifying data   19
Where will I find my data?   21
What type of question will I ask?   22
How will I manage my data?   23
How will I know the quality of my data?   23
What will my research look like?   24
What happens if I want to use numbers?   26
Why should I do qualitative secondary research?   27
How do I know if qualitative secondary research is for me?   32

2   Preparing for Qualitative Secondary Research   35
Why do you want to study this topic?   36
Beginning your research   37
Reading to support your research   41
Developing skills of critical appraisal   44
Creating research questions, aims and objectives   45
Creating a research proposal   51
The development of skills and attitudes   52
Developing a research 'mindset'   53
Being 'CLEAR'   54

3 The Role of Theory in Qualitative Secondary Research 57
Why do you need to know about theory? 58
Understanding research positions 60
Understanding theory and concepts 63
Your influence on your research 71
Where do I write about theory and concepts in my study? 73

4 Designing Qualitative Secondary Research 77
What is a qualitative secondary research design? 78
Designing your qualitative secondary research 79
Exploring criteria for research quality 89
How to write up your methodology 94
What happens when things go wrong? 96

5 Ethics in Qualitative Secondary Research 99
Why do I need to think about ethics? 100
What are the main ethical principles? 101
Ethics committees 113
Ethical and legal access to data 114
Being an ethical qualitative secondary researcher 116
Ethics checklist 117

6 Exploring Documents as Data 121
What are qualitative data? 122
Making important decisions about data 123
Ethical approaches to data 124
Exploring documents as sources of data 125
Deciding how to use documents as sources of data 139
Selecting methods of analysis 140
Understanding your influence on data selection 141

7 Locating your Data 144
What type of data am I searching for? 145
Ethical searching 146
How do I find data? 147
Where do I find data? 154
Accessing quantitative data 162

8 Securing Quality over Quantity 165
Why do I need to reduce my data? 166
How do I achieve data quality? 167
Understanding the quality of your data 168

Knowing your data   170
What are sampling strategies?   178
Seeking research quality   185

 9 **Constructing a Literature Review**   188
What is a literature review?   189
Conducting your literature review   190
Writing your literature review   197
A checklist for completing your review   208

10 **Managing your Data**   211
What is data management?   212
Generating a data management plan   213
Managing the collection of bibliographic data   217
Strategies for organising your data   219
Understanding data ownership   220
Thinking about data security   226
Planning your data disposal   228

11 **Analysing Data**   231
Why do I need to analyse my data?   232
Analysing data using constant comparison   233
Analysing data using framework analysis   243
Understanding theory first approaches   246
Using computers to analyse data   247
Making an interpretation   248
Exploring different methods of analysis   248
Data analysis and research rigour   252
Advice and guidance for analysing your data   252

12 **Working with Numbers**   256
Why do I need numbers when working with qualitative data?   257
How do I begin to create meaning from numbers?   258
How can statistics create meaning?   260
Descriptive statistics   263
How do I use descriptive statistics in my research?   270

13 **Presenting your Findings and Forming Conclusions**   277
What happens after your analysis?   278
What is a findings section?   278
Writing your findings section   281
Communicating your findings effectively   289

Data display and visualisation   291
Writing your conclusion   295
Writing your recommendations   296
Final considerations   297

14 Being a Qualitative Secondary Researcher   301
What makes a 'good' qualitative secondary researcher?   302
Why should I reflect on my research project?   302
Using a completion checklist   306
What have I learnt as a qualitative secondary researcher?   312
How can I disseminate my research?   314

Glossary   319
References   328
Index   344

LIST OF FIGURES AND TABLES

FIGURES

1.1	Difference between primary and secondary research	15
1.2	Reasons for undertaking qualitative secondary research	17
1.3	Examples of sources of data	18
1.4	Classifying sources of data	20
1.5	Sorting your sources of data	21
1.6	Understanding the context of data construction	23
1.7	Components of qualitative secondary research	25
1.8	A decision table	32
2.1	Creating your research rationale	36
2.2	Question mapping	37
2.3	Mind mapping	38
2.4	Concept mapping	39
2.5	Using a research diary as a daily planner	41
2.6	A reading loop	42
2.7	Questioning your sources	43
2.8	Knowing your research direction	45
2.9	Different approaches to stating your research problem	46
2.10	LASER acronym	47
2.11	Ensuring your question is feasible, relevant and within your capabilities	48
2.12	Examples of research aims	48
2.13	Examples of research objectives	49
2.14	Potential components of a proposal for qualitative secondary research	51
2.15	Areas of skill development	53
2.16	CLEAR research skills	54
3.1	Influences on your research	58
3.2	Deconstructing theory	59
3.3	Defining ontology and epistemology	60

3.4   Research paradigms   61
3.5   The intersecting influence of ontology, epistemology and methodology   62
3.6   An example of a conceptual framework   64
3.7   Examples of theoretical perspectives   67
3.8   Examples of middle level theories   68
3.9   The role of theory and analysis   70
3.10 Understanding forms of bias in qualitative secondary research   73

4.1   Key components of a qualitative secondary research methodology   78
4.2   Research ingredients and relevant book chapters   79
4.3   The influence of theory on your research   80
4.4   Three research strategies   82
4.5   A single research strategy   83
4.6   A combined research strategy   84
4.7   A multiple research strategy   86
4 8   Examples of possible approaches to data analysis   88
4.9   Strategies to support research quality (adapted from Lincoln & Guba 1985)   90
4.10 A checklist for reviewing your methodology   95
4.11 Considerations when writing up your methodology   96

5.1   Overview of ethics in qualitative secondary research   100
5.2   Basic ethical considerations   101
5.3   Weighing up risk against benefit within research   103
5.4   Types of sensitive and personal data   103
5.5   Direct and indirect identifiers   104
5.6   Data privacy checklist   105
5.7   Being an ethical researcher   117
5.8   Ethics checklist   118

6.1   Examples of qualitative data   122
6.2   Exploring the function of your sources of data   123
6.3   Examples of popular culture sources of data   129
6.4   Examples of strategies designed to mislead   132
6.5   Questions to ask of web-based news providers   132
6.6   Weighing up the benefits of using visual sources as data   137
6.7   Visual data and artefact checklist   138

7.1   Different search pathways   145
7.2   Four principles of quality (Scott 1990)   146
7.3   Generating useful keywords   148
7.4   Examples of field settings   149
7.5   Tips for conducting online searches   151
7.6   Examples of domain names and associated organisations   151
7.7   Criteria to assess website quality   152

7.8   Examples of basic search precautions   154
7.9   Categorising documents as data   155

8.1   Reducing your data   167
8.2   Aspects of data quality (adapted from Wang and Strong 1996)   168
8.3   CARS checklist   173
8.4   Visual data and artefact checklist   174
8.5   Checklist adapted from Scott (1990)   175
8.6   Knowing the role of your data   177
8.7   An illustration of a population and sample frame   178
8.8   Main categories of sampling   179
8.9   An example of a random number table   180
8.10 Examples of types of probability (randomised)
      sampling techniques   182
8.11 Purposeful sampling strategies   182

9.1   Knowing what a literature is NOT   189
9.2   Using questions to begin your literature review   191
9.3   An example of a literature matrix template   191
9.4   Using sources as data in your qualitative secondary research   192
9.5   Classifying sources of data for your literature review   194
9.6   Basic components for establishing data quality   195
9.7   Showcasing your skills in your literature review   196
9.8   Key attributes of a well-written literature review   197
9.9   Organisational structures for writing your review   198
9.10 Constructing your review   199
9.11 A synthesis matrix of research exploring mature women
      entering higher education   201
9.12 The relationship between critical reading and critical writing   202
9.13 Signposting arguments using key words   205
9.14 Verb strengths   206
9.15 A checklist for completing your literature review   209

10.1 A definition of data management   212
10.2 The benefits of effective data management   213
10.3 The role of a data management plan   214
10.4 Data management plan considerations   215
10.5 Generating a data management plan: questions and prompts
      to aid completion   216
10.6 Examples of data storage   219
10.7 Questions to ask about your data   221
10.8 File and tracking strategies   223
10.9 Causes of data loss   224

10.10 Data security tips   227
10.11 Erasing data   228

11.1   Different approaches to the use of theory   232
11.2   Immersing yourself in your data   234
11.3   Examples of events, instances or behaviour that can be identified
       in your document   236
11.4   Important coding advice   237
11.5   An example of a coding table   240
11.6   Tips for successful coding   241
11.7   A hierarchy tree   242
11.8   A findings matrix   243
11.9   An overview of thematic or framework analysis   244
11.10 Creating an index table   244
11.11 Recording tagged or indexed data   245
11.12 Creating main themes   245
11.13 Adapted from Fairclough's Three-dimensional model of discourse (1989)   249
11.14 Layers of meaning when analysing images   251
11.15 A checklist for analysis   254

12.1   Identifying quantitative and qualitative data   258
12.2   Outlining common examples of quantitative data   258
12.3   Questions to ask about your data   259
12.4   The role of statistics   261
12.5   Defining statistical approaches   261
12.6   Defining meta-analysis   262
12.7   Statistical measures within descriptive statistics   263
12.8   Measures of central tendency   265
12.9   Calculating the average percentage   266
12.10 Frequency distribution table 1   267
12.11 Frequency distribution table 2   268
12.12 Working with Excel   269
12.13 An example of a normal distribution graph   270
12.14 Five steps to descriptive statistical analysis   270
12.15 Questioning your data   272
12.16 Laptop questionnaire responses   273
12.17 Laptop questionnaire responses by category frequency   274
12.18 Frequency bar chart of laptop comments by category   274

13.1   What to include in your findings section   279
13.2   Key factors to consider when selecting your key findings for discussion 280
13.3   A justification matrix   281
13.4   Three ways to present your findings, analysis and discussion   282

13.5	Asking questions of your findings (based on Patton 2002)	285
13.6	Justifying your research findings	286
13.7	Evaluating research findings	288
13:8	Comparing effective and ineffective discussions of findings	289
13.9	Using verbs to support your discussion	290
13.10	Defining the benefits of effective visual display	293
13.11	Word chart	293
13.12	Visual display of an example of qualitative secondary research exploring social housing policy in the UK	294
13.13	Presenting findings as a list to begin a discussion	294
13.14	Tips for using an appendix	295
13.15	The benefits of identifying your research limitations	296
13.16	Creating recommendations	297
13.17	A checklist to support the presentation of your findings	298
14.1	Reflecting on your research process	303
14.2	Checklist for your research project completion	306
14.3	TAPE: exploring the skills and attitudes you may develop from your research	309
14.4	Disseminating your research findings	314
14.5	Examples of Blogs	315
14.6	What will you do next?	317

TABLE

8.1	Inclusion/exclusion criteria applied	176

ABOUT THE AUTHORS

Dr Claire Largan, BEd, MA, PhD, is an Independent Consultant specialising in research on education policy and practice.

Claire's career embraces UK and international contexts with its basis firmly within the realm of education, learning, teaching and research. Formerly a lecturer in education at University College Birmingham, Claire is now an independent consultant working within the field of education policy and practice.

She began her career as an early years and primary school teacher in the UK before gaining significant international experience teaching overseas in schools in Dubai and Taiwan and on English programmes offered by the British Council in Dubai. As an experienced lecturer, she has developed, designed and worked on a range of undergraduate and postgraduate programmes and been an external examiner for well-known UK institutions.

With over ten years' experience of teaching research methods at undergraduate and postgraduate levels, Claire has supported students both in UK and international contexts, specialising in working with students undertaking secondary research projects. Her own specialised research expertise lies in the use of visual methods of data collection and in 2016 she was awarded her PhD by the University of Birmingham where she also received a Postgraduate Diploma in Research in Education.

Her substantial experience of working with students from diverse educational, linguistic and cultural backgrounds led her to co-write this research book aiming to demystify secondary research processes and practice and do this in an academic, informative, accessible and student-focused way.

Dr Theresa M. Morris, BSc, MA, PhD is Assistant Director of Teaching and Learning Enhancement at University College Birmingham.

Theresa's teaching career has encompassed secondary school, sixth form colleges and further and higher education institutions. Theresa is currently an Assistant Director of Teaching and Learning Enhancement at University College Birmingham. Since 2003, she has designed, delivered and managed both degree and postgraduate degree level programmes in teaching and learning. This has culminated in leading the UCB Post Graduate teacher-training programme in vocational studies.

Theresa is a UCB lead teacher on undergraduate and postgraduate research modules delivered on UCB programmes across the world. Theresa's teaching specialisms include research design, methods and data analysis. Teaching a wide variety of national and international students, she also supervises undergraduate and postgraduate dissertations from across a range of varied vocational disciplines.

Theresa has always maintained a professional and personal interest in research. The University of Birmingham's School of Education awarded Theresa her PhD in 2010.

As well as having considerable national and international external examining and educational advisory experience, in 2014, Theresa was awarded the status of Senior Fellow from Advanced HE (previously the Higher Educational Academy) in recognition of her commitment to enhancing the student learning experience.

Theresa's extensive andragogical and educational quality assurance experiences have made clear to her the need for research textbooks to be written in a clear, accessible and user-friendly manner. She passionately believes that demystifying research is not 'dumbing it down', but empowering wider access.

INTRODUCTION

This book was written in response to the rising numbers of students, who for a range of reasons, were opting to conduct secondary research but finding it challenging to find a book that guided them through the secondary research process. Whilst, there are many excellent texts currently available that focus on the reuse of existing research data, this is often from a quantitative perspective. For those students who want to use a range of innovative, exciting and non-numerical data, guidance in the use of qualitative secondary research process is extremely hard to find; therefore, we decided to write our own and deliver the practical advice and guidance required.

As well as trying to fill what we feel is a sizeable gap in the research field, we also provide a grounded and practical approach to the research process; one that steps away from discussing research as mystical and obscure and moves toward seeing the research process as vibrant and extremely relevant to the way the world in the 21st century can be explored and understood. This is evident in the practical approaches to qualitative secondary research we reflect in all of the chapters presented.

The book is written in a style that is both informative and accessible, with a vast array of figures, exemplars and samples to underpin the concepts and processes we explore. This highly visual approach underpins the goal of this book which is to enhance both your research skills and your level of confidence in conducting a robust piece of qualitative secondary research.

We have written this book to cross disciplinary boundaries to provide an interdisciplinary text for students engaged in a wide range of national and international fields. The examples employed to illustrate qualitative secondary research approaches are drawn from a variety of fields. This exposure to different subject areas is deliber-ate as it will aid your understanding of the wider impact and implications of research decisions. It will also provide a solid support framework to transdisciplinary institu-tions as a resource for their research centres, study skills centres and academic support units.

WHAT IS QUALITATIVE SECONDARY RESEARCH?

All research has similar features; it begins with a problem which leads to the formulation of a research question(s) and/or aim(s). It requires you to provide a context within which to put this problem and it requires you to set out on a process to find some resolution to your problem. Undertaking qualitative secondary research requires you to adopt the same approach but instead of using methods to gain data from participants, you are applying a critical gaze to data that already exists in some form. In this book we argue strongly that qualitative secondary research is a robust and systematic research design but it is one that is less examined, considered and written about.

A strong driving force behind this book was to provide students with a clear and definitive statement of what qualitative secondary research design is. When we trialled this book on a range of undergraduate and postgraduate students, they were all gratified that we had provided such a clear definition. Feedback from these students indicated that often definitions are unclear or expressed in terms of what something is not rather than what it is. Therefore, in Chapter 1 we set out our clear and unambiguous definition:

> Qualitative secondary research is a systematic approach to the use of existing data to provide ways of understanding that may be additional to or different from the data's original purpose.

Our definition of qualitative secondary research means that you are using data that you have not solicited or been involved in its creation. This is the main difference between primary and secondary research. In primary research you utilise methods to seek and gather data from live participants but, in secondary research, you are using data that already exist. This is why it is secondary as your data already exists as documents in the real world. These data can be found within historically focused documents or within those that are very contemporary; the key to what you use lies in the question(s) and/or aim(s) you set for your research.

In this book we consider all sources of information as possible and potential data for your research. These sources of information are called documents and they exist in many forms. We explore what this means in great detail in Chapter 6 but it basically means that everything and anything can be utilised as a source of data, from something deemed potentially as trivial as a shopping list to existing research undertaken by well-known researchers conducted on a large scale. Anything and everything in between has the possibility of being data for your project. However, as we reiterate in this book, this does not mean we can ignore the need to create trustworthy and credible research and at the heart of the systematic approach we advocate to qualitative secondary research is the adoption of processes and strategies to secure data quality. Throughout this book, we refer to the need to apply appraisal processes and to always be aware of your data's production.

We focus on the use of the Internet to locate your sources of data and it seems an understatement to say that the Internet is a powerful tool for this purpose. Significant technological advances have widened access to a wealth of data and this can be easily demonstrated by simply typing in a key word in a search engine bar and seeing how many millions of results flood back in a fraction of a second. Yet this ease of access needs to be considered with caution as you will need to make important choices in the selection, inclusion and exclusion of your data. This is not just in terms of data quality but also by being able to use data that exists already in the world you should be responsive to ethical and legal aspects of existing data usage. This means not causing harm to others when accessing or using their data and not transgressing any legal frameworks.

HOW WE USE SPECIFIC FEATURES IN THIS BOOK

We would love it if you were to read this book in full from cover to cover but we also recognise that this may not be the way you want to use it, so we have provided 14 essential chapters with clearly signposted text that enables you to dip in and out and move around this book so you can make sense of the qualitative secondary research process in a way that suits you and your needs. To further aid your understanding, we have also created a glossary of key terms that is written specifically with you as a qualitative secondary researcher in mind.

As highly qualified and experienced lecturers, we know that there is a strong relationship between the development of deep learning and reflection which is why we offer a range of carefully positioned reflection and learning points which encourage you to think in more depth. We call these 'pause for thought' boxes as they provide clarification, additional information or aspects of further challenge. We provide these to enhance your learning experience and to encourage you to feel more empowered in the choices you make. We want you to feel confident in the defence and justification of the approach you need to take to your qualitative secondary research.

As reflection is an important part of our approach to this book, we also provide clear learning intentions at the beginning of each chapter and we revisit these at the end, asking you focused questions to stimulate your recollection of what you have explored and to encourage you to engage in critical reflection on your learning.

Using examples to stimulate deep learning

We believe passionately that people learn best when they are fully engaged so we have provided examples of secondary research within this book; not always included as examples of good practice but sometimes as useful or cautionary reminders of the challenges involved and what can go wrong. These examples have a key role; for instance, in Chapter 5 we explore ethical concerns within research and, as you will see, some of the examples we provide are quite disconcerting. We also illustrate, through an example, how fake news and falsified information is generated and spread. These we use to reiterate our claims that the data you select for use must be fully appraised and evaluated for authenticity, credibility representativeness and meaning (Scott 1990).

Practical strategies

As authors, our intent is to provide a practical guide that offers examples and clearly described procedures and approaches. These should allow you to gain control of your learning and research process and also to feel you can explore and experiment. We do not ever say there is just one way to do things, so we provide guidance and offer some 'wiggle room' where you can find your own way to conduct your qualitative secondary research within the scaffolded support provided.

Highly visual approach

When we were designing this book, we listened to students who said they wanted a book that did not just offer pages and pages of text but also offered the possibly of gaining a quick overview from well-designed images inserted at key points within the text to amplify the meaning they were making of the information being presented. We have provided this, adopting a complementary approach within which we balance text against image to support and inform learning. All the diagrams we provide act as a visual pedagogy to illustrate a key point or to extend ones being made. In student trials, feedback indicated that the visual narrative we adopt aids the learning process.

Guidance and advice

We offer plenty of guidance and advice and sometimes this is in the form of a checklist or as a statement within the text where we impart specific advice. An example of this is in the advice we offer regarding the taking of a one size fits all approach. The experience we have amassed between us means we are aware of the diversity of research processes and we openly acknowledge that we are unable to provide a definitive template for your research. We advise you to check your institution's or funding body's guidelines and to discuss key issues and concerns with your supervisor. Different institutions and different supervisors have different perspectives and expectations; we always advise you to seek out what is expected of you and to build a constructive relationship with your supervisor.

EXPLORING THE BOOK'S CONTENTS

This book has a clear narrative that focuses on key parts of the research process. Each chapter builds on from the one before offering practical guidance and advice on each aspect of the qualitative secondary research process. The narrative we create is set out in brief below.

- **Preparation:** We begin in Chapter 1 with an overview of the research process that sets the scene and prepares you for the journey ahead. Then in Chapter 2, we move to the preparatory processes of planning and question formulation.
- **Constructing:** In Chapters 3 and 4, we provide the engine house of the process as these chapters set out the underpinning theory and the design of your research. This is where you will construct your approach to your inquiry. Next, we offer Chapter 5 which explores the ethical and legal aspects that should guide and shape the way you access and work with your data within your research project.
- **Searching:** In the following two chapters, Chapters 6 and 7, we consider sources of data and where and how to find these. This is followed by Chapter 8 where we present approaches to data quality and sampling strategies because you may have found useful data but you need to know if it is credible and trustworthy.
- **Contextualising:** Knowing how to apply processes of critical evaluation and appraisal is important when you come to construct a robust, academically orientated and well-informed literature review, and this is discussed in Chapter 9. The sources of information you use within this will be used to confirm or debate the findings you generate.
- **Managing:** Although, you will have been handling data before you get to Chapter 10, we included this chapter here as you will need to have your data management fully secure as you start to analyse your data, and this is fully reviewed in Chapter 10.
- **Analysing:** Data analysis is considered in Chapters 11 and 12. Chapter 11 explores qualitative methods of analysis and Chapter 12 provides an overview of statistical procedures. We see these as offering different yet complementary approaches to data analysis.
- **Completing:** The final two chapters in our research narrative, Chapters 13 and 14, provide a considered conclusion to your research process as we discuss in Chapter 13 how to present your findings and conclusions and, in Chapter 14, we ask you to reflect on what you have completed and what you have learned and consider your next steps.

Chapter 1 Introducing Qualitative Secondary Research

In Chapter 1, we provide our definition and offer you a thorough overview of processes involved within qualitative secondary research. It explores possible sources of data and reflects on the benefits offered by this approach to qualitative research. We offer a final checklist to make sure you want to conduct this type of research.

In this chapter we encourage you to consider:

- What is secondary research?
- What does it involve?
- What are the benefits?
- Is qualitative secondary research for me?

Chapter 2 Preparing for Qualitative Secondary Research

In Chapter 2 we focus much more on the beginning of your research process. This second chapter supports the practicalities involved in the planning and preparation of your research. This includes the development of your research question(s) and/or aim(s). It also explores the composition of research proposals and the types of support you should access during the research process. We advise you in this chapter and in others that it is important to be fully aware of the expectations and requirements that you may need to adhere to.

In this chapter we encourage you to consider:

- Why is reading so important?
- How do I formulate my questions, aim and objectives?
- What is a research proposal?
- What skills do I need as a secondary researcher?

Chapter 3 The Role of Theory in Qualitative Secondary Research

This is a key chapter as it provides guidance on theory and your theoretical framework, and examines how you and your 'positioning' influence your research. It explores how to minimise this influence through a process of *reflexivity* that when employed can enhance the rigour and credibility of your research. We also examine the development of theoretical and conceptual frameworks and the significant role of these within your data analysis. This chapter provides the underpinning for your methodology and does so in a clear and meaningful way.

In this chapter we encourage you to consider:

- What is the role of theory in research?
- What is my research position?
- What influences research?
- What is reflexivity?

Chapter 4 Designing Qualitative Secondary Research

This chapter provides the blueprint for the creation and production of your qualitative secondary research. It defines qualitative secondary research as a research design and explores relevant components required in this design necessary to conduct your research. This leads to a discussion as to how to create a robust methodology. Additionally, we review in some depth, strategies within qualitative secondary research that can be employed to contribute towards claims of research quality and rigour.

In this chapter we encourage you to consider:

- How is secondary research designed?
- How do I write the methodology?
- What is research quality?

Chapter 5 Ethics in Qualitative Secondary Research

This chapter considers a range of ethical and legal considerations necessary within your undertaking of qualitative secondary research. We explore arguments surrounding informed consent when using data provided by others and we consider the need to adhere to and comply with ethical codes of conduct, whether these are institutionally focused, or discipline based. We also consider how it is imperative for all researchers to behave in an ethical way when they conduct any form of research.

In this chapter we encourage you to consider:

- Do I need permission to use the data set?
- What are the potential legal issues?
- How do I ensure I am an ethical researcher?

Chapter 6 Exploring Documents as Data

In this chapter, we explore the vast range of documents that can become sources of your data. We use a classification system that breaks away from traditional notions of primary, secondary and tertiary sources and explores documents as naturally occurring within specific domains; therefore, data can be obtained from public, popular culture, academic, personal, visual and physical artefact sources. We also encourage you to reflect on how you can influence your selection of data.

In this chapter we encourage you to consider:

* What are qualitative data?
* How do I use documents as data in my project?
* What can I use as sources for my data?
* What influences my selection of data?

Chapter 7 Locating your Data

As you are using data provided by others, it is important that you know where this can be located, so in this chapter, we outline a range of strategies to locate and retrieve sources of data. These search strategies encourage you to search for your data ethically and safely. To do this, we explore aspects of location and site credibility by exploring some of the 'tricks of the trade' and offer advice as to how to assess website credibility. We also provide a range of interesting and unusual locations for you to search for data.

In this chapter we encourage you to consider:

* What is the best way to find data?
* Where are the best places?
* Why might I need to protect myself from data?

Chapter 8 Securing Quality over Quantity

This chapter examines strategies to reduce the amount of data you may need to work with through the application of processes and procedures of data evaluation and appraisal. When we work with data provided by others, we need to ensure that what we are using is trustworthy and this is why in this chapter we encourage you to understand the context of your data's production. Additionally, and as part of a process of data reduction, we also explore how you can reduce the amount of data you may find using sampling strategies. These sampling strategies support possible claims for the representativeness of your data and for the transferability of your findings.

In this chapter we encourage you to consider:

- How can I tell if the data is trustworthy?
- How can I get to know my data?
- How do I know if my data are representative?

Chapter 9 Constructing a Literature Review

This chapter explores the highly essential role of the literature review within your research project and it begins by explaining that qualitative secondary research is more than a review of literature. Further to this, we articulate the purpose of a literature review and provide guidance on its construction, offering practical strategies such as the use of a literature and synthesis matrices to ensure you maximise the benefit of your targeted and focused reading. This guidance also includes advice on how to use language effectively to support your constructed arguments and we emphasise the importance of taking time to draft and edit your work.

In this chapter we encourage you to consider:

- What is the difference between secondary research and a literature review?
- How do I write a literature review?
- What is synthesis?

Chapter 10 Managing your Data

As you will most likely accumulate a huge volume of data, this chapter outlines the practical strategies of the governance of data. The chapter explains how having a data management plan can be a valuable tool that can make your research more efficient and effective. Therefore, we explore how robust data management practices can minimise potential risk, in relation to how you access, process and store your data and, when it is redundant, how you can delete it. We show how engaging with your data in a clear and systematic way increases research transparency and the integrity of your research.

In this chapter we encourage you to consider:

- How can I manage my data during the short term?
- Do I need to consider what happens to my data after my research has finished?
- What are the potential issues that need addressing?

Chapter 11 Analysing Data

This chapter explores approaches you can take to the analysis of your data. We explore the role of constant comparison and framework (thematic) analysis as meeting the needs of most when faced with trying to make sense of a wide range of data. We offer a procedural account that shows how data can be reduced and coded to create relevance and meaning. Towards the end of the chapter we offer a range of more specialised but also highly appropriate methods of analysis including discourse, content and narrative analysis. We also provide advice and guidance as how to find the best method of analysis suitable for the questions you ask of your data.

In this chapter we encourage you to consider:

- Why does data need to be analysed?
- How are data analysed?
- What method of analysis is suitable for the question I ask?

Chapter 12 Working with Numbers

In this chapter we explore ways that you could use numerical data within qualitative secondary research. We demonstrate how numbers can play a significant role in both illustrating and clarifying your qualitative analyses. We show how a statistical approach can be applied to qualitative data and this includes the application of mathematical measures (*e.g. means and dispersions*) that can help to summarise, interpret and present your data.

In this chapter we encourage you to consider:

- Do I have to use numbers?
- What are descriptive statistics?
- How do I use numbers in qualitative secondary research?

Chapter 13 Presenting your Findings and Forming Conclusions

You have conducted your research, analysed your results so, the next task is the presentation and discussion of your findings. This chapter outlines different strategies to present your findings as clearly and concisely as possible to your audience, so you can effectively convey the key outcomes of your research. This effective communication can include being honest and open in your research and discusses factors that may have impacted on the credibility of your findings and the conclusions you form. We also provide a spotlight on the often undervalued but highly pivotal role of recommendations that you may need to present to signpost for future research possibilities. Additionally, as communicating your findings effectively is essential, we explore how you can use quotations and images adeptly to enable your reader to fully comprehend all you have accomplished.

In this chapter we encourage you to consider:

- What is the best way to present the results of my research?
- Should I mention things that did not work out?
- How honest should I be in my write up?

Chapter 14 Being a Qualitative Secondary Researcher

This chapter encourages you to reflect on what it means to be a researcher and on your completed research project. As such, it represents the final checking stage in your research journey as we provide a completion checklist where we encourage you to reflect on the project you have completed before you submit it for assessment. This part of your reflection process is arguably the most important as, if you do not write up your research effectively and ensure it is complete, then much of your effort in the research process may be wasted.

We also ask you to consider the skills you have developed and how these can be used to support your employability. In addition, we encourage you not to think of the submission process as the end of your research and we encourage you to consider the dissemination of your research findings at conferences, through peer reviewed articles and through the Internet using blogs.

In this chapter we encourage you to consider:

- What does it mean to be a researcher?
- What have I learnt?
- What happens after I have completed my research?

Finally, ...

Research is an exciting process and one that brings benefit to you as a researcher. This can be in the skills you develop and the knowledge you can add to your subject area and discipline. It may seem strange discussing the end of your project just as you are about to begin but it is worth knowing that when you have finished you will have amassed significant knowledge and many relevant skills. Therefore, as you begin your research process try to keep this in mind – that you will be learning something about your subject and about yourself. Conducting research can be an enjoyable process as you work your way through a problem and resolve this for yourself. We hope you look back on your research project with pride and a sense of achievement and, as you begin, do so with an open and curious mind.

1

INTRODUCING QUALITATIVE SECONDARY RESEARCH

THIS CHAPTER SUPPORTS YOUR ABILITY TO

define qualitative secondary research

appreciate the range of data possible for use

identify key components of qualitative secondary research

check if qualitative secondary research is for you

CHAPTER OVERVIEW

This chapter introduces you to qualitative secondary research and we begin this book with a clear and concise definition. We define qualitative secondary research as a robust form of enquiry that is systematic and analytical in its approach to the use of existing data. The key to our definition of secondary research is that the data you use will not have been instigated by you or you will not have been involved in its creation. Therefore, the data you use already exists in some form in a multitude of locations.

In this chapter, we provide an overview of the processes involved in qualitative secondary research and we spend some time considering the vast array of data it is possible to use. This is data that exists as documents provided by people and can include personal or first-hand sources of information, as well as public and academic data and be in many forms such as social media postings, advertising images, government reports and news. Therefore, you have the potential to answer your research question(s) and/or aim(s) by drawing on the diversity of data available for use within the 21st century. We aim to show that qualitative secondary research offers many benefits and one of these is the ability to use a vast array of data.

This chapter also examines some of the key research decisions you may need to make as a secondary qualitative researcher, and how making these early on can support and shape your research project. To support you in this decision making we set out the key components in qualitative secondary research and illustrate how these fit together to create a coherent and consistent methodology.

WHAT IS QUALITATIVE SECONDARY RESEARCH?

When you start reading about qualitative secondary research it becomes clear quite early on that there are plenty of definitions and some of these are hard to apply in a qualitative research context. Therefore, we begin this chapter with a clear and unambiguous definition:

> Qualitative secondary research is a systematic approach to the use of existing data to provide ways of understanding that may be additional to or different from the data's original purpose.

We can explore this definition using three main concepts:

Qualitative: This reflects the research approach taken and as we explore in Chapter 3, the way you may see the world. Knowing that your research is qualitative means you may want to use a certain type of data; for example, you may use data that is descriptive and categorical and not numerically orientated which enables you to interpret rather than measure. This is the sort of data that allows you to focus on the socially constructed nature of reality and enable you to explore contexts or phenomena that can shape or constrain people's reality (Denzin & Lincoln 2005).

Secondary: This is the way you will conduct your research as whilst primary research involves collecting data based on first-hand engagement with participants, in qualitative secondary research you are using data that has already been created and already exists. As we explore later, the data you may use is available in many forms and can be accessed from a multitude of places. Therefore, when you undertake secondary research you are using, as Stewart and Kamins (1993: 3) assert, pre-existing data or information that is *'not the responsibility of the analyst'*. In other words, this is data that you have not instigated or been a part of its creation in any way. Figure 1.1 clarifies the difference between secondary and primary approaches to research as relating to the relationship that the researcher has to the generation of their data. The distinction being that in secondary research data exists at least one step away from you as the secondary researcher in that you are accessing the data almost 'second hand' as it has already been created.

Research: This refers to the act of finding something new in a systematic way and this is a significant part of the qualitative secondary research process. A systematic approach is one that adopts systems, strategies and techniques to ensure you achieve a piece of research that has value, is meaningful and adds to your discipline's or subject's field of knowledge. Being systematic when you engage in qualitative secondary research begins with you viewing the data you have selected through a critical lens. This is achieved by asking a new question(s) and/or having new aim(s), and/or applying a new method of analysis or theoretical framework. Therefore, qualitative secondary research is a systematic approach to using data that already exist.

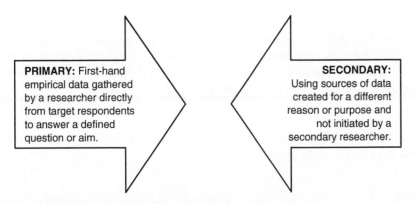

Figure 1.1   Differences between primary and secondary research

Exploring criticisms of qualitative secondary research

There are some criticisms thrown at qualitative secondary research (Heaton 1998; 2004) and we aim to repel these in this book as these criticisms reflect common misunderstandings and misconceptions around the use of existing or re-purposed data. We address two such criticisms below:

How do you know if your data is of the 'right' quality?

This criticism is often made to doubt that qualitative secondary research is credible, dependable, transferable and confirmable (Guba 1981; Lincoln & Guba 1985). We offer a range of strategies and advice to the creation of quality or research rigour in your research. This begins with the significant emphasis we place on you as qualitative secondary researcher understanding the means of your data's production. For qualitative secondary researchers, understanding the 'who', 'what', 'when', 'where', 'how' and 'why' of data production is paramount. Therefore, we encourage you to focus on Scott's (1990) approach to assessing documents and their quality which we examine in more depth in Chapter 8 but an overview is provided below:

- **Authenticity:** Is the evidence genuine?
- **Credibility:** Is the evidence accurate?
- **Representativeness:** Is the evidence typical or untypical of its kind?
- **Meaning:** Is it clear and comprehensible?

To further support your ability to assess the quality of your sources of data, we provide strategies in Chapter 8 to support crucial evaluation and appraisals that, when used effectively, can promote the dependability of your work and thus, support the credibility of your findings.

In addition, to ensure your research reflects quality we explore sampling strategies so your data can be selected and appraised for its typicality or representativeness. Applying strategies like this can support research quality and support the transferability or applicability of your findings and thus, the value of your research. Employing effective strategies to secure research quality should encourage others to have confidence in your research.

Qualitative secondary research is like doing a literature review; it is not real research is it?

Such criticism is why we are very keen to emphasise that qualitative secondary research is a robust research approach that goes beyond the mere reuse of existing data in a literature review or a report. In qualitative secondary research, you will undertake a review of existing literature on your topic focus but qualitative secondary research goes beyond this. Qualitative secondary research requires you to adopt a systematic approach which begins when you pose specific and focused research question(s) and/or aims(s). This systematic process includes the employment of a range of strategies to support effective data selection; it uses methods of data analysis, involves highly competent data management skills and a sharp focus on the ethical conduct of your research. To enhance the confirmability of your research, we encourage you to consider the influence that you may exert on your research and promote the use of research diaries and reflexivity.

Qualitative secondary research involves the same level of critical and analytical engagement as is expected within all forms of primary research. The most significant difference is that you are using data you have not instigated or generated; your data already exists in the world.

CONSIDERING THE BENEFITS OF QUALITATIVE SECONDARY RESEARCH

We cover many of the reasons why conducting qualitative secondary research should be considered as a viable and significant alternative to primary research later in this chapter but Figure 1.2 sets out some of these benefits early to reinforce our argument that it is an approach to research that is really worth taking.

As well as these benefits, when you undertake qualitative secondary research, you are enhancing and adding to your academic and employability skill set as you are:

- using critical thinking skills as you appraise and evaluate data and strengthening your media and information literacy understanding;
- gaining contemporary oversight of ethical codes of conduct as you learn to use existing data;
- enhancing your information search skills and making judgements as to data credibility;
- advancing your communication skills through processes of analysis, synthesis and evaluation;

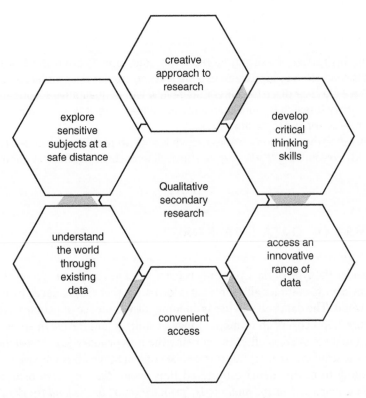

Figure 1.2   Reasons for undertaking qualitative secondary research

- developing effective data management strategies and understanding data storage and security needs;
- engaging in processes of data analysis.

We aim to show in this book that, like primary research, qualitative secondary research is a systematic form of inquiry that contains processes and strategies to promote research quality (see Chapter 4). As you read this book, we trust you will find that secondary research is not any easier or harder than primary research, it is just different.

PAUSE FOR THOUGHT

Is a literature review the same as qualitative secondary research?

In both primary and secondary research, you need to provide a context or research background for your enquiry. This is your literature review which provides a place in which to demonstrate a 'progressive narrowing of the topic' (Hart 1998: 13). Whether you are undertaking primary or

(Continued)

(Continued)

secondary research, this review of existing literature on your topic is often the first stage of a research project. It is conducted to locate and explore existing studies on a subject as a precursor to your research. There is a clear place for a literature review within qualitative secondary research but qualitative secondary research is more than a review of literature. It is a systematic process of investigation and analysis applied to existing data.

Therefore, the answer to the question we asked above 'Is a literature review the same as qualitative secondary research?' is a resounding NO! We explore these differences in-depth throughout this book (see Chapter 9).

WHAT TYPES OF DATA CAN I USE?

Before we consider the type of data you may use, we need to clarify our use of the term 'data'. We use the term 'data' to embrace all sources of information that are produced by people as they engage in the world. The data you will use is documentary evidence of people's lives and, as we explore in Figure 1.3, it covers an immense range of sources and forms. In some books terms are used to define these sources often categorising them as primary (*e.g. first-hand narratives*) or secondary (*e.g. scholarly articles*) but this can be confusing which is why we adopt the term 'data' to step away from this demarcation and thus avoid '*the confusion of trying to decide whether the data employed in an analysis is "primary data" or "secondary data"*' (Cheng & Phillips 2014: 371). We argue that all forms of human documentary evidence exist as possible sources of data and therefore, can be used within your qualitative secondary research. The most important considerations when you are selecting your sources as data should be:

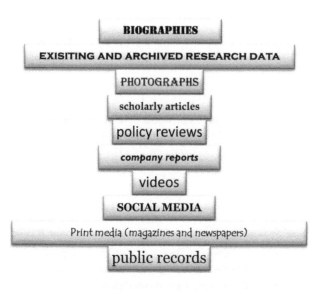

- What data do I want to use?
- How does this source of data enable me to answer my question(s) and/or aim(s)?
- Can I use this data?

In qualitative research you are trying to understand 'how', 'why', 'when', 'where' and in 'what' way people experience the world. Therefore, to do this you need sources of data that provide evidence of

Figure 1.3 Examples of sources of data

the way people interact and live in the world. You may want to use these sources to allow you to explore legal systems, forms of educational practice, personal narratives found within social media, paintings, artefacts, news media and so on because the list is really endless. When you use data like this, you are using documents as the *'material traces'* of people's lives (Hodder 1994: 393) and as sources of data, these are just *'"out there" waiting to be assembled and analysed'* (Bryman 2012: 543).

Consequently, as we show in Figure 1.3, the range of possible sources of data is huge and in qualitative secondary research you can find and use sources of data to explore diverse social and cultural topics. Therefore, the wealth of documents you have the potential to access promotes the possibility of rich and informative research that opens up opportunities to see in to the lives of others with some clarity. When you undertake qualitative secondary research, you can use documents as sources of data to explore opinions, feelings, experiences and understand social phenomena as they occur naturally. As an example of this, Box 1.1 presents research conducted by Charlotte Barlow (2016) who accessed a range of socially and culturally appropriate sources of data to explore the way women within the criminal system are represented within the media.

> **BOX 1.1 'COERCION AND WOMEN CO-OFFENDERS: A GENDERED PATHWAY INTO CRIME' BY BARLOW (2016)**
>
> Barlow set out to research women co-accused of committing a range of crimes. She accessed British newspapers' coverage of in-scope cases and compared this with the records made in the legal proceedings of these cases. The documents used included police interview transcripts, prosecution and defence arguments, sections of the trial transcripts, personal letters and judges' opening and closing statements.
>
> These documents were analysed using a combination of news, court and case file analysis which allowed a compare and contrast approach to explore varying versions of the same events. Through this process it was found that journalists presented women within distorted and gendered narratives. The combination of data (*combining newspaper and case file analysis*) revealed useful insights as to the visibility or invisibility of the women's voices.
>
> She found that a combination of both forms of data produced a more inclusive account of the women's stories and that pre-existing documents are a useful source of data in criminological research.

CLASSIFYING DATA

Whilst sources of data are plentiful, classifying them so we can understand their function can be complex and this is mainly because of the sheer diversity of information available to access within the 21st century. Some of the documents as data you may use within your research may have been previously worked on or analysed (*e.g. existing research findings*); some of it will exist as a process of second hand inquiry (*e.g. journalistic outputs or news media*); some of it may be the result of state or governmental policy reviews or reports and some of it may be 'found' sources of data such as that available as online forms of social media data created by people as first-hand narratives.

We encourage you to consider documents not just as inert things as all documents have a purpose and a function. In qualitative secondary research, you need to consider what the author or creator wanted to do with the document. One of the ways we ask you to consider this is in the expectancy of the author or producer of the sources of data as to the audience it is designed to have. In Chapter 6, we advise you to consider documents as either produced deliberately or inadvertently (Duffy 2005).

- **Deliberate:** Some documents are deliberate in their publication and have clearly defined audiences; for example, a television programme, a newspaper, a website or government report.
- **Inadvertent:** Some documents are inadvertent in their production as the author's or creator's intention as to the audience these documents should have is less clear. Documents that are inadvertent may not have been produced for a specific audience; for example, some social media postings, discarded notes and personal sources such as diaries or letters.

To help you explore possible and potential sources of data, in Chapter 6 we classify data using an approach informed by Merriam and Tisdell (2016) under the headings set out in Figure 1.4.

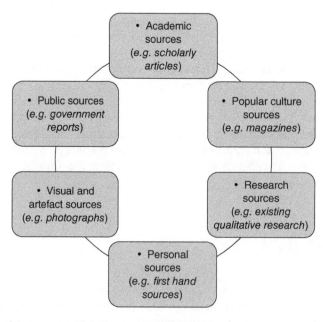

Figure 1. 4 Classifying sources of data

Different types of data for different purposes

In qualitative secondary research, as we show in Figure 1.5, we use documents as sources of data in two main ways; within your literature review and your analysis.

Your literature review provides both a context for your research and a showcase for your skills and knowledge. In your literature review, you will use sources to demonstrate the conceptual boundaries of your research as these sources will reflect your awareness of

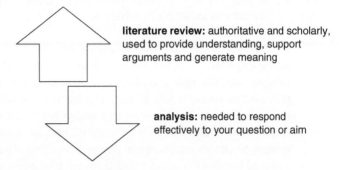

literature review: authoritative and scholarly, used to provide understanding, support arguments and generate meaning

analysis: needed to respond effectively to your question or aim

Figure 1.5   Sorting your sources of data

your subject area and research that has gone before. You should show key theorists and commentators and reflect a balanced approach offering alternative perspectives as well as ones that reflect your view. The literature as sources of data you select will play a significant role when you interpret your findings and link what you have found to other ways of understanding your topic. Making sure you have the most credible sources for this purpose is therefore, essential to the trustworthiness and overall quality of the findings you produce.

Your choice of data for your analysis is very much defined by your question(s) and/or aim(s), the theoretical framework you apply and the way you want to analyse your data (see Chapter 11). As quality is important, you will need to consider this data for its authenticity, credibility, representativeness and meaning (Scott 1990). We will refer to these criteria throughout this book to encourage you to understand the context of your data's production to support your ability to defend its use.

There are strengths and weaknesses to all forms and sources of data and this will become clear when you start searching for it (see Chapters 6 and 7). But we maintain that with careful consideration, all sources of data can be utilised within a research context. To aid your utilisation of diverse sources of data, we explore ethical approaches in some depth (see Chapter 5) and provide approaches to critical appraisal to enhance research quality and rigour (see Chapter 8).

WHERE WILL I FIND MY DATA?

Chapter 7 explores this in more depth but the data you may use exists within many physical and virtual locations. Examples of physical locations include:

- Libraries: if you want to use local or community focused data;
- Archives: if you want to use stored documents relating to well-known people or records of specific events;

- Museums: if you want to find specific visual data (*drawings, prints or photographs*) or artefacts (*ceramics, jewellery, toys, sculpture*);
- County halls or local government offices: if you want to find town planning documents or documents exploring local history.

It is also very likely that you will use the Internet to search for and access your sources of data as the introduction of the digital age has brought major changes in the ways information can be obtained. Vast amounts of data can be accessed by the touch of a button and it may be that this ease of access is one of the reasons why you want to undertake qualitative secondary research. As a qualitative secondary researcher, you are no longer constrained by geographical concerns or boundaries as access to the Internet means that you can approach your research question from an international perspective. This offers you the possibility of breaking out of national borders to consider global research possibilities as the example we provide in Box 1.3 illustrates.

As you begin thinking about your research, you need to consider some of the ethical issues you may need to navigate. This could be in terms of access to your data and your moral and legal right to use it. Just because there is a wealth of data available it does not mean it is there for you to use. As we explore in Chapters 5 and 10, when searching on the Internet you need to be aware of data ownership and consider issues with copyright. This may mean navigating your way through understanding open access and creative commons agreements.

We will also encourage you to consider issues relating to informed consent and data protection. Data gained from sources such as Twitter feeds, social media narratives and blogs can provide useful social and cultural research material, but this type of data can be laden with ethical issues pertaining to access permissions and data ownership. Accessing increasingly diverse sources of data via the Internet increases the scope for flexibility and creativity but with this comes the responsibility to be vigilant in not disrespecting the rights of others.

WHAT TYPE OF QUESTION WILL I ASK?

Knowing what to ask, how to ask it and why it should be asked can be complex at any level of study. However, we offer advice and strategies to support question and aim formulation as being focused in what you want to study and how you want to study it early on in your research process should enable you to complete your project on time. Therefore, in Chapter 2 we offer advice and strategies that should enable you to create LASER focused questions.

- **Linked:** if using multiple questions and/or aims that they are connected in some way;
- **Answerable:** not too broad in scope;
- **Specific:** see what data needs to be obtained;
- **Easily understood:** it is clear and well stated;
- **Relevant:** worthwhile asking.

We also set out the clear relationship between the development of a clear and focused research question(s) and/or aim(s) and your engagement with reading. We refer to this as 'looping' as your reading informs your question and your question informs your reading. In Chapter 3, we explore how your deep engagement with reading supports the development of your theoretical frameworks and, in Chapter 9, we show how this reading underpins your ability to construct a strong literature review.

HOW WILL I MANAGE MY DATA?

When you conduct qualitative secondary research, you will need to consider effective data management. We consider data storage as both an ethical condition of your research and as practical ways to manage the amount of data you might collect. We also encourage you to focus on citation management, so you can acknowledge all used sources.

HOW WILL I KNOW THE QUALITY OF MY DATA?

Knowing the quality of your data is of crucial importance to a qualitative secondary researcher and we have already indicated that we will urge you to consider data for its authenticity, credibility, representativeness and meaning (Scott 1990). This requires you to know as much about your sources of data as possible so, as we outline in Figure 1.6, you should ask questions to explore the context of data's construction.

Data can be found in a multitude of places but it is becoming more likely that you will access some or most of your data via the Internet. Although vast amounts of information are available very easily, it is worth considering that this ease of access needs to be countered by a pragmatic, critical, questioning and sceptical approach to your selection of your sources of data. We encourage you to ask, 'How do I know if what I am accessing is useful, credible and, significantly, mine to access?'. Although data that can be used in qualitative secondary research provides us with significant choice, we need to remember that quantity does not always indicate quality (Denscombe 2007). You need to be prepared to apply rigorous quality filters to justify how and why your selected data were chosen (see Chapter 8). In Chapter 6, we consider some of the

what: data type

who: data's author, creator, producer

when: date of creation

where: location where it was created

how: construction (materials or methods)

why: data purpose

Figure 1.6   Understanding the context of data construction

limitations that some sources of data offer, but we also explore the many benefits. As we state throughout this book, it is possible to use all forms of data, but it is important to know where possible, the conditions and context of your data's production to understand its quality (Mauthner, Parry & Backett-Milburn 1998).

PAUSE FOR THOUGHT

A word of caution

In this book, we focus on the need to adopt a sharp and critical focus to your sources of data (see Chapter 8). It is very easy to be fooled by presented information such as *'disguised or native advertising'* where an advertisement presents itself as a news item or research report. As in all forms of research, you need to ask yourself some searching questions of your data and we will prompt you to ask the following throughout this book:

- How is the data produced?
- Why is it produced?
- Where it is found?
- Do I have ethical and legal access to this data?

WHAT WILL MY RESEARCH LOOK LIKE?

The diversity of the courses, disciplines and contexts in which you will undertake your study make it impossible to provide an absolute template for you to apply to your qualitative secondary research. In this book we offer practical examples and advice that guides your thinking. We are aware that each field or subject discipline and institution may have its own approach, therefore, throughout this book we will advise you to check with your institution's or funder's guidelines to ensure you are approaching your research in a manner that meets these expectations.

In Chapter 4, we explore aspects of research design and consider the creation of a research methodology. The aim of research design is to produce a clear and well-constructed approach to the inquiry process that is coherent within the theoretical frameworks you adopt. Therefore, when we discuss the creation of your methodology, we promote a systematic approach that includes the key research components shown in Figure 1.7.

We use a metaphor to indicate the flexibility of qualitative secondary research and consider your methodology as a recipe and the components shown in Figure 1.7 as the ingredients you can use to create this recipe. This cooking metaphor should indicate that like all good recipes, you need to adjust these ingredients according to your taste. So, while we cover all of these key ingredients, what, how, and why you use them will be determined by you and your

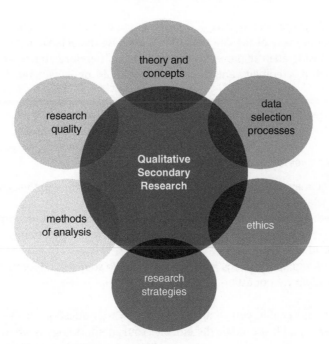

Figure 1.7   Components of qualitative secondary research

research question(s) and/or aim(s). In this section we offer a brief overview of these research ingredients, but you will find these explored in depth in the chapters we have included in this book. We begin with theory as this underpins your research.

Theory: In Chapter 3, theory is presented as functioning in your research as follows:

- Theory of knowledge which creates your world view or research position. This way of seeing the world influences the shape and scope of your inquiry.
- Theory as sets of beliefs and concepts that are created by you because of who you are and your reading, and potentially informed by known theory such as feminist theory or self-efficacy theory.

Data selection processes: In Chapter 8, we explore strategies of critical appraisal and sampling as ways to reduce data into something that is credible, relevant and manageable.

Ethics: In Chapter 5, we ask you to consider the ethical and legal requirements of researching using existing data.

Analysis: In Chapter 11, we offer a comprehensive consideration of the underlying principles for the analysis of data within qualitative research which are processes of coding, categorisation and theme creation. Depending on the approach you take to your research we also present the use of descriptive statistics (see Chapter 12) which have relevance if you want to access numerical data as a complementary data set.

Research quality: Research quality or rigour is explored explicitly in Chapter 4 but we return to this concept in many of the chapters. This is because the achievement of research quality needs to be considered in all processes you undertake. Therefore, strategies to address criteria for quality such as credibility and dependability should be considered as you design your research.

Research strategies: We introduce research strategies in Chapter 4 and refer to them in many of the chapters. These are design frames which provide a structure for the way you want to conduct your research. They offer ways of thinking about your research and support your decision making in terms of strategies for research quality, types and amount of data.

- **Single:** You may want to answer your research question through the exploration of one piece of data. This would afford a deep and critical gaze.
- **Combined:** You may want to answer your research question through processes of comparison as you compare two pieces of data exploring patterns, differences and commonalities.
- **Multiple:** A multiple strategy is the use of multiple sources and forms of data that are used to answer your question.

Each strategy should enable you to answer your research question in the way you think it should be answered and it should be defendable. Your methodology is where you put all these research ingredients together, but they have to be mixed in such a way to make sense. When you design your research and create your methodology you are aiming for research coherence. This coherence is best explained as where all the pieces of your research fit together like a jigsaw enabling a clear picture to emerge. If done well, your methodology should make your inquiry process obvious to your reader as it should demonstrate what you did, why you did it and how.

WHAT HAPPENS IF I WANT TO USE NUMBERS?

The research strategies we introduce are flexible and thus, afford the opportunity to use numerical data. If you wanted to adopt a multiple strategy, you could include a mix of qualitative and quantitative data. This approach would add complementarity to your research as several types of data could add to the richness of your research answer.

When we explore the analysis of your data, we ask you to reflect on the question you ask as this can define the approach you take. It is possible that you want to generate a numerical understanding of a phenomenon such as the frequency of specific words, images or signs. To do this you could employ content analysis which would provide numerical findings from the analysis of your data (see Chapter 11). Analysing data is about making sense of it and you need to decide *what* data you want and *how* this should be analysed to allow you to answer your research question(s) and/or aim(s).

PAUSE FOR THOUGHT

It is never too early to …

It is never too early to start thinking about your research. You may have a set deadline to work to so making sure you have considered some key questions in good time will support your confidence in the completion of your research.

- Develop a strong and effective research question or questions.
- Think about your analytical strategy.
- Begin to consider the types of data you may need to use.

We advise you to check you know what is required of you and, if you have any concerns, seek support and guidance from your supervisor, funding agency or institution. Please do not suffer in silence; if you need help seek it out.

WHY SHOULD I DO QUALITATIVE SECONDARY RESEARCH?

We have tried to persuade you of the merits of conducting qualitative secondary research to answer your research question(s) and/or aim(s) and this section will try harder. We present reasons why you should consider doing qualitative secondary research but the only person who can make this decision is you.

You can be creative and innovative

One thing that we do not want to restrict is your creative response to your research and, as qualitative secondary research is a flexible research design, it is possible that there are many ways for you to construct your research study and present your results. What we emphasise when you are deciding on how to conduct your research is to focus on your research question(s) and/or aim(s) (see Chapter 2). Your choice of research approach should be based on this.

In qualitative secondary research, your creativity can shine through in your choice of data, the research strategy you adopt and the way you approach your analysis. We offer examples that show this creative approach whether it is the analysis of teen fiction to the use of legal documents. There is a form of data and a way of understanding this that should get your interest.

You can explore diverse types of data

As we explored above, all forms and sources of data may be used within your research. As we explore in Chapter 6, anything that is a record of people's experiences and existence falls under this label. Therefore, this increases potential to engage with innovative data as you could explore paintings, websites, apps, books, poems, jewellery, photographs, vlogs, academic texts or archived manuscripts; the choice is immense.

You could explore historical contexts and access archived research to support your inquiry (Corti & Thompson 1995). You might want to focus on a specific individual or on a specific event that is social, political, economic or cultural (see Box 1.2). With qualitative secondary research, it is possible to gain in-depth perspectives through an exploration of historical data (Gillies & Edwards 2005). Approaching data in this way means you can experience 'new for old' understandings as the existing data can be reviewed using a new question. This can offer the gift of hindsight, as old ways of thinking are exposed to the new.

BOX 1.2 EXAMINING CHANGES TO WOMEN'S FASHION IN THE 1940S

As a researcher interested in women's fashion you want to examine the influence of the Second World War (WW2) on this topic. You decide that you will adopt a multiple strategy and explore a broad range of sources and forms of data. You access mass media outputs of that period (*e.g. films, news reels, books, newspapers and magazines*).

You decide to approach your research in this way as multiple forms of data provide diverse perspectives (*e.g. before, during and after and in domestic and work environments*). You analyse this data using a thematic approach to analysis that requires you to code and categorise changes in what women wear.

You find that women needed to wear practical clothes because they entered the workforce to take up the jobs of men who went to war. You conclude that it became socially acceptable for women to wear trousers as women had to adapt to the changing social and cultural landscape. Therefore, wearing trousers signposted a response to rapid social change.

You can use exising data

Secondary research offers researchers a chance to test ideas and theories which have been created through empirical research: a process that Heaton (2004: 9) calls a means of '*verifying, refuting or refining the findings of primary studies*'. This means you can use pre-existing research to answer your own question even if this question is different to the original (Polit, Beck & Hungler 2001). Using data in this way means that we can re-interpret the findings, possibly reveal new insights and reveal hidden or unforeseen relationships. Approaching research in this way has the potential to generate new or additional knowledge as you are using a new research question. This enables you to explore existing research from a new perspective (Hinds, Vogel & Clarke-Steffen 1997). You can learn from the expertise of others and in so doing, stand on the shoulders of giants as you learn from them. Consequently, exploring the research created by others can be an excellent training ground.

PAUSE FOR THOUGHT

What is secondary analysis?

The term 'secondary analysis' is often associated with secondary research. Secondary analysis is a form of secondary research that focuses *exclusively* on the re-analysis of data generated by empirical research. This is data that exists as questionnaires, interview transcripts or data within scholarly journal articles that have been analysed by a previous researcher (Heaton 2004). If you conduct a secondary analysis of data this means that you are re-analysing data that has already been analysed.

It is still secondary research but it uses a specific source of existing research data.

Accessing data collected by key experts is an underrated reason for conducting secondary research. These experts could include leading industry professionals and specialist consultants who may have very specific and specialised research competences. Glaser (1963: 11) uses the term '*economies of interest*' as other more qualified researchers may have already explored your topic and you may gain directly from this pre-existing knowledge and expertise.

You can save time and it is convenient

Factors such as time and cost are common reasons to undertake qualitative secondary research. Access to existing data can speed up the research process as some of the most time-consuming steps of a typical research project such as data collection have been eliminated (Doolan & Froelicher 2009). This is why qualitative secondary research is also known as 'desk research' as information (*data*) can be collected remotely, usually facilitated through computer assistance. Providing you have a means of access to your sources of data, you could work anywhere. This is one of the main benefits of qualitative secondary research as you can be flexible in how and where you work. Accessing your data using the Internet means you have increased access to a vast amount of data and this can be accessed from your home or library using a range of devices. This means you can research anytime, anyplace and anywhere. It also means you can provide a global response to your research question as you are no longer constrained by your geographic location. As we illustrate in Box 1.3, you could undertake research on a range of international or global topics.

BOX 1.3 HEALTHY LIVES, HEALTHY PEOPLE: A CALL TO ACTION ON OBESITY IN ENGLAND (2011)

Healthy Eating is one of many campaigns in the UK designed to encourage the consumption of at least five portions of fruit and vegetables each day to contribute to our health (www.gov.uk/). If you wanted to research answers to questions regarding barriers to healthy eating and to investigate strategies that work in other countries, you could conduct a global study. This study could explore practices or views about the consumption of fruits and vegetables among adolescents.

To conduct this type of primary research would usually require a huge amount of time and resources. However, large international studies have already been conducted by many others. This means you could access this data and explore the research study of Al Ani, Al Subhi and Bose (2016) as they conducted a multinational comparison of eleven countries in the Eastern Mediterranean Region. In addition, you could access Thomsen & Hansen's (2015) research. This involved an online consumer panel consisting of approximately 30,000 Danish consumers who were asked about their perceptions of healthy food consumption. To add to this, you could investigate research that compared 569 young USA and Chinese consumers to explore if personality trait factors influenced prevalence of a healthy diet.

You can tackle sensitive topics

You may want to study a sensitive topic and for this qualitative secondary research may the most appropriate approach for you to take. Sensitive topics are those that are filled with emotion or that have the potential to be intimate, discreditable or incriminating (Lee 1993). One way to approach sensitive topics is to use existing research outputs on your topic created by experienced researchers who have already gained ethical clearance for their work. Exploring research undertaken by researchers who may have skills and the authority to explore sensitive issues creates some form of distance from the research participants.

For you as a researcher, you may be able to gain unobtrusive access to sensitive situations without having direct contact with the research participants (Kwek & Kogut 2015). However, as we discuss in Chapter 5, there is still a strong ethical duty placed on any researcher to ensure confidentiality, privacy, and the right for those who offered their data not to be exposed to any harm.

A topic based on death and people's grief may be too challenging for some researchers. As well as the emotional aspect there are research concerns such as gaining access to grieving families that would be ethically challenging to achieve. However, if you wanted to explore subjects such as organ donation, as we show in the example of a sensitive research topic in Box 1.4, then secondary research presents itself as the most appropriate approach.

> **BOX 1.4   'ORGAN AND TISSUE DONATION: EXPLORING THE NEEDS OF FAMILIES' BY SQUE, LONG AND PAYNE (2003)**
>
> Sensitive topics such as family members' experiences of brain-stem death in relation to organ donation could be researched. Sque, Long and Payne (2003) conducted a three-year study commissioned by the British Organ Donor Society, funded by the National Lottery Community Fund to examine the experiences of bereaved adults with whom organ donation was discussed. The data collection methods included: face-to-face interviews, at 3–5 months, 13–15 months and 15–26 months after bereavement. Single interviews also took place approximately 13 months post-bereavement for families who declined donation.

It is worth reflecting on the need to safeguard yourself as you need to consider the impact of a sensitive topic on you as the researcher. There are also some forms of sensitive research (*e.g. exploring illegal activities*) that can place you as a researcher at significant risk. If you have any concerns as to the nature of your topic, it is always best to discuss this with your supervisor or identify any perceived concerns in your research proposal.

You can understand the world through existing data

Because you can access the Internet you can explore global perspectives and gain contemporary reactions to world events. You could investigate international newsfeeds, explore international advertising campaigns, study tourist information and investigate political situations.

You can see the world through the eyes of people who have created your data. If you use personal documents as your source of data you have first-hand accounts of people's lives. Using this type of data is a privilege; therefore you need to respond to this with increased ethical consideration and care.

You can develop critical thinking skills

Undertaking qualitative secondary research requires the use of a sharp and critical gaze to your data. Understanding its quality though knowing its context of production is essential and this requires the use of critical thinking skills and strategies. These are skills of critical judgement and evaluation that are supported by measures of quality such as appraisal checklists. Using these critical approaches means data can be reviewed for its credibility. When undertaking qualitative secondary research, we urge you to approach all data with healthy scepticism. Rapid changes in production, circulation and consumption of information should increase your vigilance in the way you use information in your daily lives and in your research.

HOW DO I KNOW IF QUALITATIVE SECONDARY RESEARCH IS FOR ME?

Qualitative secondary research can make significant contributions to the development of knowledge within your chosen field of study. This was recognised long ago when Glaser (1963: 11) claimed secondary research can *'lend new strength to the body of fundamental social knowledge'*. But it must be the 'right' choice for you as a researcher and for the research question(s) and/or aim(s) you set.

This chapter has provided an overview of qualitative secondary research and some of the reasons why you should adopt this research approach, but just in case you are still unsure, we provide a set of statements in Figure 1.8 for you to consider.

Reasons	✓	X
Your research does not need to engage first hand with people or institutions. You do not need or want to be involved as an interviewer, observer, chronicler or participant.		
You want to explore something that could be too sensitive to undertake first hand with people and institutions (e.g. explore cases of whistle blowing in companies or large organisations).		
You may be unable to access the people or number of people you want to interview (e.g. you are constrained by where you live and the time you have available).		
You need to access and collect data quickly to support policy and/or professional practice.		
You may want to develop, learn, create and use a range of creative approaches to information (data) collection, analysis and display that can be transferred to other forms of academic and professional practice.		

Figure 1.8   A decision table

If you agreed to most if not all of the statements in Figure 1.8, then secondary research is the approach you should consider taking.

PAUSE FOR THOUGHT

Making the right decision

It is important that you make the right decision regarding your choice of research. As researchers we need to know we are answering our research question, conducting a piece of 'original' research and that our research has value and meaning. Hopefully, you have a clear understanding of why and how this research design will enable you to answer your research question(s).

   If you are still not sure, then you will need to seek advice and support from your tutor, your institution's research team or the research commissioning team; seek advice earlier rather than later.

REFLECTION AND FURTHER READING

At the beginning of the chapter we set out what you should be able to do when you reached the end of this chapter. To aid your reflection on all we have covered we ask some chapter specific questions. If you are unsure of any of your answers to these questions, please go back to the relevant section to review this aspect.

REFLECTING ON CHAPTER 1

In this chapter we have:

- **Defined qualitative secondary research:** Can you define qualitative secondary research?
- **Appreciated the range of data it is possible to use:** Are you aware of the range of data you could use? Do you know how to check the quality of your data?
- **Identified key components of qualitative secondary research:** Do you know how each component works within your secondary research? Do you know where to find a discussion of these components in this book?
- **Checked if qualitative secondary research is for you:** Do you want to conduct qualitative secondary research? Do you know why?

WE RECOMMEND FOR FURTHER READING:

Bell, J., & Water, S. (2014) *Doing your Research Project: A Guide for First Time Researchers* (6th edn). Maidenhead, Berkshire: Open University Press.

(Continued)

(Continued)

This book has something to offer researchers at all levels of experience. The sections we recommend are Section 6 in Part I: 'Preparing the Ground' which offers an accessible overview of the role and function of a literature review and Section 7 in Part II: 'The Analysis of Documentary Evidence' which provides an overview of approaches to documentary sources.

Bornat, J. (2008) Crossing Boundaries with Secondary Analysis: Implications for Archived Oral History Data. Paper given at the ESRC National Council for Research Methods Network for Methodological Innovation, 2008, University of Essex.
Joanna Bornat provides an overview of her approach to the analysis of oral history. She identifies some of the ethical issues, specifically those faced when trying to understand another person's data.

Payne, G., & Payne, J. (2004) *Key Concepts in Social Research*. London: SAGE Publications Ltd.
This book provides an overview of key research concepts and we advise you to look at the section on Documentary Methods.

Scott, J. (1990) *A Matter of Record: Documentary Sources in Social Research*. Cambridge: Polity Press.
Although published some time ago, this remains a classic text on the use of documents. We recommend Chapters 1 and 2.

2
PREPARING FOR QUALITATIVE SECONDARY RESEARCH

THIS CHAPTER SUPPORTS YOUR ABILITY TO

explore effective reading and planning strategies

create relevant research questions, aims and objectives

complete a research proposal

recognise your developing research skills

CHAPTER OVERVIEW

This chapter sets the scene for your research success and it begins by asking why you want to study your selected topic for your research. Knowing why you have chosen this sets you off on your inquiry. To aid you in the realisation of this thinking, we offer a range of practical supporting strategies.

The strategies we offer relate to planning, reading, effective question and aim construction and the development of a research proposal. They are centred on helping you manage the amount of reading you are likely to undertake and on supporting your planning, so you can manage the delivery of your research project in the time you have available. We also examine ways to create feasible, relevant and achievable research question(s) and/or aims(s) and link these to the development of your conceptual framework. Towards the end of this chapter, we explore the function of a research proposal and outline some of the key ingredients your proposal could include.

You may want to go straight into your research, but we ask you to invest time and consideration in this early part of your research process. Effective planning and preparation are vital when you begin your research and devoting sufficient time to this will undoubtedly be one of the best investments you will make

WHY DO YOU WANT TO STUDY THIS TOPIC?

As you set off on your research journey make sure you keep thinking about *what* you want to study, *why* you want to study it and *how* you will undertake your research. It is easy to be swept up in the excitement of the research process without ensuring you have these basic questions answered. Knowing why you want to research your subject supports your ability to construct an appropriate research question and aim. This motivation to conduct your research will underpin your research process, including the data you may select and the method of analysis you apply. Therefore, it is worth taking time to make sure you really know why you want to do this project. You also need to know why this topic has relevance and meaning because you may need to write a section in your project called a research rationale. This is where you set out the drivers for your study in a clear, informed and persuasive way.

Developing a rationale

Creating a compelling rationale is important as it provides a context in which your research should be understood. A rationale is a section in your research that outlines the 'what' and the 'why' of your research. It may be that you have identified a gap in existing literature or you may want to explore a new way of thinking about your topic. The most important thing to consider is that you are trying to establish reasons why your research is important and provide a context for your reasons by referring to existing literature, research or practice in which your reasons can be understood. In other words, you are justifying your research and your approach, and trying to persuade your reader that reading your research project is worthwhile. Therefore, your rationale should contain your answers to certain questions outlined in Figure 2.1.

Why are you doing this piece of research?	*Is there a gap in existing research and/or literature?*
	Is it a current topic of debate or tension?
Why it is important?	*Is it something that concerns you professionally or academically?*
	Will it improve practice and/or policy?
How does your study add to what is already known?	*Are you asking a new question?*
	Are you using a new form of data to explore an existing question?
	Will you apply a new theory or form of analysis?
	Will it contribute to thinking about your topic in a new way?

Figure 2.1   Creating your research rationale

This section of your project enables you to hook your reader in as you show your knowledge and provide a robust justification for your research on the topic. the research does not need to 're-invent the wheel' as drawing on what others have done is an important part of the research process. Showing you are aware of how others have approached this topic adds to your research authority as you can draw on what they have generated and attempt a new way of thinking.

PAUSE FOR THOUGHT

Your rationale and your proposal

You may have to submit a research proposal to your institution's research committee or ethics board. Your proposal as a clear and concise overview of your planned research study enables judgements to be made on its feasibility and relevance. Therefore, having a robust and well-informed rationale will help you justify the need for your research.

BEGINNING YOUR RESEARCH

A specific interest in a subject or topic usually sparks the beginning of your research process, but this interest needs to be developed, extended and structured so your approach makes sense. Academic research does not just happen, it needs to be planned, designed and systematically executed. As stated above, you need to consider 'what' you want to study, 'why' you want to do it and now you need to consider 'how' this should be done.

Using planning strategies

Adopting methods that promote effective planning helps you develop the scope and sequence of your research project. This could mean you plan in a way that permits you to see your project from different perspectives. This could be as a big overall plan where you can see how each part fits together or it could be where you plan for smaller sections (see Figure 2.2). When you plan well, you encourage an ongoing dialogue with yourself as you challenge and question your topic choice, your question and your

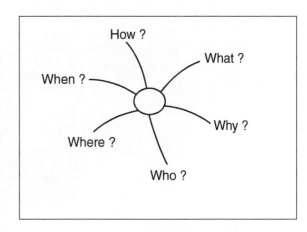

Figure 2.2 Question mapping

approach. This process of challenging and self-questioning should enable you to plug any knowledge gaps or flaws in your understanding. Planning is rarely a 'one-shot' process as it is something you should return to as you read and learn new things about your topic. Thus, your original pristine plan may become overwritten, drawn on or ripped up as you begin again. We advocate that a practical approach to planning does not have to be complicated. Sometimes the most effective plans are those created by drawing, mapping or writing your ideas out on paper (see Figure 2.2).

This planning approach is based on asking broad questions to get you thinking about your whole project or a specific part. For instance, you could ask these questions to narrow down your approach to your literature review:

- **How** do I access my data?
- **What** type of data?
- **Who** are the main theorists or commentators in my research area?
- **Where** will I access my data?
- **When** do I need to have my literature review completed?

An approach such as mind mapping that shows how concepts can be created and linked within your research can be useful (see Figure 2.3). This form of planning shows how concepts can be generated and linked, often as the result of your knowledge of your subject and that gained from your reading.

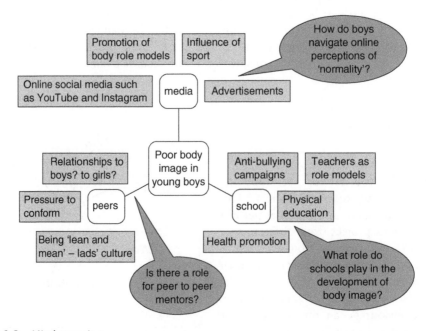

Figure 2.3   Mind mapping

You could also create a concept map which is similar to mind mapping (see Figure 2.4). Drawing maps of your key concepts and ideas can be a particularly useful visual-spatial tactic as they are, as De Simone (2007: 33) describes, a strategy *particularly suited to identifying relationships between ideas*.

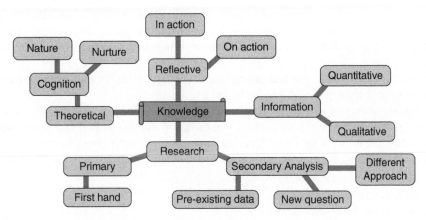

Figure 2.4 Concept mapping

You begin your map with your main research idea and then apply branches outwards to show how this main idea can be broken down to identify other new concepts that connect them. A map like this can promote the big and small picture planning we discussed previously as it can show the conceptual underpinning of your whole project or it can show the micro linkages made within one specific concept. As it is a non-linear diagram it can represent words or ideas linked to and arranged around a central concept or subject. This can highlight relationships between key words or phrases. Being able to highlight key words early on in your planning can support your key word searches and it can form the basis of your approach to data analysis (see Chapters 3 and 11).

There are more sophisticated planning tools available to access in formats like apps or online programs. Some of these programs offer free or limited free access but you will need to check before using and always check they are safe to download. However, you may not respond to mind maps as not everyone does. You may prefer a linear format and there are online tools available for you to do this or you can use the heading functions within word processing packages such as MS Word.

You may also want to use paper, pens, highlighters and sticky notes as these can be useful low-tech alternatives. It is worth exploring a variety of planning approaches as only you will know what works for you. In your decision process consider that a method that works for you must be one that allows you to see the structure of your inquiry as you see it and enable you to make connections and linkages. Do not be afraid to interact with your plans, to annotate them and draw on them and do not be afraid to show others. Having someone you trust apply a critical gaze to your work early on can save you going down blind alleys. It is also called peer review as your peers provide informed judgement on your approach to your research.

There are also some general points to consider when you start out on your research journey and these are about you planning your time effectively and taking care of yourself.

- Use a wall calendar so you can see key dates. Sometimes having a visual reminder can keep you focused on deadlines. If you record other personal or social commitments on this wall calendar such as birthdays you should be able to manage your time more effectively, so you can enjoy these.
- Be realistic in how much time you can devote to your study. Do not push yourself too hard and remember to keep a work and life balance.
- Know how, when and where you like to work. Self-knowledge like this is invaluable when planning your opportunities for study as you can plan your day around your study habits.
- Take regular breaks; try to set a timer for every hour so you move and refresh your focus. This also means taking breaks from staring at a computer screen and you could apply the 20-20-20 rule.
    - Every 20 minutes look away from your computer;
    - Look at an object 20 feet away (*about 6 metres*);
    - And do this for at least 20 seconds.

PAUSE FOR THOUGHT

Consider time management

A good plan should include time management targets that encourage you to set realistic goals for your research project completion. It can be tempting to leave everything to the last minute but meeting clear and realistic deadlines will ensure you feel in control and this can help to reduce stress. Try to see yourself as the manager in charge of the process. Ask yourself:

- **What is my time frame?** Be clear about your deadline and always factor in some time for reflection.
- **What do I need to complete and in what order?** You could use a program like Excel to create a Gantt chart. This will show you what is happening and when, allowing you to track your progress.

Keeping a research diary

One more way to support your planning and your understanding of your research process is to keep a research diary. This can be an informal log completed on paper, on a computer or written as an online journal to record the decisions and choices you make. You can use a diary in any way to suit your way of working but it can work well if you use it to set yourself clear, realistic and achievable goals that can be reviewed regularly. An approach like this can show you that your project is moving at a pace you can define and this can increase your sense of control. Figure 2.5 illustrates the daily use of a diary and shows how asking a few questions can create a structure that helps you keep track of your project.

What did I do today?	e.g. I completed my research question in rough.
What is its status?	e.g. Need to check a couple of issues – not sure it's specific enough.
What do I do next?	e.g. Continue to work on this tomorrow – must call my supervisor to arrange a meeting to discuss this.

Figure 2.5 Using a research diary as a daily planner

You can also use your diary to note down and highlight eureka moments or to track how you came to key decisions. This could include keeping track of any anonymisation processes and to provide information about the codes you create when you are analysing your data. A research diary should be a working document that records your planning and decision making in your research but it can also be a document that supports your reflection. You may need to refer to it if you are expected to write about your research experiences in a concluding section of your research project. Therefore, your diary can be a document for self-reflection that, as Lin (2016: 171) suggests, '*grows*' with you and encourages self-directed learning.

READING TO SUPPORT YOUR RESEARCH

One of the most important ways you can prepare yourself for your research project is to comprehensively read around your subject area. You will need to do this before you complete a research proposal as when you submit this you need to show you are aware of key sources of literature, key thinkers on your topic or any other literature or policy that supports the currency and relevance of your research question(s) and/or aim(s). Therefore, right from the start of your project you need to be involved in wide and diverse reading as this is central to your project's success. This is because:

- As you read you can appreciate and understand how others have attempted research in your subject area.
- The reading you undertake should expose you to diverse sources of data and, significantly, ways of thinking about your topic.
- As you read you should be able to identify key concepts and theories that appear within your research area.
- The reading you undertake facilitates the construction of your literature review as you will identify scholarly and academic texts that enable you to provide a strong context for your research inquiry.

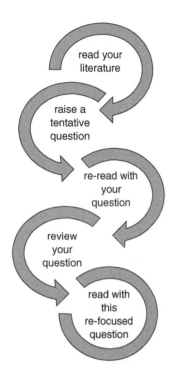

Figure 2.6 A reading loop

Creating reading loops

There is a strong relationship between your reading and the formulation of your research questions. Cameron and Price (2009: 292) describe this as '*looping*' which is a process of re-visiting and re-exploring available literature to refine your understanding of the topic. The aim of this looping process is to ensure you have a clear and focused question(s) and/or aim(s). This iterative process supports the creation of your conceptual framework which is informed by you but also significantly by your selection of reading material. Using a looping process like this can reinforce the strength of your conceptual framework and Figure 2.6 offers guidance on how you can apply a reading loop.

Using reading strategies

Although you should be used to reading whilst studying, reading for research purposes can be challenging. You may feel overwhelmed by the volume of literature you have to read and you may feel there is not enough time in which to do it. Reading for your qualitative secondary research project does not mean you have to read every book, every article and every document on your topic from the start to the end. Reading should widen your existing knowledge but, to do this effectively, you need to retain the information you read and be able to use this to form new connections. This requires an 'active' approach to reading which requires you to engage with your texts to promote deep rather than surface learning. It requires you to 'do' something with your reading to increase its meaning to you. Here are some active reading techniques:

- **Goal setting:** Ask yourself, what do you want to get out of the text. If it does not meet your goal, then move on to a new piece of reading.
- **Key word collecting:** Make a note of any new terminology or words and the context in which they appear. This is an effective way to develop key words which can be used within your data searches (see Chapter 7). You can also find key words under abstracts in journal articles; keeping a note of these can be a useful way of developing a conceptual framework for your study.
- **Visualisation techniques:** You can create a concept map using the key words you have identified. Note down the concepts explored and use connecting lines when you can make links between them. Use highlighters to colour code concepts or use coloured sticky post-it notes.

- **Direct your vision:** If you are using a hard copy of a book, article or document, use your fingers, a ruler or a piece of paper to mask the other text when you read. This will help you as you scan your text and help you home in on key words. If you are reading online, trace the words with the mouse and highlight as you read.
- **Question:** You could prepare a set of questions to ask when you begin reading. These could be questions such as those offered in Figure 2.7:

What is this text helping me understand?	Identify briefly the information this source is giving you.
How is this source supporting my understanding?	Is this source providing a visual model for you to follow? Could this source be a key text and central to your understanding?
What are the key points made?	Try to summarise your text and use bullet points to capture its essence.
Are there any issues raised for me to review?	Start to identify any arguments, debates or tensions it raises. Have any other sources of data raised these?
Are there any cited sources that could be useful for me to review?	This is citation chaining or snowballing (see Chapter 7) and it is an effective way to create a literature or data bank.
Identify one key point you have gained from this text	There may be many other points made and you should record these as well, but focusing on one key point will aid recall and retention. It will also support your ability to see connections between the various texts you will read.

Figure 2.7 Questioning your sources

It is also important that you read sources of information that challenge your views or offer alternative perspectives (see Chapter 9). Using sources of literature that confirm your argument is important but so is using sources that offer conflicting views. In your literature review you need to create balanced arguments to create a rounded understanding of your topic but also to refute claims of confirmation bias (*only including evidence that agrees with your point of view*).

- **Summarise:** Like the question technique above, being active here is based on you summarising what you have read. Try to reduce each article or chapter you have read into one clear summary. If you can do this in one paragraph, then you are doing well. You do not have to write everything down; you could record your summary on to your phone or other preferred recording device. It should then be possible to use speech-to-text software to change this into a text-based summary.

In addition to these techniques there are some more traditional tools such as 'scanning' and 'skimming' that can encourage an active approach to your reading:

Scanning: This is a process used when you search for specific information on a page. You can scan for key words, phrases and diagrams. You can also scan key sections of a book as you can scan the contents page, the reference list, the subject index, the abstract, or jump to the conclusions and findings. When you scan you are making a judgement as to the value of this source and your judgement may be based on your ability to identify key words or specific terminology.

Skim reading: This is a useful strategy to get the feel or gist of a key text. You may only need to read the first few sentences to see if the text you are reading is appropriate in content and reading level. Skim reading can be part of this looping process we discussed as you might skim read something before you interrogate it in more depth. When you skim read you are actively deciding if this text has relevance to you and your research topic.

Do not be afraid to close the book, leave a web page or reject an article if it is of no use. It is impossible to read everything and part of being an effective and active reader is making informed judgements so you can focus on reading sources of data that are relevant and meaningful to you and your study.

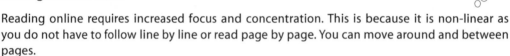

PAUSE FOR THOUGHT

Reading literature online

Reading online requires increased focus and concentration. This is because it is non-linear as you do not have to follow line by line or read page by page. You can move around and between pages.

Web pages often have adverts, additional links and other distractions which can direct or hijack your reading path (Kress 2003). Be aware of these and try to work against them. Try not to be tempted to go off piste. Deviating from your intended reading can make you lose focus and this can lead to frustration.

DEVELOPING SKILLS OF CRITICAL APPRAISAL

It is impossible to read everything written on your topic, especially as some of it may not be relevant or reflect the level of scholarship you need. Your understanding of your chosen topic will be based on the literature you access so ensuring this reflects the standard you aspire to is essential (see Chapter 9). This means considering issues such as the quality and credibility of your source; checking that the content is relevant and accurate. When doing this you are engaging in critical thinking, which can be enhanced by tools for critical appraisal (see Chapter 8). Critical appraisal encourages you to read with 'reasonable scepticism' (Wallace & Wray 2011: 5) which requires that you only accept evidence if the authors can support the claims they make. Always ask questions of your data and find the what, where, when, how and why of its production.

CREATING RESEARCH QUESTIONS, AIMS AND OBJECTIVES

Your research should have a clear purpose and, as an intellectual problem, it should be reflected in the question(s) and aim(s) you create. Questions, aims and objectives all have specific functions within a research project in demonstrating a research intention and direction. When formulated well, they provide a scaffold within which the research can develop (see Box 2.1). Therefore, creating a well-phrased question or aim is essential because it guides the direction of your research and keeps you focused on what you are trying to achieve. This may sound a bit basic to state but if you are researching a topic for a significant period of time, having a clear question of intent in mind will aid your ability to maintain your project's consistency and coherence (see Figure 2.8).

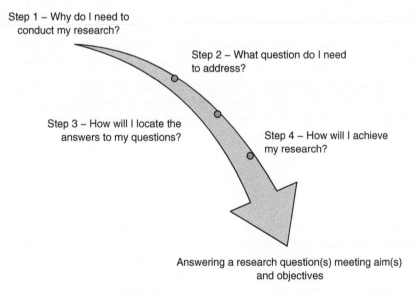

Step 1 – Why do I need to conduct my research?

Step 2 – What question do I need to address?

Step 3 – How will I locate the answers to my questions?

Step 4 – How will I achieve my research?

Answering a research question(s) meeting aim(s) and objectives

Figure 2.8   Knowing your research direction

Developing research questions

Your research question or statement is the intellectual problem you want to explore. It needs to consider the '*what*', '*who*', '*when*' and '*where*' of your problem for you to know '*how*' and '*why*' you will undertake this research. As we indicated above, reading is an essential part of your research process as it widens your knowledge base but it could also create the spark that ignites your interest or curiosity or increases your interest in a topic already selected. As the list below shows, your research question can come from a variety of places:

- It is formed at the start based on your curiosity and interest.
- It emerges as you begin to engage in reading around your topic.
- It is supplied to you by a funding body or supervisor.
- It is based on an area of concern (*e.g. vocational, professional or academic*).
- It stems from a situation you want to improve.

Descriptive or explanatory questions?

Your research questions can be 'descriptive' or 'explanatory' of the phenomena you wish to examine.

Descriptive research questions: These questions start with 'what', 'when', 'who', 'where', or 'how'. For example, How do adults access adult literacy sessions in Scotland? Using a synonym finder shows the word 'how' synonymous with 'in what way' and 'by what means'. Therefore, descriptive research questions are straightforward questions that try to understand or explore a phenomenon.

Explanatory research questions: These questions start with 'why'. For example, Why do adults access adult literacy sessions in Scotland? Using a synonym finder, shows the word 'why' synonymous with 'for what reason' and 'to what end'. Therefore, explanatory questions try to understand causes for a phenomenon.

Statements or questions?

You may need to create a question and/or a statement. The differences between the two are clear when you see them written down. A statement is 'declarative' as it declares what your research is about and interrogative is where you ask a question (see Figure 2.9).

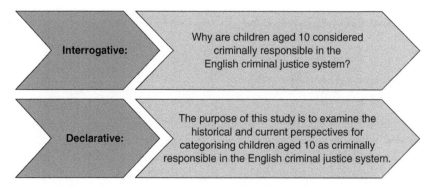

Interrogative: Why are children aged 10 considered criminally responsible in the English criminal justice system?

Declarative: The purpose of this study is to examine the historical and current perspectives for categorising children aged 10 as criminally responsible in the English criminal justice system.

Figure 2.9   Different approaches to stating your research problem

The form you use may be decided by the remit you have to follow, your supervisor's or institution's guidelines. Irrespective of the type of question you require, it should clearly signal the content and purpose of the research. Formulating an effective research question can take time and it is worth considering that there is no *'foolproof way of generating research questions'* (Robson 2002: 54). This stage of your research needs to be carefully considered and whilst your question can emerge through your immersion in relevant literature, it can also be formed by discussion with others. You could discuss your topic with your supervisor or share your ideas with your peers. Talking your question through with others in this way could help you develop *'good'* research questions (Punch 2013: 76). Figure 2.10 illustrates what effective research questions should be.

The word 'worthwhile' is important to consider (in Figure 2.10) because tempting as it may be to rush ahead with your project, time needs to be taken to ensure that the question or problem you have set yourself is actually 'worthwhile' answering. Ask yourself:

- Is there too much written on my subject? *If you answer yes, consider if your inquiry can be approached in a new way. If you are just repeating what has already been done it is difficult to justify why your inquiry should take place. However, you may consider that investigating your topic using qualitative secondary research can add a distinct perspective and therefore, this research design enables you to add to existing knowledge.*
- Can I answer my question using yes or no? *If you can, then this is not a strong research question and it needs to be considered. You could try to refocus your question using 'how' or 'why'.*

L **Linked:** if using multiple questions, they need to be connected in some way.

A **Answerable:** you can see what data is required and how this will be obtained.

S **Specific:** the concepts offered are specific enough to link to data indicators.

E **Easily:** understood and not ambiguous.

R **Relevant:** the questions you ask are interesting and **worthwhile**.

Figure 2.10 LASER acronym

Making sure your research is worthwhile is important as you need to defend why your research needs to take place (*the rationale*) and this means you should consider if your question is 'feasible', 'relevant' and within your 'capabilities' (see Figure 2.11).

Feasible	Relevant	Capabilities
• Within a clear and achievable time frame. • You can access the data you need. • It is not *too big* or *too sensitive* to handle.	• It meets your discipline's and institution's expections for a research project. • It adds to the field of knowledge.	• You have the research skills needed to complete the project. • You are persistent and resilient. • You can manage your time.

Figure 2.11   Ensuring your question is feasible, relevant and within your capabilities

Developing research aims

An aim is a statement that sets out the purpose of the enquiry. It is a declaration of your anticipated intentions that 'paints the picture', directs the focus of your research and states what you aim to achieve. Depending on your research and the expectations of your institution, you may have more than one aim. An aim is easy to identify as it usually begins with an infinitive of a verb such as 'to explore' or 'to investigate'. Figure 2.12 illustrates how writing aims in this way reflects a clear purpose of action and intent as the infinitive used indicates the approach you will take to your research.

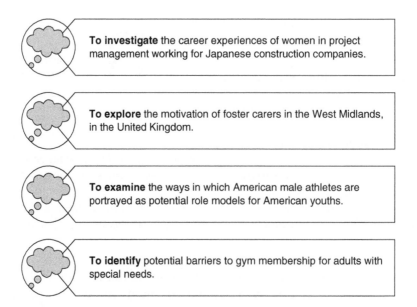

To investigate the career experiences of women in project management working for Japanese construction companies.

To explore the motivation of foster carers in the West Midlands, in the United Kingdom.

To examine the ways in which American male athletes are portrayed as potential role models for American youths.

To identify potential barriers to gym membership for adults with special needs.

Figure 2.12   Examples of research aims

Developing research objectives

Objectives are the steps that you take towards achieving your aim(s) or answering your question(s). They can be specific to each part of your research process (see Figure 2.13). You may have objectives for the methodology; for example, the approach taken to data analysis, defining key terms or to provide a critical consideration of the underpinning theory you plan to employ. They tend to have a practical tone as they indicate that you are going to 'do' something within your research (Needham 2016). Therefore, objectives generally indicate actions that are required to complete your study and function to outline key steps in your research. Like aims, they often begin with the infinitive of key verbs; for example, to *analyse*, to *access*, *to calculate*, to *compare*, to *determine*, to *establish*, to *measure* and to *provide*. This can be seen in the examples offered in Figure 2.13.

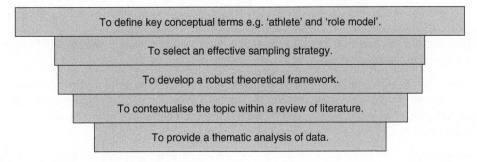

To define key conceptual terms e.g. 'athlete' and 'role model'.

To select an effective sampling strategy.

To develop a robust theoretical framework.

To contextualise the topic within a review of literature.

To provide a thematic analysis of data.

Figure 2.13   Examples of research objectives

PAUSE FOR THOUGHT

Testing your question or aim

When constructing your question or aim, you could apply the 'Goldilocks test' (Clough & Nutbrown 2012: 43). This is a test to see if your question is 'just right'. To do this, they suggest you ask yourself the following questions:

Is my question or aim?

'too big'? – Can this question be tackled in the size of the study I have to do?

'too small'? – Is there enough substance to this study to make it worthwhile?

'too hot'? – Is the subject selected too sensitive?

Making your questions and aims clear and specific

An effective research question is one which makes '*explicit the precise area of an investigation; it identifies, within the area of general concern, the specific aspect(s) which is or are of particular interest*' (Lewis & Munn 1987: 7). This level of specificity is important for you and your reader. Your question(s) can provide a scaffold that keeps you focused on your research task and underpins your conceptual framework (see Chapter 3). The words you use in your question(s) and/or aims(s) can have '*methodological implications*' (Punch 2013: 23). Using a question to support methodological processes can be seen in the example offered in Box 2.1. A good question or aim should provide clearly defined concepts that can be easily identified and thus, explored in your reading.

BOX 2.1 THE IMPORTANCE OF FORMULATING CLEAR AND PRECISE QUESTIONS

If you were researching specific aspects of working with young offenders and to do this, you formulated the question '**How** does **Art therapy support** the **rehabilitation** of **young offenders** in **institutions** in the **North East of England**?' it would be possible to deconstruct your question to inform parts of your research process. Every word highlighted in bold within the question has a pivotal role in your answering your question.

How – This is a descriptive question suggesting you want to understand how art therapy supports young offenders. In your rationale, you may state that you are a youth worker or a person within the youth justice system and this question needs answering because it supports your practice or may inform a review of current policy.

Art therapy – This sets out two key concepts, **art** and **therapy** but you will need to define and explore '**art therapy**' as a therapeutic experience.

Rehabilitation – This is another key concept and it will need defining both legally and socially.

Support – This is where you would need to define '**support**' which may be considered from a financial, emotional or behavioural perspective.

Young offenders – The age range for '**young**' needs defining and this would need a legal definition rather than a social one. In the same way, you would need to consider what is meant by '**offenders**'. You may explore social definitions and consider how these differ to the legal ones you found.

Institutions – As a concept, institutions would need defining and this may require both legal and social definitions.

North East of England – This is a very specific geographic area and its significance would need exploring in relation to the other key concepts. This significance of this area might appear in your rationale as you discuss the relevance of your research; for example, to your profession, to policy, to key arguments or to aspects of social change.

CREATING A RESEARCH PROPOSAL

Most academic or formal research projects expect you to complete and submit a research proposal. This research proposal should be a concise and coherent summary of your proposed research. It typically should include a succinct summary of the existing understanding on the topic and recent debates. This should then indicate some of the central issues or questions that you aim to address and persuade your reviewer that your research is worthwhile and the outcomes worth knowing. There are many ways to construct and compose a research proposal and Figure 2.14 sets out some of the key components you may need to consider.

Title:	• This may be very tentative at the beginning and change as you develop your ideas.
Aim or research questions:	• The requirements for this section may depend on your subject area, on your institution and/or supervisor.
	• In general, your aim(s) and/or question(s) should be as specific and as focused as they can be at this early stage, but they may change (see Chapter 2).
Objectives:	• You may or may not have to use objectives but, if you do, these guide your research activities. They say what you are going to do to achieve your aim (see Chapter 2).
Rationale or justification:	• You may have a section that asks you to justify why your question is worth asking and therefore, answering. You should explain why your research is important and identify the contribution it will make.
	• It should justify why your topic should be explored or investigated (see Chapter 2).
Research context (literature review):	• You may need to provide a context that explains the broad background against which you will conduct your research.
	• Provide a concise overview of the area you wish to explore, and a critical evaluation of existing knowledge may be needed.
	• You may need to offer an understanding of theory or identify key texts you may draw upon (see Chapters 3, 4 and 9).
Methodology:	• You may need to describe your approach to data collection and selection (see Chapters 7 and 8).
	• It is best to identify your research strategy (*single, combined or multiple* – see Chapter 4) and set out the type of data you will use within this (*qualitative data only or a mix of qualitative and quantitative*).
	• State how your approach to data analysis will support your research (see Chapters 4, 11 and 12).
Ethics:	• You should disclose if you are selecting a sensitive topic or if you need to access sensitive data.
	• You may need to discuss issues of informed consent and confidentiality (see Chapter 5), data storage and, possibly, submit a separate Data Management Plan (see Chapter 10).

Figure 2.14 Potential components of a proposal for qualitative secondary research

You may or may not have to formally submit a research proposal but, if you do, focus on its importance as it demonstrates the following skills and attributes:

- **your academic skill set:** concision, clarity of thought, ability to analyse and synthesise substantial amounts of data;
- **your research skills:** understanding and using key research terminology and processes in practice;
- **your ability to plan and lead your study:** reflected in the scope and sequence of your study.

Your proposal should be as well-structured as it is possible to create so early on in your research but it should provide some flexibility. It is very rare for research to always go as planned. Even if you do not need to submit a formal research proposal, it can still be an effective way to plan. It may support your ability to set clear completion targets to keep your research on track.

You may also need to submit a Data Management Plan (see Chapter 10) but this will depend on the requirements of your institution or organisation. Even if this is not a compulsory part of your research process, it is worth considering completing a data management plan as this will help you focus on some of the key issues in your research process. A good data management plan encourages you to consider legal and ethical issues and can provide evidence of your adherence to your institution's or discipline's ethical code of conduct, specifically as it relates to data collection and storage.

PAUSE FOR THOUGHT

Check that you know what to do

It may be tempting to jump right in to your project but it is worth taking time to read any information supplied to you about your project (*e.g. your school or academic handbook or research guidelines provided by your institution*). For example, before you begin you may need to check the following:

- Do you need to create questions, aims, objectives or a mix of these?
- Do you need to create a research proposal?
- Do you need a data management plan?
- Do you need to include a bibliography and/or a reference list?
- Do you know who your supervisor is and how to contact them?

THE DEVELOPMENT OF SKILLS AND ATTITUDES

We thought we would begin and end (see Chapter 14) this book with a consideration of you and the skills you will develop. When you undertake any form of research, you will develop key skills which are eminently transferable into other aspects of your academic experiences and future employment. In conducting qualitative secondary research, you can develop a wide variety of skills. These could be your capacity for investigation, analysis, critical thinking, effective data management and key organisational skills. Some of the specific key skills and attributes you may develop are outlined below (see Figure 2.15).

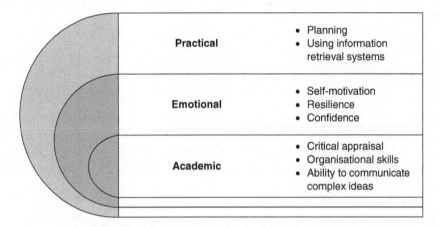

Figure 2.15   Areas of skill development

Some of these skills you may already have as you begin your research journey and some you will develop as you progress. This is called capacity building as you grow in your capacity to complete your research, developing the skills and attitudes we have identified (see Figure 2.15).

DEVELOPING A RESEARCH 'MINDSET'

Being open-minded and prepared to take risks is part of being a researcher as not every decision we make will be a good one and not every piece of data you select will be the best. Being able to recognise that with risk comes the ability to grow and develop reflects a 'growth mindset' (Dweck 2006). It means being open to possibilities that could expose you to failure but accepting that if failure happens you can learn from it. This approach to thinking about yourself is linked to enhanced creativity, problem solving and strongly linked to resilience. Adopting a growth mindset will enable you to withstand challenges and if problems do occur in your research, you will be more likely to resolve these. One of the key aspects of a 'growth mindset' is the ability to accept feedback and use it to grow. Therefore, try to embrace the feedback you are offered and use it constructively to develop yourself as a researcher.

PAUSE FOR THOUGHT

Do not attempt this on your own!

Try to establish a good working relationship with your supervisor or mentor. Your supervisor knows what you should do. They can offer guidance and support on all aspects of the research process. As Bell (2005: 36) warns *'few researchers, inexperienced and experienced, can go it alone and expect to produce quality research'.*

BEING 'CLEAR'

As you begin to think about your study, take some time to reflect on the skills you have and the skills you need to complete it. Completing a research project requires being able to work in a logical and structured way. The acronym **CLEAR** is used to illustrate the skills you may have or may need (see Figure 2.16). As you start to plan or complete your proposal have these words in the back of your mind.

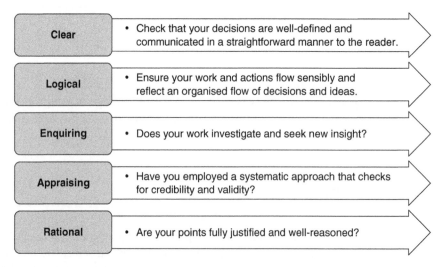

Figure 2.16   CLEAR research skills

What happens if things do not go to plan?

As a final word, your plan and your questions may be clear and appropriate but sometimes things happen that lead to amendments and revisions. It may be that the data you were hoping to analyse is not available, or you may encounter a new piece of information or a new concept while undertaking a literature search that makes you rethink the basis of your research question. If this happens you should always talk to your supervisor before you make any substantial revision to your plans and explain why you think you need to make the change.

REFLECTION AND FURTHER READING

At the beginning of the chapter we set out what you should be able to do when you reached the end of this chapter. To aid your reflection on all we have covered we ask some chapter specific questions. If you are unsure of any of your answers to these questions, please go back to the relevant section to review this aspect.

REFLECTING ON CHAPTER 2

In this chapter we have:

- **Explored a selection of reading strategies:** Is there one strategy that you felt you could use to enhance your approach to reading?
- **Examined the role of planning:** Do you have a preferred way to plan? How does this help you see the big and small picture of your research?
- **Set out in depth the formulation of research questions, aims and objectives:** Do you know how to create LASER focused research question(s), aim(s) and objectives?
- **Provided an overview of research proposals and their completion:** Could you complete a qualitative secondary research proposal?
- **Discussed the creation of research skills and the need for a growth mindset:** Are you aware of the skill set you bring to your research and the skill set you could develop?

WE RECOMMEND FOR FURTHER READING:

Abdulai, R.T., & Owusu-Ansah, A. (2014) Essential ingredients of a good research proposal for undergraduate and postgraduate students in the social sciences. *SAGE Open*, *4*(3), 1–15. This article offers advice on the creation of an undergraduate research proposal.

(Continued)

(Continued)

Emerald Publishing (2018) *How to use mind maps to revolutionize your note-taking.* Available at: www.emeraldgrouppublishing.com/learning/study_skills/skills/mind_maps.htm.
This site offers a comprehensive overview of mind mapping techniques.

Green, N., & Stoneman, P. (2016) Formulating and refining a research question. In N. Gilbert & P. Stoneman (eds), *Researching Social Life* (4th edn) (pp. 44–59). London: SAGE Publications Ltd.
Chapter 3 contains a wealth of information that complements that offered in this chapter. Of special note is section 3.3 'The characteristics of social research questions'.

O'Leary, Z. (2017) *The Essential Guide to Doing Research* (3rd edn). London: SAGE Publications Ltd.
Chapter 3 is strongly recommended as it explores research question construction.

Ortlip, M. (2008) Keeping and using reflective journals in the qualitative research process. *The Qualitative Report, 13(4)*, 695–705.
Michelle Ortlip offers an open and reflective account of her use of a research journal (diary) and how this added insight to her own research persona and skills.

University of Leicester (2018) *Gantt Charts.* Available at: www2.le.ac.uk/offices/ld/resources/dissertations/getting-started/your-time-management/gantt-charts.
The University of Leicester student learning development website has a section on using Gantt charts to support your project management.

3

THE ROLE OF THEORY IN QUALITATIVE SECONDARY RESEARCH

THIS CHAPTER SUPPORTS YOUR ABILITY TO

- know about positionality

- understand the role of theory

- understand the role of concepts

- consider how theory supports your analysis

- recognise your influence on your research

CHAPTER OVERVIEW

This chapter aims to add some clarity to what can be a complex and confusing aspect of the research process. We begin with a consideration of positionality as a way of understanding how who you are as a person has the potential to influence the research you conduct. This leads to a consideration of your theory of knowledge which, as a way of understanding how you consider knowledge is generated, underpins your decision to conduct qualitative secondary research.

We also explore the dynamic relationship between concepts and theory within your research and consider the function of theory as known or existing ways of understanding the world (e.g. Marxism or social learning theory).

We end this chapter with a discussion of 'reflexivity' which, as a process of critical self-awareness, acknowledges your influence on the research you produce and types of possible bias which can occur if you are not alert to the possibilities of your influence. By the end of this chapter, you should understand the role and function of theoretical and conceptual frameworks and how they support the design of your qualitative secondary research.

WHY DO YOU NEED TO KNOW ABOUT THEORY?

The answer to this question is that theory explains what is happening in the world. It explains who we are and how we think this because the active engagement you have in the world leads you to create knowledge that is unique to you. As you learn through this active engagement, you can make predictions or theories of the world. You may create basic theories in your life, such as it always rains on your birthday or bread always falls butter side down, to more significant theories based on not going to the 'right' school or having the 'right' clothes and explaining this within theories of social and cultural disadvantage.

When we discuss theory in research we need to consider the role of concepts as the two are tightly bound in a dynamic relationship. Concepts are your thoughts or ideas created as you interact in the world and as such they are the building blocks of your knowledge. However, you need to construct some form of explanation that enables you to makes sense of your concepts. Theory is therefore, an explanation that makes sense of your concepts and organises them into something meaningful. In research, it is the explanation as to why you will explore certain subjects, why you ask specific questions and how you understand your findings.

As your beliefs, concepts and theories are influenced by your interaction in the world, the research you produce has the potential to be influenced by who you are as a person and consequently, as a researcher. This influence is constructed in many ways and as you are an individual so is the influence you bring. Your influence can be felt in the question(s) you ask or aim(s) you set or it can be in the sources of data you select or the method of analysis you want to apply to understand your data. We show some of these influences on research in Figure 3.1.

Figure 3.1   Influences on your research

Some of the influence that you bring to your research may be quite subtle and some will be very powerful but this will depend on who you are and the nature of your experiences. This influence also pertains to the values you bring to your research. These are your beliefs formed by your family and personal life, your religion, or your politics. Your influence is therefore felt strongly on an approach to research such as qualitative research which is based on interpretation. The interpretation you make of your data can be influenced by you and, therefore, there is a need to disclose this influence in case it distorts or alters the interpretation you make. Declaring who you are and what you are in your research is called stating your 'positionality'. Your research is therefore, influenced by you and your theory of the world as it shapes your choices in the following ways:

- **What you study**
- **Why you study it**
- **How you will study it**
- **Formulation of your question(s) and/or aim(s)**
- **The data you select for analysis and the literature you are drawn to for your literature review**
- **The method of analysis you employ**
- **Your interpretation of your findings**

Theory is therefore, a set of concepts or beliefs that enable us to explain or to test something that exists in the world. These concepts and beliefs form a critical lens through which you see the world and, in research, this lens is applied to the way you design your research and the findings you will generate. Hence, knowing what theory is, what it does and what it looks like is pivotal to you as a researcher because it can provide a rationale for the way your research is conducted and, above all else, it should help you explain what you have found out.

Theory is often presented as complex and explored differently by various authors so in this chapter, we will approach theory in a practical and straightforward way. It can be very easy to talk about theory in an abstract way but we aim to deconstruct this large 'thing' called theory into more meaningful and relevant parts to show how it functions in your qualitative secondary research project. As we show in Figure 3.2, we divide theory into three core components to illustrate how it functions in your research.

In this chapter we explore theory as having a key role in your qualitative secondary research in three ways:

- Explaining why you conduct your research the way you do – your theory of knowledge;
- How theory works to make sense of your concepts;
- How theory can explain your findings.

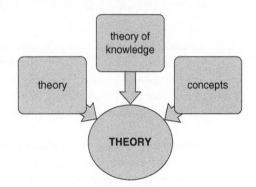

Figure 3.2 Deconstructing theory

UNDERSTANDING RESEARCH POSITIONS

Your theory of knowledge is your worldview or research position as it is how who you are as a person influences the way you think knowledge is created. It is your explanation for the way you will conduct your research. In research, your theory of knowledge has two main aspects: one is ontology (*what things are*) and the other is epistemology (*how things are*) (see Figure 3.3). Knowing 'what' and 'how' things exist in the world guides and shapes your research in many ways. It directs you to a type of research, to a source of data and it can signpost how you may use theory to aid your understanding of your research findings. Therefore, knowing your research position can be a powerful tool when you construct your research methodology as it can defend some of the research decisions you make.

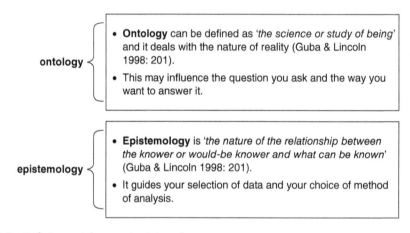

Figure 3.3   Defining ontology and epistemology

How research positions influence your research

To understand what your research position means to your research, we begin by exploring two basic ontological research positions; 'objectivity' and 'subjectivity'. These two extremes of research positions reflect how you can see yourself in the world and how this can be translated into a way of thinking about the research you create. We link these research positions to epistemology (*how knowledge is created*).

Objectivity: Seeing the world objectively (*your ontology*) can lead to a positivist research position (*your epistemology*). This is because you accept that knowledge in the world can be measured or quantified in some way. Striving for pure objectivity makes you endeavour to conduct your research without the influence of the researcher as you want to ensure your research is value-free. Therefore, it is more likely you will use numerical data that lends itself to categorisation or forms of measurement and not data that offers rich descriptions.

Subjectivity: If you believe that reality is subjective (*your ontology*) and open to interpretation then you may adopt a post-positivist or interpretive position (*your epistemology*). This research position accepts that understanding the world is based on multiple realities which are constructed through human interaction in the social world. In this research approach, there is a relationship between you as the researcher and what you are researching. This is where the 'who', 'what' and 'where' of your researcher identify is important. You believe that because of who you are (*e.g. your gender, your age, ethnicity*), what you are (*e.g. teacher, student, parent*) will in some way influence the research you produce. In qualitative research you may adopt 'reflexivity' to acknowledge your influence on your research (O' Leary 2004). As you believe that the world can be interpreted, you may use documents as sources of data as these provide insight into people's lives (see Chapter 6 for examples of qualitative data). Your aim is for description not accurate and objective measurement.

If you look at Figure 3.4, you will see there is a third way of knowing. This is called 'pragmatic' (Onwuegbuzie & Leech 2005) which reflects a more realistic research reality as most people do not exist in the two extremes of positivism (*objectivity*) and interpretivism (*subjectivity*) or within polarised paradigms (*qualitative or quantitative*); most are some way in between. This being 'in between' accepts that you need to approach your research in a way that leads to an appropriate answer.

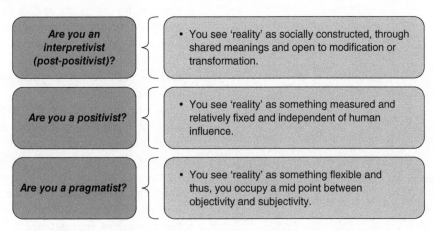

Figure 3.4   Research paradigms

Pragmatism: Being a pragmatist is a 'third alternative' as it is a mid-point between positivism and interpretivism (Tashakkori & Creswell 2007). Pragmatists respond to the question(s) and/or aim(s) they set and do not feel they should be restricted to specific forms of data. Adopting a pragmatic approach can provide benefits within your research as it can support data and methodological triangulation, adding to the rigour of your research (Patton 2002) (see Chapter 4).

Research paradigms

As indicated in Figure 3.4, the research positions 'positivist', 'post-positivist', 'interpretivist' and 'pragmatist' can also be referred to as research paradigms. Paradigms are sets of known and common research beliefs and agreements that indicate how your research problem or aim should be understood and addressed (Kuhn 1970). Knowing about research paradigms is useful because they are research shorthand that enables the research community and your reader to understand how your study is designed. As you have decided to research using qualitative data, you may declare an interpretivist or post-positivist research position but you may also be a pragmatist.

Why should I identify my research position?

Knowing how you see the world indicates your relationship to all parts of the research process. As shown in Figure 3.5, your research position or worldview (*your ontology*), your research paradigm (*epistemology*) and your methodology are linked. By developing an increased appreciation of this link, you should develop a greater understanding of the research process and the significance of your influence on your data (Neuman 1997). Understanding your theory of knowledge can be challenging, but do not give up as there is significant value in knowing this. You will need to defend the way you constructed your research and knowing that it begins with your worldview and research positions can increase the strength of your defence.

We have provided a condensed overview of research positions and there are many informative research texts (see further reading) that can add to the research perspectives we have explored.

Figure 3.5   The intersecting influence of ontology, epistemology and methodology

Knowing who you are as a researcher is the basis of the defence you make for the how and why of your research design. Our aim in discussing this theory here is to get you thinking about this defence.

PAUSE FOR THOUGHT

Defending your approach to theory

Your methodology is where you defend your approach to theory and this defence should begin with you understanding your theory of knowledge or worldview. However, not all institutions may expect you to include this theoretical aspect and therefore, we advise you to check with your institution guidelines or research handbook to check what is expected.

If you have a choice, we strongly advise you to embrace this concept as it makes sense of processes such as reflexivity and other strategies to secure research quality that we explore in Chapter 4.

UNDERSTANDING THEORY AND CONCEPTS

In this section we explore the role of concepts as the ideas and beliefs that you have as informed by your interaction in the world and that underpin the whole of your research. In Chapter 2, we explored how your research question could be deconstructed to understand the concepts you needed to explore in your inquiry. This process demonstrated the role of concepts as the building blocks of your research and how, when clearly defined, these can provide a conceptual framework. Your conceptual framework is therefore a collection of key concepts, ideas, thoughts and beliefs about your inquiry and is created by you as a person with experience of your subject, by your academic engagement with your subject and by your reading.

Concepts provide an organisational structure to your research as they narrow down the scope of your inquiry (see Chapter 2). You can only include concepts in your research that are relevant to answering your research question, and this requires you to make critical judgements about what to include and what to reject. This process is based on your understanding of your subject and it is an essential part of your inquiry process as it is impossible to include everything. Hence the importance of your reading, as this is where you are guided in what to include or exclude.

What you include in your study and what you omit inform your reader as to the depth and breadth of your knowledge and understanding. Therefore, when clearly articulated, a conceptual framework is a powerful tool as it sets out what is explored in your inquiry process illustrating logic and clarity in your selection. Your conceptual framework sets out the boundaries of your research (see Chapter 2) and as Miles and Huberman (1994: 440) state, it '*lays out the key factors, constructs, or variables, and presumes relationships among them*'. When viewed in this way, your conceptual framework forms the spine of your research as it supports the whole structure.

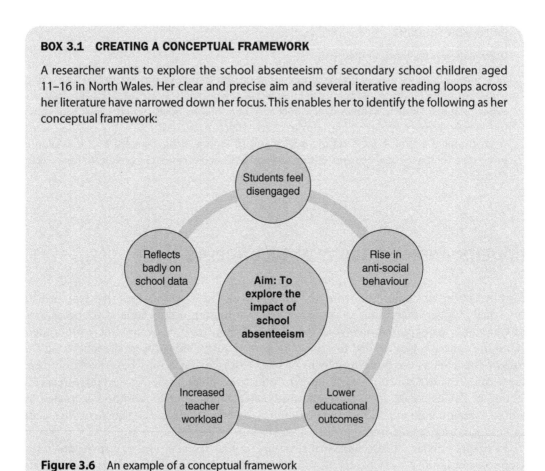

BOX 3.1   CREATING A CONCEPTUAL FRAMEWORK

A researcher wants to explore the school absenteeism of secondary school children aged 11–16 in North Wales. Her clear and precise aim and several iterative reading loops across her literature have narrowed down her focus. This enables her to identify the following as her conceptual framework:

Figure 3.6   An example of a conceptual framework

The concepts she has defined through her reading guide the way she thinks about her research topic and she can use these concepts to facilitate the construction of her literature review, employing her identified concepts as headings. When used in this way, her conceptual framework provides a structure for her inquiry. When she analyses her data her conceptual framework supports her ability to identify emerging themes.

To support the interpretation of her findings she could apply a critical spotlight offered by theoretical constructs such as poverty, social exclusion, community and class. She could also apply known theory such Maslow's (1943, 1954) Hierarchy of Needs to understand factors that create barriers to children's school attendance.

This example highlights the relationship that exists between concepts and theory. Concepts identify 'what' is happening but you need to be able to explain 'why' and this is the role of theory. Theory is, therefore, central 'to the quest for ongoing knowledge development' (Fox, Gardner & Osborne 2015: 70), as it takes you away from simple observations of what is happening to more in-depth clarifications and insight. Theory provides a lens through which you can see your findings and make sense of them so you can 'stand back and view phenomena critically' (Kelly 2010: 285).

Working with theory is very much an individual consideration because the concepts you create will be informed by who you are and by your reading and the knowledge you have gained while studying. This academic engagement may have led you to specific theoretical perspectives provided by key thinkers and pivotal ways of understanding your subject. The section that follows explores how theoretical perspectives as known and existing theories can inform your conceptual understanding of your research topic.

The influence of known theory

Known or existing views of the world exist because of a logical or systematic process of observation and inquiry and they can be large theoretical perspectives – e.g. feminism, Marxism – or more focused theory that can be applied to explain your findings – e.g. social learning theory, attachment theory.

This known theory has its use which we can see when we consider Einstein's theory of relativity and Newton's law of gravity. These provide ways of understanding the world that have become accepted over time. We might not use Einstein's theory in general conversation but we are all aware of the forces of gravity especially when we drop something valuable. This theory provides a general understanding for the phenomenon of dropping something and as such it allows us to make sense of the act. We do not need to go out and experiment to know how gravity works as this has already been done and it is now accepted. We can apply this to other ways of explaining what is happening in the world and we may feel that theoretical constructs such as race, gender and poverty offer explanations for what happens in the world. Creswell (2009: 61) defines this use of theory as providing a broad explanation for behaviour and attitudes.

Theory should facilitate your understanding of the phenomena you seek to explore and known or existing theory can help to explain the concepts you identify within your research. In Box 3.2, we provide an example of a researcher interested in exploring women returning to work. In this example, it is possible to see that she brings her own conceptual understanding because she is a woman with similar characteristics to the people she wants to study. She also finds feminist theory that adds to her knowledge and increases her conceptual understanding of the topic. Her use of known theory informs her wider understanding of her topic and thus, it forms a theoretical framework for her study.

BOX 3.2   EXPLORING THEORY

A researcher aims to explore the narratives provided in an online blog created by a group of women who have returned to work after a long break caring full-time for their children. She is a woman, has children and has experienced career breaks herself. She is therefore, influenced in her choice of topic by her identity and experiences.

   As she begins her research she creates a conceptual framework in which age, gender, ethnicity, domestic role and professional or vocational status all influence women as they study. However, as she continues to read she comes across feminist theory and this provides her with a critical lens through which to consider social forces that act on women and the choices they make.

Your use of theory is very much researcher defined and you may have a theory to help you understand your data when you commence your study or it may be something that evolves as you read and engage with your subject area in more depth. However, as you read and immerse yourself in the literature on and around your subject area, it will soon be clear that there are a multitude of known theories and many ways to create a conceptual understanding of your topic. We have broken this large category of theory into two; one is a larger theoretical perspective and the other is mid-level and more specific theory.

Types of theory

Theoretical perspectives are '*schools of thought*' (Cooper & Meadows 2016: 13) that offer a big picture or broad perspective of the world. Theoretical constructs such as power, race and oppression can be reflected in theoretical perspectives like functionalism and Marxism. These are accepted as theoretical perspectives or paradigms because they are 'beliefs, values, techniques, and so on shared by the members of a given community' (Kuhn 1970: 175). We offer examples of these perspectives in Figure 3.7.

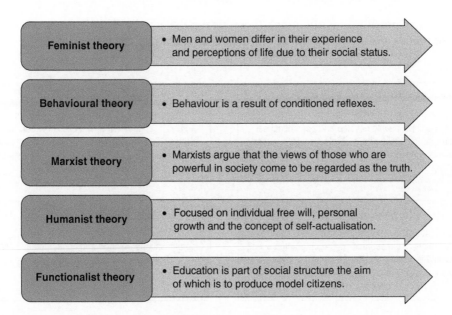

Figure 3.7 Examples of theoretical perspectives

These perspectives (see Figure 3.7) provide a critical lens to your subject as they offer specific ways in which you can view your research findings. For example, adopting a functionalist perspective to secondary research on families with children where both parents work may reveal children are struggling at school. Your theory would provide a critical response to your findings where you may consider changes in social order (e.g. both parents working) has led to a decline in school standards as parents are not around to support their children when they do their homework.

If you begin your research within a functionalist perspective, this will inform your conceptual understanding and will influence your selection of data. When you have generated findings, you will explain these through your functionalist critical lens. Employing a known theory provides a spotlight on how your topic can be conceptualised as evidenced in the example of the woman researcher and her use of feminism as a critical lens. The concepts her theory exposed supported her ability to explain the lives of women. However, there are also more focused ways of understanding theory.

This is relevant as these larger well-known theories may not be able to provide the sharpness of conceptual understanding to use as a critical lens. This is where we need to turn to 'middle range' theory (Merton 1967). This is the theory that has the potential to be more specific in supporting your understanding of your research topic and your findings. Presented in Figure 3.8 are just a few well-known examples out of a vast range of possible and potential middle range theoretical perspectives. This is again a huge category of theory and we could not cover all and do them justice.

Transformative learning theory: This theory, developed by Mezirow (1978, 1991), describes how people develop and use critical self-reflection to consider their beliefs and experiences and, over time, change the way they see themselves and the world.	**Social learning theory:** This theory based on the work of Bandura (1977b) suggests that we learn new behaviour through a process of observation and imitation. Thus, learning is more efficient when behaviour required is modelled.
Critical race theory: As a theoretical framework this provides a spotlight to issues relating to race, racism, and other intersecting aspects. It is linked to social justice and social change and because it is critical, it explores the role and function of power.	**Resource-dependence theory:** This theory provides a focus on how organisations manage and control relationships. It is used to explore relationship building.
Self-efficacy theory: The theory of self-efficacy (Bandura 1977a, 1997) assumes that psychological factors create and strengthen expectations of personal worth or value.	**Communities of practice:** First theorised by Lave and Wenger (1991) and developed further by Wenger (1998), communities of practice can be employed to explore how people engage in collective processes, when learning or working together.

Figure 3.8   Examples of middle level theories

If you wanted to conduct qualitative secondary research on adults applying for employment you may consider this within a broad behavioural perspective that identifies concepts focused on motivation, sense of worth, confidence. However, this may not enable you to understand the nuances at play, so you identify self-efficacy as a theory that embraces the conceptual understanding you need. This theory becomes useful because your findings indicate that adults' sense of self is related to their surroundings. This theory is very clear in explaining how people's 'self-system' enables them to have some control over their thoughts, feelings, motivation, and actions. This system is influenced by what they know about themselves, what they feel about themselves and the environment they are in, and this is known as triadic reciprocity. Therefore, this theory may help you understand the conditions of people's unemployment status and their success or lack of it when applying for future employment possibilities. Because of your use of this theory, your understanding of your topic has increased. It has created a clarity in your understanding that was not there before you found it.

Interdisciplinary nature of theory

As you read, you will find that some theories have relevance beyond a specific subject or discipline boundary. These can be interdisciplinary theories as the main principles of a certain theory can be used in different subject areas (see Box 3.3). We advise you not to pick any old theory 'off the shelf' but to make sure it is relevant to your research question(s) or aim(s) and appropriate for your subject area. Whilst there is some transferability in theoretical perspectives, you need theory in a way that reflects your subject area or discipline.

BOX 3.3   EXPLORING THEORY IN RESEARCH

If you were researching secondary data to answer a research question that seeks to understand the principles of collaborative working, you could use the same theory (*communities of practice*) across two distinct subject domains:

Travel and Tourism: e.g. communities of practice – exploring planning reports and meeting notes to explore how hotel owners worked collaboratively to rebuild tourism following natural disasters.

Education: e.g. communities of practice – examining school policy documents to explore the mentoring processes for student teachers.

The main premises of the theory would remain consistent but how this is applied would be different.

Working with more than one theory

Theory as an organising conceptual structure should be used in a way that supports your ability to make sense of your research or your findings. Therefore, it is possible to use more than one theory as there are some research topics that need to have a widened perspective and need to be understood in different ways. This may be relevant when you are using a multiple research strategy as we explore in Chapter 4. Such an approach can have benefits as it can:

- widen your exploration of the topic under review;
- provide a more distinct interpretation within the findings;
- be used to support theoretical triangulation as a strategy to promote research credibility.

How does theory function in the analysis of data?

Theory can be employed in a variety of ways by researchers, for example theories can be applied or created. When employed in the analysis of your research this can be realised via the application of 'theory first' (deductive) and 'theory after' (inductive) approaches. In a 'theory first' approach, theory that fits the phenomenon being studied is utilised as a framework or as something that needs to be tested. This use of theory has relevance when you are looking for something specific such as specialised terminology or key words.

However, most qualitative research creates findings emerging from processes of concept or theme building. This 'theory after' or data driven approach suggests you will analyse your data using processes of constant comparison (see Chapter 11) as you interrogate your data for meaning. When you have exhausted this, you will create findings and these will be explained by your use of theory. This is often referred to as generating theory as you '*construct potential explanations for your forthcoming findings*' (Thomas 2011: 3–4).

While qualitative research is usually associated with a 'theory after' approach (Denscombe 2010), there may be times when you need to apply 'theory first'. Therefore, before you begin your research, consider the role and function of theory not just in your analysis but throughout your research (see Figure 3.9).

- apply theory to the analysis of your data
- intepret this application of theory

theory first (deductive)

- findings emerge from your data
- you draw on existing theory to construct new meaning

theory after (inductive)

Figure 3.9 The role of theory and analysis

PAUSE FOR THOUGHT

Which framework do I use?

Your theoretical and conceptual framework functions as '*spectacles through which to see the world, at the same time, it places boundaries on one's vision and horizons*' (Imenda 2014: 185).

Therefore, it is not a choice of one or the other, as your frameworks provide a supporting structure for the way your research is conducted and both function to:

1. Identify the main concepts in your research;
2. Support your decision to the overall research approach;
3. Influence your approach to data collection and interpretation.

YOUR INFLUENCE ON YOUR RESEARCH

Lincoln and Guba (1985: 161) declare research to be influenced '*by the values of the inquirer*' and we began this chapter by exploring 'positionality' which is who you are in relation to the research you create (see Figure 3.1) and the potential influence you may have on your research and the findings you generate.

This discussion arises because it is linked to the way we undertake research. When we explored theory of knowledge we identified ontological research positions as those who seek objectivity and those who accept subjectivity. As we explored, in an objective position you want to claim that the research you create is values free and neutral and to do this, you need to remove yourself from the research, engage in measurement not interpretation and employ '*procedural*' objectivity (Hammersley 2013: 10). However, for those who want to use documents as data and interpret these, this removal of the researcher is not the goal of the inquiry process. As qualitative secondary researchers who want to interpret documents as data, there is an acceptance of some subjectivity in the way you approach your research because you are a human being handling human documents.

But with this influence comes the threat of bias and knowledge distortion which can arise when we are unaware of our influence and thus, do not engage in processes or strategies to limit or understand this in the research we produce. Findings should not depend on who did the research, but on what was there to be found. Therefore, using strategies to manage and counter your perceived influence can reduce your ability to distort your findings.

Your researcher influence should be managed and tamed by being rigorous in the way you approach your research; you may not be able to aim for research neutrality but you should aim to attain research credibility. Being honest and open about your influence is an important step in striving for research credibility. We explore strategies to enhance research quality to seek credibility in Chapter 4 but in this chapter, we focus on the role of reflexivity as a mechanism to disclose your potential influence on your research.

Creating a reflexive account

Researchers are increasingly prepared to inform readers of their influence and that of their values on the research process and subsequent findings. This informing of the reader of researcher influence is called 'reflexivity' and in qualitative approaches to research it is a process of critical self-reflection or conscious '*self-scrutiny*' (Hellawell 2006: 486). Through reflexivity, you demonstrate your awareness of who you are and how this has the potential to influence the research you produce. Therefore, taking time to acknowledge your relationship to your data indicates you are aware of how who you are can permeate your research (Lather 1991). Therefore, reflexivity allows you to consider how aspects of your researcher identity – for example, your gender, class, nationality, ethnicity, level of education and your religious and political beliefs – may influence the choices you make and the findings you generate. This is also where, if you were an insider researcher you would identify your role and acknowledge this as affording certain privileges in relation to the knowledge you can attain.

Reflexivity does not absolve you from claims of bias and contamination as you will need to engage in strategies to minimise these to achieve research credibility, but used effectively it can indicate that you are aware of your influence on your research. As Payne and Payne (2004: 191) indicate, this explicit '*self-aware and self-critical approach*' is important as it is part of a wider approach to research credibility and validity. Therefore, reflexivity is an integral part of ensuring the transparency and quality of qualitative research enhancing the trustworthiness of your findings.

Understanding bias

Bias is the consequence of the researcher on the research or in other words as defined by the Oxford Dictionary it is, '*an inclination or prejudice for or against one person or group, especially in a way considered to be unfair*'; it is '*a concentration on an interest in one particular area or subject*'. Therefore, understanding and responding to issues of bias within any type of research is important because as Norris (1997: 173) states:

> Researchers are fallible. They make mistakes and get things wrong. There is no paradigm solution to the elimination of error and bias. Different forms of research may be prone to different sources of error, but clearly none are immune.

In the previous section we explored positionality and researcher influence on research and considered reflexivity as a way of openly admitting this potential for influence. To reduce this influence, we discussed the need to engage in verification processes or strategies to minimise researcher influence and achieve credible research (see Chapter 4). In this section we consider the possible consequence of an unchecked or unacknowledged influence on your research. Not knowing how you influence your qualitative secondary research can lead to biased processes within your research. In Figure 3.10, we offer three main forms of bias within qualitative secondary research that you need to be aware of and defend yourself against, and we offer you advice to support your defence.

BIAS	CONSIDER
Researcher bias: This is where you influence your research and every aspect of it, thus making the findings fit your story. You do not engage in any attempts to mitigate this influence and do not acknowledge any concerns.	• Engage in reflexivity to raise awareness of your presence in your research. • Adopt the strategies we propose in Chapter 4. • Acknowledge all deviant or discrepant findings. • Approach your research in an open and transparent way – show how you analysed your data.

BIAS	CONSIDER
Confirmation bias: This is where you only adopt perspectives that match your own version of reality. This is in the selection of sources for literature review and how you analyse your findings as you only present those that match your view of your research.	• Engage in reflexivity to raise awareness of your presence in your research. • Read widely and consider divergent perspectives and arguments. • Engage in process of critical appraisal to show you understand your data and to widen your choice-making process. • Make sure you acknowledge all findings and show how these emerged through your analysis. • Approach your research in an open and transparent way – show how you analysed your data.
Selection bias: Not selecting a representative sample but this is not always possible and is often dependent on the type of data and research strategy adopted.	• Engage in reflexivity to raise awareness of your presence in your research. • Engage in sampling strategies identified in Chapter 8. • Engage in critical appraisal processes as representativeness may not be possible but you still need to show you have approached your selection of data in a systematic way.

Figure 3.10   Understanding forms of bias in qualitative secondary research

PAUSE FOR THOUGHT

Keeping a research diary

One of the tools we discuss when we explore research quality is the use of a reflective research diary (see Chapter 2) as this is where you can reflect on your research process (Blaxter, Hughes & Tight 2010). This is a diary where a researcher makes regular entries during the research process, possibly recording methodological decisions, or decisions about your analysis. Keeping a research diary like this can be a useful tool to aid your memory when you come to write your methodology.

WHERE DO I WRITE ABOUT THEORY AND CONCEPTS IN MY STUDY?

We cannot provide a template for your research, so we advise you to consult your research guidelines to check the expectations placed on you in this process. There are some recognised places in your research where you should consider writing about your theoretical and conceptual frameworks:

Methodology: This is the main section in your research where you explore your understanding of theory in terms of your theory of knowledge and your positionality. As we explore in Chapter 4, your methodology is a recipe for your research and theory and concepts are two of the ingredients. In your methodology, you should discuss how theory was used in your research and to help with this, please consider the following questions:

- What theory did I use?
- How did this help me understand my data? (*e.g. explanation of your findings after your analysis*)
- How did I apply my theory? (*theory first/theory after?*)
- Why did I apply theory like this?

Rationale: Theory can be a driving force for your research. You should identify your key concepts, disclose the use of a named theory (*e.g. self-efficacy*), larger theoretical perspective (*e.g. feminism*) or organising constructs (*e.g. power within identity construction*). Setting your theoretical position out clearly in your rationale adds to the justification for your research (see Chapter 2).

Literature review: Your literature review should provide a context for study and this includes any theory/theories you select and, as such, it should expose your conceptual framework. This is important to do as you need to help your reader understand your research as much as possible. You may draw on theory provided from previous researchers who have approached their work in a comparable way. You may critique this and argue why your theoretical approach has more relevance. Theory is a way of explaining your research and your literature review is where you cover all aspects that can aid this explanation.

Analysis: You may use theory to explain your findings after your analysis but it may also be something you need to apply.

Findings: In your discussion of your findings, you will create your theory of your research as you explain what your findings mean. This will be linked to the reading you generated in your literature review. This is where you either confirm or refute what you have found.

Conclusion: Theory will be in your conclusion as you have generated an explanation for your findings. In addition, theory can also be in your recommendations; you could recommend that your theory is used again or that a different theory is explored.

REFLECTION AND FURTHER READING

At the beginning of the chapter we set out what you should be able to do when you reached the end of this chapter. To aid your reflection on all we have covered we ask some chapter specific questions. If you are unsure of any of your answers to these questions, please go back to the relevant section to review this aspect.

REFLECTING ON CHAPTER 3

In this chapter we have:

- **Explored how research positions influence your research:** Can you say what your research position is? If you can, do you know how this may impact on your research?
- **Provided an overview of the role of theory:** Do you know what theory is? Do you know how to work with theory?
- **Provided an overview of the role of concepts:** Do you know what a conceptual framework is? Do you know where your concepts can come from?
- **Examined the role of reflexivity as a mechanism to disclose researcher influence:** How could you influence your research? What could this mean to your research credibility?
- **Explored where theory and concepts appear in your research project:** Do you know how theory functions in your analysis and findings section?

WE RECOMMEND FOR FURTHER READING:

Becker, H. (1998) *Tricks of the Trade: How to Think about Your Research While You Are Doing It.* Chicago: University of Chicago Press.
This text is a classic of its type and well worth a read. We recommend Chapter 4, CONCEPTS where, on page 120, Becker identifies concept identification 'tricks'.

Crotty, M. (1998) *The Foundations of Social Research: Meaning and Perspective in the Research Process.* Thousand Oaks, CA: SAGE Publications, Inc.
While an older text, this book provides a wealth of relevant information on research theory.

Grant, C. & Osanloo, A. (2014) Understanding, selecting, and integrating a theoretical framework in dissertation research: Creating the blueprint for your 'house'. *Administrative Issues Journal: Connecting Education, Practice, and Research, 4*(2), 12–26.
Using a metaphor of building a house, this article provides an accessible account of research philosophy.

Hammersley, M. (2012) Methodological paradigms in educational research. *British Educational Research Association* online resource. Available at: www.bera.ac.uk/researchers-resources/publications/methodological-paradigms-in-educational-research.
This article offers an accessible account of research positions and provides a useful glossary of key terms. This is highly recommended.

(Continued)

(Continued)

Saunders, M., Lewis, P. & Thornhill, A. (2009) *Research Methods for Business Students* (5th edn). Harlow, Essex: Pearson Education Limited.
This offers a comprehensive overview of research processes. We recommend Chapters 4 and 5 to extend your research knowledge.

Thomas, G. (2017) *How to do Your Research Project* (3rd edn). London: SAGE Publications Ltd.
We recommend Chapter 5 as this offers a very informative account of 'ologies' and frameworks.

University of Southern California (2018) *Organizing Your Social Sciences Research Paper: Theoretical Framework*. Available at: http://libguides.usc.edu/writingguide/theoreticalframework.
This presents some useful information relating to the construction of your theoretical framework.

4
DESIGNING QUALITATIVE SECONDARY RESEARCH

THIS CHAPTER SUPPORTS YOUR ABILITY TO

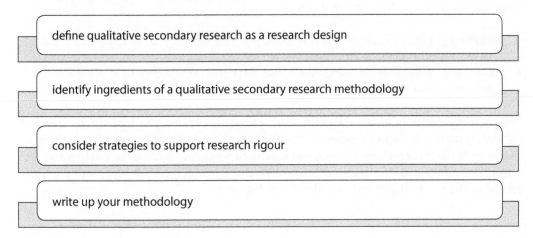

define qualitative secondary research as a research design

identify ingredients of a qualitative secondary research methodology

consider strategies to support research rigour

write up your methodology

CHAPTER OVERVIEW

This chapter begins by exploring qualitative secondary research as a research design that provides a plan of action indicating how you will conduct your inquiry. For you as a qualitative secondary researcher your design is the use of existing documents as data that can help you to understand people and their lives and experiences. This leads to an examination of the key components of your research design and a consideration of the importance of ethics, sampling processes, your use of theory, methods of analysis and research strategies within the creation of your methodology.

We emphasise the pivotal role of your methodology as the recipe for your research. It is where you select the approaches you will take and where you will defend your choices. We reiterate throughout that your methodology is where you provide a robust justification for the choices you make. This chapter ends with a consideration of strategies to secure research quality as we reflect on the need for your reader to have confidence in the research you produce. The final part of the chapter provides a spotlight on writing up your methodology and, whilst we cannot provide a specific template, we offer a list of questions to support its effective construction.

WHAT IS A QUALITATIVE SECONDARY RESEARCH DESIGN?

Qualitative secondary is a research design because it provides a clear supporting structure for the way you will undertake your research and it sets the parameters for your study indicating it will be conducted in a specific way. This design becomes, as Burns and Grove (2003: 195) describe, '*a blueprint for conducting a study*' which for you as a secondary researcher, is no more complicated than knowing that you are:

- engaging in a form of inquiry that is secondary to your data as you are using information that already exists in the world;
- conducting your research using qualitative data that allows you to explore human phenomena and interaction in the world.

Therefore, by deciding to use data that you have not generated you have already made a significant design decision or '*general orientation*' as to how you will conduct your research (Bryman 2012: 35). Knowing that you are conducting your research as qualitative and secondary provides substantial support for your research decisions. These decisions are those related to the research elements we identify in Figure 4.1.

Figure 4.1   Key components of a qualitative secondary research methodology

DESIGNING YOUR QUALITATIVE SECONDARY RESEARCH

When you begin to think about your research project, it may be difficult to think of it as a finished product with a clear beginning, middle and end but right from the start you need to be concerned about the way it is constructed. Thinking of the key components we identified in Figure 4.1, a well-constructed piece of research requires you to have a clear understanding of which of these aspects you need to include, and how and why they need to be included. For this reason, we encourage you to start thinking of your research plan and proposal (see Chapter 2) as forming the basis of your methodology, as this is where you begin to structure your approach.

We will reiterate many times in this chapter the importance of creating an effective methodology. Your methodology is where your research makes sense as it 'joins the dots' of your thinking and this, as Wellington (2000: 22) declares, is essential because *'no one can assess or judge the value of a piece of research without knowing its methodology'*. Therefore, your methodology is a key section in your research project because it turns your research question(s) and/or aim(s) into coherent and logical projects (Robson 2002).

A 'methodology' is, as established perspectives dictate, the theory and practice of how your research is undertaken (Saunders, Lewis & Thornhill 2009) and we consider it as the recipe of your research. In your methodology or research recipe you place the 'ingredients' we provided in Figure 4.1 in such a way that they are combined to create an effective qualitative secondary research project.

In the following section, we explore each of the 'ingredients' indicated in Figure 4.1 and review some in more depth than others not because they are less important, but because they appear in much more depth in later chapters. To aid your navigation, Figure 4.2 provides an overview of the components and their respective chapters.

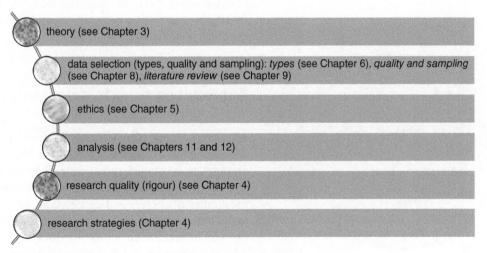

theory (see Chapter 3)

data selection (types, quality and sampling): *types* (see Chapter 6), *quality and sampling* (see Chapter 8), *literature review* (see Chapter 9)

ethics (see Chapter 5)

analysis (see Chapters 11 and 12)

research quality (rigour) (see Chapter 4)

research strategies (Chapter 4)

Figure 4.2   Research ingredients and relevant book chapters

PAUSE FOR THOUGHT

Do you know what is expected of you?

We have stated a few times that we cannot prescribe a specific template for any part of your research process but we can offer advice and guidance. Before you begin your methodology, we encourage you to check your institution's or funder's research guidelines or handbook to familiarise yourself with what you may need to do.

Research position and theoretical frameworks

One of the main components or ingredients in your methodology is your discussion of the role and influence of theory. As we explored in Chapter 3, deciding to undertake qualitative secondary research means you wish to answer your research question within a particular paradigm. This paradigm is one that encourages an exploration of the qualities of human phenomenon and interaction in the world. This we described as reflecting your research position and this should be declared within your methodology as an underpinning principle on which your research is based. As we show in Figure 4.3, how you see your world and how this perspective influences the research you produce is too important to remain hidden and, as Creswell (2009: 5) attests, it should be clearly stated.

Theory has a strong influence on your research as who you are as a person and researcher exerts influence on the way you approach and conduct your research and as your methodology is where you discuss this influence. Knowing that there is a connection between theory and the other parts of your research process forms the foundation of your research coherence and consistency.

Approaches to data selection

Another key ingredient is a consideration of data. In qualitative secondary research all information can be considered as potential data for you to use. This can leave you faced with making a range of choices and decisions about what to include or omit. One of the first decisions you will be faced with is filtering documents as data for inclusion in your literature review or deciding on these as data for your analysis

Figure 4.3   The influence of theory on your research

theoretical
framework

types of data
and choice of
literature

approach to
analysis

(see Chapter 6) and/or literature review (see Chapter 9). In both cases, making this decision requires a critical gaze gained through the application of evaluation and appraisal checklists and being able to reduce data through effective sampling procedures. We refer to the use of Scott's (1990) fours aspects of quality:

- **Authenticity:** Is it real?
- **Representativeness:** Is it typical?
- **Credibility:** Is it believable?
- **Meaningful:** Does it make sense?

We advise you to adopt a sceptical approach to your sources of data and never to assume they conform to Scott's assessment of quality. In your methodology you should defend your selection processes and if you sample your sources, you will need to justify the sampling strategy adopted. Knowing if your data are considered typical or representative of the phenomenon you want to understand can support the transferability and generalisability of your findings and thus, suggest they have the potential for relevance; but not all data can be appraised as typical of their context. Therefore, your methodology is where you identify the approaches you take as you select your literature and where you defend these as robustly as possible.

- **Literature review:** Your literature review requires a specific type of data and your methodology is where you identify the approaches you employed to select this. In your review you should select authoritative sources of evidence. These should be scholarly academic journal articles that have been peer-reviewed and needed in your literature review to demonstrate your subject knowledge, awareness of key theories and show you are apprised of key arguments and debates. Knowing you can defend your selection of sources is important, as the literature you select enables you to make sense of your findings (see Chapter 8). Therefore, selecting sources for your literature review with diligence is paramount.
- **Data for analysis:** The main consideration when selecting data for analysis is the question(s) and/or aim(s) you set. However, you also need to consider the relationship between your data and how it can be analysed (see Chapters 11 and 12). If you select visual data, you need to defend your method of analysis. Ultimately, the choice of data and how they can be analysed is grounded in the question(s) and/or aim(s) you set.

Approaches to ethics

Your methodology is where you provide evidence of your compliance with codes of conduct and, as we explored in Chapter 5, these can be institutional, or discipline focused. Your defence should include how you accessed your data and responded to key ethical considerations relating to informed consent and data confidentiality. We advise you to consider your methodology as providing an arena in which you demonstrate that you and your research have caused no harm.

Research strategies

In qualitative secondary research it is possible to use approaches or 'research strategies' that are specific and focused inquiry structures that guide and shape the research you conduct. These strategies can be used to create research that is intimate and small-scale study, up to projects that use larger and multiple data sets. Research strategies are an approach to your inquiry that enables you to consider the following:

- the type of sources of data needed;
- the quantity needed;
- your approach to data analysis.

Figure 4.4 identifies these strategies as 'single', 'combined' and 'multiple'. Each strategy has merits when used to answer your research question(s) and/or aim(s).

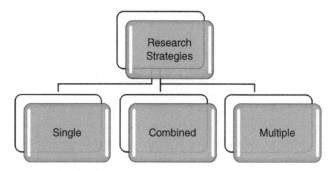

Figure 4.4   Three research strategies

As we explore in the following sections, each strategy provides a clear and logical approach to your research inquiry. They can guide your selection of data, your approach to data analysis and your use of theory. Consequently, once you have decided on your 'research strategy' you can begin to provide an effective response to your research question(s) and/or aim(s).

What is a single strategy?

If you answer yes to the question asked in Figure 4.5, then you may decide to conduct a 'single strategy'. A single strategy could involve one piece of documentary data that is explored in great depth and can be from more than one theoretical or analytical perspective. This can be a useful way of exploring your research question using a single critical gaze to create a deep and focused consideration (see Box 4.1).

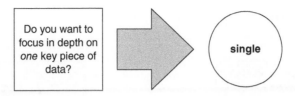

Figure 4.5   A single research strategy

BOX 4.1   SINGLE STRATEGY

You wish to analyse a famous and influential film screenplay to explore the role of motivation in the film. You begin by categorising characters identified in the script as main or subsidiary and labelling each with identity markers (*e.g. gender, age, ethnicity*). You create a framework analysis using these concepts as headings. You review your data, coding the script for instances of motivational behaviour (*e.g. speech, action, thought*). You plot this against the chart you have already created and generate a matrix of your findings. You interpret your findings using Maslow's (1943, 1954) Hierarchy of Needs as this theory enables you to make sense of the motivational aspects of your data.

The example offered in Box 4.1 illustrates how one piece of data can be used within this strategy but it is advisable to find something that meets your research question(s) and or aim(s) and is large enough to mine enough data for your project. Using one piece of data can provide a creative and effective response to your research question(s) and/or aim(s) but you would need to defend your approach and demonstrate how you are seeking research credibility. Providing a rigorous response to the critical questions we ask can support your defence from accusations of researcher bias as your inquiry is focused on a sole source of data (Patton 2002). Your defence of this strategy can be supported by asking yourself questions such as these:

- How do you know the quality of your data?
- How do you know if the data you have selected are representative of the focus of your study?
- Do your data need to be typical or representative?
- Can exploring one source of data facilitate the transferability of your findings?
- How would you manage the influence you may exert on this data?
- How will you analyse your data?
- How will theory help you understand your data?

Even with these concerns, a single strategy can be used to explore your research question in depth rather than breadth. It can also lead to data immersion where you engage so deeply with your data that you can comprehend its meaning in its entirety (Crabtree & Miller 1999).

What is a combined strategy?

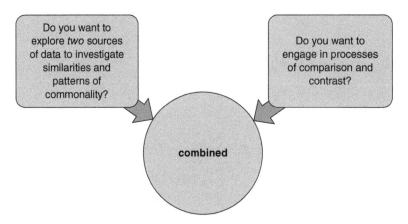

Figure 4.6   A combined research strategy

If you answered yes to the questions asked in Figure 4.6, then you could conduct a 'combined strategy'. A combined strategy is the combination of two sets of data that can either complement or contrast. You could explore two sources of data to enable you to identify differences that have occurred across a span of time. You may consider using two scholarly research articles to trace theory development or explore two blogs, images or videos. This approach offers scope for a wide variety of possibilities.

You could compare two sources of data as indicated in Box 4.2 that enable you to understand differences in arguments and debates. The main consideration is that you select data that supports your ability to answer your research question(s) and/or aim(s) you set. There are some clear positives with this approach as it can:

- support your ability to present your analyses in a clear and focused way (*e.g. the use of tabular comparison charts or maps indicating commonalities*);
- afford the opportunity to immerse yourself with a restricted range of data as you seek depth not breadth;
- strengthen your arguments by the clarity of the processes involved;
- support your exploration of a wide range of historical, social and cultural context and perspectives (*based on the data you select and the question you ask*).

However, as in the single strategy you will need to be able to defend your choice of data and approach against the critical questions asked above.

- How do you know you have quality data?
- How do you know if the data you have selected is representative of the focus of your study?

- Does your data need to be typical or representative?
- Can exploring two sources of data facilitate the transferability of your findings?
- How would you manage the influence you may exert on this data?
- How will you analyse your data?
- How will theory help you understand your data?

As we indicated above, the choice of data and strategy is yours to make but you must be able to defend it. You need to demonstrate that you are aware of the concerns within these critical questions and provide strategies to counter these.

BOX 4.2   COMBINED STRATEGY

As a researcher you are interested in manifestations of nationalism and you wish to focus on responses to National Anthems. You locate two journal articles published at similar times that explore this phenomenon within one country. One explores people's motives for standing and the other reflects motives given by those who are against standing. These two articles offer competing views and this enables you to compare and contrast the supporting arguments offered. You could apply different forms of analysis (*e.g. content and discourse*) and adopt diverse theoretical perspectives (*e.g. social learning theory and communities of practice*).

Your categorisation and coding process would be the same for both articles and the themes you create following this would be those that shape your comparison.

Comparative thinking is one of our first and most natural forms of thought as it underpins our ability to make sense of the world in terms of the basic judgements we make – we recognise what is the same and what is different. Therefore, a research project that focuses on these fundamental ways of understanding the world could provide insight into the way the world is constructed and how people engage in it.

What is a multiple strategy?

If you answer yes to the question in Figure 4.7 you could conduct a 'multiple strategy'. In this strategy, you will analyse multiple sets of data and this would be appropriate if you wanted to conduct larger-scale research that involves analysing different data sets (*e.g. verbal and visual data, qualitative and quantitative*). It also enables you to engage in aspects of focused research rigour as this approach facilitates the use of '*different but complementary data on the same topic*' (Morse 1991: 122) (see Box 4.3). Like the combined strategy, it is also possible for you to engage in comparative analysis using more than two sources of data.

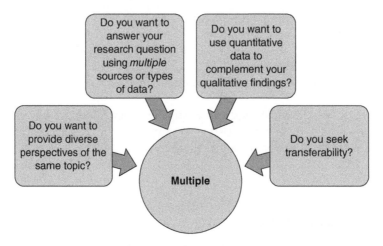

Figure 4.7   A multiple research strategy

Adopting a multiple strategy widens the amount of data you can access and analyse. It enables you to integrate a wealth of data (*e.g. reports, videos, interviews or academic texts*) and it can enable a mixed approach to analysis that leads to the use of quantitative data.

The focus of this multiple approach to data is to offer a comprehensive exploration through multiple perspectives. You could engage in both data and methodological triangulation as you could employ both qualitative and quantitative data, potentially enhancing your research credibility. Therefore, the strength of this approach is in the depth of exploration offered by the multiple perspectives provided.

It is also important to consider how you will justify your selection of the data. Being able to use several types of data to answer your research question offers a wealth of analytical possibilities and complexities. However, be mindful as Morse (2003) warns, of a liberal, ad hoc and mix and match approach that does not reflect methodological congruence. As for the strategies discussed above, you will need to defend your choices against the critical questions you need to ask:

- How do you know if you have quality data?
- How do you know if the data you have selected are representative of the focus of your study?
- Do your data need to be typical or representative?
- Can exploring multiple sources of data facilitate the transferability of your findings?
- If so, how?
- How would you manage the influence you may exert on this data?
- How will you analyse your data?
- How will theory help you understand your data?

> **BOX 4.3   MULTIPLE STRATEGY**
>
> You want to investigate the way various media report on one piece of news. You want to explore differences in the language used and if this can be related to a target audience. You isolate one event that has been widely covered and provide a representative sample of news-feeds, print media, television coverage and Twitter feeds from key political figures.
>
> You decide to analyse your data performing content analysis as this enables you to identify the frequency of key words in the news. The context is also offered so you can begin to build up a consistent view of what is happening, when and where. To fully understand your data, you apply discourse analysis to comprehend the social and cultural function of the language used.

Taking a mixed approach to your inquiry: mixing words and numbers

It is possible to approach your combined and multi strategy using both qualitative and quantitative data. This is an approach akin to mixed methods research as it crosses over paradigmatic boundaries (*i.e. qualitative and quantitative*) and where the approach taken is solely dependent on the question asked. It could be argued that this pragmatic approach is a more natural way to engage in research as it does not adhere to polarised research paradigms (Bryman 2012) (*i.e. positivism and interpretivism*). The distinction between quantitative and qualitative data can be quite artificial as in qualitative studies it is common to count units or instances of a category in a descriptive way using words like 'often' and 'frequently'. In quantitative studies, the statistical approach we explore is one that focuses on description and often requires a narrative account to help us understand what is happening. Whilst this book focuses on the use of qualitative data, we advise you to select the data you need to answer your research question(s) and /or aim(s). Adopting a blended approach is pragmatic, can add complementarity and increase confidence in your research findings through data and methodological triangulation (see Box 4.4).

> **BOX 4.4   USING NUMBERS TO ADD EMPHASIS AND MEANING**
>
> In the UK in 2018, the word 'plastic' was declared children's word of the year. This was determined following an analysis undertaken by the Oxford University Press of stories submitted to the BBC's children's short story competition which is aimed at children aged 5 to 13. They performed content analysis and the word 'plastic' was the most prevalent word, as
>
> *(Continued)*

(Continued)

it was counted 3,359 times in the 134,790 stories submitted. This is an increase of 100 per cent from the previous year. In 2017, the word of the year was 'Trump' and in 2016, it was the word 'refugee'. Being able to count words like this provides a snapshot of children's understanding of the world as it says *what* influences their thoughts but it does not say *why* or *how*.

To gain this additional information, we could explore the word 'plastic' using discourse analysis to consider the social context in which the children used these words. We might find that issues such as pollution, global warming and natural disasters emerge from the children's stories and are linked to the use of the word 'plastic'. The complementary data we can gain by a combination of these two approaches may allow us to understand children's thinking. Using a dual approach to data adds not just complementarity, but it can add rigour (Seale & Silverman 1997) through the application of methodological triangulation.

Sourced from: www.bbc.co.uk/news/uk-44372686 (Accessed 2018).

Methods of analysis

Being able to make sense of your data is integral to the success of your inquiry and your defence of your methods of analysis is, therefore, crucial. In qualitative secondary research *'nothing becomes data without the intervention of a researcher'* (Wolcott 1994: 3). This statement clearly identifies the dynamic relationship between your data and you as the researcher. When you construct your methodology, you will need to provide a clearly articulated justification for the analytical approach you take and defend its choice for the data you have selected. If you are using more than one source of data and need to apply different methods of analysis, you need to explain why and how this approach enabled you to answer your research question(s) and/or aim(s) you have set.

There are no fixed templates for analysis but analysis is a process of meaning making where you try to understand and make sense of the data you have collected. Qualitative secondary research suggests the use of methods of analysis to uncover themes, patterns, concepts, insights and understandings (Patton 2002). Therefore, your methodological defence may

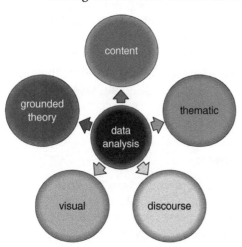

Figure 4.8 Examples of possible approaches to data analysis

be based on how your chosen method of analysis affords a better understanding of people's experiences in the world (Denzin 1978). Figure 4.8 offers examples of possible methods of analysis and we explore this in more depth in Chapter 11 which considers the principles and processes of qualitative data analysis and in Chapter 12, where we examine the use of quantitative approaches to analysis.

PAUSE FOR THOUGHT

Being clear and logical

As we have emphasised throughout this chapter and this book, when you design your research please be guided in your choices by:

- the question(s) you ask;
- the aim(s) your set;
- your research intentions;
- your institution's or organisation's guidelines
- advice and guidance offered by your supervisor.

Whatever decisions you make, you must be able to defend these!

EXPLORING CRITERIA FOR RESEARCH QUALITY

Early on in this chapter we explored a methodology as being the recipe for your research and the ingredients are the core components discussed earlier in this chapter (see Figure 4.1). However, just putting these in your research does not necessarily mean your research will be credible. Each of the ingredients within your methodology needs to be 'mixed in' so that it adds to the quality and worth of your research. This mixing process is where you try to attain research rigour or research quality as you are trying to show how your approach to aspects like sampling, ethics, your research strategy and methods of analysis make the findings generated from your research trustworthy.

Having a clear understanding of how to achieve trustworthiness within your research means considering ways in which you can ascertain its quality or rigour which, as Morse et al. (2002: 14) declare, is essential because *'without rigor, research is worthless, becomes fiction, and loses its utility'*. Therefore, when working with existing data you need to provide considerable evidence of your attempts to address and secure research rigour and quality. This means demonstrating you have employed a range of strategies that ensure that the research you produce is trustworthy (Seale & Silverman 1997). These strategies create methodological coherence and consistency as they offer appropriate responses to quality within qualitative research.

Strategies for research quality

Qualitative secondary research should provide strategies that when used enable your reader to make judgements as to the quality of your research. To support this, the criteria offered by Guba (1981) and Lincoln and Guba (1985) can be used effectively to provide a way of approaching and securing quality research. The criteria they propose are 'credibility', 'transferability', 'dependability' and 'confirmability', but these are not meant to be strict categories. As we explore in the section below, there is an overlap within qualitative secondary research as dependability and confirmability can utilise the same strategies. This should not be considered problematic as all the strategies that can be used within qualitative secondary research are used to the same end, to promote research quality and the confidence that your reader can have in your research. In the following section, we explore aspects of research quality, examining the criteria and strategies used within qualitative secondary research. Figure 4.9 illustrates these criteria and shows the role they have in your research.

CRITERION	STRATEGY	GUIDING QUESTIONS
Credibility	Triangulation (methods, data, analyst, theory) Audit trail Prolonged engagement – data transparency and the role of critical appraisal processes	This relates to the truth of your research: How can I have confidence in my findings?
Transferability	Sampling processes	This relates to the applicability of your research: Do my findings have relevance for other contexts?
Dependability	Research diary Analytical transparency Sampling processes Data selection processes Audit trail Clearly written methodology (thick description)	This relates to the consistency of your research: Am I being clear enough in the methods and processes used so that results can be repeated and are consistent?
Confirmability	Reflexivity Peer scrutiny Research diary Audit trail	This relates to the neutrality of your research: How can I show that my findings are shaped by my data and not by me as the researcher?

Figure 4.9   Strategies to support research quality (adapted from Lincoln & Guba 1985)

Source: Lincoln, Y.S. & Guba, E.G. (1985) *Naturalistic Inquiry.* Newbury Park, CA: SAGE Publications Inc.

Credibility

As we stated above, credibility relates to the truth of your research and how believable your findings are based on the research processes you have undertaken. The credibility of research is something that needs to be demonstrated and as Denscombe (2010: 297) states '*researchers should not assume that people are naïve and will take their findings at face value*'. The following are some of the ways that credibility within research can be approached:

Prolonged engagement: In qualitative primary research, being in the field, knowing your participants and being immersed in their environment and exploring what they can provide is called prolonged engagement. This is not possible to do within qualitative secondary research, but it is possible to attain prolonged engagement by spending time getting to know your data as well as you can; this can be when you search for it, when you read or explore it and it is in knowing the 'what', 'when', 'where', 'how', 'who' and 'why' of its production. This prolonged engagement is also possible when you analyse your data in processes of data immersion and familiarisation.

Triangulation: Triangulation is a method of research quality based on the practice of viewing things from more than one perspective. Triangulation involves a set of strategies that form an approach to the attainment of research rigour (Denzin 1978). When used appropriately, these strategies can help guard against accusations that your findings may in some way be flawed. Therefore, as a suite of strategies, triangulation can support your ability to demonstrate that your work is trustworthy because, as Denzin (2009: 149) warns, if the research is not '"*credible*" the whole house of cards falls down'.

- **Triangulation of sources:** The validity of findings can be checked by using diverse sources of data. This can mean comparing several types of data (*e.g. text, visual, online offline*) and if this is relevant, it can be data that are collected at different times (*e.g. time triangulation*). This may have some relevance if you are tracking posts on a blog. A key consideration is the use of context triangulation (*e.g. using data that are from different social, geographic, or cultural contexts*). This would depend on the question you ask and the data you access but seeing your question answered through multiple sources may increase your confidence in the findings you create.
- **Analyst triangulation:** This is where you can gain the perspectives of other observers (*e.g. peers and colleagues*) to ensure you are not engaging in selective perception and making assumptions. It can be a very effective check against forms of bias. Asking colleagues, peers or your supervisor to check aspects of your work can support your claims for transparency. You could ask them to review your approach to analysis and even small review processes such as proof reading can be part of this peer-checking process because it opens your research to multiple scrutinising views. This strategy can contribute towards the dependability of your research.
- **Theoretical triangulation:** As we explored in Chapter 3, it is possible to use more than one known theory within your research to analyse your data and this can be the basis for theory triangulation. As we considered in Chapter 3, theories can shape your selection of data, the

way they are analysed and the way they are understood. Therefore, applying different theoretical perspectives can provide increased insight and begin to confirm if what you are finding is relevant and significant.

- **Methodological triangulation:** As a secondary researcher, this applies to both the types of data you access (*qualitative and quantitative*) and the method of analysis adopted (*qualitative or quantitative*). The use of alternative methods allows the findings from one method to be contrasted with the findings from another.
- **Data transparency and critical appraisal processes:** These are explored in Chapter 8 as strategies to support your understanding of your data and to enable you to make judgements as to data quality. Critical appraisal checklists and the use of inclusion and exclusion criteria can be used to provide evidence of your critical thinking and thus, can support both research credibility and dependability. Knowing how your data was selected is important as your reader needs to understand the processes you adopted to add to the trustworthiness of your research. Issues such as the age of your data, the place of publication and even the type of data all exert some influence of the findings you create, or the literature review you will construct. Poor quality sources detract from the quality of your research and if this is the case, its validity and credibility may be questioned.

Transferability

Transferability is a contested form of quality as it suggests there is a certain and specific 'normal' benchmark to which your data can be compared. This may not be the case when certain types of data are accessed for your research as we explore in Chapter 6; the representativeness of personal documents such as diaries and letters can be hard to determine. However, it is possible to demonstrate transferability of your research by engaging in strategies that can indicate how the sample of data you have gathered can be generalised to, or seen to be true of, the larger population from which the sample is drawn. This may be needed if you are using news reports or specific types of fiction (see Chapter 6). The transferability of your research can be supported by paying close attention to the way you select and sample your sources of data.

Sampling processes: Sampling processes are used to reduce the amount of data you could work with but they also reflect approaches to the transferability or generalisation of your research and can add to its dependability and its confirmability. When you sample, you identify data that is representative of the focus of your inquiry. The strategies we explore in Chapter 7 should enable you to consider how you can select data that can be considered as representative or typical of the focus of your inquiry. However, there are some data, for instance that gained from personal documents, that may be hard to sample and consider as representative; this should not dissuade you from using these data but you will have to defend your choice. One defence could be uniqueness, as we can learn from atypical events in the world as much as we can from typical.

Transferability can also be demonstrated in varying degrees by you as a researcher being able to demonstrate how you achieved your findings. In the following section we examine how dependability can be seen as engaging in processes that not only aid transferability but also reveal how these can support its confirmability.

Dependability and confirmability

We have placed these two criteria together as they work to confirm the 'truth' of your findings. Dependability is the way in which the process you engage in to 'measure' the quality of your work and the decisions made within your research are consistent. Dependability is something that can be gained through methodological protocols such as effective data selection processes, and a methodical approach to data analysis which we promote as inherent within a systematic and logical approach to inquiry. Confirmability relies on these protocols and others such as peer review to account for researcher influence. Confirmability is often equated with reliability and objectivity in quantitative research but this objectivity is not the aspiration of qualitative research. Therefore, as we explore below, to gain confirmation of the research you produce you need to be open and transparent in how research was conducted.

Thick description: Being clear and precise in the way you approach your research is an essential part of the quality process and this requires you as a researcher providing a 'thick description'. This means you provide your reader with a full account of the context, and the procedures used within your study. This approach should enable your reader to make their own judgements as to the credibility, transferability, dependability and confirmability of your research. This can be no more complicated than engaging in the strategies that we offer below:

- **A clearly written methodology:** This can lead to increased research rigour as providing a well-written methodology also promotes trustworthiness, as revealing your research processes makes them accessible to your reader enabling then to judge your findings on these. This is what Geertz (1973) and Lincoln and Guba (1985: 125) define as a *'thick description'* where you provide all the information your reader needs to know to understand your findings. Such clarity supports research replication as you should provide enough detailed information so that your research could be repeated (*or replicated*). If the research is replicable, then it provides some evidence towards the dependability of your research and thus, its quality.
- **Research diary:** There are many benefits to keeping a research diary. It can be used to note down your reflection on the research process, illustrate how and when key decisions were made and be used to record your coding procedures when you analyse your data. These records of your research process could indicate that if required, your research could be replicated. As we explore below, they can support the creation of an audit trail which exposes key decision-making moments and records of key processes and procedures.
- **Analytic transparency:** We consider analytic transparency to be an essential component of understanding the confirmability and dependability of your research. Your reader and the wider research community should know how you have analysed your data, so your results

can be understood and, if required, reproduced. It also means acknowledging when data does not fit your research question. It is as important to know how data answer your question as it is to know how they may not. Engaging in analytic transparency is acknowledging this and we recommend in Chapter 13 that you capitalise on any data that seem outside of your analysis and use these to signpost the need for further research and inquiry.

• **Acknowledging researcher influence through reflexivity:** This is linked to the confirmability or neutrality of your research. In qualitative research disclosing your researcher relationship to the research you create is an acknowledgement that *'the researcher influence disturbs and affects what is being researched in the natural world'* (Wellington 2000: 41). Your research may never be truly objective or *'value free or neutral'* (Davies et al. 2004) but being open about the possibilities of your influence can increase the confidence that can be had in your research. It allows your reader to consider and judge your findings knowing the context of their production. Therefore, this self-awareness or reflexivity (see Chapter 3) becomes a powerful strategy as it encourages an open and honest discussion about the influence of the researcher on their research.

Research transparency

The criteria we explored above are all strategies to gain the confidence of your reader and one key approach is the use of thick description. This thick description represents as commitment by you to your research to provide transparency. At its most basic, transparency is making your research decisions, procedures and processes clear and explicit enough for others to replicate. This is research that opens itself up to scrutiny and shows the underlying processes within its creation.

Therefore, research diaries have relevance as they can add to this transparency and create an audit trail. When used in this way they can offer an *'account of procedures and methods, showing the readers in as much detail as possible the lines of enquiry that led to particular conclusions'* (Seale 1999: 157). A key part of this transparency is in your acknowledgement of the possible influence of your researcher identity on your research so that your reader can evaluate your findings based on your self-disclosure (see Chapter 3).

When considering how you can create confidence in your research it is worth considering that Lincoln and Guba (1985: 329) conclude: *'naturalistic inquiry operates as an open system; no amount of member checking, triangulation, persistent observation, auditing, or whatever can ever compel; it can at best persuade'.*

HOW TO WRITE UP YOUR METHODOLOGY

In this chapter, we have explored some of the key components or ingredients of your qualitative secondary research that need to be considered in the construction of your methodology. However, when it comes to writing up your methodology, we can only offer guidance.

We provide this guidance by asking some methodological questions (see Figure 4.10). We have called this section of your research project the recipe as it is where you set out all you did as systematically and as logically as you can because your methodology is where you should provide 'thick' description. As we discussed above, it is where you make your research transparent and explicit and state *what* you did, *why* and *how* you did it and if necessary, *where* and *when*.

Methodological questions	What these mean and where to seek support in this book
How do I explain the way knowledge is created?	This is asking about your research position and how this influences the research you will undertake. Please see Chapter 3.
How did this influence my theoretical position?	This is how your research position or worldview influences your theoretical and conceptual frameworks. Please see Chapter 3.
What type of data did I select and why?	This is where you reveal your decision making as to the data used for your literature review and analysis. It is based on the question(s) you ask and/or the aim(s) you set, and it is influenced by your theoretical and conceptual framework. Please see Chapters 3, 8 and 9.
How did I select this data, what were my sampling strategies and why were they used?	This is how you selected your data using quality checklists and how, if necessary, you were able to seek representativeness in your sample. Please see Chapter 8.
What method of analysis made sense within my theoretical perspective and to my data?	This is how you approached the analysis of your data. Please see Chapters 11 and 12.
How did I approach ethics in my research?	This is how you complied with your ethical code of conduct and engaged in practices of informed consent, data anonymity and confidentiality. Please see Chapter 5.
How do I ensure my research is valid and credible?	This explores strategies and techniques to secure research rigour. Please see Chapter 4.

Figure 4.10   A checklist for reviewing your methodology

Most of the questions we ask in Figure 4.10 are phrased in the past tense as when you write your methodology you do this as something that has happened; you have defined your question, identified your theoretical perspective, selected and analysed your work. Notice your research position or worldview is written in the present tense to reflect an ongoing form of knowing. To support your ability to respond to these questions we have provided the relevant chapters where this information is explored in depth.

Writing your methodology

As you write your methodology, Booth, Colomb and Williams (2008) advise that you should consider the roles that you create for yourself and your reader. When you write your methodology, you do this from a position of authority as you are the person in charge of your research.

Thinking of yourself as the expert of your own study might sound daunting but it should enable you to feel a sense of ownership, academic authority and autonomy. Your reader for a range of reasons wants to know about your work. It may be that they have paid for it as you were funded by an organisation; it may be that this research is for an assessed component of a degree or higher learning course; but irrespective of the reasons why you created the research, you need to assume your reader (*funder, colleague or marker*) wants to know about it.

Guba and Lincoln (1994) explain that a methodology is where you as the researcher can answer questions based on your process of inquiry. Your reader wants to know the 'what', 'why', 'when' and 'how' of your approach to answering your research question. So, it makes sense that when you write your methodology you will write it as an expert on the research you have conducted. Your methodology therefore, needs to be written not just with great clarity but also with some authority and skill. Figure 4.11 provides a few tips to consider when writing up your methodology.

It can be written in the past tense as it describes what you did and not what you are going to do.
Defend your decisions: How did you go about your research? What overall strategy did you adopt and why? What design and techniques did you use? Why those and not others?
Demonstrate your research knowledge; your methodology is where you can show your investment in understanding the art and craft of research.
Be clear; make sure you are using terminology in a consistent way. If you are referring to specialised terminology make sure you direct your reader to a footnote or a glossary where they can be informed of its meaning and usage.
Gain ownership; as we stated above, this is your work, no one knows it as well as you.
Do not over explain: assume your reader has some knowledge so you do not go into the micro detail of all you did. As Labaree (2018) states, focus on how you *applied a method,* not on the mechanics of *doing a method*.

Figure 4.11   Considerations when writing up your methodology

WHAT HAPPENS WHEN THINGS GO WRONG?

Your methodology should be a space where you can report and reflect on the inquiry processes you created and employed within your research. However, as any researcher will tell you, things can and do go wrong when you conduct research. Being an ethical researcher means acknowledging the difficulties or issues faced no matter how painful this is. When we do this, we are aiming for research transparency as disclosing any issues clearly and objectively enables our work to be judged accepting the limitations it offers. However, being open and honest should not be considered as creating vulnerability, as being open in exploring the issues faced can enhance your claims for credibility and trustworthiness. Remember that if any problems arise:

- Describe the ways in which you responded to these concerns. This can be a good way to indicate your research knowledge and skills.
- Indicate if the problems created had any impact on your findings in any meaningful way. If you do not identify these, your reader will!
- Use any issues to your benefit: in your conclusion and recommendation sections indicate if these issues led you to think about undertaking this or future research in a new way.

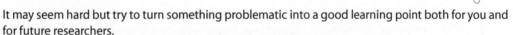

PAUSE FOR THOUGHT

Accentuate the positive

It may seem hard but try to turn something problematic into a good learning point both for you and for future researchers.

Being able to demonstrate how you overcame obstacles reflects your skills and credibility as an effective secondary researcher.

REFLECTION AND FURTHER READING

At the beginning of the chapter we set out what you should be able to do when you reached the end of this chapter. To aid your reflection on all we have covered we ask some chapter specific questions. If you are unsure of any of your answers to these questions, please go back to the relevant section to review this aspect.

REFLECTING ON CHAPTER 4

In this chapter we have:

- **Defined qualitative secondary research as a research design:** Why is qualitative secondary research described as a design?
- **Identified key ingredients of a qualitative secondary research methodology:** What is the role of a methodology? How can it aid your claims for your research to be considered credible?

- **Considered a range of strategies that can be used to support your attainment of research quality and rigour:** What is the purpose of triangulation? How can you try to ensure your research is confirmable?
- **Explored how to construct your methodology:** Why do we focus on your ability to defend your methodological choices? In what tense should you write your methodology?

WE RECOMMEND FOR FURTHER READING:

Clough, P. & Nutbrown, C. (2012) *A Student's Guide to Methodology: Justifying Enquiry* (3rd edn). London: SAGE Publications Ltd.

This book offers an accessible overview of the research process. Written for clarity, Part 1: Research is Methodology, presents some key questions within the research process and they begin by asking 'What is research?'. We also recommend the second part: The Pervasive Nature of Methodology, as it explores how knowledge is constructed and explores the influence of the researcher in the research process.

Golafshani, N. (2003) Understanding reliability and validity in qualitative research. *The Qualitative Report*, *8*(4), 597–606. Available at: https://nsuworks.nova.edu/tqr/vol8/iss4/6.

This article presents an informative overview of processes to secure research rigour. It is written for researchers at any level and is well worth reading.

Knafl, K.A. & Breitmayer, B.J. (1991) Triangulation in qualitative research: Issues of clarity and purpose. In J. Morse (ed.), *Qualitative Nursing Research* (2nd edn) (pp. 226–239). California: SAGE Publications, Inc.

Although quite old in terms of the date of publishing, this chapter (13) offers a clear and comprehensive approach to issues of reliability and validity in qualitative research.

Morrow, S.L. (2005) Quality and trustworthiness in qualitative research in counseling psychology. *Journal of Counseling Psychology*, *52*(2), 250–260.

Morrow considers the trustworthiness, or credibility, of qualitative research and offers some guidelines for writing qualitative research.

Tracy, S.J. (2010) Qualitative quality: Eight 'big-tent' criteria for excellent qualitative research. *Qualitative Inquiry*, *16*, 837–851.

Tracy offers an alternative approach to research quality within qualitative research.

5
ETHICS IN QUALITATIVE SECONDARY RESEARCH

THIS CHAPTER SUPPORTS YOUR ABILITY TO

define ethics within qualitative secondary research

consider issues relating to the right to privacy

investigate legal issues in accessing and using data

identify ethical researcher behaviour

CHAPTER OVERVIEW

This chapter considers the ethical intricacies that can surround qualitative secondary research and, to do this, it provides guidance to ensure that exacting standards of ethical conduct are met. We begin by setting out some basic principles, consider the complexities of informed consent and explore issues relating to confidentiality and anonymity. The potential for direct and indirect identification is examined for all data but we provide a specific spotlight to data found online.

We discuss legal responsibilities to the data you may use and encourage you to meet your obligations to ethical research practice by adhering to copyright and intellectual property and data protection legislation. We also discuss ethical researchers as acknowledging and respecting the contributions of others in their research. Therefore, by the end of this chapter, you should have a clear overview of some of the ethical and legal responsibilities of a qualitative secondary researcher.

WHY DO I NEED TO THINK ABOUT ETHICS?

Ethics are a set of beliefs or behaviours that guide and inform the research process to ensure researchers behave appropriately. This means understanding and undertaking the duties and responsibilities we indicate in Figure 5.1. Whilst you are a qualitative secondary researcher and are not using 'live' participants, there is still a need to engage in ethical behaviour because as Mauthner (2012: 173) affirms, we all have '*ethical and moral responsibilities as researchers*'.

In qualitative secondary research, ethics defines your relationship to your research as it is:

- predicated on appropriate behaviour *in* and *to* your research. This approach reflects the rise in seeing ethics as more than behaviour to others; it is about the behaviour you show to your research (*e.g. being open and transparent, acknowledging your influence*);
- conforming to codes of conduct (*e.g. institutional, discipline or professional*);
- following legal frameworks (*e.g. data protection legislation*).

Consequently, ethics in qualitative secondary research should reflect the same principles as those provided for all types of research. As a researcher working with data provided by others, you need to show that you have considered and responded to the components we identify in Figure 5.1. This means addressing issues of respect, not causing any harm, seeking consent where this is possible and safeguarding privacy.

As we have already suggested, ethics is more than just a code of conduct to protect others; it is also a way of behaving within your research. To reflect this belief, we consider ethics as integral to all parts of the research process and we discuss ethics in Chapter 2 (*research proposals*), Chapter 3 (*reflexivity*), Chapter 4 (*strategies for research quality*), Chapter 10 (*secure and safe data storage*), Chapter 11 (*analysing data*) and Chapter 13 (*the presentation of your findings*). We advocate that ethics is more than engaging in ethical processes such as a passive tick list process; it is an active commitment to ensuring high-quality research.

Therefore, we need to know about ethics in qualitative secondary research because as Stake (2005: 459) reminds us '*Qualitative researchers are guests in the private spaces of the world. Their manners should be good and their code of ethics strict*'.

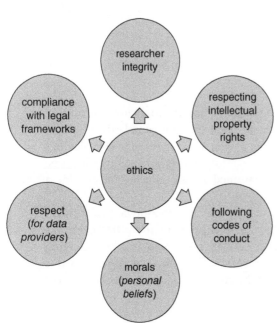

Figure 5.1 Overview of ethics in qualitative secondary research

WHAT ARE THE MAIN ETHICAL PRINCIPLES?

In the section above we identified the three main principles or research respect that you as a qualitative secondary research must adhere to. These principles (see Figure 5.2) are enshrined within codes of conduct and form the basis of institution and organisation research guidelines. These principles hold true for all forms of research.

The three main principles identified in Figure 5.2, emerged as a direct response to terrible atrocities performed in the name of scientific research that came to light in the aftermath of the Second World War. Evidence of dehumanising research was presented during the American Military Tribunals that took place in Nuremberg between 1945 and 1946. This evidence contained extreme cases of unregulated

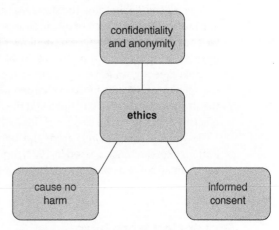

Figure 5.2   Basic ethical considerations

medical research and this led the judges at Nuremberg to respond to the need to protect humans within research. To do this they defined a set of 10 research principles (*the Nuremberg Code – see NIH.gov*) designed to safeguard those taking part in research.

The first principle of this code is '*the voluntary consent of the human subject is absolutely essential*'. This vital contribution, along with the merger of the medical practitioner's Hippocratic Oath '*first do no harm*' serves as a blueprint for codes of ethical research conduct used today. Both the Nuremberg Code and the Helsinki Declaration (WMAGA, 1964) established by the World Medical Association to monitor research involving human subjects form the foundations of ethical practice within research (Israel & Hay 2006). In this chapter, to highlight the need for ethical research we offer examples that do not reflect the exacting standards of ethical conduct and integrity we have come to expect. We begin with the Tuskegee Syphilis study (see Box 5.1).

BOX 5.1   TUSKEGEE SYPHILIS STUDY (1932 TO 1972)

In Alabama in the United States of America, the Public Health Service conducted the Tuskegee Syphilis Study to study the effect of untreated syphilis. Over a period of 40 years a total of 600 men were offered free medical care in exchange for their medical data. No informed consent was gained. None were told that they had syphilis and when the study began, no proven treatments for the disease existed.

(Continued)

(Continued)

When penicillin became the standard treatment for the disease in 1947, this was withheld and many of the men died of the disease. Some unknowingly transmitted the disease to their wives and children. When a whistleblower leaked the story to the national press in America, news of the study set in motion a national and international public outcry.

Subsequently, an Advisory Panel, comprising representatives from areas such as health, law, religion and education, was charged with reviewing this study. The panel concluded that the study was ethically unjustified and the Assistant Secretary for Health and Scientific Affairs officially announced the closure of the Tuskegee Study in 1972.

Because of the findings from the panel and the public backlash that followed, the National Research Act, passed in 1974, required all USA federally-funded proposed research with human subjects be approved by an institutional review board (IRB).

Protection from harm

The example in Box 5.1, illustrates the harm that can be done to human participants in research but harm may be less obvious when you are using existing data provided by others. Therefore, the first main ethical principle 'protection from harm' needs to be considered alongside the source of the data you wish to use. Using data that is in the public realm or within popular culture may present fewer opportunities for causing distress, whereas using personal documents could reveal private and sensitive data and present increased potential for harm. Therefore, right from the beginning of your research, you should consider how you can access and use data without causing the people or organisations that provide it any harm or distress. This may require you to make a judgement where you weigh up the rights of the individual who owns the data against the benefits to you and the wider research community of your doing the research (see Figure 5.3).This is something Beyrer and Kass (2002) indicate as a balance between risks and benefits. Thus, the judgement you employ is an ethical, moral, and legal duty to ensure your inquiry does not cause harm. Whilst not exhaustive, here are some examples of possible harm:

- **Reputational:** through the inadvertent disclosure of sensitive or confidential data (*e.g. disclosing an individual's political beliefs*);
- **Organisation/Business:** abusing copyright or terms and conditions (*e.g. using an image from a commercial company and not complying with the terms of use*);
- **Researcher harm:** accessing some sensitive or 'hot' topics may create emotional harm (*e.g. data on child exploitation, modern slavery or extremist views*).

Therefore, to safeguard yourself and others from possible harm and distress, we advise you to read your relevant codes of conduct and ethical guidelines. They may not be the most interesting reading material but reading them carefully can help you make informed choices when you consider potential risks within your research study.

Confidentiality and anonymity

The second main principle focuses on privacy and data protection. This is also dependent on the type of data you wish to access. If the text is by a published author, they have the right to be acknowledged as the intellectual owner of your data but if you are accessing information provided by people in online spaces then anonymity should be considered. Therefore, the way you approach aspects of confidentiality and anonymity can depend on the data you want to use.

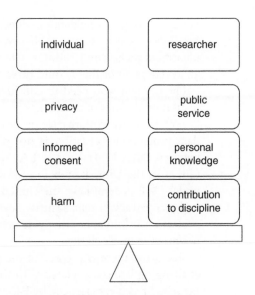

Figure 5.3   Weighing up risk against benefit within research

As we consider towards the end of the chapter when we discuss current UK data protection, exploring strategies for anonymising data is essential to remove the possibility of an individual being identified. Disclosure may accidentally happen: for example, when you access photographic data in a local newspaper or use a blog. Therefore, as a qualitative secondary researcher, ensuring that any of the data you access cannot lead to deliberate or non-deliberate disclosure is imperative as an ethical and legal duty. The sources of data identified in Figure 5.4 indicate some possible identifiers.

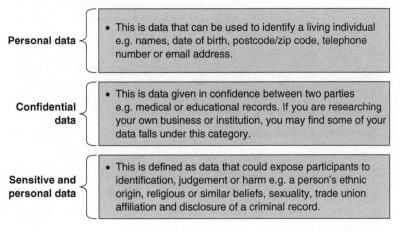

Figure 5.4   Types of sensitive and personal data

For a researcher using data provided by others, being aware of the possibilities and potential for disclosure is important. When you access online data, disclosure can occur when you use identifiers such as an IP address (*Internet protocol address*), an email address, screen name or an avatar as all of these could directly identify a person. Although some of these are in the public domain, you need to consider your compliance with data protection legislation and institutional codes of conduct.

Whilst, as we explore later in the chapter, there is very clear data protection law in the UK, data protection legislation is not always clear and consistent between countries or even between states in America (DLA Piper 2017). According to the global law firm DLA Piper (2017) in the United Arab Emirates (UAE), the concept of 'personal data' is not reflected under UAE Federal Law; the United States has about 20 sector-specific or medium-specific national privacy or data security laws and there is no specific legislation on privacy and data protection in India. So, the wide array of international data protection and privacy laws do not provide much clarity.

Ensuring there is privacy in the online domain remains one of the most enduring and challenging issues associated with the Internet. This issue was brought into focus following the data breach experienced by Facebook in 2015 (reported in 2018) when an analytics company, Cambridge Analytica, was able to harvest the private information of more than 50 million individuals (Cadwalladr & Graham-Harrison 2018).

In existing research data, some qualitative researchers use rich descriptions. These rich descriptions are in data when a researcher has provided details about a person's life or situation that are personal and specific. Therefore, we advise you to be rigorous and always check your data to ensure that it is not inadvertently disclosing any personal, confidential or sensitive data such as that identified in Figure 5.5.

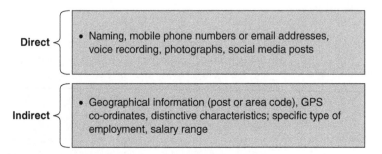

Figure 5.5   Direct and indirect identifiers

If you want to access archived research data or research found in scholarly journals, it may be possible to check that the original researcher has adhered to and complied with ethical guidelines. If an organisation has funded them, evidence of ethical conduct will have been one of the conditions of the research.

There is a wealth of valuable qualitative data available online such as that found in blogs or social media sites but be vigilant and check for personal identifiers. As we discussed above (see Figures 5.4 and 5.5), when faced with data harvested from the Internet, we need to balance the ease of availability it offers and our desire to use it against the rights of the individual who owns it. Just because the data is there for us to see and access does not mean we should use it without careful consideration. There is a growing awareness of the need to regulate Internet research and the Association of Internet Researchers (AoIR) provides specific guidance on ethical approaches to research using the Internet (see https://aoir.org/aoir_ethics_graphic_2016/). In the chart they offer for those researching using the Internet they suggest the following questions:

- Could analysis, publication, redistribution, or dissemination of content harm the subject in any way?
- If the content of a subject's communication were to become known beyond the confines of the venue being studied would the likely result cause harm?
- Does the author/participant consider a personal network of connections sensitive information?
- Does the author/participant consider the presentation of information or venue to be private or public?
- Do the terms of service conflict with ethical principles?
- Is the author/subject a minor?

The final question is hard to answer as the anonymity of data provided on the Internet can make authorship hard to ascertain. As we explore later in this chapter, if you have any concerns as to the authenticity of your data or of the people who created it, leave it out. Therefore, in Figure 5.6 we offer advice to keep you and your participants safe from harm

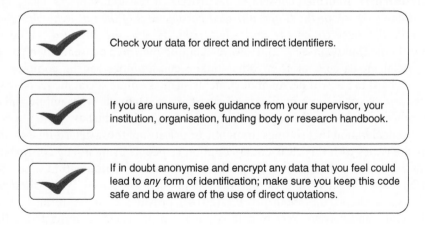

Figure 5.6   Data privacy checklist

PAUSE FOR THOUGHT

Anonymisation

There are many ways to employ anonymisation techniques to provide data security. There are basic approaches such as numbering your data and keeping a code book or anonymisation log to record this process (Corti et al. 2014). This creates a paper trail indicating your anonymisation strategy and ethical adherence. You could use the following:

- Use pseudonyms, which is the application of a new name or word to describe a person, location or organisation (*e.g. Manchester in the UK becomes 'Northern' city*).
- Provide an age range rather than a specific age (*e.g. 30–40 instead of 32*). Keeping data like this general rather than specific is essential when using data that discloses a specific religion, ethnic origin, political affiliation or a person's sexuality. The UK Data Protection Act (2018) considers data such as this as 'sensitive data' and it should therefore be treated with great care.

There is a range of open source software which can be used to support anonymisation processes. You will need to check if the program you select is sufficient for your needs by seeking advice from your supervisor, institution or funding organisation.

Informed consent

This is the third main principle and the most challenging to adhere to for qualitative secondary researchers. Informed consent is the process of research subjects being '*informed fully about the purpose, methods and intended possible uses of the research, what their participation in the research entails and what risks, if any, are involved*' (ESRC: www. ethicsguidebook.ac.uk/Consent-72). However, gaining informed consent when you harvest data on social media sites or from other online communities can be complex. This is because it is hard to know if personal documents such as online social media or first-hand narratives (*e.g. blogs*) are in a public or private domain. Defining what public and private mean in times of mass data sharing is difficult and codes of conduct are trying to catch up. There is a consideration that settings for public or private are those determined by the user, but there are issues with this clear-cut assumption as people using a range of social media platforms may assume that, as they are publishing their information within what they perceive to be a specific site, the data they offer is private. The social media site Facebook (https://en-gb.facebook.com/about/privacy (2018)) provides clear definitions of what is deemed 'public' and private'. Private data is password protected or restricted within site settings, but public data is defined as the following:

When you choose to share something with **Public** (ex: when you select **Public** from the audience selector), it's considered public information. If you share something and you don't see an audience selector or another privacy setting, that information is also public.

We propose that one way to consider whether data is in the public or private domain is to consider the level of expectancy of privacy. A clear example of this is when a password is used as this creates an expectation of privacy but a blog that is freely available online to read or an open Twitter discussion does not have the same level or expectation for privacy.

The American Educational Research Association (AERA 2011: 151 section c) clearly states that '*researchers may conduct research in public places or use publicly available information about individuals (e.g. naturalistic observations in public places, analysis of public records, or archival research) without obtaining consent*'. However, this is not the view shared by the British Education Research Association (BERA 2018: 7) who state that researchers using social media and online communities need to remember that digital information is generated by individuals. They continue:

> Researchers should not assume that the name given and/or identity presented by participants in online fora or media is a 'real' name: it might be an avatar. This avatar could represent a human or a bot, but behind either will be one or more human creators responsible for it, who could therefore be regarded as participants; whether and how these potential participants might be traceable should be considered.

It is no wonder that Bryman (2012: 138) describes this ethical concern as '*hotly contested*' as even ethical codes of conduct cannot present agreement. To guide you in this, we offer the following advice to help you work with your social media data ethically:

- Try to seek permission where you can.
- Always anonymise your data as fully as possible to remove the possibility of any direct or indirect disclosure. This also means not using direct quotations from any harvested text.

Most social media information could be described as mundane as it explores the everyday aspects of people's lives, but some can be considered sensitive if it discloses personal feelings, illegal activities or different and controversial beliefs. As Eynon, Fry and Shroeder (2008: 37) firmly state, decisions as to the type of data you access have very complex legal and moral connotations and that the researcher needs to '*respect context and intentions online*'. Gaining informed consent is therefore something difficult to secure for personal, unregulated, or found online data. BERA (2018) in their latest ethical code recognise that gaining consent is difficult but they expect researchers to provide evidence of their attempt to address this. However, before you think it is impossible to research using data found online, please refer to the example of blog research (see Box 5.2) and consider how this researcher resolved some of the ethical tensions in her research.

You may need to seek consent in other ways. This may be when you are using data that is owned by someone and not in the public domain. This means offering 'informed' consent to owners of other forms of data. This may be required when the data is an object such as a painting in a private collection or private documents in an archive. You need to provide details of your research and how you plan to use their property. You may also need to seek permission to access and use some forms of data to comply with copyright law. However, your use may be defined as subject to policies termed 'fair use' as it relates to non-commercial research activity.

You should also be aware that harvesting data may lead you to contravene the terms and service provided within some websites and, inadvertently, infringe data protection and privacy laws. It is always advisable to check your use of any data if you are unsure of your right of access.

What about using existing research data?

There is a move towards informing participants who have participated in primary research studies that their data may be shared. In the UK, the Data Protection Act (1998) stated that all participants should be asked if they were willing for their data to be archived and made available for further research. The more recent Data Protection Act (2018) adds to this stating that all data processing should be lawful, fair and transparent. Additionally, professional codes of ethics such as those of the American Educational Research Association (AERA 2011) require researchers to inform participants of the immediate and future use of the material. Some of the large data archives, such as UK Data Archive (www.data-archive.ac.uk/) have this as a condition for the sharing of data. Large data archives and repositories are beginning to address issues with data sharing but this may not be the case when accessing individual studies such as those in institutional repositories (*e.g. unpublished master's or doctoral theses*). It may be difficult to check if their participants were informed of possible data reuse.

BOX 5.2 'YOUTH RESEARCH IN WEB 2.0: A CASE STUDY IN BLOG ANALYSIS' BY SNEE (2012)

Helene Snee used blogs to examine stories told by young people about their gap years. Whilst she felt this was a good way to understand their narratives she experienced some ethical concerns: namely two key issues the needed to be resolved:

1. **Are blogs public or private?**

This she identified as 'blurred' as when people write online they may not be aware that anyone else may read it. This may create a false sense of privacy. She also wondered if the author had considered who the audience would be and whether they had considered that it may be a researcher. She also encountered issues with confidentiality as some of the sampled blogs contained personal information such as a name and an email address.

2. **Should the blogger's anonymity be protected or do they have a right to be recognised as authors?**

Her debate involved considering the nature of the data revealed in the blog as this suggested the need for some form of anonymity but this approach was difficult because this form of online data can be easily found using any search engine. She also raised a significant point which is that some bloggers might actually want to be recognised for the work that has gone into their blogs. She wonders if they should therefore be treated in the same way as a journalist, in other words, acknowledging the rights of intellectual ownership to the published material. If this is the case, then she would need to recognise the author by providing a link to their blog when writing up the research.

She resolved her concerns as follows:

- She felt there was a strong case for considering the gap year blogs as public data as they were publicly accessible and she felt no informed consent was needed.
- However, even though the data was considered as in the public domain, she applied a level of disguise to protect the blogger's identity which she felt was more important than recognising them as authors. When she used quotes from the blogs she altered any identifiable details.
- She later contacted some of the bloggers for interviews and they confirmed they were aware that the blogs were not totally private.

Codes of conduct

Codes of conduct can be provided by a specific discipline, by an academic or training institution or by an employer but they are important to follow as they set out how you as a researcher need to engage with your research. The responsibility of any researcher, irrespective of discipline, profession and institution is to ensure specific codes, standards of behaviour and conduct are upheld. Many organisations provide their own discipline focused ethical guides and framework. Organisations such as those listed below provide a vast amount of information of ethical conduct.

- **British Educational Research Association:** www.bera.ac.uk/researchers-resources/resources-for-researchers
- **Australian Association for Research in Education:** www.aare.edu.au/pages/aare-code-of-ethics.html
- **American Educational Research Association:** www.aera.net/Portals/38/docs/About_AERA/CodeOfEthics(1).pdf
- **Canadian Association of Social Workers:** www.casw-acts.ca/sites/default/files/attachements/casw_code_of_ethics.pdf

These frameworks and codes of ethics are useful starting points but they have a strong leaning towards primary research. As a qualitative secondary researcher, knowing and understanding these codes of conduct is imperative, but as Creswell (2009: 88) emphasises, ethical practices need to go beyond the *'following of static guidelines'*. Being active in ethical practices means embracing ethics as a philosophy to guide all parts of the research process.

PAUSE FOR THOUGHT

Ethics is a changing field

The Tuskegee Syphilis Study illustrated how ethics have developed and the field of ethics is still developing. Some of this development relates to new forms of data access and technological advances. Therefore, we advise you to access the most current version of your institution's, funding body's or professional code of conduct.

• Do you know how to access the latest version of your required code?

One recent development in some disciplines, such as education, nursing and social work, is to adopt an *'ethics of care'* (Held 2006:10).

When things go 'wrong'

The following examples are not specifically of qualitative secondary research that went wrong yet they are well-known studies that exemplify the need for codes of ethical conduct. The first example in Box 5.3 is the *'Monster Study'* by Wendell Johnson (1939). It is included to illustrate unethical research practice in the mistreatment of vulnerable children. Whilst it is distressing to read, it should be noted that this research was undertaken before the Nuremberg Code.

BOX 5.3   'MONSTER STUDY' BY WENDELL JOHNSON (1939)

Wendell Johnson was a speech pathologist from the University of Iowa, USA who, assisted by one of his graduate students Mary Tudor, conducted an experiment on 22 orphan children to test his new theory on the cause of stuttering. Johnson wanted to challenge the existing belief that stuttering was an inborn trait.

The children selected were randomly assigned to a control group or an experimental group. The children in the 'control group' were given positive speech therapy and praise for the fluency of their speech. The other half in the 'experimental stuttering group' were demeaned and belittled every time they made a speech imperfection, no matter how slight.

The results found that children who were not stutterers in the stuttering group developed a stutter by the time the experiment ended and those that did stutter ended up with a more pronounced stutter than before. Johnson established that a negative focus on stuttering makes the condition worse, indicating a developmental causation rather than innate trait.

Despite efforts to reverse the process, many of the children who developed stutters could not recover from this experiment. The University of Iowa publicly apologised for the Monster Study in 2001. Six of the orphan children were awarded damages for the psychological and emotional scars caused by the experiment. The American Speech-Language-Hearing Association prohibits experimentation on children when there exists a significant chance of causing lasting harmful consequences.

What this example shows (see Box 5.3) is the power held by researchers over the children as participants least able to protect themselves. Whilst this research may have been conducted before a formal consideration of research ethics, there is still evidence of morally dubious behaviour. If you were undertaking an exploration on the development of children's speech and language concerns, you would need to consider if and how you could or would include research such as this as data.

In the next example, presented in Box 5.4, 'When Contact Changes Minds: An Experiment of Transmission of Support for Gay Equality' by LaCour and Green (2014) the focus is not on the mistreatment of participants but on researcher behaviour. It provides an example of what happens when the integrity of the data is, in some way, compromised. Although, the claimed 'results' inspired a greater conversation about gay rights, the underpinning evidence for the claims made was declared as flawed.

BOX 5.4   'WHEN CONTACT CHANGES MINDS: AN EXPERIMENT OF TRANSMISSION OF SUPPORT FOR GAY EQUALITY' BY LACOUR AND GREEN (2014)

This research published in *Science* (Volume 346, Issue 6215) in December 2014 claimed that a 20-minute conversation involving the telling of a personal story with a gay canvasser could create positive shifts in attitudes towards gay people. The results argued that whilst both gay and straight canvassers produced large attitude changes, only gay canvassers could sustain a positive mood change over 3-weekly, 6-weekly and 9-monthly checks. Significantly, it was the enduring nature of this change that became so influential.

When LaCour's research was examined by other researchers, 'irregularities' were found. It was asserted that LaCour could not have collected the data in the way he said he did and it was identified that he had used data from an existing data set. Combined with this, the survey

(Continued)

(Continued)

company LaCour claimed he worked with also found no record of him. He never showed anyone his raw data so that someone else could independently confirm the validity of the reported findings. He withheld the data claiming that it was too 'sensitive' and that he had to destroy the data after analysing the findings. This research was redacted by Green who was a co-author.

The above example is interesting as it challenges the status of the 'gold standard' peer review process (Baverstock 2016). The research paper written about this study was reviewed by academic and knowledgeable professionals. But the anomalies later identified in this research were not detected (see Box 6.1 in Chapter 6). Peer review has long been considered by all researchers as the closest thing possible to ensuring quality in research. As a qualitative secondary researcher, you are encouraged to access peer-reviewed sources of evidence but as with all forms of evidence it pays to be critically evaluative (see Chapter 8).

The final example, in Box 5.5, is from the UK. It is the study *'Ileal-lymphoid-nodular hyperplasia, non-specific colitis and pervasive developmental disorder in children'* by Wakefield et al. (1998 – there are 12 co-authors).

BOX 5.5   'ILEAL-LYMPHOID-NODULAR HYPERPLASIA, NON-SPECIFIC COLITIS AND PERVASIVE DEVELOPMENTAL DISORDER IN CHILDREN' BY WAKEFIELD ET AL. (1998)

This research paper was published in *The Lancet* and it claimed that there was a direct link between the MMR (measles, mumps and rubella) inoculation jab and the increased prevalence of bowel inflammation and pervasive development disorder in children (a form of autism).

The findings of this research were challenged due to limitations in the size of the case (12), the lack of a control group and claims based on the reliance on parental recall and beliefs. What emerged later was that Dr Wakefield did not disclose his relationship to an anti-vaccine group, which was a clear conflict of interest.

Debates concerning the validity of Dr Wakefield's claims still abound and whilst his co-authors retracted their work, Wakefield chose not to. At the time, this research was influential as the claims made by this research led to a fall in the vaccination rate in the UK and US and made parents feel they had 'given' their child autism (Hilton et al. 2007).

When published, this article created a media storm as it reported a proposed link between the measles, mumps and rubella vaccine given to children in the UK and the development of autism behaviours in children. The research supporting this claim was declared as limited and potentially flawed but this research became more infamous for its consequences as it was criticised for being responsible for the reduction in vaccination rates and potentially exposing children to increased risk of disease.

PAUSE FOR THOUGHT

Considering the ethical practice of others

As the examples outlined above indicate, as well as considering your ethical practice, you also need to review the ethical practices of other researchers. This is because you may be using their data as a foundation for your research.

We cannot stress enough that it is worth taking time to consider the type and quality of the data you select for analysis. If you use the 'wrong' type of data you may end up with the 'wrong' findings.

ETHICS COMMITTEES

In Chapter 2, we explored the completion of a research proposal and a key part of your proposal is showing how you will address any ethical issues and concerns. When writing a proposal, showing that you have a firm grasp of ethical approaches to data is essential. You may need to submit your proposal to an ethical committee for review. These committees are gatekeepers for the ethical conduct of research and are there to protect research participants, and in secondary research these are the people who provide your data. Their responsibility is also to protect the institution where you may be studying and ensure you do not engage in unethical behaviour that could compromise the institution's reputation. Most universities, institutions and professional associations have committees like these to explore the risks and benefits of the research you propose. In the UK these may be called Research Ethics Committees (RECs) and, in the US, there are Institutional Review Boards (IRBs) and Independent Ethics Committees (IECs).

PAUSE FOR THOUGHT

Demonstrating an ethical approach

You will need to show you have adopted an ethical approach to data when you submit your research proposal. Consider how you will:

- discuss issues of informed consent;
- explore concerns regarding forms of disclosure;
- manage and store your data (see Chapter 10).

Your proposal sets out *what*, *why* and *how* you want to explore your research question. In the ethics section you are demonstrating your respect for the data provided by others.

ETHICAL AND LEGAL ACCESS TO DATA

The Internet offers a vast amount of data which can offer ease of access. But this ease also creates challenges. The Internet as a global phenomenon has widened the research field. But it has created gaps in legislation as information is no longer defined by national borders and their respective legal frameworks. Some legal concerns need to be considered even for a small-scale researcher; for example, storing data in the cloud can be seen as taking data outside of national borders and this can infringe some data protection legislation (Kuan Hon, Millard & Walden 2011).

For those researchers who are doing small-scale studies, issues such as the migration of data across borders might seem a bit alarmist. However, the main point to consider is that personal, sensitive and confidential data is legally protected as are intellectual and ownership rights. As a qualitative secondary researcher, you will have to show that you are aware of this legal protection. This needs to be explicitly stated on your research proposal and/or data management plan.

Whilst the Internet offers many benefits there is a chasm between advances in technology and policies that need to keep pace with it (Parry & Mauthner 2004). Carusi and Jirotka (2009: 288) describe the reality of this technological expansion as *'pushing us beyond existing practice and … challenging its moral grounds'*. Therefore, tread carefully when using the Internet to harvest your data and be aware that with new forms of data come new ethical challenges.

Data protection legislation

In the UK, the Data Protection Act 2018 (*the UK's implementation of the General Data Protection Regulation GDPR*) sets out very clear rights for data owners and responsibilities for data users. This act specifies that personal data is any information relating to a living individual who can be identified, directly or indirectly by a name, an identification number, location data or an online identifier. It goes further, stating that this identification could also be factors specific to the physical, physiological, genetic, mental, economic, cultural or social identity of the individual. In other words, any information that is clearly about a person, and it states that sensitive data needs to be handled with extra security. These categories of sensitive data are:

- Racial or ethnic origin;
- Political opinions;
- Religious or philosophical beliefs;
- Trade union membership;
- Genetic data;
- Biometric data (*where processed to uniquely identify someone*).

The Data Protection Act (2018) requires data be handled in a way that is fair, proportionate, secure, and justified. For research purposes, it is possible to use such data as long as anonymisation processes have been undertaken and the data cannot be linked to a living individual in any way. The UK's Information Commissioner's Office (ICO) describes anonymisation as '*the process of turning data into a form which does not identify individuals and where identification is not likely to take place*'. But it must be 'truly' anonymised as the ICO states, '*pseudonymised data can help reduce privacy risks by making it more difficult to identify individuals, but it is still personal data*'. Further information can be found within the guide provided as recommended reading and we advise you to discuss any issues relating to data protection with your supervisor and access your institution's code of conduct.

Copyright and intellectual property

Being ethical means approaching your qualitative secondary research in a way that is morally, ethically and legally appropriate. This necessitates thinking about the authors, creators and researchers who own the sources of data. Recognising the intellectual property rights of others is an important ethical duty and a legal one, as some of the data you may access can be covered by copyright legislation. Intellectual property was first protected by the Berne Convention for the Protection of Literary and Artistic Works, first adopted in 1886 and the current version of the convention is the Paris Act of 1971 (WIPO). One hundred and sixty-four countries have signed up to the convention and, under this convention, the author has the right to claim authorship and object to any treatment of the work which could damage her/his honour or reputation. In the US there is the Copyright Act of 1976 which grants five rights to the owner of the copyright. In the EU, more recent directives (*Directive 2001/29/EC of the European Parliament and of the Council of 22 May 2001*) are beginning to acknowledge the influence of technological advances on intellectual property (McCarthy 2013).

Issues relating to intellectual property are becoming increasingly relevant due to the increased sharing of copyrighted material on the Internet. As a qualitative secondary researcher, knowing how to access your sources ethically and legally is paramount. The rise of movements such as open access and Creative Commons whilst widening access have also made issues relating to intellectual property ownership less clear.

Therefore, there is a legal responsibility on you to care about who owns the data you may want to use. However, the levels of your responsibility can vary and for some, acknowledging source and giving fair attribution are all that is required but for others, you may need to check your data is legally yours to use. Most of your data needs may fall under the category 'fair use'; however, it is best to check, especially if you are using images, films or any brand or known copyrighted material (*denoted with the symbol* ©). Here are four probable conditions of access you may come across:

Copyright: This is a legal right that exists globally for the creator of an original work to claim exclusive rights. This enables the creator or owner to decide whether, and under what conditions, others may use the work. Sometimes copyright is denoted by a symbol © but not always.

Fair use: This is a policy that permits the use of copyrighted material without having to first get permission from the copyright holder. Fair use is called a *'limitations to copyright'* which is an attempt to keep the rights of the creators (*copyright holders*) in balance with the public interest in the wider distribution (UK Copyright Service 2017).

Creative Commons (CC): This is an organisation that seeks to increase access to the range of intellectual property that can be legally shared. The organisation has released a variety of Creative Commons licenses which indicate how the works of others can be used free of charge or penalty.

Public domain: These are the work of others that are not covered by copyright. The rights to the work may have expired (*in the UK this is after 70 years*) or been given away by the creator or owner.

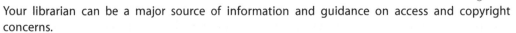

PAUSE FOR THOUGHT

Are you making the most of your library and its staff?

Your librarian can be a major source of information and guidance on access and copyright concerns.

Familiarise yourself with any resources or courses available to support your information gathering and/or referencing skills. Many institutions offer courses online. Before you start your research, it is advisable to explore the range of help available to you.

BEING AN ETHICAL QUALITATIVE SECONDARY RESEARCHER

Ethical behaviour for a qualitative secondary researcher can begin with your recording of all source material and data accurately (see Chapters 2 and 10). Keeping a record of your sources of data is not just a form of good practice; when this is done well, it should also safeguard you from any challenges that could damage your reputation and dismiss the credibility of your research. Acknowledging your sources and giving credit to authors who have added to your knowledge is essential for all those engaged in academic practice. Making sure that you follow your institution's referencing guidelines should protect your professional reputation and show your respect for the intellectual property of others.

Thomas (2009) states an ethical researcher is one that avoids causing reputational harm. Therefore, any professional criticism should not be derogatory (Parry & Mauthner 2004). Being able to use other people's knowledge and data is a privilege and, as such, it should be treated with respect.

Depending on the research question you ask, you may find yourself classed as an 'insider researcher'. This is where you research an institution that is known to you, possibly as a student, intern, volunteer or employee. If you are an insider, you have privileged access to your data. Conducting research in a familiar context presents specific ethical challenges. These are related to data ownership, maintaining anonymity and confidentiality (Breen 2007). Therefore, seek permission before any data (*e.g. company records, promotional material, policies and procedures*) is used. This holds true even if the data is available online and published in the public domain. This permission should also inform your institution about the type of data you want to use. Contact the data 'gatekeeper' who may be the head of department, manager or owner of the company and seek advice before you begin your research study.

An ethical researcher conducts their inquiry 'in the open' and this means being clear and transparent in the processes and strategies you use. Ensuring you have trustworthy research is reliant on the decisions you make and showing how and why these were made. In Chapter 4, we consider strategies to aid research quality and this is where ethics and rigour or research quality overlap. Whilst not exhaustive, Figure 5.7 presents some of the attributes of ethical researchers.

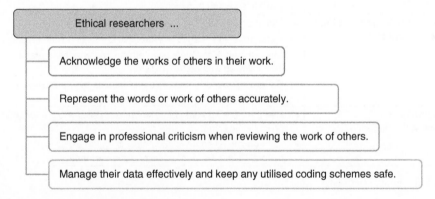

Figure 5.7   Being an ethical researcher

ETHICS CHECKLIST

Whilst being an ethical qualitative secondary researcher requires the same level of adherence as primary research, it can demand a different way of thinking about some ethical processes. In Figure 5.8, we provide a checklist to prompt your thinking about ethical approaches to your qualitative secondary research.

Questions	Comments
Can I get informed consent?	• Try to show you have considered this in your proposal and offered alternatives such as enhanced processes of data anonymisation. • Check if it is possible for you can to access the providers of data if this is possible. • If using existing research, informed consent may be written into data sharing agreements – refer to this in your proposal.
How will I engage with practices and strategies to ensure anonymity and confidentiality?	• Consider processes of coding and obscuring all identifier features if using visual data (*pixelating*). • Remove all direct/indirect identifiers.
Do I have permission to access this data	• Always refer to the terms and conditions of any site you are accessing. • Try not to infringe rights of ownership or copyright.
What are the legal frameworks I need to follow?	• Follow data protection guidelines for your institution and discipline; access the legal frameworks for your region or country. • Do not infringe copyright or intellectual property rights of ownership
What codes of conduct do I need to follow?	• This depends on your subject area and discipline. • Access your institution's or funding body's ethical codes.
Am I exploring a topic that could be considered sensitive or 'hot'?	• Sensitive topics are those that have the potential to cause harm to you and your institution (e.g. terrorism or extremist data). • Your research searches may get you 'flagged' (*using words that trigger suspicion*).
How will I store my data?	• We explore this in Chapter 10, but you need to consider how to keep your data secure and safe.
Have I acknowledged all of my sources accurately?	• This process respects intellectual property ownership. • If you are using images or logos, please seek advice on copyright. • Citing the work of others is an ethical and academic practice so it is best followed with some precision. • Recording your sources of data enhances the possibility of replication (*your research can be replicated*).
Have I engaged in a professional manner?	• Use the work and data of others making sure you do not cause reputational harm. • Referencing all sources accurately is important as is not mispresenting the words of any authors or their data.

Figure 5.8   Ethics checklist

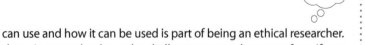

PAUSE FOR THOUGHT

If in doubt, leave it out

Making decisions as to what you can use and how it can be used is part of being an ethical researcher. As the amount and forms of data have increased so have the challenges researchers now face. If you are faced with such a dilemma that you cannot resolve, it is worth considering the saying 'if in doubt, leave it out'.

REFLECTION AND FURTHER READING

At the beginning of the chapter we set out what you should be able to do when you reached the end of this chapter. To aid your reflection on all we have covered we ask some chapter specific questions. If you are unsure of any of your answers to these questions, please go back to the relevant section to review this aspect.

REFLECTING ON CHAPTER 5

In this chapter we have:

- **Defined the role and function of ethics within qualitative secondary research:** Can you define the use of ethics for qualitative secondary researchers? Can you identify one problematic area for your research?
- **Discussed some of the complexities of anonymity, confidentiality and the role of informed consent:** How will these key principles be addressed within your research?
- **Explored the function of codes of conduct and ethics committees:** Do you know what code of conduct you should be working to? Do you have to complete a research proposal for ethical review?
- **Explored legal issues:** Are you aware of current data protection legislation? Do you know how this legislation may affect you?
- **Explored how to be an ethical researcher:** Are you aware of the relationship between ethics and research quality?

WE RECOMMEND FOR FURTHER READING:

Association of Internet Researchers (2012) *Ethical Decision Making and Internet Research: Recommendations from the AoIR Ethics Working Committee (Version 2.0).* Available at: https://aoir.org/ethics/ and https://aoir.org/aoir_ethics_graphic_2016/
This guidance provides a comprehensive overview to accessing information on the Internet and is highly recommended.

British Educational Research Association (2018) *Ethical Guidelines For Educational Research* (4th edn). Available at: www.bera.ac.uk/wp-content/uploads/2018/06/BERA-Ethical-Guidelines-for-Educational-Research_4thEdn_2018.pdf?noredirect=1
This is the recently updated version of this comprehensive account of ethics for those interested in educational research.

(Continued)

(Continued)

Charlesworth, A. (2012) Data protection, freedom of information and ethical review committee: Policies, practicalities and dilemmas. *Information, Communication & Society, 15*(1), 85–103.
This offers a useful discussion of the legalities, ethical guidelines and institutional regulations faced by researchers.

Economic and Social Research Council (nd) *The Research Ethics Guidebook*. Available at: www.ethicsguidebook.ac.uk/
This site offers a wealth of information on all aspects of ethical research. It is worth reviewing the 'principles and factors' section in some depth.

Eynon, R., Fry, J. & Schroeder, R. (2016) The ethics of internet research. In N.G. Fielding, R.M. Lee & G. Blank (eds). *The SAGE Handbook of Online Research Methods* (pp. 19–37). London: SAGE Publications Ltd.
This chapter offers a comprehensive consideration of the ethics of Internet research.

Information Commissioner's Office (2018) *Guide to the General Data Protection Regulation (GDPR)*. Available at: https://ico.org.uk/media/for-organisations/guide-to-the-general-data-protection-regulation-gdpr-1-0.pdf
This is an informative guide to current UK data protection legislation.

Kennedy, H., Elgesem, D. & Miguel, C. (2017) On fairness: User perspectives on social media data mining. *Convergence: The International Journal of Research into New Media Technologies, 23*(3), 270–288.
This paper offers a useful discussion about the issues with social media research.

Miller, T., Birch, M., Mauthner, M. & Jessop, J. (2012) *Ethics in Qualitative Research*. London: SAGE Publications Ltd.
This book includes a philosophical interpretation of the research process for those needing more depth in this argument.

6
EXPLORING DOCUMENTS AS DATA

THIS CHAPTER SUPPORTS YOUR ABILITY TO

> define qualitative data

> identify different categories of data

> make informed choices about data

> evaluate your use of research strategies in relation to your data

> understand the influence you have on the data you select

CHAPTER OVERVIEW

This chapter should help you make clear and informed decisions about the sources of data within your qualitative secondary research. We begin by defining qualitative data provided by documents created by people that can be anything from a scholarly peer-reviewed journal article, a blog, a painting or a vase to more specialised forms like archived qualitative research data.

We begin with a discussion on what constitutes the 'right' types of documents that provide the sources of data for your literature review and analysis. To help you in your decision making, we categorise data and consider how each category can be used as data for your analysis or as a source of information for your literature review. We also explore the role of your research strategies in your selection of data and ask some focused questions that should support your ability to defend your data selection in your methodology. Towards the end of this chapter we consider your influence on the data you select. Therefore, at the end of this chapter, you should have confidence in identifying sources of data for your literature review and analysis.

WHAT ARE QUALITATIVE DATA?

All information created by humans exists as data in one form or another and therefore, as resources for research that can be evaluated and analysed. As qualitative secondary researchers, it is likely that you will want to use data that enable you to understand how people engage in their social worlds. Consequently, you may be guided towards data that allow you to have insight in to people's lives and this could be in the form of words, pictures, video, audio and physical objects. Data like these describe all forms of human interaction in the world, from mundane daily routines to the highest philosophical thoughts. We call these data documents of human existence and May (1997: 157–158) describes these as '*the sedimentation of social practices*' because when we use documents as sources of qualitative data we are gaining access to people's reactions to their social and cultural world. When used in research these documents become the qualitative data that allows your research question to investigate descriptions, understandings, perceptions and attitudes.

Documents as sources of data are extremely diverse, available in vast quantities, found in many forms and in numerous locations and sites of access. They can range from documents provided by an individual and personal to those offered as public provided by immense intergovernmental organisations (IGOs) such as the United Nations. Figure 6.1 illustrates just a few examples of sources of qualitative data.

The variety and abundance of these documents as data can be both a wonder and a scourge. The wonder is in the opportunities it offers you as a secondary researcher to use innovative and exciting forms of data. The scourge is in the uncertainty of knowing if you are using credible and relevant sources and in knowing if you can access this data ethically. Another key concern could be how to reduce the amounts of data you may be faced with and how to do this in a meaningful and productive way.

Some of the documents you might think about using may be thought of as personal or private and so it is not just a question of what can I use, but also, how can I use it and whether or not I can use it. Depending on the sources of data you want to access, being a qualitative secondary researcher requires you to navigate difficulties of data access, privacy and ownership. It also means knowing about and applying processes and strategies to check the trustworthiness of your data.

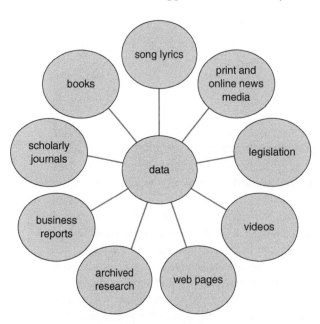

Figure 6.1   Examples of qualitative data

For qualitative secondary researchers, understanding the 'who', 'what', 'when', 'where', 'how' and 'why' of data production is paramount. Having confidence in the choices you make will enable you to defend these choices in your methodology. This confidence can come from knowing your data and its authenticity, credibility, representativeness and meaning (Scott 1990; see also Chapter 8).

MAKING IMPORTANT DECISIONS ABOUT DATA

As you begin to consider documents as sources of data, you will need to consider the sources of data you could use. To do this, you may need to reflect on the data's role, function and purpose. This might begin with complete immersion in all the data you need to explore for your topic. This immersion is the reading around your topic we explored in Chapter 2. As you read you will at some point need to decide what you want to do with the data. This means considering if the data you are searching for is to be used within your literature review or as data for your analysis. Whilst all data you select needs to be defendable to counter claims of weak credibility, selecting data for your literature review requires additional care.

Your literature review plays a pivotal role in your research project as it provides a context for the question you ask. It frames the scope of your inquiry and provides confirmation of your subject knowledge and understanding (see Chapter 9). Your review also has a pivotal function in the interpretation of your findings. The literature you select within your review should act as supporting evidence for the claims you make in your findings as you link your knowledge to that of other researchers and commentators. Therefore, sources selected for your literature review should be credible, scholarly and academic.

Searching for these sources needs to be based on more than chance and convenience and more on systematic search strategies (see Chapter 7). It also necessitates the application of a critical gaze, which we explore in Chapter 8, in the promotion of approaches to critical appraisal and evaluation. We explore the creation of your literature review in more depth in Chapter 9 but it is worth knowing a little of the process now as we explore specific types of data.

When selecting data for your analysis, knowing if there is potential to respond to your research question(s) and/or aim(s) is paramount and this requires you to view the data critically to assess usability. You may need to know the representativeness of your data and if a sampling strategy can be applied. Hence, selecting data for your qualitative secondary research requires a critical eye to make sure you use the most relevant and appropriate source of data.

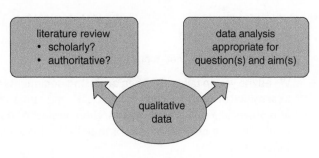

Figure 6.2 Exploring the function of your sources of data

As shown in Figure 6.2, some of the documents you can use as data in this chapter may be relevant to use within your literature review or analysis but this decision is one you need to make. We encourage you to base your decision on your research question(s) or aim(s), your knowledge of your subject area and discipline and in knowing the role and function of a literature review.

ETHICAL APPROACHES TO DATA

We explored the ethics of qualitative secondary research in significant depth in Chapter 5, but it is worth reflecting on some of the main points again as you consider the range and types of documents you can use as your data. This ethical consideration may be in making sure that you access documents fairly, reference the work of others and do not infringe copyright. But there are certain types of documents that as data may require additional consideration. These are 'personal' or first-hand sources that you may find in online communities, personal blogs or social media sites. In Chapter 5, we reviewed some of the complexities inherent in using these documents as data but we also encouraged you to persevere ethically. The list below provides a brief overview of some ethical considerations:

- Make sure you do not use any private or sensitive data within your documents that can directly or indirectly disclose any personal or confidential information. This could be in the use of an avatar, screen name, IP address, date of birth, postcode/zip code, telephone number or email address, or any information that identifies sexual orientation, race or political beliefs. You need to handle information provided in personal documents with some care.
- Check you have the right to access the information you want to use (*e.g. not gaining access via private sites*).
- Be aware of copyright and intellectual property rights.
- Accurately record the bibliographic information of your sources.

PAUSE FOR THOUGHT

Studying sensitive or 'hot' topics

We advise you to take care when accessing documents to explore topics that could be described as sensitive or 'hot' (e.g. child abuse, death and human trafficking). Complex topics such as these and others like sexual exploitation, child neglect or domestic violence can be 'laden with emotion' or 'inspire feelings of awe or dread' (Lee 1993: 6) and it may be difficult not to feel some influence.

Also, consider safeguarding yourself if you want to explore 'hot' topics, especially if you need to access websites that might be associated with illegal activities such as terrorist/extremist organisations. Some sites associated with these organisations may be subject to police or authority surveillance. The UK has many laws that prohibit the downloading or circulation of certain material (Universities UK 2012).

If you have any concerns regarding the data you want to access please consult your supervisor.

EXPLORING DOCUMENTS AS SOURCES OF DATA

Before you begin to consider documents as sources of data you should reflect on your research question and decide on the genre of research you are conducting. Ask yourself some fundamental questions such as:

- Are you doing historical research?
- Will you need to access archived research data?
- Will you take an education focus?
- Do you want to undertake arts-based research?

Making sure you have set some boundaries will narrow down your focus considerably. Another way to narrow down your selection of data is to consider adopting a research strategy and we review this towards the end of this chapter.

We begin an exploration of documents as data by considering ways in which these documents can be classified. This is a useful process as it highlights possible access concerns. For instance, documents described as personal suggests that these need to be considered with increased sensitivity whereas access to public data could be considered as 'fair game'. There are many ways to classify and categorise documents which can be utilised as data but applying a classification system that embraces all types is very difficult to achieve. Documents as sources of data are very diverse; they can be personal, official, public and private, as well as verbal or image based and exist digitally and in the real world. However, one critical aspect to consider is the need to know how and why your document was produced; therefore, thinking about documents as being deliberately and inadvertently created Duffy (2005) adds a useful dimension to understanding the context of their production:

- **Deliberate:** These are documents that are created for a specific purpose with some expectancy that these data would be accessed and used. Examples could be: government documents, information posted online by charities, books, articles and paintings.
- **Inadvertent:** These are documents that the producers may not have expected were to be used for any other purpose than for what it was intended. Examples could be: social media data, personal letters, emails and personal photographs.

In this section, we classify documents as sources of data using an approach informed by Merriam and Tisdell (2016) and explore these under the following headings:

- Academic sources (*e.g. scholarly articles*);
- Research sources (*e.g. existing qualitative research*);
- Popular culture sources (*e.g. magazines*);
- Personal sources (*e.g. blogs*);
- Public sources (*e.g. government reports*);
- Visual sources (*e.g. photographs*);
- Artefacts as sources (*e.g. ceramics*).

The sections that follow can only explore a snapshot of these types of potential sources of data but we examine interesting examples and review how each source category could be used for your literature review or analysis. As you consider documents as potential sources of data, we advise you to focus on the context of production and know *what your data is, who created it, when, how, why* and *under what conditions.*

Academic sources

Academic sources in the form of academic texts and peer-reviewed scholarly articles are essential to provide the robust underpinning your research project requires. This set of data has a high-level of authenticity, credibility and meaning as it is most likely that they will have undergone various review and editorial processes to confirm levels of scholarship and accuracy of content. Often associated with higher levels of study, documents such as this are called *scholarly* or *learned* as they are often the result of the author's substantial academic engagement within their subject area or discipline. These sources have specific relevance to your literature review as they can provide the theoretical and conceptual underpinning for your research and give any knowledge claims you make within your findings some credibility.

Scholarly articles as sources

Scholarly or peer reviewed (*refereed*) journal articles are deemed to be an academic and credible source for both your literature review and data for analysis. This is because the peer-review process ensures that articles have met benchmarks for credibility (Soloman 2007). Scholarly articles often have diverse forms of content. They can be articles written for discussion or review; they can report on completed or ongoing research and offer a theoretical or historical consideration of a topic. As a source of data for your analysis, scholarly articles offer the possibility of exploring methodological differences or the re-analysis of any presented data.

Scholarly data like this produces '*metrics*' or an '*impact factor*' which indicates how many times a source of data has been read, downloaded or cited by others. Information such as this can add an additional layer of reliability when assessing the authenticity and credibility of your sources. As the journals in which scholarly articles are housed are published regularly, scholarly articles can have some currency in the content they offer.

Not all published journals should be considered as equal in quality. The rise of 'open-access' has changed the way journals and articles are published, leaving the 'gold standard' peer-review process under threat. Some published work may not have been rigorously peer-reviewed and some articles or papers can be published because the author has paid for the privilege (Bohannon 2013). If you are looking for the most credible sources of data for your research, you should do some ground work and check that the journal that hosts your selected article has a robust peer review and editorial process. As the example in Box 6.1 indicates, the submission processes for some journals may not be as impeccable as we assume.

BOX 6.1   'WHO'S AFRAID OF PEER REVIEW?' BY JOHN BOHANNON (2013)

John Bohannon was so concerned as to the standard of peer review in open-access journals he decided to check the process for himself. He created a credible scientific paper using a fictitious name and workplace and generated a scientific research paper that contained significant errors. These errors were so evident that they should have been easily identifiable by a competent peer reviewer. He sent out 304 versions to open-access journals and found that 157 journals accepted the paper, failing to notice its fatal flaws, and 98 rejected it. The remaining 49 were either out of business or took too long to review the paper. Of the 255 papers that underwent the entire editing process to acceptance or rejection, about 60 per cent of the final decisions occurred with no sign of peer review. He states that many of these open-access journals are hosted by some of the largest and prestigious publishers.

Academic books as sources

Academic books are varied and plentiful but as key texts they need to be critically evaluated for their currency and relevance. However, there are some books that are central to your subject's way of thinking that even though they are over 50 years old, still offer a way of thinking about the focus of your inquiry that is foundational to the way it is understood. Academic books can offer a wealth of information to support your understanding of the research context, specific theory or identify subject specific ways of thinking but you need to appraise their merits. Using a checklist as a form of critical appraisal should encourage you to check for key information such as the date of publication and where it is published. Knowing where and when a key text is published should alert you to check the currency and relevance of the terminology and main concepts used.

Existing research sources

Recent years have seen an increased emphasis on researchers 'data sharing' with research data being made available through the rise in online archives and repositories. Existing research can provide a strong source of data as it is possible to have some knowledge of the context of its production. You could re-analyse the data either to replicate the original research findings (Hinds et al. 1997) or to apply your own question (Polit et al. 2001). There are some significant benefits such as having access to larger data sets or those collected in a different country. One important benefit of using data collected by others is that many of the time issues involved in research become redundant as you do not have to recruit or gain access to participants (Corti et al. 2014).

Knowing the 'what', 'when', 'where', 'how' and 'why' of existing research data can support your decision making as you can assess your data's usability, currency and relevance. This can be further helped if you know the following:

- If the research was funded and by whom;
- The purpose of the research;
- If the research was published in any way and, if it was, where it can be found;
- The original researcher's question(s) or aim(s).

Not all research data will have been analysed and it is possible to find unpublished or 'raw' data to use (*e.g. field notes or research diaries*); however, knowing how it was produced and why is still important. Researching existing interview data, research diaries, field notes is a convenient way of using data provided by researchers, but to do this you should have some understanding of the data's context.

To illustrate how using existing data can support your research, we offer an example in Box 6.2. This example presents the research conducted by Libby Bishop and it concludes with a reflection on the research she conducted.

BOX 6.2   'A REFLEXIVE ACCOUNT OF REUSING QUALITATIVE DATA: BEYOND PRIMARY/ SECONDARY DUALISM' BY BISHOP (2007)

Bishop (2007) researched existing empirical research studies that explored the use of convenience food to examine the way meals were eaten at home. She explored two historical qualitative data sets: Blaxter's *Mothers and Daughters* (2004) and Thompson's (2005) *The Edwardians* to examine attitudes and practices about early forms of processed foods and 'sociality and food choices at meal times'.

After reading around this subject, she generated a list of questions for the research project. She then began to read the existing data and, as she did this, she applied a detailed coding scheme. She used computer software Atlas.ti 5.0 for data management and thematic coding. Her coding categories included: *types of foods, cooking techniques, attitudes about (and definitions of) good foods,* the *role of food in health, references to some specific foods (fruits and vegetables), any discussions of good, homemade, and proper food.* The data were then examined for reasons and justifications given for using convenience food.

Reflecting on her approach to her research she says, '*I found the actual practice of doing secondary analysis very similar to working with primary data. What was most familiar was the sense of always working back and forth: from questions to data and back, from one data source to another, and from data to explanations (hypotheses, concepts or mere hunches) and back*' (section 11.1).

Popular culture sources

This category includes a vast range of potential sources of data and as we show in Figure 6.3, it can be anything produced by forms of mass communication (*e.g. newsfeeds, magazines*), websites, television programmes to books that are self-published and cartoons. The data in this category can provide insights into the way a society functions and experiences the world. The global nature and relative ease of access to these data makes it an appealing but immense category of data and creates the need to consider processes of data reduction to ensure you get the 'right' data and that it reflects the quality you need. However, the sheer diversity of this category means it could open up your research to wider forms of data that you may not have considered using before. An example of research using popular culture documents is provided in Box 6.5 and in Figure 6.3 we indicate the range of data choices this category affords.

There are significant strengths to this category of data, so it should not be dismissed. You could explore the role of television in shaping the beliefs and attitudes of young people or investigate how a television programme can lead to a possible uptake of a specific career or pastime. You could explore representations of evil in superhero comics or, as Da-Silva et al. (2014) explored, you could consider character construction in superhero comics. They investigated Marvel and DC Characters inspired by arachnids and found 84 Marvel Comics characters and 40 DC Comics characters and that most of

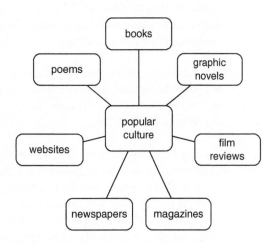

Figure 6.3   Examples of popular culture sources of data

these arachnid-inspired characters had been created since the 1990s. You could also explore political themes like Hardy and Phillips (1999) who researched social responses to refugees and the Canadian refugee system using political cartoons.

Using news sources

News media as a source of data can provide social, cultural and historical perspectives at a local level with specifically targeted news (*e.g. local or site specific – schools, businesses*), at community or state level and at national and international levels of focus. Historical reports as documents can provide glimpses into past lives and ways of living that no longer exist. Accessing newspapers or news sites means you can explore more than news content as you could consider the use of advertising, headline generation, presentation and layout and, depending on the format of your news source, the use of personal advertisements or obituaries. The global nature of news as a source of data can widen the possible focus of your inquiry to embrace international viewpoints. Therefore, news media as popular culture data can provide varied, diverse and easily accessible data.

Many well established and respected newspapers have an online presence, but access to them is often through subscription or payment to access sites, therefore the increased use of free-to-access online news platforms, such as BuzzFeed, has changed the way people access news content. However, with increased access come concerns relating to the quality of this news. These issues are mainly those pertaining to authenticity as fake news or the reporting of untrue or alternative facts causes great concern. So much so that this concern provoked members of the UK parliament to write a report (House of Commons, *Disinformation and 'fake news': Interim Report*, 29 July 2018) claiming that fake news was undermining democracy. The spread of fake news has recently been reported in research by Vosoughi, Roy and Aral (2018). They investigated the spread of fake news within Twitter and identified the following:

- false news stories were 70 per cent more likely to be re-tweeted than true stories;
- true stories took around six times longer to reach 1,500 people;
- true stories were rarely shared beyond 1,000 people, but the most popular false news could reach up to 100,000 ...

leaving them to conclude that it was the degree of novelty and the emotional reactions of recipients that may be responsible for the differences observed.

Not all news will be fake but being able to make any assessment on its credibility can depend on the sites where you access your news data. In some cases, the authenticity of this category of data can be difficult to ascertain as knowing who created the information you wish to use can be hard to determine. Additionally, it is not always possible to know if the person who has created it has any authority to speak on the subject. Therefore, as a potential consumer of this data, you need to engage with it as critically as possible. Misleading data can look credible and come from locations that we feel we can trust (*e.g. news feeds, political organisations*). The example of misleading and 'fake' news found in Box 6.3 illustrates how 'news' was taken at face value with very little credibility checking. This unquestioning acceptance of 'news' is highlighted in this example as the website that created this 'news' never purported to be a 'real' news site. The 'news' spread because of its sensational content, and without the context of its production being fully explored.

BOX 6.3   'POPE FRANCIS SHOCKS WORLD, ENDORSES DONALD TRUMP FOR PRESIDENT'

There was a story widely reported on some social media sites stating that Pope Francis had decided to endorse Donald Trump for president of the United States of America. However, there was no truth to this story and this became one of many pieces of fake news generated in 2016. This 'news' originated from a site called WTOE 5 News which looks like an authentic newsfeed provider.

However, when you access the 'about us' tab, WTOE 5 News very openly describe themselves as a '*fantasy news website*' and that '*most articles on wtoe5news.com are satire or pure fantasy*', indicating how trusting people can be of sites that claim to offer news.

Silverman and Alexander (2018) investigated the phenomenon of fake news further and found that some of this 'news' was generated by Macedonian teenagers trying to earn money as they obtained advertising income from the visitors who accessed the site that published this 'news'. These teenagers found that the best way to make money was to publish highly sensational stories on Facebook. The more sensational the stories, the more money they earned.

When using news documents as a source of data try to be aware of some of the 'tricks of the trade'. Figure 6.4 contains three common examples of ways in which you can be misled into believing what you are reading,

News media can add a current and social perspective to your literature review but they are not the most credible of sources. We have explored the possibility of 'fake' news but there are other issues such as media bias where external forces such as government, owners, editors and some journalists can exert influence over what is reported and how it is reported. There is also reporting bias as not every news story can be covered. News in all of its many forms should be used to provide a social, cultural or historical dimension to your literature review but we advise you to be sceptical and wary of using it to support any claims you make within your findings. Figure 6.5 provides some questions you need to ask when selecting news documents as data for your research.

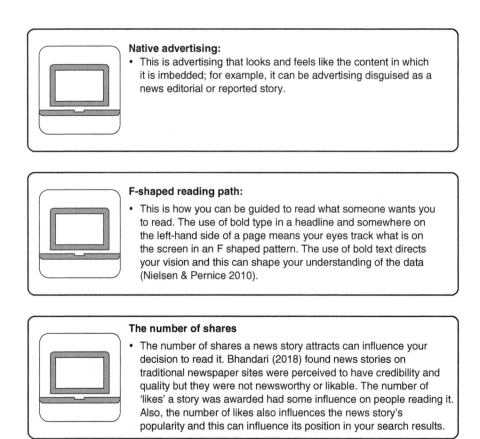

Native advertising:

- This is advertising that looks and feels like the content in which it is imbedded; for example, it can be advertising disguised as a news editorial or reported story.

F-shaped reading path:

- This is how you can be guided to read what someone wants you to read. The use of bold type in a headline and somewhere on the left-hand side of a page means your eyes track what is on the screen in an F shaped pattern. The use of bold text directs your vision and this can shape your understanding of the data (Nielsen & Pernice 2010).

The number of shares

- The number of shares a news story attracts can influence your decision to read it. Bhandari (2018) found news stories on traditional newspaper sites were perceived to have credibility and quality but they were not newsworthy or likable. The number of 'likes' a story was awarded had some influence on people reading it. Also, the number of likes also influences the news story's popularity and this can influence its position in your search results.

Figure 6.4   Examples of strategies designed to mislead

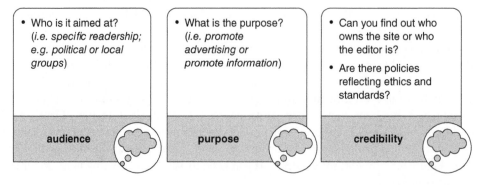

- Who is it aimed at? (*i.e. specific readership; e.g. political or local groups*)

- What is the purpose? (*i.e. promote advertising or promote information*)

- Can you find out who owns the site or who the editor is?
- Are there policies reflecting ethics and standards?

audience   **purpose**   **credibility**

Figure 6.5   Questions to ask of web-based news providers

For all sources of data within this popular culture, you need to consider how you can select or sample your data. You may need to confirm if your data are representative of the topic you want to explore. However, knowing if the data are typical or atypical of other data may also be difficult to ascertain (Scott 1990). These are the dilemmas offered by this category of data and the critical appraisal and sampling strategies discussed in Chapter 8 should help you apply some quality control to your selection.

Magazines as sources

One specific form of popular culture data are magazines either as lifestyle, leisure or professionally orientated and as print and online media. As sources of data, they can offer a social and cultural understanding of everyday life. Professional or trade magazines may have reports and reviews on current events which can identify areas of possible tension and debate in your subject area. Most articles in trade or professional magazines may have undergone some form of editorial process but you would need to consider the strength of this process when considering their credibility as a source of data for your literature review. They can provide a supporting vocational or practical focus for your review. As Box 6.4 indicates, depending on your question(s) and/or aim(s) they can be used as data for analysis in many ways.

BOX 6.4 USING MAGAZINES AS DATA

You can use magazines (*online or print media*) as data to explore language and image usage within specific sites of practice (*e.g. health, beauty, education, sports*). Depending on how you construct your question(s) and/or aim(s), you could:

- explore magazines for professional discourse using Fairclough's (1989, 1992) three-dimensional model of discourse (see Chapter 11). You may see terminology being used in specific contexts.
- perform content analysis to assess the frequency of key words to understand the development of professional terminology.
- explore the images contained within them (*e.g. photographs and advertisements*) and undertake semiotic visual analysis to see how professional identify is presented.

Published fiction books as sources

Books as works of fiction can be an exciting source of data for analysis as the example offered by Collins and Carmody (2011) illustrates (Box 6.5). In this example, the researchers performed content analysis on the four books in the *Twilight* series (authored by Stephanie Meyer). Interesting in this example is the way they were able to generate a specific sample of influential teen fiction based on publication sales and the popularity of the films based on the book. Whilst offering valuable data for your analysis, fiction books such as these do not reflect a scholarly source of evidence for your literature review.

BOX 6.5 'DEADLY LOVE: IMAGES OF DATING VIOLENCE IN THE "TWILIGHT SAGA"' BY COLLINS AND CARMODY (2011)

Researchers Collins and Carmody (2011) wanted to explore representations of dating violence. They began with the premise that teens in the United States faced an elevated risk of dating violence and the authors hypothesised that this was influenced by behaviours reflected in media such as books, movies, and video games that target a teen audience. This led them to study the presentation of dating violence in *The Twilight Saga* (a book series by Stephanie Meyer) selected due to its widespread popularity and thus, its perceived influence on teens. Since 2005, the *Twilight* books have sold over 40 million copies worldwide and have been made into extremely popular films with the second film reportedly grossing $72.2 million on its opening day (Gray 2009). The researchers performed content analysis across the four books using the Duluth Model of Power and Control as a theoretical framework to aid their coding. Their results revealed examples of behaviours and attitudes that they identified as conducive to dating violence. They conclude that their findings were troubling as the series had been praised for its 'wholesome' presentation of teen romance.

Personal documents as sources

This category covers personal documents created as first-person accounts (Merriam & Tisdell 2016) usually reflecting one person's view of the world and, because it is personal to someone, we need to ensure there are no personal data identifiers within any personal documents you want to use. This category of data offers valuable insight into people's lives and it can embrace the hand-written personal diaries of famous or notable people located in museum archives or repositories to the mass of personal documents available as data found on the Internet. Increasingly any discussion about personal documents usually equates to the information that people share online as first-hand data within social media. Micro blogs (*e.g. Twitter*) and Weblogs (*blogs*) are key places to access this type of data and as the global use of social media grows, so too does the harvesting of these personal documents as data for insights into the opinions, moods, networks and relationships of ordinary users (Kennedy, Elgesem & Miguel 2017). These data are usually provided as a verbal post but can also include images, audio, video, and interactive links to other online sites such as Instagram (Joosten 2017). Data found in blogs, Wikis, Twitter and social media platforms can offer a wealth of social and cultural data.

This source of data offers many benefits to a qualitative secondary researcher but there are some complexities mainly because its authenticity is hard to prove. The anonymity the Internet offers can make it very difficult to know how your data were produced, for what reason and by whom. Additionally, the individualised nature of this data source may render knowing if it is typical or atypical impossible. For all forms of personal documents representativeness is something you will need to consider. Consider how you can assess whether a person's life when set out in a diary is representative of all lives offered in diaries. However, it may be that knowing if your selected personal documents are typical of other such documents may not be the goal of your selection. But it is important to consider that the personal nature of these documents leaves them exposed to fraudulent representation (*e.g. fake profiles*). Therefore, knowing if the data you access is credible is essential. Whilst there are some ethical issues that need to be navigated, these concerns are not specific to online data as researchers who want to explore all forms of personal documents (*e.g. diaries and letters*) face similar concerns.

Personal documents can offer rich insights into the lives of others and can capture immediate and contemporary reactions to what is happening in the world. It may be challenging to use as a source within your literature review because it lacks a robust academic tone and its credibility can be challenged. But if used as data for analysis, it could provide contemporary insights at global, national and personal levels. Whilst we have explored some of the negatives, this does not mean you should not use it. Box 6.6 explores how blogs could be used as data.

BOX 6.6   USING WEBLOGS AS DATA

As Snee illustrates (Chapter 5, Box 5.1) Weblogs (blogs) can provide a rich and abundant source of publicly available data. They can offer insights into the experiences, thoughts and understandings of an individual as they engage in a global world. This is because the data blogs present can form a commentary where it is possible to explore past and present posts and links made to other bloggers. Therefore, it is possible to embrace the individuated nature of this data and explore both large and small social and cultural influences on everyday life. In your research it can offer an international perspective where it would be possible to explore personal reactions through blogs to national or world events.

Public sources

This category contains documents that offer more formalised records of the social world. These are documents for public consumption and can be public records (*e.g. births, marriages and deaths*), school board records, some government reports or reviews, conference presentations, theses, charity information and open data. The definition of open data is that it is '*data that can be freely used, re-used and redistributed by anyone – subject only, at most, to the requirement to attribute and share alike' (Open Data Handbook nd).* In Chapter 7, we discuss open data created by intergovernmental organisations (IGOs) such as the Organisation for Economic Co-operation and Development (OECD) and United Nations Educational, Scientific and Cultural Organization (UNESCO) and non-governmental organisations (NGOs) *(e.g. charities and pressure groups)* as producers of a vast amount of valuable data.

The documents produced within this category can be used to explore local, state, national and international perspectives. You could use public documents as data to explore school improvement in the UK and this could be achieved by accessing Ofsted reports. In the US, you could explore overseas schools and access documents from the Office of Overseas Schools. Public documents like this can provide insight into a wide range of social and cultural issues but as it is a diverse category, you would need to be specific when you set your question to refine your selection.

Unlike most popular culture documents, public documents provide more information about the context of their production. This can make this category of potential data more trustworthy as it is possible to authenticate it with some ease but it should still be appraised for its credibility. As Atkinson and Coffey (2011) argue, documents in the public realm should not be assumed as accurate records of reality as they have been written with distinctive purposes in mind. Therefore, as with all forms of data, you need to understand the context of its production and question 'what', 'when', 'where', 'why' and 'how' of your data.

This possible form of data may have some relevance to you within your literature review as it can offer a contemporary understanding and demonstrate a rapid response to aspects of social and cultural change. It is often used to indicate the relationship of theory to practice so it should not be dismissed. Therefore, you could draw on government or federal documents, explore national and international charity websites, refer to professional organisations and legislation to supplement the information offered through your use of more scholarly sources in your literature review. As data they can be used to explore a wide range of social and cultural contexts.

PAUSE FOR THOUGHT

Influences on data

No form of data is immune from some form of influence. As human beings we tend to insert ourselves in some way into whatever we create. The role of critical appraisal is to try to understand how and in what way this influence exists.

When you are looking for data to answer your research question(s) and/or aim(s) please consider that every personal or first-hand source will be biased as it is the writer's personal perspective.

If you use a public source such as a government report you still need to consider the possibilities of bias. All governments have ideological perspectives and the reports and policies they create will reflect this.

Knowing that data is influenced by those that create it should not stop you from using qualitative data, but we hope it adds to your healthy scepticism. Adopting a critical approach to your data to explore bias and knowledge distortion is essential. As a qualitative secondary researcher, knowing your data as well as you can will support your ability to use it effectively.

Visual sources

There is less research conducted using visual forms of data and this may be due to concerns over authenticity or fears as to how to approach its analysis (see Chapter 11). Visual documents have many strengths and can provide ways of understanding the world, socially, culturally, historically that can be different from that gained from verbal forms of data. For instance, a social network site such as Pinterest affords powerful visually informed insight into people's worlds and, very specifically, it can afford insight into the way people choose to curate the image of themselves they want to project.

Photographs as sources of visual data are, as Bryman (2012) emphasises, useful when exploring topics that can be difficult to access. Using visual data found online or accessed via archives can be considered as non-intrusive data as you can experience personal moments without being there. However, there are issues relating to rights of access and ethics of use. Therefore, if you are using images of other people you would need to think about issues surrounding informed consent and, if this is not possible, how you can minimise any possible harm and anonymise your data.

It is possible to access a wide range of pre-existing images in an expanding set of locations. You could use maps, diagrams, advertisements, drawings, paintings and photographs. What you decide to use depends on your subject, the questions(s) and/or aim(s) you have set. Figure 6.6 provides an overview of some aspects to consider when deciding whether to use visual sources as data.

There are some concerns as to authenticity and credibility. All digitally created visual data can, with relatively simple software, be altered with some ease. This makes it vulnerable to alteration and misrepresentation. You should also consider the purpose and intent of the image because visual data can be anything that is commercial (*e.g. advertisements, illustrations*), a work of art (*e.g. photograph, print*) or first-hand personal data (*e.g. photographs posted on social media*). Therefore, consider the '*production, distribution or "circulation" of these images*' (Hand 2017: 216) with increased scrutiny. Where an

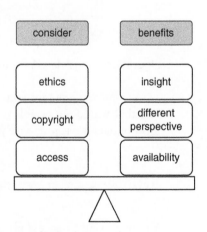

Figure 6.6 Weighing up the benefits of using visual sources as data

image is found is often very relevant to its meaning. Consider the difference in context between a famous painting hanging in an internationally renowned gallery and a selfie posted on social media. Both have relevance as data within qualitative secondary research, but to use them well in your research you would need to know how each functions as an image in the context in which it is provided. In Figure 6.7 we provide some prompts to promote critical appraisal of visual forms of data.

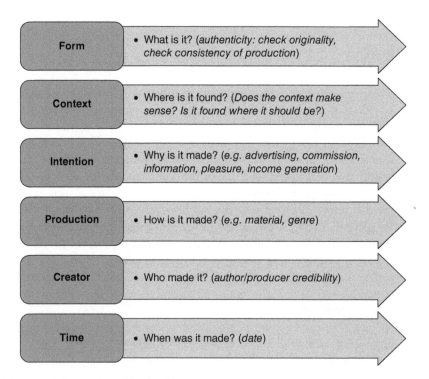

Form
- What is it? (*authenticity: check originality, check consistency of production*)

Context
- Where is it found? (*Does the context make sense? Is it found where it should be?*)

Intention
- Why is it made? (*e.g. advertising, commission, information, pleasure, income generation*)

Production
- How is it made? (*e.g. material, genre*)

Creator
- Who made it? (*author/producer credibility*)

Time
- When was it made? (*date*)

Figure 6.7 Visual data and artefact checklist

As a form of data for your literature review, it may have illustrative usage but as it is non-verbal, it would not be able to provide the academic contextualisation needed. However, as a form of data it has immense potential.

Artefacts as sources of data

You may want to access physical objects as data. These are still called documents but the way these are created, the materials used and their three-dimensionality leads them to be called artefacts. As data, they are concrete and tangible sources of evidence (Hodder 1994). Like all the sources of data we have explored above, this category is diverse as it includes toys, pottery, jewellery, clothing, furniture and even, tombstones (Norum 2008). Artefacts disclose much about the development of societies in their means of production and in the social, cultural and historical perspectives they afford (see Box 6.7). As a source of data for your literature review, this form of data offers little benefit, but they can offer a rich form of data for your analysis. There are some concerns to navigate relating to copyright if you want to reproduce artefacts as images but it is most likely you will be covered by fair use policies; it is wise to check this before you download, take or use any images. As with all forms of data, it is advisable to be rigorous and check its authenticity, credibility, representativeness and meaning (Scott 1990) and the checklist we offer in Figure 6.7 can be used to support your appraisal process.

BOX 6.7   USING VASES AS DATA

Ceramics are a valuable source of data. They offer social and cultural information across vast timescales and diverse means and processes of construction. If you were exploring representations of masculinity it could be possible to explore anything from Grayson Perry's vase *'Aspects of Myself'* (2001) to Greek vases painted in the mid-8th century BC.

Vases are objects of material culture and it is possible as with all text and images to approach them at different levels or layers. When exploring vases, you could focus on the aesthetics (*i.e. what it looks like and how it is valued*); Its materiality (*i.e. what it is made of and how*); its function (*e.g. container, decorative or ceremonial item*); context (*i.e. who it was made for and in what context*); and how it is understood within society. You could compare vases of diverse cultures and across time frames.

DECIDING HOW TO USE DOCUMENTS AS SOURCES OF DATA

The data you may want to use can be plentiful and varied, so knowing what you want to select and why is imperative so as not to waste time as you begin your research. Therefore, the development of a strong and LASER orientated research question(s) and/or aim(s) is important (see Chapter 2). As we explored in Chapter 2, a well formulated aim reflects your conceptual framework and this can guide the selection of data. One other part of the research process that can guide how you will use your data is your use of a research strategy. Knowing which strategy you may adopt and why can support your choices as to the amount of data you need and potentially, how this will be analysed.

In Chapter 4, we offered research strategies as approaches to your research that can guide and shape the form of your inquiry. Selecting your research strategy early on in your research process will help you narrow down your search for data, allowing you to focus on selecting the amount and type of sources required to answer your research problem. We provide an example of these in action in Box 6.8.

BOX: 6.8   RESEARCH STRATEGIES AND DATA

If you wanted to explore a topic on immigration through key aspects of legislation, you could use research strategies in the following ways:

Single strategy: You could explore one piece of legislation in great depth focusing on distinct parts: its structure, its language and its social and legal function. Applying discourse analysis, you could consider the legal definition of immigration in this one piece of legislation; explore the language used focusing on specific units (*e.g. words and sentence structure, but also the terminology used and the way the piece of legislation is presented*).

Combined strategy: You could compare and contrast two pieces of legislation exploring immigration policy from different countries, different historical periods or from different government or administration perspectives.

Multiple strategy: You could consider a timeline of legislation and policy and review critical points on this. You could consider using policy documents, committee reports, news reports, television interviews, politician's Twitter feeds.

To aid you in this process, we provide some questions to support your decision making because whatever strategy you decide to adopt, you will need to provide a robust defence for its use in your methodology (see Chapter 4).

- What strategy will you use?
- How does your strategy help you answer your research question?
- What data will you use?
- If you are using a combined or multiple strategy, will you use quantitative data? If you are, why is this needed and how will it be used?
- How can you ensure your data for this strategy are credible and authentic?
- Do you need your data to be typical and representative of your topic?
- How can you demonstrate if your data are typical or representative of your topic?
- Why is representativeness significant or not?

SELECTING METHODS OF ANALYSIS

In Chapter 11 we review an array of methods of analysis but as you are thinking of the sources of data you need to select, consider why you want to select these and how you will make sense of this. For instance, you want to explore images of young adults on educational charity websites but before you select your data you should ask yourself 'What do I want to know?'

- Is it the literal meaning of these images? In other words, is it that there are young adults presented in specific contexts. If it is, then thematic analysis or constant comparison may help you with this.
- Is it the social and cultural meaning? Do you want to go beyond the literal presentation to a deeper subtext? If you do then discourse analysis could be useful as could visual analysis (*semiotics*).
- Is it their frequency? Do you want to ascertain a demographic count i.e., representation by gender or ethnicity? If it is, then content analysis could be useful.

This brief example shows how one source of data can be analysed in many ways; therefore, choosing your data with a clear understanding of what you want to do with it will inform your search and also guide you in your choice of method of analysis.

UNDERSTANDING YOUR INFLUENCE ON DATA SELECTION

We encourage you to be aware of your influence on your data selection. In Chapters 3 and 4 we explored how who you are as a researcher has the potential to influence every aspect of the research you conduct. This includes the data you select. We proposed reflexivity as a process of self-disclosure where you identify your possible influence on the research you conduct and the findings you generate. This process is not a 'get out of jail card' as it does not make your influence disappear. It does however, alert you to your possible influence so you can mitigate it in some way and enable your reader to understand your research knowing your potential levels of influence. We offer reflexivity as one process out of many you can employ to vouchsafe research quality.

Knowing how you may influence your data and how this can compromise the credibility and trustworthiness of your research is important. As we explored in Chapter 4, your methodology is where you make your decisions and choices transparent and this includes how you selected your data. In your methodology, you may need to consider how you can defend yourself against possible claims of selection and confirmation bias and this may be by utilising sampling strategies as we explore in Chapter 8.

REFLECTION AND FURTHER READING

At the beginning of the chapter we set out what you should be able to do when you reached the end of this chapter. To aid your reflection on all we have covered we ask some chapter specific questions. If you are unsure of any of your answers to these questions, please go back to the relevant section to review this aspect.

REFLECTING ON CHAPTER 6

In this chapter we have:

- **Defined qualitative data:** Can you provide a one-sentence definition of qualitative data?
- **Identified different categories of data:** What type of data do you want to use? Can you defend this decision?
- **Encouraged you to make informed decisions concerning the role of data in your research:** What are the strengths and weaknesses of using popular culture data? How can you check the quality of visual data?
- **Evaluated the use of research strategies in relation to the data you decide to use:** Which research strategy will you use and why? What types of data will you use? How will this help you answer your research question?
- **Explored your influence on the data you select:** How could you influence your choice of data?

WE RECOMMEND FOR FURTHER READING:

Central Queensland University (2018) *Evaluating Books, Journals, Journal Articles and Websites*. Available at: https://libguides.library.cqu.edu.au/evaluating-resources.
This is a clearly laid out website that offers a brief overview of advantages and disadvantages of a range of data sources.

Corti, L., Van den Eynden, V., Bishop, L., & Wollard, M. (2014) *Managing and Sharing Research Data*. London: SAGE Publications Ltd.
We suggest this book as a key text for anyone who wishes to use existing research data. Specifically, we recommend the overview provided in Chapter 2 'The Research Data Lifecycle', and Chapter 10 'Making Use of Other People's Research Data: Opportunities and Limitations' for further reading on the use of existing data.

Duffy, B. (2005) The analysis of documentary evidence. In J. Bell (ed.), *Doing Your Research Project* (4th edn) (pp. 122–136). Berkshire, England: Open University Press.
This chapter provides a very useful checklist that can be used to aid your selection of sources.

Hookway, N. (2008) 'Entering the Blogosphere': Some strategies for using blogs in social research. *Qualitative Research*, 8(1), 91–113.
This article provides a comprehensive approach to the use of blogs for the social researcher. It covers ethics, sampling and methods of analysis.

Mitchell, C. & de Lange, N. (2011) Data collections and building a democratic archive: 'No more pictures without a context'. In C. Michell (ed.), *Doing Visual Research* (pp. 116–134). London: SAGE Publications Ltd.
This chapter focuses on the need to provide a context for the images you select. It draws on past studies to support this argument.

The Open University (2018) *Comparing Academic Sources*. Available at: www2.open.ac.uk/students/skillsforstudy/comparing-academic-sources.php.
A useful contribution to understanding the advantages and disadvantages of sources of data.

7

LOCATING YOUR DATA

THIS CHAPTER SUPPORTS YOUR ABILITY TO

recognise the need for ethical searching

develop effective search skills

evaluate website credibility

explore possible locations for sources of data

CHAPTER OVERVIEW

We begin by asking you to consider what type of data you require and ask you to reflect on where it will be used in your project. This means deciding if you are searching for data for your literature review or for your analysis. We then provide some practical and effective search strategies designed to increase your accuracy when searching the Internet. This includes using field searches when interrogating your library subscription database and search tips for Internet searching. We also offer advice for assessing website credibility and ask you to be alert to the use of domain names and search result positions.

At the end of this chapter we offer guidance on where you can find data and suggest some less well-known sites that reflect the diversity of data possible to use within qualitative secondary research. This chapter covers a wide range of information and it should provide you with the foundation and confidence to begin your data collection process.

WHAT TYPE OF DATA AM I SEARCHING FOR?

In Chapter 6 we provide an overview of possible sources of data. We describe this data as coming from documents that reflect all forms of human existence. This means you could be searching for data from a vast range of possible sources including public, personal (*e.g. first-hand*), visual, artefacts, popular culture data, academic and existing research. The diversity of your choice of data is mirrored by the multitude of places where you could locate it.

Your search for data begins as you commence your preparatory reading. In Chapter 2, we explored this as an iterative process where you read to define your research question(s) and/or aim(s) and in turn, these guide your reading. Engaging in a process like this can provide you with a firm foundation for your project as you can identify current and past debates and tensions, recognise key theorists, respond to new ways of thinking and develop relevant terminology. When you search for data for your research project you are trying to ensure you access the most pertinent sources you can find. This means making carefully considered choices as to the role sources of data will play in your research (see Figure 7.1).

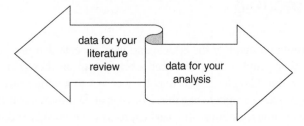

Figure 7.1 Different search pathways

This may lead you to create two specific search pathways. We say 'may' as there could be one search. This could happen if you were using scholarly articles for your data as these would also be required reading for your literature review. Whilst all of your data needs to be reviewed and evaluated for credibility, the sources you select for your literature review need to be viewed with a heightened analytical gaze. These sources act as supporting evidence in your rationale where you justify the relevance of your work. They also underpin the arguments you provide within your review. Therefore, making sure you make the 'right' choices and find the 'right' data is paramount.

To aid in this decision-making process, we explore strategies to promote the quality control of data in Chapter 8 and we encourage you to review and use these. As you search for your data, please keep in mind the four main principles of quality as defined by Scott (1990) (see Figure 7.2).

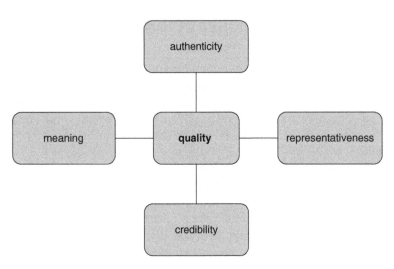

Figure 7.2   Four principles of quality (Scott 1990)

ETHICAL SEARCHING

In Chapter 5 we presented many of the ethical and legal aspects that need to be considered by researchers using other people's data. We offer a brief recap on these here as you begin your search. As we explored in Chapter 5, you may have access to a wide range of information but that does not mean you have a right to use this. The type of data source you search for and where this is found will determine the ethical and legal approaches you need to adopt; for example, you could access a freely available video on YouTube but you would need to consider how you could comply with your ethical duty to secure anonymity and data confidentiality. You could access freely available school inspection reports that may be considered as 'fair game' because they are in the public domain but it is highly likely your institution would require you to redact the school's name and anonymise this data in case there is a risk of reputational harm.

In Chapter 5, we set out three core principles: protection from harm, informed consent and anonymity and confidentiality and your legal duty to your data and those who provide it. Therefore, when you access sources of data for your research be mindful of how they should be used. Here are a few reminders:

- Check you have the right to access your data.
- Check you have permission to use your data. Under copyright law, you may need to have consent to access and use some of your data.
- Remember to record sources accurately. This is an academic and ethical responsibility to show ownership (see Chapter 10).
- Be careful what you access and this means be aware of 'hot' and sensitive topics explored in your sources of data.

HOW DO I FIND DATA?

As past or current students who have produced formal academic work at any level of study, it is highly likely that you will be familiar with a variety of search techniques and strategies. Therefore, you should be acquainted with searching for data in an effective and responsible way. However, when you conduct your research, you may find yourself searching for diverse types and forms of data and for substantial amounts. The scale of your data searches may now mean that the strategies you employed in the past need to be reviewed or revised.

Searching on the Internet requires you to have effective search skills. The one thing that you cannot be is vague and this can be exemplified by typing the word *play* into Google's search box. Just typing the word *play* receives over 9,000,000,000 results in 0.65 seconds. Whilst it is amazing to have so much information returned so quickly, it can be very frustrating when most of it is irrelevant and of mediocre quality. There is just too much to search through. This '*data deluge*' (Rambo 2015: 2) is just one of the consequences of living in an information rich age. The time saved on gaining access to data is now spent on filtering, classifying and evaluating the data our search has returned.

The Internet has created a digital environment that offers us copious amounts of data, but this needs to be matched by your use of search tools and strategies that facilitate your ability to find the right data to answer your research question and finding this requires a structured, systematic and critical approach.

PAUSE FOR THOUGHT

Using your library effectively

Make sure you access your library, its staff and any resources it provides when you undertake your research. Libraries have a relevant and valuable place in the research process. They are staffed by trained professionals who can offer guidance and support.

- Check if your institution's library provides courses on information literacy as these may help you navigate some of the complexity of online searching.
- When beginning any literature or data search ensure you explore your institution's online resources as fully as possible.

Using effective search skills for locating your data

As a qualitative secondary researcher, you need to develop tools that facilitate your ability to manage, record and search for this data. In Chapter 10 we explored data management and, in this section, we explore strategies to support clear, structured and systematic searching.

The vast amount of data on the Internet requires the strategic use of search engines. Here are some useful search approaches you can take:

Using key words

In Chapter 2, we discussed a 'looping' approach which is where you link your research question to the literature you read and vice versa in your quest for a well-informed and conceived piece of research. This iterative and immersive process should throw up 'keywords'. These are called '*topic guidance criteria*' (Onwuegbuzie and Frels 2016: 88) as they are words that have heighted relevance due to the frequency of usage and their appearance in key texts.

To generate key words, you could go back to your lecture notes or discuss your topic with your peers or colleagues. Keywords, when used effectively, can help you retrieve the data you want for your research project. This can be seen in the example we offer in Figure 7.3 which shows useful keywords needed if you wanted to address the aim 'to explore the impact of tourism on the Maasai culture in Kenya'.

The UK Data Service provides HASSET, which is a data set index which acts as a thesaurus that generates alternative research terms and signposts you to their data archive for relevant data (https://hasset. ukdataservice.ac.uk/). You can also find key words presented under scholarly articles and these can support your search process. Using keywords is a basic form of a serial search but it can be a very effective one once you have perfected your words (Bell 2005). To generate keywords, you could go back to your lecture notes or discuss your topic with your peers or colleagues. Keywords are worth pursing as these may form the conceptual building blocks of your research topic.

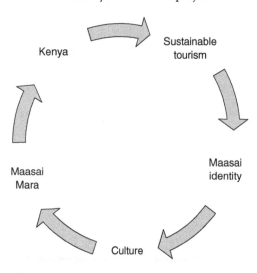

Figure 7.3   Generating useful keywords

Applying filters and limiters

If you are affiliated to a specific institution or organisation, there is a strong likelihood that you will be able to search your institution's library subscription site. This site should contain a wealth of information for you to access but there may be too much. To aid this narrowing of your search, you can apply 'filters' and 'limiters'. When used in a systematic way, they can increase the amount of valuable data you receive. It can take practice to set these so you return your required results but it is worth persevering as these can speed up your search processes and encourage more relevant responses.

- **Limiters:** These set specific parameters such as age, place of publication and type of source (*e.g. book, article, brochure*) and peer review. You may need to consider setting a geographic limit (*e.g. USA*) and specifying a language (*e.g. English*). When used effectively, these limit the number of returns within a specific search. Always try to set a limiter to include access full text articles.
- **Field searches:** These are often associated with searching for specialised sources such as those found within academic journal sites. When you use a field search, you are telling the database where to look for a certain phrase or keyword. For example, you can direct the database to look for an author's name or tell it to find a specific phrase such as 'tourism in Malaysia' in the titles of articles. Fields function as data reduction tools that relate to a specific part of a book or article. Figure 7.4 provides some examples of the fields you may experience when you search.

All Text: Search every part of the article and the information about it (full text, title, abstract, etc.).
Author: Type in an author's name to find articles only by this author.
Date: Search for the date of publication or a date range.
Title: Look for keywords that you want to appear in the titles of each result.
Subject Terms: You need to know the term you want to look for and exactly how that database uses the term.
Abstract: Look for your search terms in the abstract of an article.

Figure 7.4   Examples of field settings

Snowballing

Snowballing is an effective way to find your literature for your literature review. It begins with a key data source that you have read and understood. This could be a source of data given in a lecture, on your course notes, something you discussed with peers or with your supervisor. We use the word 'key' as you need to begin with a source that is known to be an authority in the field and can be considered a credible and valuable source. Using this source as your first point of reference, you access the list of references or bibliography to find other relevant titles on your subject. You can then access the reference lists or bibliographies of these articles and so on until you have found enough. This can be a useful method for gaining a large amount of data quickly and it gets you immersed within your specific academic field.

Daisy or citation chain

Using a process similar to that of snowballing, citation or daisy chaining means searching backwards and forwards in time for materials that are cited by and also that cite an article or resource you already have. One resource links you to another, which links you to another, and so on to create a chain of relevant literature. This can be an adept way to build a bank of pertinent literature for your literature review.

You can create a backwards chain as you trace the citations back through literature or forwards where you start with the oldest source and work your way through to the most recent citation. You can use data bases such as Google Scholar to support this chaining process. If you are new to this process of chaining, it is worth investing some of your time in exploring how this works.

Bookmarks

If you use the Internet to search for most of your data, it is advisable to use 'bookmarks'. Bookmark is a Web browser tool that records the URL (*Uniform Resource Locator – URL*) of the website or file you want to access. It is an extremely effective filing system that enables you to save and categorise your URL addresses in a way that is meaningful to you. If you are unfamiliar with this feature, it is worth trying as it can save frantic and often frustrating searches when you try to find the useful website you found last week. You can find this feature on or near the search bar using a star as a symbol.

Using search engines effectively

There is a wealth of guidance available on the Internet as to how to search using search engines. Search engines are large databases of web pages connected by software called spiders or web crawlers. You type in keywords or phrases and receive your results as a list of Web content or search engine results page (SERP). These pages are ranked not just by relevance but also popularity so there is no guarantee that your first few results will be what you want or even credible sources. In Chapter 6 (see Box 6.3), we explored how fake news could be spread and one key factor was its popularity.

Search engine capabilities are developing rapidly so we advise you to explore what your search engine can do. This may also require you to explore the use of cookies and to review your search history. A search engine such as Google can make predictive searches based on your previous searches. If you do not want this to happen, you will need to delete your search history. If you have a preferred website, we advise you to use the 'advanced' settings where you can apply limits and restrictions to your search. Most have a 'safe search' facility if you want to avoid some Internet content. Figure 7.5 provides some tips for conducting online searches.

Remember to read around your topic first so that you have a range of subject-specific words to use as 'topic guidance criteria' (Onwuegbuzie & Frels 2016: 88).
Remember to 'daisy chain' or 'citation chain' references so you can use these in your searches. This way you will increase your knowledge and your repertoire of key authors and theorists.
Try to reduce your search by using a plus sign + in front of a key topic word. This will ensure that the word with the + is also included in the search results.
If you are struggling with your search, check your spelling. Some search engines will offer you the option of a corrected spelling but please check this carefully and do not assume it has guessed correctly.
You can search for a specific domain. In the search bar type: site:.gov or site:.edu and your results will only be in your specified domain.
You can try using a multiple keyword search by placing " " around the most important keywords. This will create a search phrase. Doing this will make sure that the whole phrase is searched for not, just individual words.
The WWW is where the content is found and the Internet enables you to search this but neither are mind readers; what you get back is based on what you type in. Be as accurate and as precise as you can be.

Figure 7.5 Tips for conducting online searches

Exploring website credibility

In a time of increased Internet usage, it is important to know what you are searching for and if it can be trusted. Seeking credibility when using websites can be challenging as it is not always easy to determine whether the information they contain is trustworthy. Although not foolproof, you can check the domain names which are part of the website's address. Using this as a guide can offer some indication of the type of sites you have found and the possible type of data the site claims to contain. Figure 7.6 provides some examples of domain name and corresponding organisation.

Whilst there is no certainty, it is important to know that domains such as .gov, .edu and .ac can only be registered by government and educational institutions. It is possible to search for your data within specific domains and this is shown in Figure 7.6. Knowing that it is possible to authenticate some domains may provide you with some confidence and make you feel less concerned as to their validity but you still need to be vigilant. We will always advise you to be sceptical and approach all unknown sites with some caution. Here are some issues to be aware of:

Domain	Organisation
.gov	Government agencies
.com	Commercial businesses
.ac	Academic Institutions
.edu	Educational Institutions
.net	Network Organisations
.org	Organisations (non-profit)
.ca	A country (ca=Canada)

Figure 7.6 Examples of domain names and associated organisations

- **Domain bias:** This occurs when too much emphasis is placed in the domain suffix (*e.g. .org or .gov*) (Leong et al. 2012). This can sometimes lead to misplaced trust as you can be guided to the sites that seem to belong to a recognisable and reputable organisation.
- **Snippet bias:** You can be led to open a link because the snippet (*the small section of text that appears under the web page results on a Search Engine Results Page (SERP)*) includes your search terms in bold. Beware of these as they are not always what they present themselves to be and you can find yourself directed to unwanted sites and pages.
- **Position bias:** It may be that you are more tempted to click on a result when it is placed higher on the results page (Yue, Patel & Roehrig 2010). As we stated above, sometimes the results are not ranked on relevance but on popularity.

There are some strategies that you can employ to aid your assessment of unknown websites. Research by Ahmad et al. (2010) assessed people's credibility judgements when searching for websites. Their findings indicate that people are more likely to visit a site and think it is trustworthy when:

- advertisements were limited;
- there was evidence of good grammar;
- the information seemed up to date.

These findings reflect some of the accepted criteria related to website credibility as we show in Figure 7.7:

Figure 7.7   Criteria to assess website quality

- **Currency:** Is the information up to date?
- **Credibility:** Does the author or producer have some authority on the topic they present?
- **Purpose:** Why is the website there? Is it self-promotion? Is it a political group? Is the site trying to sell something?
- **Accuracy:** is it grammatically correct? Are there formatting concerns?
- **Check advertising:** Are there too many advertisements? Do they flash or pop-up?

We explore criteria to check source credibility in more depth in Chapter 8. Whilst these are not foolproof checks, these criteria and the awareness of domain names are some basic steps that you can take.

Conducting safe searches

When using a library, you have a certain amount of control. This control is in handling the books or texts you select, knowing where they came from and, if you borrow them, you know for how long and under what terms. There is also a person who is employed to support you in this process (*the librarian*) so there is little personal risk involved. However, being on the Internet may mean searching without the aid of a safety net. Whilst the Internet has democratised knowledge sharing and gathering, you need to be vigilant and safety-conscious. Whilst no strategies can be claimed as perfect, Figure 7.8 outlines some examples of basic search precautions.

1.	Ensure your hardware is protected by up-to-date Internet security software.
2.	Check before you begin a search that your work is backed up to the last version; an ill-timed crash will not help your blood pressure.
3.	Make sure your supervisor is fully aware of the topic you are studying, particularly if it is one that may be perceived as sensitive or 'hot'.
4.	Familiarise yourself with your browser's privacy setting so you understand the role of cookies and tracking software. Make sure you protect your privacy and seek support from your institution's or organisation's IT department if you need further guidance.
5.	Do not be tempted to click on an unexpected image or headline as this could be click bait. Click bait can take you into unsafe territory so, remain in control of your searching and try not to be tempted to go 'off piste'. Also, be aware of the rise of 'native advertising': that is advertising that looks like news but it is just trying to sell or promote a product (*or a range of other things*).
6.	Be ethical when you search which means being aware of your responsibility to the privacy and protection of those whose data you seek to use. Check you are not infringing copyright or breaching any privacy laws.

(Continued)

Figure 7.8 (Continued)

7.	Be alert to fake news which is now an ever-present aspect of being on the Internet. If you are in any doubt as to the truthfulness of the source, always triangulate it, which means look for it in different places and by different authorities.
8.	Finally, read the small print when you download any software you feel might be useful or if you sign up to access any sites. It takes time to check and it can be frustrating but you should know what you are signing up for and how the site or company will use your data.

Figure 7.8 Examples of basic search precautions

PAUSE FOR THOUGHT

Knowing the context of your data's production

In Chapter 6 we explored some 'fake news' (see Box 6.3) and how with some simple detection work, this 'news' could have been revealed as 'fake'. Therefore, if accessing data from a website, try to find the context of your data's production. There are a few places on a website that can help you understand 'what', 'when', 'where', 'why', 'who' and 'how' your your data were created.

• Look for information tabs or icons on the side bars that offer information about mission statements, start-up dates and any tab that says:

'About us'

'Philosophy'

'Background'

'Biography'

This is a process of critical appraisal as you are applying judgements to the information you can find out about your data.

WHERE DO I FIND DATA?

Data exist in the 'real' world in many places and where you can find it depends on what you want to use. You may want to use data from local or national libraries, or from your own institutional library. You may want to visit museums and galleries that offer private, local and national collections and you may want to use data found in specialist archives. It would be impossible to cover all locations so in this section we explore a range of possible sites on the Internet where documents as data can be found. In Chapter 1, when we explored why qualitative secondary research was such a strong and relevant research design, we argued that accessing data online means that you are no longer restricted to data locations that are near to you; your geography is no longer the constraining force it once was and so now your choice of what you can use and where you can find it has increased. However, this does mean you need to have very firm ideas about what you are looking for as there is just too much to trawl through so we encourage you to remain on your research intentions and keep your research question(s) and/or aim(s) firmly in view. To guide or inform your selection, we have tried to find places where you could access sources of data reflective of the diversity available in the 21st century.

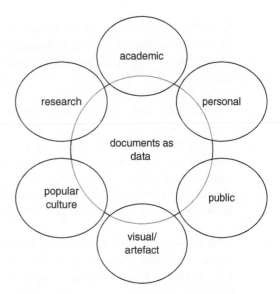

Figure 7.9   Categorising documents as data

We offer a few words of caution, as whilst we have attempted to provide free or open access data, there are some locations that require logins, subscription through your institution or payment for full access. Different sites and repositories function in diverse ways. Depending on the type of data you want to access, some sites provide an online catalogue for the documents they have available but often these can only be viewed when you visit the archive or storage centre. Therefore, be clear when you start about what you want and what you do not want. Set yourself some clear parameters and see what there is to find. We present these sites using the headings we identified in Chapter 6 (see Figure 7.9).

When you search we advise you to keep in mind the ethical issues we covered in Chapter 5 and again briefly at the beginning of this chapter. Make sure you have permission to access the data and if you want to select it for your work, ensure you have permission to use it. We also advise you to reflect on the data management processes we explore in Chapter 10 and record your locations of interest and all sources accurately. This will save you time and frustration in the long run. When you begin your searches the best advice we can offer is to:

- make sure your computer is safe from any Internet based attack (*anti-virus and malware protected*);
- be armed with effective search strategies;
- record your sites of interest and any resulting data (*use bookmarks*);
- always adopt a sharp and critical gaze (see Chapter 8).

Research sources

You can find a range of existing research in research archives and repositories. Digital data repositories, data archives or data centres store and disseminate research data. Whilst there is an emphasis on quantitative data there are a range of social science archives providing qualitative data:

CESSDA (*Consortium of European Social Science Data Archives*) (www.cessda.eu/): CESSDA provides large-scale, integrated and sustainable data services to the social sciences from archives across Europe. It is worth exploring their 'data impact blog' for additional information.

The UK Data Archive (www.data-archive.ac.uk/): The UK Data Archive provide this site and it is worth exploring. Try using the thesaurus 'HASSET' (https://hasset.ukdataservice.ac.uk/). This is a data indexing function which works as a thesaurus. It provides a full description of your keywords and links to a wide range of social science data. There is also the international multi-lingual version (https://elsst.ukdataservice.ac.uk/). The UK Data Service operate the Qualidata archive which is where you will find a range of open and safeguarded data. Please review their data usage policy to ensure you have full access.

re3data.org (https://www.re3data.org/):This is a global registry of research data repositories that covers different academic disciplines. It offers permanent storage and access to researchers, funding bodies, publishers and scholarly institutions. It has an effective search and browse function.

Qualitative Data Repository (QDR) (https://qdr.syr.edu/): QDR is a recently created data storage facility for storing and sharing digital data (and accompanying documentation). Most of the data it houses are generated or collected through qualitative and multi-method research in the social sciences (QDR 2017). It offers a range of interesting subjects from maps, legal records and ephemera (popular culture) and you will need to register to access the data.

Academic sources

You may have access to an institution subscription database, and if you do, then you should find a wealth of academically focused sources for your literature review of data. If you have any concerns finding this information, please seek advice from your librarian as they have knowledge and skills in data searching. There are an increasing number of open access locations which provide access to scholarly articles and research. We offer a brief consideration of what is available to you.

Open access

An open access journal is where the publisher of the journal makes all articles and related content available for free on the journal's website. Open access began in the Budapest Open Access Initiative (2002) and so far, two main ways of open access have been agreed; 'gratis', which is completely free to use and 'libre' which has conditions attached. Open access arrangements have been hailed as creating an 'internet of the mind' which has opened up knowledge to wider groups of people. However, even though these journals are open and many articles can be located on the Internet, authors still have rights as to how their material is used. This means acknowledging citations fully.

As we explored in Chapter 6 there are some issues with some journal publishing houses. Whilst some have undergone peer review and are accepted as being of a required academic standard, some may not. As we have advised, check the editorial process and if you have any doubts cross reference the journal within an Internet search to see if there are any reported issues. Most open access journals indicate that some form of peer review has occurred but it is possible to check the processes they use by clicking on links to the journal home pages. Then look for links that provide an overview of their editorial process or peer review. There is still some debate as to whether these are the 'real' thing but checking how they are reviewed can provide some reassurance. Positive outcomes are that open access has benefited the wider research community as researchers are gaining increasing measures of impact for their articles and research is reaching a wider audience. If you want to explore the value or worth of an article, you can explore the 'Impact Factor' to see if the journal or article has been viewed before and if/when it has been cited by others. Here are three well known providers of open access sources:

Elsevier (www.elsevier.com/about/open-science/open-access/open-access-journals): Elsevier claim that all of the articles published by Elsevier in open access journals have undergone peer review. They offer published articles within open access as permanently free for everyone to read and download.

Wiley (www.wileyopenaccess.com/view/index.html): Wiley offer a range of open access journals and indicate that processes of peer review are performed.

Springer (www.springeropen.com/journals): Springer offer a transparent approach to open access. They will publish the names of the peer reviewers alongside the article as part of a 'pre-publication history'. Upon request, they will also provide previous versions of the manuscript and all author responses to the reviewer's comments.

The following providers offer a significant amount of data that is mainly academic in focus but as we explore in Chapter 8, you must adopt a clear critical gaze to ensure quality.

CORE: There are other sites such as CORE (https://core.ac.uk/) that collect open access research outputs from repositories and journals worldwide and then make them available to the public. Data is usually provided as full-text content (*typically a PDF*).

Semantic Scholar: You could explore Semantic Scholar (www.semanticscholar.org/) which is a free non-profit search engine from Allen Institute for Artificial Intelligence. It has some very useful features that can be used to consider article impact and to support source credibility.

Google Scholar (https://scholar.google.co.uk/) Google Scholar is a search engine which locates mainly academic papers or books. Some may be available for you to access and others may require you to log in through your institution's internal data base. You need to apply filters and search systematically to find what you need but this search engine offers an interesting feature called 'metrics' which can be accessed from the search bar (https://scholar.google.co.uk/intl/en/ scholar/metrics.html). A tool like this can be used to defend your selection of sources, especially in your sampling processes. It offers evidence as to their impact; for example, how many times the source is cited and viewed by others.

Not all online databases are open access but some do offer a selection of documents for you to access without needing to be affiliated to a specific institution. You could explore a site such as ERIC.

ERIC (*Educational Resource Information Center*) (https://eric.ed.gov/): ERIC is an online digital library sponsored by the Institute of Education Sciences of the United States Department of Education. It provides a wide range of journal and non-journal focused information and you can search for articles by selecting 'peer review' only.

Personal sources

You could search for data described as personal or first-hand narrative data. These are data found within social media platforms and micro blogging sites. You could also access blogs which are diaries recounting an individual's or organisation's experiences. We reviewed some of the ethical concerns faced with accessing social media data online but it is possible to find publicly available first-hand data from a range of social media platforms. Micro blogs such as Twitter can be searched using https://twitter.com/search-home?lang=en-gb and websites such as https://www.all-hashtag.com/index.php offer a range of tools to explore tweets but please check you can use these and that they are safe to access.

Personal documents such as diaries, letters and journals from famous people can be found online but most sites offer an online catalogue, but to view the stored documents, you may need to visit the specialist archive. There are some interesting first-hand data sites such as a website that offers a vast amount of personal documentation from Queen Victoria: www. queenvictoriasjournals.org/home.do. You will also find Samuel Pepys' diary online at www. pepysdiary.com/ and a large array of personal documents, letters, and journals from Winston Churchill at www.churchillarchive.com/.

Public sources

This is a wide category of data and includes reports from local, national and international and global level. It is freely available on the Internet and is often found in sites referred to as 'open data'. As a movement, open data is about releasing and making available substantial amounts of important and reliable data to all users. One key aim of this movement is to provide data that is traceable, so you know where it originates, thus allowing people to make judgements as to whether it can be trusted. Sites like the examples below aim to increase transparency within the sharing of data.

Canada (http://open.canada.ca/en): This site encourages you to explore widely to find data and digital records.

United Kingdom (https://data.gov.uk/data/search): This site houses a large amount of public and open data provided by the UK government.

Enigma (https://public.enigma.com/): This site offers a vast array of publicly available data including topics as diverse as art and agriculture to Switzerland's economic affairs.

Google (www.google.com/publicdata/directory): This is a large directory of public data sites with some very informative visualisation tools.

You should be able to find local sources of public data such as births, marriages and deaths as well as records at local government level. These might relate to town planning, health or school inspection reports. There are large international agencies that produce an immense amount of data. These are data that can be country or event specific and, for those seeking to explore international comparisons, this may be the type of data you need to explore. It is worth considering the social media presence of organisations that generate this data. They may have Facebook pages and Twitter accounts and these can provide a contemporary commentary or updates on current events.

Intergovernmental agencies

These are called IGOs as they are large international agencies established by treaty or other agreement. Notable examples of organisations that produce vast amounts of public data are the United Nations or the European Union. The United Nations is the single largest IGO in the world (http://data.un.org/). It has several specialised agencies such as:

UNESCO (*United Nations Educational, Scientific and Cultural Organization*) (https://en.unesco. org/): UNESCO is an organisation which was established with the aim to build peace through international cooperation in Education, the Sciences and Culture. They have a well curated Twitter account so you can add to any information you find using this regularly updated feed.

OECD (*Organisation for Economic Co-operation and Development*) (www.oecd.org): The Organisation for Economic Co-operation and Development (OECD) is an intergovernmental organisation that works to improve the economic and social well-being of people around the world. They provide a vast array of data which could be useful for internationally focused comparative projects. If you go to the 'publishing' tab you will be directed to an online bookshop, a site promoting their published reports and other partner organisation's iLibraries.

Non-governmental organisations

These are called NGOs and produce a vast amount of data that is independent of any government. These are data that cover social or political issues and could be from charities or movements for social change. You could access data from organisations such as:

Oxfam (www.oxfam.org.uk/): A charitable organisation fighting poverty.

World Wild Life Fund (www.wwf.org.uk/): This is an organisation that fights to preserve wildlife and aims to reduce human impact on the environment.

International Rescue Committee (www.rescue.org/who-we-are): IRC offer support to people who have been affected by disaster and they offer thought provoking information on the state of the world. To access this, go to the tab marked 'what we do' and access 'reports and resources'.

National archives

There are a wide variety of National Archives found on the Internet for you to explore. They offer both historical and contemporary international perspectives of people's lives. These are public data and can offer significant amounts of interesting data. The following are examples:

The UK National Archive (https://images.nationalarchives.gov.uk/assetbank-nationalarchives/action/viewHome): This site offers a huge range of images but check you have permission to use what is available.

National Archives of Australia (www.naa.gov.au/): This site is described as a nation's memories and in one search we found this homage to board games; useful if you wanted to explore pre-computer age social interaction: www.naa.gov.au/collection/snapshots/Games/index.aspx.

The Library and Archives Canada (LAC) (www.bac-lac.gc.ca/eng/Pages/home.aspx): This site contains a huge collection of images and documents spanning 140 years. Whilst searching for interesting data we found the Virtual Gramophone index which has historical audio recordings: www.bac-lac.gc.ca/eng/Pages/home.aspx.

Popular culture sources

Some of these data may need to be accessed by payment or subscription and we advise you to check the ownership and copyright of this type of data very closely. As we indicated in Chapter 6, this is a large category of data including genres such as books, newspapers, films, cartoons and YouTube. There is always some form of crossover within categories of data and, as we considered above, it is possible to access social media data to complement any other online data you collect. Here are a couple of examples:

Comicsgrid (www.comicsgrid.com/): This site offers peer-reviewed articles for those interested in exploring comics or 'the appreciation of graphic narrative'.

Wikimedia (https://wikimediafoundation.org/research/): The Wikimedia Foundation is a non-profit organisation designed to promote free information for all. They have many projects including the well-known Wikipedia, to Wikiquote and Wikidata. The Foundation site itself contains many interesting documents such as those of the organisation's mission statement, policies of free speech.

eBook and Digital Libraries

There are some geographic copyright issues when using web-based eBook libraries so it is best to check the terms and conditions. We include a few examples for you to consider:

The Internet Archive (https://archive.org/details/texts): This is a non-profit library containing a vast variety of free books. Currently, there are over 20,000,000 downloadable ebooks and texts. There may be some limitations on use so check the terms and conditions.

Google books (https://books.google.co.uk/): Google had an ambitious project to digitise millions of books but there were issues with intellectual property and copyright; however, under the 'snippet' arrangement you can preview about 20 per cent of a book.

The World Digital Library (WDL) (www.wdl.org/en/publications/): This is a project of the US Library of Congress carried out with the support of the United Nations Educational, Cultural and Scientific Organization (UNESCO). It features some interesting timelines and interactive maps.

The British Film Institute Regional and National Archive (www.bfi.org.uk/britain-on-film/regional-national-archives): This site contains a vast array of film and television output. It offers a fascinating glimpse into UK social and cultural history.

The British Library (www.bl.uk/subjects/news-media): Some of the information is available online and for some you may need to visit the reading room but you can explore archived websites, news media, notebooks from Leonardo Da Vinci and a wealth of other interesting subjects. It is well worth searching through the catalogue.

BBC (www.bbc.co.uk/writersroom/scripts): This site allows you to explore scripts from well-known BBC shows.

Visual and artefact sources

We have only provided a small amount of what you could search for on the Internet. As with all the searches we have considered, you need to consider if you have the right to access and the right to use. Most of the images and works of art are covered by some form of copyright but 'fair use' may be indicated. Here are a few museums and large online visual collections to consider:

The Getty Research Institute (www.getty.edu/research/institute/): The Getty Research Institute provides diverse open content. See: www.getty.edu/about/whatwedo/opencontent.html and access to the J. Paul Getty Museum at www.getty.edu/art/collection/.

The Victoria and Albert Museum (www.vam.ac.uk/): This is a huge museum with a large online catalogue. The section on sculpture is worth visiting at www.vam.ac.uk/collections/sculpture.

MOMA (Museum of Modern Art) (www.moma.org/): This has a vast online selection.

Wikipedia Commons (https://commons.wikimedia.org/wiki/Category:Image): This site offers many images under the Creative Commons licence of Attribution and ShareAlike (CC BY-SA 3.0). This means you must give credit but you can copy and adapt.

ACCESSING QUANTITATIVE DATA

Depending on how you are approaching your research study (*i.e. combined or multiple strategy*) you may want to access numerical or quantitative data. This can be data that is generated by surveys and collected and published as census data. You may want to access websites such as www.census.gov (*US Census Bureau*) and www.abs.gov.au/ (*Australian Bureau of Statistics*) as these can yield large amounts of data. However, as with all searches, you need to invest some time in exploring what sites like these can offer. Sites such as the World Values Survey (www.worldvaluessurvey.org) provide the possibility of international comparisons as does the website produced by the European Commission (http://ec.europa.eu/eurostat).

PAUSE FOR THOUGHT

Online security

Make sure you are protecting yourself, your computer and your institution when searching for information in the public domain.

- Do you have up-to-date and effective virus and Internet security software?
- Do you know how to activate the privacy and security settings on your browser?
- Have you followed your institution's guide to Internet usage?

When accessing sources of information on the Internet ensure you are aware of some of the basic rules of Internet safety. Check your institution's data policy and ensure you act within its guidance, especially if you are accessing information on topics that could be considered sensitive or *too hot*. If in doubt, always check with your supervisor.

REFLECTION AND FURTHER READING

At the beginning of the chapter we set out what you should be able to do when you reached the end of this chapter. To aid your reflection on all we have covered we ask some chapter specific questions. If you are unsure of any of your answers to these questions, please go back to the relevant section to review this aspect.

REFLECTING ON CHAPTER 7

In this chapter we have:

- **Revisited the need to consider the ethical and legal access and use of data:** What are the three core principles within ethics? What is the relationship between levels of access and your ability to use data?
- **Provided strategies to develop effective search skills:** Why are key words so important? How can citation chaining improve your literature searches?
- **Considered the credibility of websites and searches:** Which website do you feel would have more credibility: .com or.edu? Can you defend your answer and say why? Why should you check the use of advertising when using websites?
- **Presented possible locations for your sources of data:** Where would you find information on intergovernmental initiatives? Where could you access archived research data? What does open access mean to you as a researcher?

WE RECOMMEND FOR FURTHER READING:

Adolphus, M. (2018) *How to ... use search engines effectively.* Available at: www.emeraldgroup publishing.com/research/guides/management/new_search_engines.htm.
This site provides very clear and easy-to-follow steps towards effective searching, particularly for those with institutional access to a subscription database.

(Continued)

(Continued)

Bradley, P. (2017) *Expert Internet Searching* (5th edn). London: Facet Publishing.
An informative read that provides more depth on the aspects explored in this chapter.

Hart, C. (2001) *Doing a Literature Search: A Comprehensive Guide for the Social Sciences.*
London: SAGE Publications Ltd.
Hart's book offers a vast range of relevant advice and support.

Jesson, J., Matheson, L. & Lacey, F.M. (2011) *Doing Your Literature Review: Traditional and
Systematic Techniques.* London: SAGE Publications Ltd.
We recommend Chapter 2 which focuses on searching for literature, and Chapter 3 that
explores a range of reading strategies that complement the ones we reviewed in Chapter 2
(this volume).

University of Bristol (2016) How to use search engines effectively: Google and beyond. Available at: www.bristol.ac.uk/library/support/findinginfo/search-engines/.
This site offers a wealth of pertinent information which is well worth exploring.

University of Leeds (2017) *Developing your search strategy*. Available at: https://library.leeds.
ac.uk/researcher-literature-search-strategy.
This site offers practical and relevant search advice for all levels of researcher.

8
SECURING QUALITY OVER QUANTITY

THIS CHAPTER SUPPORTS YOUR ABILITY TO

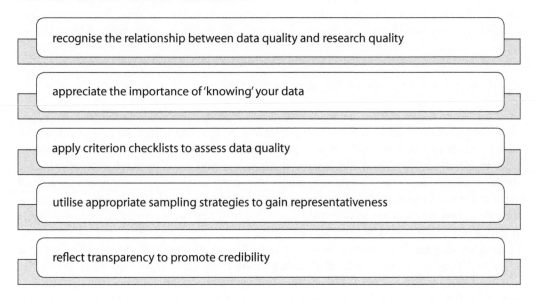

- recognise the relationship between data quality and research quality
- appreciate the importance of 'knowing' your data
- apply criterion checklists to assess data quality
- utilise appropriate sampling strategies to gain representativeness
- reflect transparency to promote credibility

CHAPTER OVERVIEW

As we explored in Chapter 7, due to the mass of potential data available to you it is vital that the outcome of your data searching is quality over quantity. Therefore, the focus of this chapter is to guide you in techniques to reduce your data to reflect this goal. We review processes to secure data quality, namely; evaluation and critical appraisal approaches and sampling strategies. The chapter explores how both of these processes are linked to ensuring the quality of your research.

When using existing data, you need to know as much about it as possible because whilst you may have access to enormous amounts of data the quality of this can vary. In this chapter, we provide a spotlight to strategies that when used effectively will assist you in being able to filter your data. Strategies such as informed judgement, critical appraisal checklists and the use of inclusion and exclusion criteria should enable you to check the quality of your sources and make effective decisions about the data you use for your analysis and that you need to include in your review.

Additionally, this chapter explores the role of sampling strategies that are also closely linked to aspects of research quality and rigour. Sampling strategies enable you to obtain a representative or relevant sample from the initial sources identified through the application of your quality review. We emphasise throughout that it is through being able to understand, respond and record your steps in the selection of your data that adds not only to the credibility of your research, but to its replicability and transferability (generalisability) therefore increasing the meaning and contribution to the field of knowledge.

WHY DO I NEED TO REDUCE MY DATA?

As we outlined in Chapter 6, you could potentially be working with a very large amount of data which can be both useful to your research and demanding to manage. It may be impossible to effectively handle all the data you access, so you need to employ some effective decision-making processes to reduce and filter your data. Issues of data quality can arise in all types of data and therefore we encourage you to implement quality control procedures, not as a single action when locating your data (see Chapter 7) but as an ongoing part of all your research responsibilities (UK Data Service 2018).

In this chapter, we present reducing data based on the making of effective and informed choices. These are basic decisions indicating what stays and what should be removed. This is the focus of this chapter, but we have covered aspects in Chapters 6, 7 and 9. In Chapter 9, we discuss the decision you have to make regarding sources that should constitute your literature review. This choice needs to reflect scholarly and robust sources of data to confirm the meaning and utility of the findings you generate. This means knowing that the sources of data you have selected are scholarly, robust and can confirm your findings. There are other decisions that need to be made when we work with existing data. These are:

- Decisions relating to data quality.
- Decisions about data as representative, transferable or generalisable.

As a qualitative secondary researcher, you need to be aware of any possible problematic data characteristics you may face when collecting your data. Therefore, it is important to be aware of the potential for data distortion that can be presented in a range of forms and put in place mitigating strategies to reduce or combat this distortion. This can begin with checking your sources for quality as knowing that you have quality data adds to the confidence in your research. The quality of your data is vital to the success of your research.

HOW DO I ACHIEVE DATA QUALITY?

You can achieve quality data through the adoption of a sceptical and questioning approach. This needs to be applied to all forms of data but it may be required to be more rigidly applied to some data than others. This applies to data such as that found on the Internet, as advertising, newsfeeds and in magazines but this may also need to be directed at existing research data. Even though there is a presumption that these data may in some way be of greater quality, it is misguided to assume this. When working with existing research data, issues of quality can arise. Sometimes the lack of quality can be intentional, for example, when a researcher has deliberately misrepresented their research. However, issues relating to the trustworthiness of pre-existing data have been identified (Andrews et al. 2012; Elliott 2015). Therefore, we advise you not to assume that data are credible and trustworthy. There are steps you can take to aid your development of a detailed contextual knowledge about the circumstances of data production.

These steps include examining your data to assess what it can bring to your answering of your research question. By employing strategies and processes to inspect and evaluate your data you are focusing on the prevention of quality issues. When used, such strategies can contribute

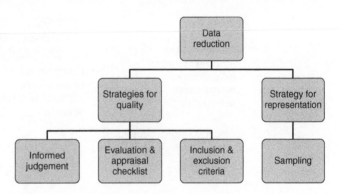

Figure 8.1   Reducing your data

to your research integrity, increasing the dependability of what you produce and generally enhancing its credibility. This is because your research is based on 'quality' data. Therefore, we emphasise that making sure you have quality data should underpin the whole of the research process. Not having quality data is like building a house on sand; it might look good but the foundations will not be strong. Therefore, when we use data reduction strategies, we are trying to:

- **reduce data overload** (*i.e. eliminate irrelevant or weak data*);
- **focus on sources that are relevant to your study** (*i.e. needed to answer your question or needed in your review to provide meaningful context for research*);
- **provide research quality and rigour** (*i.e. to provide credibility, dependability, transparency in processes used*).

When we use data reduction strategies we should use them with clearly defined functions in mind (see Figure 8.1).

UNDERSTANDING THE QUALITY OF YOUR DATA

The search processes we explored in Chapter 7 will only have benefit if these result in accurate and high-quality data. However, knowing what 'quality' is can be challenging but the definition offered by Wang and Strong (1996: 6) adds some clarity. Wang and Strong (1996: 6) define data quality as '*data that are fit for use by data consumers*' and they describe the seeking of data quality as '*a set of data quality attributes that represent a single aspect or construct of data quality*'. As shown in Figure 8.2, they suggest that you can think of quality as having three aspects.

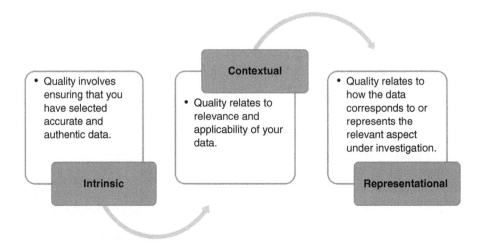

Figure 8.2   Aspects of data quality (adapted from Wang and Strong 1996)

Therefore, when we think about quality we should have some understanding of what this looks like. To do this we consider what Scott (1990) asserts are the four main criteria of data quality:

- **Authenticity:** Is the data authentic?
- **Credibility:** Can the data be believed? Is it credible?
- **Representativeness:** Is the data representative? Can we generalise and make claims to inform practice and policy making decisions?
- **Meaning:** Does the data have meaning? Can it be understood? Does it make sense?

Authenticity: Being able to know if data are authentic can depend on the data you are using; for example, if you are researching medieval illuminated manuscripts then knowing you have a real version and not a forgery would be essential. You could perform some basic checks such as checking records to know where it came from; you could look for signs of age and wear; and you would know by the materials used. However, if you are using media from online communities or social media your ability to perform these checks would be challenging. One key issue to navigate would be if the data were produced by a bot or a human. There are some sources where there is a data trail that could enable more effective judgements as to the authenticity of data to be made. These might be if the data are published and you can track the bibliographic data; it might be if it comes from a website with a known and more trusted domain. You may be able to get more knowledge about data authenticity if your data is published or produced from a source such as a government organisation or a well-known charity. However, when it comes to assessing whether something is authentic or not, then you can only make a judgement on the information you have available. In Chapter 7, we explored strategies such as checking domain names and in Chapter 6, we encouraged you to check information provided on websites to understand your data as much as you are able.

Credibility: Credibility refers to the accuracy of your data, its sincerity and the reliability of the producer of the document. This relates to the content of your data and the level at which it can be believed. In Chapter 6 we explored the influences on data and we explored issues such as media bias which is not fully reporting the 'truth' just a version of the 'truth'. Issues with credibility are more profound when we consider first-hand accounts of the world. Data created by people about their lives will inevitably be produced from their perspective and thus, reflect their way of knowing (see Chapter 3). This means data from personal Twitter feeds, blogs, diaries and most first-person narratives are subjective views of the world and need to be accepted as such. There are other forms of influence from government or political ideology, persuasive advertising to charities needing to get your money. All sources need to be reviewed with this possibility and potential for bias and distortion. This does not mean you do not use your data, but you know what you are using and how it can be used.

There is also a need not to assume that sources are credible because of where they are produced. In Chapters 5 and 6 we provided examples of some issues with peer review. Peer review is held as a gold standard approach to knowledge production but this needs to be checked. As we explored, new ways of publishing academic sources have led to a need for increased vigilance. There are other aspects to consider such as knowing when the data were created as ways of thinking change. Your data may not have been inaccurate when it was produced but time has altered its relevance and meaning.

Representativeness: This is linked to typicality which is whether your data can be considered as typical or representative of similar forms of data. Knowing if you require your data to be typical or not is important in terms of what you search for and how you defend your selection of data. For example, if you want to research one painting by one artist in great depth, then its typicality to all other paintings of its type may not be relevant. The same may be true if you were using the personal letters of a famous person or if you were contrasting the narratives used in two very specific blogs. In cases like these it would be very difficult to ascertain the typicality of these data. Therefore, representativeness may not be the aspiration of your data selection. Whereas, representativeness may have increased relevance if you are doing a larger scale piece of research using existing research data, then you may need to know how these data are in some way typical of a wider population.

Meaning: Data has a literal meaning and we can check this by asking questions such as what is it? and, what does it do? Does it make sense? But there is also the meaning created when the data are in use. This is the social and cultural meaning of your data. This means understanding the context in which your data are meant to be understood and considering the domain in which your documents have meaning and relevance. For example, when we discuss legal documents, we expect a certain way of writing and presentation and we know they are written for a specific audience. We know they have to be understood in this way in this context; but take them out of that context and the meaning can change. In Chapter 11, we explore discourse analysis which is an attempt to understand this social and cultural meaning of data as 'discursive practices'.

BOX 8.1 THE HITLER DIARIES

In April 1983, the West German news magazine *Stern* published excerpts from sixty journals supposedly written as a diary by Adolf Hitler. It was alleged that these journals had been smuggled from a crash site in Dresden. However, *Stern* were suspicious so they sent one page to handwriting experts in Europe and the USA. This page was compared with known samples of Hitler's handwriting and the experts concluded that both the diaries and the samples were written by the same hand. They also had noted historians check and confirm the diaries' authenticity. However, even though these diaries had been checked by handwriting experts and verified by leading historians, doubts still existed. This led to additional tests and when analysed further, the diaries were proclaimed as fake.

(Sourced from: Levy 2010 and Lusher 2018)

The example in Box 8.1 illustrates the need for vigilance when faced with data that may seem authentic but is in some way flawed. Therefore, we need to use strategies such as critical evaluation and appraisal to encourage you to interrogate your sources and to encourage you to be sceptical and challenge your data. To support your assessment of data, it is possible to employ relevant criteria and strategies. We will explore these starting with the need to understand and know your data.

KNOWING YOUR DATA

Knowing your data leads to your ability to reduce it in quantity and refining it for quality. As a qualitative secondary researcher, you may have no control over the production of your data, but you do have control over its selection and usage. Just using existing data because it is easily and readily available may challenge the validity and authenticity of the research. Therefore, your role in the data reduction process is to minimise potential flaws in relation to the data you have collated for analysis. This can be achieved through a systematic approach to the collection and selection of the sample for analysis by the application of appropriate data reduction strategies. As Morris (2009: 178) states:

> This predicament may be linked to internal validity and the conduct of the researcher with regard to the extent of the actual procedures and techniques and implementation which may compromise results.

Ensuring that you apply a systematic and transparent approach to the selection of your final data set for analysis reduces the risk of excluding key information (Nickerson & Sloan 2002). Ultimately the goal of data reduction is to gain a range of data that enables you to answer your research question and in doing this you demonstrate credibility and validity in your research. In Chapter 4, we discussed how effective secondary researchers defend themselves against claims of bias and possible knowledge distortion. Without such protection there would be little confidence in the research findings and conclusions produced. The following section explores strategies that can support your ability to reduce your data quality and provide confidence as to its quality.

Using strategies to explore data quality

Demonstrating transparency in your decision making is about ensuring any research you produce is credible and meaningful. Therefore, you need to adopt a *'process of systematically examining research evidence to assess its validity, results and relevance before using it'* (Hill & Spittlehouse 2003: 1). Reducing the amount of data you have into more manageable and meaningful quantities should enable you to reflect your commitment to quality over quantity.

This begins with the application of techniques and strategies to support you as you sift through your data, enabling you to both reduce the quantity and search for quality. This sifting needs to be performed in a systematic way using a critical gaze to refine your choices and support your ability to make effective and reasoned decisions. This is not just a process of guess work. You need to know how and why you are employing these strategies as you will need to defend the data you have selected in your methodology (see Chapter 4).

Adopting a focused approach to your data is essential for you as a secondary researcher because, as we have stated throughout this book, just because data are available to you, this does not mean that you should use it. To answer your research question and meet your aim, you need to find sources that can be considered as both relevant and trustworthy.

The sections below provide three data reduction strategies for you to employ. These are not placed in a hierarchical order, but as a collection of guides to support your actions. What you decide to use may be dependent on the type of data you select, and whether they are used as sources for your literature review or for your data analysis. However, we also ask you to be aware of being overly rigid or too prescriptive; the techniques we offer should add rigour to your research, but they should not define or confine your selection of data.

Informed judgement

You can select sources based on your *informed judgement* – this means deciding about sources of data based on what you know and not just your gut feeling. This approach to data quality acknowledges the importance of reflexivity and contextualisation in the assessment, as judgement is made for a specific purpose (Boud & Falchikov 2007). In other words, this approach accepts that who you are, and what you are, can be important determiners in what you select as data and how you consider its quality. In all parts of our life we regularly make informed judgements but when we undertake research these can be based on:

- professional judgement from experience;
- knowing about policy, legislation and research from a previous study;
- talking and discussing your topic with peers;
- key texts supplied as course reading;
- lecture handouts;
- information on course website;
- metrics and impact factors;
- snowball data and daisy chaining – using one source to understand the importance of another (see Chapter 7).

However, you need to consider if this strategy of applying your *informed judgement* offers a robust defence for your selection of data. You need to consider if you can defend yourself from claims of bias and knowledge distortion. Making decisions can be highly complex and, whilst drawing on your own informed judgement might guide you to a specific range of sources for your research, you may need to step back and reflect on the difference between your informed judgement and your making of assumptions. These assumptions can be that all sources of data provided on a .gov website are credible and that scholarly journals are always credible but, as we explored in Chapters 5 and 6, this is not always the case.

PAUSE FOR THOUGHT

Using your informed judgement

Your informed judgement is informed by who you are and what you are and by the reading you undertake. This means that the criteria you use to make your judgement willalso be guided by your conceptual framework. Therefore, we advise you to try to record the concepts that you think will inform your judgement in your research diary (see Chapter 2).

Being able to isolate and identify these factors can give you more confidence in the selection of your data.

Evaluation or critical appraisal tools

When locating sources in Chapter 6, you were asked to consider the question prompts *'what'*, *'why'*, *'when'* *'where'*, and *'how'* to guide your selection of sources. This approach demonstrates critical thinking as you are challenging and questioning your evidence. But these questions need to be applied in a more robust way if you are going to be able to defend your decisions and offer a critical consideration of all the sources you wish to use (Cottrell 2005). Being able to defend and justify your selection of data whether for your literature review or your analysis is important

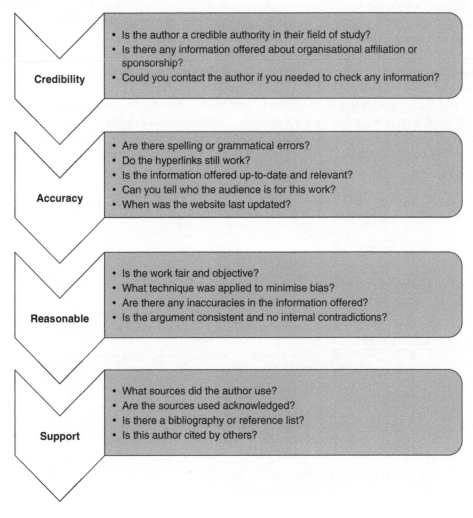

Credibility
- Is the author a credible authority in their field of study?
- Is there any information offered about organisational affiliation or sponsorship?
- Could you contact the author if you needed to check any information?

Accuracy
- Are there spelling or grammatical errors?
- Do the hyperlinks still work?
- Is the information offered up-to-date and relevant?
- Can you tell who the audience is for this work?
- When was the website last updated?

Reasonable
- Is the work fair and objective?
- What technique was applied to minimise bias?
- Are there any inaccuracies in the information offered?
- Is the argument consistent and no internal contradictions?

Support
- What sources did the author use?
- Are the sources used acknowledged?
- Is there a bibliography or reference list?
- Is this author cited by others?

Figure 8.3   CARS checklist

and this defence can be aided by the utilisation and implementation of evaluation checklists. These are sets of criteria that can be applied or created to filter your data before you make your final selection. Critical appraisal checklists can aid your ability to make clear and analytical judgements as to your source's credibility, accuracy, relevance and overall robustness.

We offer an approach to critical appraisal known by the acronym CARS (Figure 8.3). Checklists like this can be found on many library and study guide sites and we provide a modified example to embrace a range of online sources. It offers four quality measures with each one seeking to assess the usefulness of the source you have found.

However, there are some sources of data for which this checklist may be redundant. This would depend on the data you had selected. If you decided to explore artefacts as data or want to use vlogs this approach would not enable you to explore the materiality of the data (*how it is created and of what material*) and the context of the data's production in sufficient depth. Therefore, a checklist like Figure 8.4, as provided in Chapter 6 could be adapted to meet your crucial appraisal.

You could generate your own using Scott's (1990) criteria as a framework. This approach enables you to generate tailor-made criteria to assess the quality of your data. Figure 8.5 presents a checklist we have created:

Whilst there are a variety of checklists to explore, it is possible that you may want to amalgamate what is on offer and/or create your own. To facilitate your ability to do this, in the next section we identify key elements to support your decision making. These start with knowing what to include and exclude.

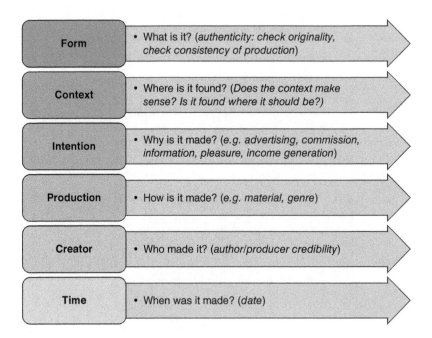

Figure 8.4   Visual data and artefact checklist

Authenticity

- Do we know who created the data?

- Where are the data found?

- Have the data been edited or transformed in any way?

- Could we find the data again?

Credibility

- Are the data sincere?

- Are the data free from forms of distortion or bias?

- Are the data believable?

- Are the data relevant?

Representativeness

- Are the data typical of other instances of this type of data?

- Can we create a meaningful sample?

- Does this data need to be typical?

Meaning

- Are the data clear?

- Does the data make sense out of context (*can it stand on its own*)?

- In what way does the data add to our understanding (from past, or current perspectives)?

Figure 8.5   Checklist adapted from Scott (1990)

Inclusion and exclusion criteria

You can apply a more discerning and selective approach to your data by setting clear parameters. These are termed inclusion/exclusion criteria that aid data reduction and, as a classification system, they can support a quest for rigour in your research. This rigour can exist because you have applied criteria that minimises the inclusion of biased, outdated and irrelevant data sources. Reducing the inclusion of flawed data lessens the possibility of the production of defective research (Conn & Rantz 2003). Establishing firm reasons for including or excluding particular types or classifications of data can increase the credibility and aid support of the confirmability of your research findings. Hence, it is important that you carefully consider your selected criteria. Consider the prompts provided below:

What are your key elements for source evaluation? Is it:

- The key ideas, arguments or conclusions put forward?
- The substantial evidence?
- The engagement with contemporary evidence?
- The methods or approach taken?
- That the authors are key commentators/specialists in field?
- The population sample and ability to generalise?
- The line of reasoning?

Are there other aspects you could use to review the robustness of sources?:

- Experience from your professional practice?
- Agreement from others to increase the reliability?
- National or international consensus?
- Use of qualitative or quantitative data?
- Metrics in journals' sites' citation indices?
- Book sales?

The example offered in Box 8.2 demonstrates the application of inclusion criteria and as you can show your choices as a table, you can open up your research process to the scrutiny of others.

BOX 8. 2 WORKING WITH INCLUSION/EXCLUSION CRITERIA

A researcher wants to access existing research data to understand why parents in the UK are reluctant to vaccinate their child. She has identified a significant body of research outlining parental opposition to childhood vaccines (Smith et al. 2017; Al-Lela et al. 2014; Barbacariua 2014; Brunson 2013; Sheriff et al. 2012; Bean 2011; Wilson et al. 2008). But there is so much available and it needs to be reduced. She applies the following inclusion/exclusion criteria.

Table 8.1 Inclusion/exclusion criteria applied

	Inclusion Criteria	Exclusion Criteria
Date	Only data published post 2010 is considered relevant	Data published prior to 2010
Type of publication	Research Data from government departments, charities, peer-reviewed journals. Online moderated blogs	Newspapers, theoretical data or Twitter accounts
Sample size	Research with sample sizes more than 20	Research with very small sample sizes e.g. less than 20
Population	Representative sample across the United Kingdom	Research conducted outside the United Kingdom

Existing research

If you are using existing research, then accessing and evaluating relevant factors that impact on the creation of your secondary data can be challenging. However, it is important to achieve because *'the importance of this familiarity with the strengths and weaknesses of the dataset cannot be overemphasized'* (Smith, Ayanian & Covinsky et al. 2011: 926). This requires you to explore the data fully to know what, where, when, why and how the data were produced. Issues relating to sample size, theoretical perspectives and methods of data analysis also need to be considered as these influence the ways findings are generated and interpreted.

Selecting your data according to its purpose

In Chapter 6, we identified that you could be faced with hundreds if not thousands of potential sources to consider. At the beginning of this chapter we illustrated the careful choices you need to make about your data and we expand on this here in Figure 8.6.

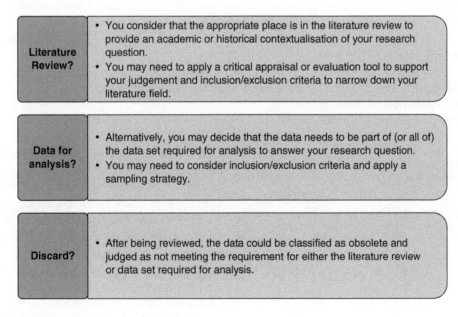

Literature Review?
- You consider that the appropriate place is in the literature review to provide an academic or historical contextualisation of your research question.
- You may need to apply a critical appraisal or evaluation tool to support your judgement and inclusion/exclusion criteria to narrow down your literature field.

Data for analysis?
- Alternatively, you may decide that the data needs to be part of (or all of) the data set required for analysis to answer your research question.
- You may need to consider inclusion/exclusion criteria and apply a sampling strategy.

Discard?
- After being reviewed, the data could be classified as obsolete and judged as not meeting the requirement for either the literature review or data set required for analysis.

Figure 8.6 Knowing the role of your data

PAUSE FOR THOUGHT

Quality over Quantity

In this chapter and throughout this book, we emphasise that there is only one major consideration when making decisions about your research data.

This is that the *quality* **of the sources should always take precedence over** *quantity*.

This is important to recognise to produce persuasive investigations. In research, we want to raise the bar, rather than produce a mediocre investigation where the credibility of your research is challenged.

WHAT ARE SAMPLING STRATEGIES?

In the first part of this chapter, we explored quality processes and, in this part, we consider how you can reduce your possible amount of data through the use of effective sampling processes. Sampling strategies are processes undertaken to select a representative group of data from all the data that are available within the scope of your inquiry. These techniques can support the production of accurate findings without accessing every document or research output on your topic or 'population'. In the section above, we considered inclusion/exclusion criteria and this results in a sampling frame as it narrows down the total population of documents into a typical but condensed selection. This sampling frame reflects three general conditions as outlined by Denscombe (2010: 27):

1. **Relevance:** only data directly linked to the research question or aim.
2. **Completeness:** all relevant items.
3. **Precision:** does not include any data that are not relevant (exclusion criteria).

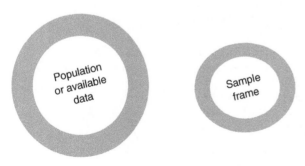

Figure 8.7   An illustration of a population and sample frame

As it can be impossible to examine every single document, a portion (*that which is reduced in number and range in relation to the total available population*) is selected for the analysis. In qualitative secondary research, this is a procedure to select '*texts for inclusion in a research project*' (Grbich 1999: 68). Therefore, sampling is the application of a strategy to extract a sample (*the data you are going to use*) from a population of interest (see Figure 8.7). The goal is to condense the data pool to obtain a conveniently sized data set, which reflects the relevant aspects found in the original whole data collection.

It is of particular importance that the reduced sample reflects, and is therefore representative of, the larger data set to ensure the retention of pertinent data from which you wish to generalise. This means that the sample frame selected must include the features and qualities of the whole data set to support the validity of the research. This is to try to ensure that the sample when analysed, would likely produce equivalent results to the analysis of the original or whole data set.

BOX 8.3   EXPLORING MUSIC CONCERT GOERS' VIEWS

If a researcher wanted to examine national data regarding the satisfaction levels of people attending concerts in the United Kingdom, the population would be *all* concert venues across England, Northern Ireland, Scotland and Wales. If they were to use as their sampling frame, just data from concert halls located in England, the information extracted from them may differ from the full population to which they wish to generalise their results back to (i.e. all concert venues in the United Kingdom).

In this case, the sample will almost certainly be biased because it does not include data from *all* venues (such as those from Northern Ireland, Scotland and Wales) and as such, the sample will differ from the population to which the research findings need to generalise back to.

Types of sampling

Figure 8.8 shows sampling techniques as broadly categorised into two major types.

Probability sampling

Probability sampling relies on the use of random selection to create representation within a sample and this approach is based on statistical theory relating to the 'normal distribution'. This type of sampling is also known as random sampling which involves some form of random selection (*randomisation*). This approach to sampling also tries to ensure that the researcher has limited influence on the selection of what needs to be in the sample.

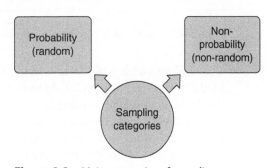

Figure 8.8   Main categories of sampling

There are different ways to achieve this claim to representation or random sampling (Creswell 1998) and one technique that supports these strategies is the use of random number tables or computer-generated numbers (see Figure 8.9). These can be applied to select individual pieces of datum and are used to minimise sampling bias in the sampling process. A number table is a filtering system that generates random data sets. They are easy to access and many statistics books and online sites contain random or computer-generated number tables. A random number table can be generated in Excel (www.excel-easy.com/examples/random-numbers.html). An example of a random number table for numbers between zero and 9,710 is shown in Figure 8.9 (*Please access http://stattrek.com/statistics/random-number-generator. aspx.for more examples*).

Random Number Table					
8	6641	818	272	25	2012
1448	574	139	11	445	171
850	86	4444	99	121	1319
10	1985	141	2797	94	45
233	1	55	9672	98	14
917	7787	1983	5934	336	591
623	7908	8133	2003	73	215
5059	4325	1619	910	419	49
6767	3092	91	289	9191	5004
789	28	3902	2011	1493	4388
8268	96	1958	473	7270	8179
2315	873	9034	2991	1919	4475
3463	7	5601	730	6204	1710
4006	869	106	78	7651	6597
1973	8027	4249	1203	4	1961

Figure 8.9   An example of a random number table

The random number table works as the numbers in the list are arranged so each digit has no predictable relationship to the digits that preceded it or to the digits that followed it. In short, the digits are *randomly* arranged.

You could use these numbers to guide your selection of sources. The example in Box 8.4 of a research study that wants to explore pre-existing research into the relationship between owning a pet snake and perceived happiness of the owners, explains how this can be achieved.

BOX 8.4   IS THERE A LINK BETWEEN HAPPINESS AND SNAKE OWNERSHIP?

A student researcher wants to conduct secondary research to explore if there is a relationship between snake ownership and the state of happiness. When inputting the key words of 'snake ownership' plus 'happiness' into a search engine, a total population of 9,710 pre-existing journal articles on the topic were identified. As this data was set out in list form, she used a Random Number Table (see Figure 8.9) to identify which articles on the list they would choose. They decided that a 1 per cent sample would suffice and selected the 97 journals using the random numbers identified in the list e.g. the 8th, 6,641th, and 818th etc., until a total of 97 data sources had been identified and extracted for secondary analysis.

The example in Box 8.4 employed a 1 per cent sample size. The sample size is dependent upon the potential size of the pre-existing data, in this case 9,710 items of data, but also the level of certainty in the results required. The higher the level of confidence in the results required, the larger a sample might need to be. It may be that whilst the 97 articles identified above from our random selection have researched snake ownership and happiness but to investigate further we may need to examine all the attributes identified across all the 9,710-population data (e.g. gender, age, class, location, number, type of snake, length of time owned, etc.). As such, an arbitrary (random) method of selection may not be successful in representing every variable within the data sampling set. The technique of employing random numbers to select the data is a type of sampling strategy categorised as *probability systematic sampling*.

Probability sampling methods, such as the random number table in Figure 8.9, are also known as *random sampling* or *representative sampling*. This is so the data or 'population' have equal chances of being included in the sample. This type of sample is considered as fending off claims of bias as the researcher does not choose the sample; the system applied governs the selection, thus reducing researcher influence. Figure 8.10 provides some examples of probability sampling methods.

As identified in our example of 'snake ownership and happiness', the random number selection may not be useful for exploring all the relevant variables which influence the relationship between snake ownership and happiness. So, although this type of sampling technique reduces the chance of sampling bias, a more representative sample may be produced by employing non-probability sampling methods, which are explored next.

Non-probability sampling

Non-probability or exploratory approaches are not randomised and involve the researcher, in some way, in the selection process of their sample. The approaches shown in Figure 8.11 are often employed in qualitative research. Non-probability sampling is also known as *judgement* or *non-random sampling* and it is possible that the researcher selects the sample using their

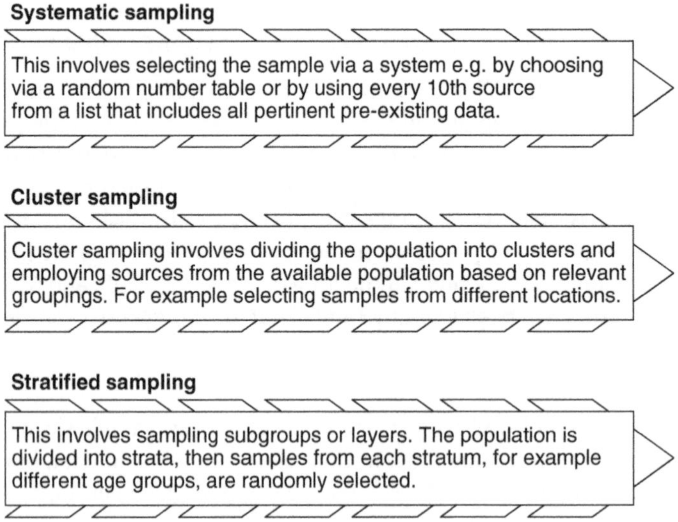

Systematic sampling

This involves selecting the sample via a system e.g. by choosing via a random number table or by using every 10th source from a list that includes all pertinent pre-existing data.

Cluster sampling

Cluster sampling involves dividing the population into clusters and employing sources from the available population based on relevant groupings. For example selecting samples from different locations.

Stratified sampling

This involves sampling subgroups or layers. The population is divided into strata, then samples from each stratum, for example different age groups, are randomly selected.

Figure 8.10   Examples of types of probability (randomised) sampling techniques

subjective judgement to meet the needs of their research (see Box 8.5). Whilst a researcher can apply a selection of mechanisms to reduce their bias in this process, the sample cannot always be claimed to be fully representative of the population. Figure 8.11 provides an overview of some of the main non-probability sampling strategies.

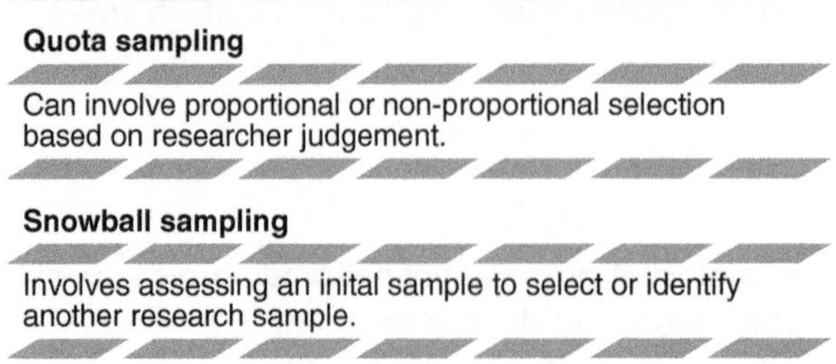

Opportunity sampling

Consists of obtaining the sample from those easily available or more convenient to access for the researcher.

Purposeful sampling

Purposive sampling relies on the researcher's judgement to select a sample based on the purpose of the study.

Quota sampling

Can involve proportional or non-proportional selection based on researcher judgement.

Snowball sampling

Involves assessing an inital sample to select or identify another research sample.

Figure 8.11   Purposeful sampling strategies

In addition to the above sampling techniques is theoretical sampling. If you are contemplating using grounded theory as an approach to your research, you might need to consider this form of non-probability sampling closely linked to grounded theory (see Chapter 11). In grounded theory, the researcher first analyses data to generate a theory, a new sample is selected to test this theory, so the new sample becomes theoretically defined. In this way, the researcher *'decides what data to collect next and where to find them, in order to develop his theory as it emerges'* (Glaser & Strauss 1967: 45).

BOX 8.5   SNOWBALL SAMPLING

A researcher may access an essential document as data. This may be because it has been produced by a leading academic scholar or key author in your chosen field (*purposive sampling*).

To select additional sources for analysis, the researcher reads the document and identifies cited authors that seem relevant and appropriate to her research. She accesses the reference list to identify the source location.

She notes these down and searches for them and repeats the process of reading, identification and searching. Each time she does this, her sample grows like a rolling snowball (*snowball sampling*) until it is considered that sufficient sources are gathered to answer the research question.

If she had a large sample to select from she could use a random number table and then apply quota sampling. This would ensure that the 'population' she wished to generalise to is represented in the sample.

PAUSE FOR THOUGHT

Reusing existing research data

If you are reusing data, you could access a research archive or repository and create a refined list using filters and limiters (see Chapter 7). When the list reflects your research focus then you have created a sampling frame (Xiao-Bai & Varghese 2008). Remember to keep a record of this to demonstrate your approach to sampling.

Sample size

A common question asked by secondary researchers is, *'how many sources do I need?'* This is akin to asking, *'how long is a length of string?'* There are generally no conventions or hard and fast rules as to the number you need; however, in quantitative research where a statistical test needs to be applied there may be a minimum number (see Chapter 12). In qualitative research, numbers may be dependent upon the methodological perspective taken. Research that involves just one interview is valid for example within oral history as single qualitative interviews can produce detailed accounts to explore (Passerini 2012).

In order to decide how many sources is enough the researcher must interrogate the research. Keep in mind that often investigations are time bound and there may be practical realistic reasons for examining only a limited sample within your secondary research. Therefore, data reduction is essential as it is not always practical to work with all the available data as it is much faster and more convenient to work with a condensed sample. Reducing your data to a manageable sample size is a practical response to data management. You need to select a sample size that meets the focus of your research question and the variables required to explore it.

Combining sampling strategies

Employing sampling strategies can be very useful for your research. However, researchers often combine more than one sampling strategy in the same research study. As mentioned, a common approach to data collection is opportunity (*convenience*) sampling, where you use data you have easy access to. This then can lead to employing a key pre-existing document which can support the adoption of another sampling technique such as snowball sampling strategy. Whilst not completely without bias, the combination of sampling strategies can be used to complement other research methods. For example, the de-employment of snowball sampling strategy can decrease some aspects of researcher bias as you are not directly selecting the sources for analysis.

However, there are some concerns when considering the mixing of samples for mixed method research. Collins, Onwuegbuzie & Jiao (2007: 269) ask:

> is it appropriate to triangulate, expand, compare, or consolidate quantitative data originating from a large, random sample with qualitative data arising from a small, purposive sample?' How much weight should researchers and/or consumers place on qualitative data compared to quantitative data?

The answers to Collins, Onwuegbuzie & Jiao (2007) lie within each particular study but as we have emphasised throughout, quality qualitative secondary research requires quality sources.

PAUSE FOR THOUGHT

Which strategy should I use?

You need to use the strategy that makes sense for your research and this may be opportunity or convenience sampling. This is a much-used form of sampling as this consists of procuring a sample that is most easily accessed and generally fits the criteria under examination. However, you still need to demonstrate the quality of your data. Just because it is 'convenient' does not mean issues such as quality should be overlooked.

SEEKING RESEARCH QUALITY

In Chapter 4 we discussed the need to consider research quality and that transparent research provides evidence of where steps have been taken to gain this. We explored how writing an effective and detailed methodology could support replicability and that selecting the 'right' type of data enables us to aim for transferability or generalisability. Therefore being able to select quality data needs to begin with processes of critical evaluation and appraisal of worth. In your literature review this is related to the inclusion/exclusion criteria we can apply to sift sources to ensure we get the ones that offer strong supporting evidence. In Chapter 4, we provided four criteria of quality, and engaging in effective sampling and quality processes can reflect the criteria as follows:

- **Credibility:** using appraisal and evaluation processes to gain sources that have been considered for their authenticity, credibility, and meaning;
- **Dependability:** consistent and systematic application of strategies to enhance data quality;
- **Transferability:** sampling processes to select sources that could be generalised to a wider set of sources;
- **Confirmability:** use of sampling processes to remove researcher influence.

PAUSE FOR THOUGHT

Recording your decisions

In Chapter 4, we considered the creation of an audit trail to enhance research transparency and promote the trust and confidence people can have in your research. Therefore, keep records of your sampling and critical appraisal decisions. You may need to have these ready for when you write your methodology as you need to defend the choices you make.

- You could use a research diary, as we discussed in Chapters 2 and 4.
- You could insert a copy of your data selection criteria in your appendix to show the thoroughness of your approach.

Please refer to your institutional handbook and guidelines for this aspect as there may be a specific way you need to approach the provision of supporting documents.

REFLECTION AND FURTHER READING

At the beginning of the chapter we set out what you should be able to do when you reached the end of this chapter. To aid your reflection on all we have covered we ask some chapter specific questions. If you are unsure of any of your answers to these questions, please go back to the relevant section to review this aspect.

REFLECTING ON CHAPTER 8

In this chapter we have:

- **Considered the importance of quality over quantity:** Is data overload going to be a potential problem in your research area?
- **Reviewed what is meant by quality data:** How well do you 'know' your data? How will you assess the quality of your data? Will you apply criterion checklists to assess data quality, if so which ones?
- **Examined strategies to reduce your data:** Which data reduction techniques suit your research data? How well do you understand the sampling strategies?
- **Considered how to secure research quality:** How can you demonstrate research is credible?

WE RECOMMEND FOR FURTHER READING:

Checkmarket (2018) *Sample Size calculator*. Available at: www.checkmarket.com/sample-size-calculator/.
This website provides guidance on sample sizes.

Cottrell, S. (2005) *Critical Thinking Skills*. Basingstoke, UK: Palgrave.
This is a user-friendly guide to critical thinking and provides examples of relevant and extremely useful critical appraisal checklists that you can use or adapt.

Daniel, J. (2012) *Sampling Essentials: Practical Guidelines for Making Sampling Choices*. Thousand Oaks. CA: SAGE Publications, Inc.
We recommend Chapter 1, as it provides a thorough overview of sampling processes.

Mason, J. (2018) *Qualitative Researching* (3rd edn). London: SAGE Publications Ltd.
We suggest you read Chapter 3 in the latest edition of this readable book. It covers the sampling of documents as data including visual data and objects, so it is highly recommended.

Robson, C. (2002) *Real World Research* (2nd edn). Oxford, UK: Blackwell.
We recommend Chapter 8, which begins with surveys and questionnaires, but continue to the end as it provides a clear overview of sampling process.

The Foundation for Critical Thinking (2017) *College and University students*. Available at: www.criticalthinking.org/pages/college-and-university-students/799.
This website offers a wide range of critical thinking resources.

Web Center for Social Research Methods (2006) *Sampling*. Available at: https://socialre-searchmethods.net/kb/sampling.php.
This site offers a concise overview of sampling approaches and terminology.

9
CONSTRUCTING A LITERATURE REVIEW

THIS CHAPTER WILL SUPPORT YOUR ABILITY TO

know the function of a literature review

identify the type of literature you need to review

create literature and synthesis matrices

write an effective literature review

CHAPTER OVERVIEW

This chapter sets out the purpose of a literature review within qualitative secondary research. We explore this purpose as a contextualisation of the research topic where key literature, concepts, arguments, theories and theorists are explored. To support your completion of your review, we offer a questioning approach to the selection of your sources that encourages you to consider the 'what', 'why', 'where', 'when' 'who' and 'how' of your source selection.

We also offer some practical strategies and advice which include the generation of literature and synthesis matrices and provide examples of how these can be used to create the logical reasoning you need to demonstrate in your literature review. Highly effective strategies are provided to support you as you write your review. Strategies such as using the right verb in the right place, writing for a known reader and drafting and editing can add to the quality of the work you produce. By the end of this chapter, you should have a clear understanding of how to conduct a literature review for your qualitative secondary research.

WHAT IS A LITERATURE REVIEW?

In Chapter 1, we stated that qualitative secondary research is much more than a review of literature on your topic. But within your qualitative secondary research project you will still need to complete a literature review. Your review should play a pivotal role in providing a meaningful context for your research question(s) and/or aim(s) and for the findings you will generate.

Your literature review is the part of your research process where sources of data are analysed, evaluated, critiqued and synthesised and, presented in a logical and coherent way. Your review is where you demonstrate your knowledge of your subject, evaluate what is known on your subject and highlight any possible gaps. Thus, a strong literature review provides a firm foundation for your inquiry and when done well, it should demonstrate how your research can contribute to knowledge in your subject area or discipline. As we outline in Figure 9.1, there are some things a literature review should not be.

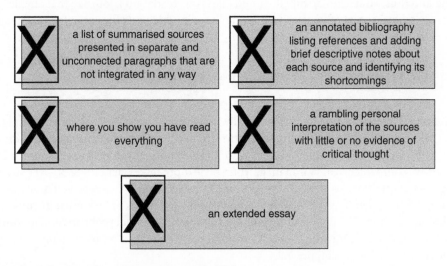

Figure 9.1   Knowing what a literature review is NOT

When you construct your literature review, you should seek existing literature that frames your research question(s) and/or aim(s). To do this, you may draw upon academic and scholarly work provided by leading researchers, theorists and commentators in your field who have explored your topic. This may be in the form of existing research studies where you can explore and critique their methodologies and findings; scholarly articles which consider the role and function of theory; or that you review arguments provided in books that set out accepted thinking about your subject. What it should not be is a description of everything there is to know on your research topic. Your review therefore, should reflect your filtered selection of key sources as you try to reduce what is written on your topic. To do this, skills of critical appraisal need to be employed as you actively seek strong and credible sources of evidence for your review.

Your review of literature is also where you should reflect current debates and tensions both in and around the subject of your research. Whilst it can be tempting to only include sources whose perspectives and argument agree with yours, you need to present a balanced critical debate. Your literature review is where you need to consider diverse opinions and alternative viewpoints to ensure you are not just creating an echo chamber of your own thoughts and opinions in your research. We discussed this in Chapter 3 as being aware of potential forms of bias; therefore, we advise you to think of your review as providing context and substance for your research and also as a forum for exploring critical perspectives and divergent views. This approach to alternative viewpoints is what Booth, Colomb and Williams (2008: 89) describe as '*looking for creative disagreement*'.

When a literature review is done well it should be a joy to read. Partly because it reflects your subject knowledge but also as it demonstrates your skills of critical reading and critical writing and thus, your scholarship. It should take your reader on a journey that enables them to appreciate the context of your chosen research topic which sets the scene for your research.

CONDUCTING YOUR LITERATURE REVIEW

Conducting a literature review is not usually something that can be winged or fudged. It should take time to select your sources and time to evaluate these for relevance and for credibility. Therefore, it is advisable to begin with a clear and focused plan (see Chapter 2) and consider ways in which you can manage your review process. Hart (1998: 30–31) advocates asking a set of questions to structure your thinking as you begin your review. These questions encourage you to identify what is already known and what needs to be known in your subject area. Using questions like these can inspire you to explore potential problems and identify and locate key arguments. Drawing on Hart's approach, we provide a set of questions to support your literature search (see Figure 9.2).

The questions we ask in Figure 9.2 encourage you to make decisions about the literature you select. This approach enables you to achieve step one of what Goldman and Schmalz (2004: 5) ascertain are four clear steps in the process of literature review creation:

1.   Making decisions about which documents to review.
2.   Reading and understanding what authors present.
3.   Evaluating any ideas, research methods and results in each publication.
4.   Writing a synthesis that includes both the content and a critical analysis of the materials.

Providing a full response to Goldman and Schmalz's (2004) steps 2 and 3 may require the completion of a literature matrix or concept map (Figure 9.3). A literature matrix is an organisational structure that encourages a structured response to the identification, recording and use of your sources (Klopper, Lubbe & Rugbeer 2007). It provides conceptual scaffolding as it

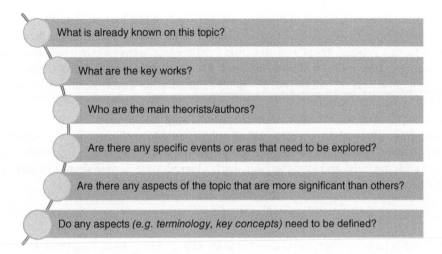

What is already known on this topic?

What are the key works?

Who are the main theorists/authors?

Are there any specific events or eras that need to be explored?

Are there any aspects of the topic that are more significant than others?

Do any aspects *(e.g. terminology, key concepts)* need to be defined?

Figure 9.2   Using questions to begin your literature review

affords a visualisation of the important sources you have identified and the main concepts they include. You can see what you are reading and this helps you make more informed choices as to what you could or should read next.

	source type	key concepts explored	main conclusions	limitations	key references	connection to research question/aim
1						
2						
3						
4						
5						

Figure 9.3   An example of a literature matrix template

How you use this matrix is dependent on how you like to work. You could create separate matrices for each concept you explore. This can help you generate a synthesis matrix, which we explore later. Matrices like this are designed to be working documents that you annotate and review. It is most unlikely that any matrix you create will remain the same and be a highly polished piece of work. As you engage in more focused and narrowed reading your matrix will change; sources will be removed and others included. Using a matrix supports your understanding of what is happening in your subject area and it enables to you to identify and locate ideas, methods and connections to your work and the work of others.

When you immerse yourself in reading, you will find yourself exposed to the existence of models, concepts, theories and findings. In Chapter 2, we explored the looping process when you read. In this process, there is a dynamic relationship between what you read and the development of your question. Therefore, having a research question(s) and/or aim(s), even if it is still in development, can be useful when you begin your search for your sources of data required for your literature review.

Your review therefore should be undertaken with diligence as it should highlight key areas of debate, draw attention to any gaps found in current and past research and signpost the direction of your research. Therefore, each article or source should be carefully selected because it adds meaning and value to your work. Overall, your review should be informative to both you and your reader (Onwuegbuzie & Frels 2016).

The difference between sources of data for your literature review and data for analysis

The main difference between data for analysis and data for your literature review is defined by your research question(s) and/or aim(s) and the sources you could include in your literature review. In Chapter 6, we explored documentary source as data and considered that there was some crossover, as data such as a government report had relevance within your literature review but it could also be used as data for analysis. To provide some clarity, in Figure 9.4, we explore the main uses of sources of data in your literature review and your analysis.

In a literature review ...	For your data analysis ...
• you select sources that contextualise your research • you are demonstrating academic engagement through your knowledge of leaders or key experts in your subject area • you are showing through your selection of sources an awareness of the main concepts for enquiry • you are providing a theoretical and conceptual framework for your question • you are building on existing research • you are appraising literature for its quality • you are showing your ability to synthesise and reduce substantial amounts of literature to form key points for discussion • you are providing supporting evidence for any findings generated and any claims made	• you will be guided by your literature review to identify data that can be analysed to understand the phenomena/phenomenon you wish to explore • you will appraise data, so it can be considered credible, authentic and trustworthy • you will analyse this data using a method of analysis to generate findings to help you answer your research question(s) and/or aim(s)

Figure 9.4   Using sources as data in your qualitative secondary research

PAUSE FOR THOUGHT

Remember to check what you need to do

Whilst we acknowledge that different disciplines have differing approaches to qualitative secondary research, we strongly advise you to include your approach to selecting your sources of evidence for your literature review in your research project. It may take the form of a criterion-based checklist which is then included in an appendix or within your methodology. Approaching your research in this way adds to its transparency (see Chapter 4) as you explain precisely how you searched for and selected the literature included in your review. Such an approach is invaluable in creating an audit trail as you can see how the research is constructed.

Sources for your literature review

The sources you need for your literature review are those that provide a solid and grounded context for the question you ask. They should provide insight, understanding and be reflective of scholarship in your subject or discipline. Hart (1998: 13) articulates what your selected documents or sources should provide in your review: '*information, ideas, data and evidence written from a particular standpoint to fulfil certain aims or express certain views on the nature of the topic and how it is to be investigated*'. The sources you select for your review reveal much about you as a researcher and an academic because your academic judgement is reflected in the sources of literature you select and, as we explore later, how you write.

When you undertake a literature review you are trying to demonstrate your information searching skills and your knowledge and understanding of your topic. To do this effectively and to provide a robust and secure foundation for your research, your literature review should include a wide range of sources such as books, scholarly articles, existing research, legislation, policy and any other sources relevant to your research focus or theory. When considering types of sources to include in your literature review, Wallace and Wray (2011) offer four useful classifications (see Figure 9.5).

There are no definitive lists as to what literature you need to or can select as this depends on your subject or discipline, the research question(s) and/or aim(s) and your identified theoretical and conceptual frameworks. However, a good literature review should engage with the most authoritative and authentic sources you can find. This quest for authority and authenticity may lead you to include many forms of data (see Chapter 6).

It can be frustrating searching for the sources of literature you need and sometimes you may think that your search has led you to a dead end, but before you tell your tutor or supervisor that you cannot find any literature on your subject, please reflect on Merriam's (2009: 72) wise claim that '*there is always some research study, some theory, some thinking related to the problem that can be reviewed to inform the study at hand*'.

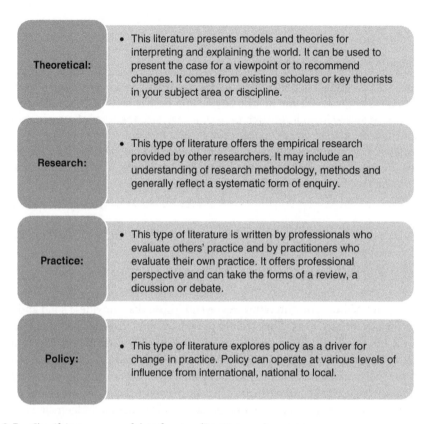

Theoretical:
- This literature presents models and theories for interpreting and explaining the world. It can be used to present the case for a viewpoint or to recommend changes. It comes from existing scholars or key theorists in your subject area or discipline.

Research:
- This type of literature offers the empirical research provided by other researchers. It may include an understanding of research methodology, methods and generally reflect a systematic form of enquiry.

Practice:
- This type of literature is written by professionals who evaluate others' practice and by practitioners who evaluate their own practice. It offers professional perspective and can take the forms of a review, a dicussion or debate.

Policy:
- This type of literature explores policy as a driver for change in practice. Policy can operate at various levels of influence from international, national to local.

Figure 9.5   Classifying sources of data for your literature review

Making a critical selection of literature

You may feel daunted by the prospect of ensuring you select quality sources for your review and, therefore, evaluation checklists can be useful as they offer a critical filter through which to review your sources, supporting the judgements you make. Using checklists to search for 'quality' literature demonstrates your awareness of the importance of having sources of data in your literature review that are authentic, credible, representative and meaningful (Scott 1990), thus adding to the trustworthiness of your research. We explored critical evaluation and appraisal in more depth in Chapter 8 but Figure 9.6 provides an overview of the main considerations needed when evaluating sources of data.

Checklists reflect your active engagement in your filtering of your data, encouraging you to consider the sources that are credible and authoritative. Only using sources that are credible and relevant is essential for your research quality because the sources you select for your literature review function in two main ways as they are:

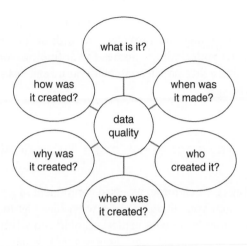

Figure 9.6 Basic components for establishing data quality

- **informative:** They provide a context for your study and identify what is known in your subject area;
- **confirmatory:** They help you make sense of your findings and situate these findings within existing knowledge of your subject area.

Therefore, making sure you have the most relevant sources for your review is crucial at the beginning of your topic and at its end.

Your influence on your source selection

It is also important to be aware of your influence on the selection, analysis and evaluation of sources. In Chapter 3, we explored researcher influence because who you are as a person and researcher frames your view of the whole research process and this includes conducting your literature review. Your influence will be felt on the range of literature you read and on your selection of sources. There is a strong relationship between what you read and the development of your conceptual and theoretical framework.

This means being aware of forms of cognitive bias that your influence can generate and, whilst we explored this in more depth in Chapter 3, consider how confirmation bias can exist in your literature review. Confirmation bias is often an unconscious act of only referring to those perspectives that reflect our pre-existing views, while at the same time ignoring or dismissing those views, beliefs or opinions that, whilst valid, can challenge our way of thinking.

Therefore, in your literature review try to demonstrate that you are aware of alternative arguments or opposing views. This approach can counter any claims of confirmation bias but it also reflects your wider understanding of your subject area. Including diverse viewpoints strengthens your line of reasoning and provides you with an increased range of literature which can help you interpret your findings. Some of your findings may answer your question and some may not. Including a diverse selection of literature enables you to make sense of any divergent findings that emerge.

Your literature review as a show case for your skills

When you are undertaking research for an assessed component of a course you need to demonstrate your scholarship and your literature review enables you to do this. Your literature review is where you can demonstrate your critical reading and writing skills; effective information search strategies; and competent data management. When you come to write your review, your ability to synthesise and generate new found connections should be obvious to your reader.

Your literature review is where you can show skills of analysis, synthesis and evaluation. These are higher order cognitive skills and are defined by Bloom et al. (1956 – and revised by Anderson et al. (2001); see Chapter 14) as the following:

- **Evaluation:** judging/appraising/assessing
- **Synthesis:** generating new ideas from existing knowledge
- **Analysis:** breaking things into smaller components
- **Application:** using information to solve problems
- **Comprehension:** understanding
- **Knowledge:** knowing

By conducting and constructing a literature review you should be able to demonstrate the skills identified in the list above. You should be able to show your knowledge and comprehension of past and current ways of thinking, key theorists within your subject area and their work. You should be able to apply this knowledge to your research question(s) and/or aim(s) and engage in processes of analysis, synthesis and evaluation. Consequently, as Figure 9.7 shows, your literature review affords an opportunity to highlight your many abilities.

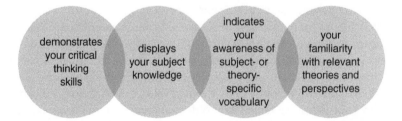

Figure 9.7   Showcasing your skills in your literature review

PAUSE FOR THOUGHT

Where do I use my selected sources of data?

There are **three** key sections where your sources of evidence may be used:

- In your introduction or rationale – to provide a justification for your choice of study;
- In your literature review – to indicate what has gone before and what is now known;
- In the discussion of your findings – where you interpret your findings.

You should include indicative reading when you complete your research proposal (see Chapter 2).
   It is possible that you will use some of the same sources in each section. Therefore, investing time and energy into finding the most appropriate sources will benefit your research project. Remember, your rationale is where you argue that your topic or study is worthy of research and your defence will be helped by some well-chosen and pertinent sources of evidence.

WRITING YOUR LITERATURE REVIEW

Ensuring you have located relevant and credible sources is essential as these are the ingredients for the review you need to write. However, turning these into a clear, coherent and logical review can be a challenging prospect and is something frequently *'poorly done'* (Randolph 2009: 1). The critical gaze you adopted when searching for your sources (see Chapter 8) now needs to be used within the construction of your review.

   As Figure 9.8 indicates, your literature review needs to have certain attributes and we cover these in more detail later in this section but, as a brief overview these are:

Authoritative: uses language to communicate knowledge and understanding in an authoritative manner;

Analysed/Synthesised/Evaluated: identifies specific aspects; identifies similarities, combines existing ideas to create new ways of thinking and appraises these ways of thinking;

Accurate/Clear: well-referenced, proofread and edited;

Logical/Signposted: uses effective language structures to indicate lines of argument;

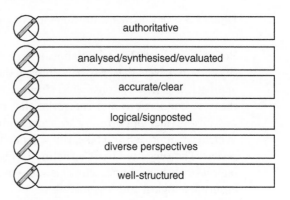

Figure 9.8   Key attributes of a well-written literature review

Diverse perspective: well-rounded response that embraces tensions and debates and accepts alternative perspectives;

Well-structured: presented with points for discussion provided in a clear and logical way.

PAUSE FOR THOUGHT

Check first before writing

There are different ways of thinking about the structure of your review. You may have some choice in this process or it may be specified in your institutional guidelines. Therefore, we advise you to check how you should approach the writing of this section before you begin to avoid any potential misconceptions and possible disruption to your study.

The following section explores how to set out your work in a clear and logical way as you need to adopt a structure that enables you to contextualise your study for your reader in an academically orientated way. To aid you in this, there are some acknowledged organisational approaches that may support the writing of your review and Figure 9.9 presents two such ways.

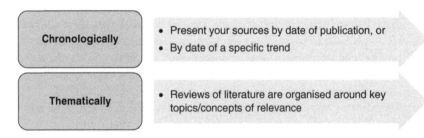

Figure 9.9   Organisational structures for writing your review

Providing a chronological timeline of your research context can be useful if you need to identify certain drivers that may have impacted on your topic. However, a thematic or conceptual approach is generally considered stronger as it affords opportunities to draw out important theories, connections and categories that could be significant within your research. It also provides greater opportunity to show your skills of synthesis and knowledge integration. Whichever approach you take, you will need to tell your reader how you are constructing your review. The suggested basic structure in Figure 9.10 would be the same for either a chronological or thematic approach. This way your review can be read as an interconnected whole ensuring a logical and reasoned flow.

When you write your introduction consider using a 'narrative hook'. This is a short piece of persuasive text that grabs your reader's attention and gets them interested. The piece of text

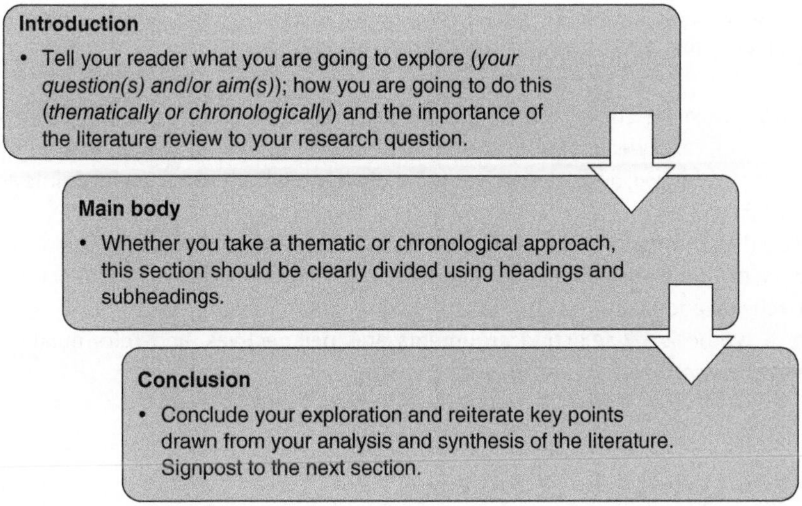

Introduction
- Tell your reader what you are going to explore (*your question(s) and/or aim(s)*); how you are going to do this (*thematically or chronologically*) and the importance of the literature review to your research question.

Main body
- Whether you take a thematic or chronological approach, this section should be clearly divided using headings and subheadings.

Conclusion
- Conclude your exploration and reiterate key points drawn from your analysis and synthesis of the literature. Signpost to the next section.

Figure 9.10   Constructing your review

in Box 9.1 uses strong and powerful language designed to elicit some response from the reader. They may not agree, or they may think you have captured the scene wonderfully but, whatever they think, at least they are thinking and therefore, engaged.

BOX 9.1   CREATING A NARRATIVE HOOK

Narrative hooks generate interest. The text below sets the scene for a study on women returning to study. It is written in an expressive way to stimulate interest but each one of the issues identified will be explored in the review.

Transition is at best a confusing process of academic and personal realignment. However, when women experience transition to academic study, they often do so within a battle for their time and identity. This battle is created by the intersecting forces of the domestic, professional and personal realms that exert pressure on them as they endeavour to navigate their way to aspired study. It is against this background that this study …

Engaging in ethical criticism

Conducting a literature review should involve aspects of academic criticism as this is inherent within processes of analysis, evaluation, interpretation and in the identification of held beliefs and views of others. However, this should be undertaken in a professional and ethically responsible way (see Chapter 5). Based on a list of characteristics of effective criticism presented by Hart (1998: 177), we offer the following guidance:

- agreeing with, or defending a position, or confirming its usefulness through an evaluation of its strengths and weaknesses;
- conceding that an existing approach or point of view has both some useful points and some less useful;
- focus on the arguments and theories not the author – it should never be personal;
- be aware of your own perspectives and standpoint and how this can influence the critical approach you adopt;
- create a synthesis by selecting arguments and perspectives, and reformulate these to generate new connections and ways of knowing.

Creating a synthesis of sources

The writing of a literature review is as Merriam (1988: 6) confirms '*an interpretation and synthesis of published work*'. Therefore in your literature review, you need to appraise and synthesise the work of others and do this in an evaluative and critical way (Saunders et al. 2009). What you are aiming for is text that demonstrates your ability to combine key concepts and thoughts of others to form new ways of thinking and new ways of knowing.

Synthesis is a process of making connections or putting things together and combining the ideas of more than one source with your own. This requires you to highlight what is important and similar across several studies to establish what is significant to your research. For example, suppose you are researching female violence. You read articles that focus on how aggression in women has been assessed as you want to explore variations in assessment. Therefore, you amalgamate what you have read to combine the information gained to reflect this focus (see Box 9.2).

BOX 9.2 RESEARCH ON FEMALE VIOLENCE

Research indicates that there are a number of approaches to assessing female aggression. One study found a higher prevalence of physical aggression committed by women (Archer 2000). A later study also found a higher prevalence of women committing physical aggression (Straus 2004). This trend is found when examining psychological aggression. Cercone, Beach and Arias (2005) found no significant differences between college men and women on the perpetration of minor (86% versus 89%, respectively) or more serious (30% versus 27%, respectively) forms of psychological aggression. However, it is recognised that this was violence involving male partners and, whilst it may appear that there are similar levels of females who are violent, women are more likely than men to be injured during domestic violence incidents and to suffer more severe injuries (Swan et al. 2008).

Strategies exist to support you in the development of this skill and an effective one to use is a synthesis matrix (see Figure 9.11). You can use your literature matrix to support this process of synthesis as it is based on similar principles but each synthesis matrix you create should contain texts indicating specific concepts, lines of argument or debate for you to review. When these are completed you can begin to see patterns and connections emerge and how these separate texts relate or do not relate to each other. Figure 9.11 is an example of a synthesis matrix generated from a narrow set of scholarly articles that explore the concept of transition for women entering university or other higher education settings.

Author	Theme 1	Theme 2	Theme 3
Brine and Waller (2004)	*Transition is not straightforward – it's a period of risk, confusion and contradiction.*	**Returning to education challenges women's identities as learners, their classed identities and their classed femininities.**	*The risk of academic failure is strong in transition. Compounds low self-esteem of those already educationally disadvantaged.*
Reay (2003)	~~The desire to 'give something back' is a motivation.~~	<u>Sacrifice of social life due to time poverty, creating a lack of time and no 'care of the self.'</u>	**Wanting to be more than their current self, creates tensions between families, women and their aspiration.**
Penketh and Goddard (2008)	A 'beset by trials' narrative emerges where competing demands of family life influence study. (p. 322)	*Transition is discussed as a time when learners may be less resilient due to personal, social and academic change.*	<u>Time management was a persistent theme in the narratives.</u>

Figure 9.11   A synthesis matrix of research exploring mature women entering higher education

The markings in Figure 9.11 indicate the connections and similarities found:

- Italicised text are those themes that focus on women and transition as a problematic process;
- Strike through text provides evidence of motivation for the transition;
- Plain text indicates the influence of transition in women's domestic, caring roles and home life;

- Bold text is how women's identities were challenged by this transition;
- Underlined text indicates the significance of time.

This matrix (see Figure 9.11) can then be used to create a piece of synthesised text (Box 9.3). This example (see also Figure 9.3) and the one provided in Box 9.2 illustrate different approaches to what Golden-Biddle and Locke (2007: 33) describe as '*synthesised coherence*' which is the skill of constructing text from ones that were previously unrelated.

BOX 9.3   USING A SYNTHESIS MATRIX: MATURE WOMEN ENTERING HIGHER EDUCATION

Using the themes gained from the matrix (see Figure 9.11), it is possible to see how some of these can be synthesised:

Research on transition from Foundation degree to higher level study for women presents a complex picture. This research suggests that the process of moving from one level of study to another can threaten women's identity (Brine & Waller 2004: Reay 2003) and compound their low self-esteem. Likewise, there is some consensus that transition exposes women to increased risk of academic failure (Brine & Waller 2004: Penketh & Goddard 2008).

Additionally, there is an influence felt on women's domestic lives as seen within research offered by Penketh and Goddard (2008) who highlight this as a significant theme within the narratives they collected. They describe women trying to study when 'beset by trials' (Penketh & Goddard 2008: 322). Other issues emerge such as concerns relating to time management and time poverty (Reay 2003). Therefore, research into women's transition to study presents this as a time of personal, academic and social change.

Creating a coherent synthesis is a skill that can take practice to develop. It is reliant on other critical skills as there is a strong relationship between being able to critically read the work of others and being able to turn this into critical writing (see Figure 9.12).

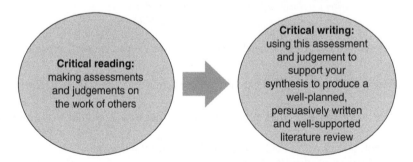

Figure 9.12   The relationship between critical reading and critical writing

Here are some questions to support your ability to synthesise sources of data within your literature review:

- Do your sources agree?
- What are the points of agreement or disagreement?
- Do they draw on different theories or concepts?
- Do they approach the topic from diverse theoretical perspectives?
- Are there clearly defined lines of debate?
- Is one source's position more persuasive than others'?
- Can these differences be easily explained?
- Are the differences related to different times, places, or subject areas?
- What conclusions can be drawn from these differences in positions?
- Does it signpost a change in thinking in your subject or topic area?

Using language effectively when writing your review

Writing for an assessed dissertation or thesis requires a formal approach that involves the use of academic stylistic conventions (*e.g. referencing protocols, correct terminology*) and a formal use of language (*e.g. no slang or colloquial expressions*). It can help to be aware of your reader's expectations and if you are being assessed, these expectations will be on your marking scheme or assessment schema. We advise you to use these criteria to inform your approach to writing. Your use of language should reflect the level of your study and the subject area or discipline. In the section below, we have identified some useful strategies to help you present your arguments clearly:

Paragraph starters

Your style of writing should reflect a flow of discussion rather than a list format. We include some starters for your paragraphs:

- Following on from this …
- Disagreeing with Smith (2017) is …
- Contradicting Cheng's (20015) argument is …
- In a similar way, Largan (2016) believes …
- Agreeing with Morris (2010) is …
- It appears that O'Grady (2015) is misguided when claiming …
- Likewise, it appears that Brown et al. (2012) may have overlooked …

Identifying important works

You can use words to signpost your understanding and acknowledgement of key texts. Onwuegbuzie and Frels (2016: 304) state that the words we have identified in italics '*establish the path of argumentation*' for your reader. If you read these out, you can hear the authoritative tone they create:

- Smith's (2017) *ground breaking theory* sets out...
- Cheng's (20015) work dismisses the *notable contribution* made by...
- Similarly, Largan's (2016) *influential* study...
- Agreeing with Morris' (2010) *classic* research is...
- It appears that in O'Grady's (2015) *pivotal* text...
- Likewise, it appears that Brown et al. (2012) may have overlooked the *cutting edge* contribution by...

Words to signpost arguments

When we write we should create text that has a clear and logical meaning. This meaning can be enhanced by words that signpost the direction of your argument. Cottrell's (2005: 40) seminal text on critical thinking describes an argument as having three key features:

- A point of view;
- An attempt to persuade others to accept this view;
- A reason why your point of view should be accepted.

To ensure you persuade people of your argument, you can use words to signpost your line of reasoning as demonstrated in Figure 9.13.

Role	Words	
To set the scene	firstly ...	to begin with ...
	initially ...	
To add more detail	additionally ...	what is more ...
	furthermore ...	equally ...
	moreover ...	indeed ...
	similarly ...	apart from this ...
	besides ...	
To contrast arguments	nevertheless ...	conversely ...
	alternatively ...	whereas ...
	on the other hand ...	despite this ...

Role	Words	
To agree with arguments	similarly …	also …
	likewise …	in addition …
	again …	
Concluding	therefore …	accordingly …
	subsequently …	as a result …
	hence …	as a consequence …
	consequently …	thus …

Figure 9.13   Signposting arguments using key words

Using verbs accurately

In this section, we explore how slight changes can make a significant impact on your written work. Using the right verb in the right place will add clarity to your analysis, evaluation or presented argument and navigate your reader through the argument you create. In Chapter 13, we encourage you to think carefully about the verbs you use when presenting your evidence. We link this to the need to remain tentative about your findings as words that indicate you have proved something are hard to defend.

In this section, we ask you to consider the verbs for speech action. This can mean trying to find alternative ways of expressing the thoughts and ideas of others without overly using the word 'states'. The word 'states' is comfortable and easy to use as it describes in a factual way what a person said or says. It is therefore a useful word for reporting a thought or statement. However, there are times when you need to use something stronger and something that reflects the argument you should provide. Therefore, we advise you to think about verbs and the strength they can add to your argument (see Figure 9.14). Using the right verb in the right place also provides insight into your knowledge of the author's work and the argument they provide. There can be authority in these words but be mindful that you know the work you are critiquing or reviewing well. The wrong verb in the wrong place can skew your argument and undermine its credibility.

Making sure that your writing has a clear and logical flow can be supported by planning (see Chapter 2). This planning is useful as you can refer to it to ensure you do not lose the thread of your argument and to help maintain your chain of thought. Another way to minimise the risk of losing your way, is to focus on not writing overly long sentences. Long sentences can get you lost within an argument and if you are lost, so is your reader. Try not to make your reader work too hard

Finally, consider the phrase 'if in doubt read it out'. Sometimes we can hear where punctuation should go better than we can see it. If you struggle with grammar, ask a colleague or friend to read your work out or employ widely available text to speech software. Hearing your work read back to you enables you to assess its readability and to check if it makes sense.

Low strength
- Words like *show*, *indicate* and *report* are very descriptive as they say exactly what the author says, thinks or does. These verbs are very important and there is a place for the procedural and functional tone they set.

Medium strength
- Words such as *infers*, *suggests*, *hypothesises* and *implies* are verbs which signpost a cautious response to a possible argument, debate or formed conclusion. They offer a tentative way of expressing knowledge.

Full strength
- Words such as *asserted*, *emphasised*, *ascertained*, *outlined* and *declared* are emphatic within their knowledge claims. These words are '*explicit*' verbs (Onwuegbuzie & Frels 2016: 322) as they reinforce the arguments and claims made.

Figure 9.14   Verb strengths

Writing for a specific audience

Knowing why you are writing and for whom can shape and guide the writing style and tone you need to project. Therefore, Randolph (2009) suggests we should consider our 'audience' carefully. If you are producing a literature review for a dissertation or thesis, then it is more than likely that your audience will be academics who are knowledgeable in your subject area or field. Therefore, you need to use sources of evidence that demonstrate your academic and scholarly judgement to meet the expectations of this audience. This is important to consider as a '*well-constructed literature review is an important criterion in establishing researcher credibility*' (O'Leary 2004: 66).

PAUSE FOR THOUGHT

Inserting images, diagrams or tables

It is possible to insert images, graphs and tables into your review, but they need to be used wisely. They can be very useful if you are using a specific model or theory in your research which can be made more accessible if presented diagrammatically.

If they are used, they should add to the narrative you create and reflect high standards of presentation and accuracy. This means clear labelling and effective signposting so the reader knows why they are there.

However, in all things, make sure you check your institution's guidelines and check with your supervisor.

Using drafting and editing processes

Whilst this is focused on your literature review, the processes of drafting and editing are relevant to all parts of your completed project. They are two skills that when used effectively can allow your words and thoughts to shine through.

Drafting

It is very rare for anyone to be able to assemble their thoughts in such a coherent and effective manner that they can write their review in one take. Most people write in stages, to sketch out ideas which eventually become more established as the writing develops. Therefore, each draft should be a refinement of what was written before. A drafting process is also a reflective process where you can think about the knowledge you are collecting, how this extends and enhances your understanding and how you can communicate this. The number of drafts needed is up to you, your writing style, possibly your supervisor and the time you have available. As we explore in Chapter 9, make sure you are saving and labelling your drafts in a systematic way.

Editing

This is the process of critical review and revision. It includes the act of proofreading where aspects such as spelling, grammar, the use of figures and terminology are reviewed for accuracy and consistency. It is difficult to spot your own mistakes so it is advisable to ask someone, preferably someone who knows nothing about your research, to review your work when it needs editing. Having an objective reader or non-subject specialist review your work means they can look for the technical aspects of your writing rather than content. This means they can focus on your sentence structure, grammar, coherence and clarity rather than the meaning of your content. If you are unable to find anyone to help there are many useful editing features within Word. Some versions of Word will read your work out loud for you, making it easier to spot errors.

PAUSE FOR THOUGHT

Writing your literature review

Including the best sources in your literature review is essential but these need to be presented reflecting a well-written and coherent assessment of your topic area. This is not just in the structure you adopt but also how each paragraph links to the other. This means you could use a process called 'signposting' which, when mastered, enhances the flow of your work and its intelligibility. Consider the following:

- **Connect** your ideas by using paragraphs that explore a single theme or an aspect of this. Keeping your paragraphs focused and linked in this way will help your readers understand your argument.
- **Signpost** each new paragraph to show how it advances your argument. Signposting is the use of a topic sentence at the beginning of a paragraph to indicate the transition from the previous paragraph. Your transitions should inform in such a way that it is easy to see how each new point or piece of evidence links by building on the one before.

A useful piece of advice is to never let your reader work too hard, especially if it is your marker!

A CHECKLIST FOR COMPLETING YOUR REVIEW

As your literature review is a key component of your research, it is worth checking to make sure you have a firm understanding of how it should be approached. Ask yourself the following questions (see Figure 9.15):

Ask yourself ...	Think ...
Does my literature review relate to my research questions?	Is this clear in your review? Are the headings linked to the concepts within your question or aim?
Is my literature review presented in a persuasive manner? **Is the structure clear, logical and coherent?**	Have you used headings and sub headings to indicate the narrowing down of the themes? Is it easy to see how one theme leads to another – is this well signposted?
Is my review written in a critically and evaluative way? **Is there evidence that I have synthesised my sources?**	Have you written a synthesised account of the literature and not just provided a list of what each article or author states?

Ask yourself …	Think …
Have I used a range of sources that are relevant to my field of study? **Have I applied a critical filter to these to ensure I have included those sources that will add benefit to my research?** **Have I referenced these correctly?**	Are you using a range of sources that indicate your awareness of your subject area or discipline? Have you used the most appropriate sources? (*academic, practice or policy orientated*). Have you selected these using a critical appraisal checklist or through the application or rigorous filters? Have you referenced and shown your academic skills in the process?
Does my literature review have an introduction, main body and a conclusion?	Have you ensured you have set the scene for your review, organised the main body for meaning and checked that your conclusion discusses the main points raised but also signpost the next part of the research project.

Figure 9.15   A checklist for completing your literature review

REFLECTION AND FURTHER READING

At the beginning of the chapter we set out what you should be able to do when you reached the end of this chapter. To aid your reflection on all we have covered we ask some chapter specific questions. If you are unsure of any of your answers to these questions, please go back to the relevant section to review this aspect.

REFLECTING ON CHAPTER 9

In this chapter we have:

- **Explained what a literature review is and its function in your research project:** Can you identify two key functions of a literature review?
- **Identified the type of literature you need to review:** Do you know what type of literature you need to include in your review? What are the two main roles performed by your sources of data in your literature review?
- **Provided examples of a literature and synthesis matrix:** Can you define the process of synthesis?
- **Offered advice on writing your review:** How will you write your review? Do you know who your audience is?

WE RECOMMEND FOR FURTHER READING:

Booth, W.C., Colomb, G.C. & Williams, J.M. (2008) *The Craft of Research* (3rd edn). Chicago: The University of Chicago Press.
We recommend Chapter 13 'Drafting your report' as it offers practical advice and strategies for writing up your work.

Levy, Y. & Ellis, T.J.A. (2006) A systems approach to conducting an effective literature review in support of information systems research, *Informing Science Journal*, 9, 181–212.
This article offers a comprehensive overview of the literature review process. It considers the vital role of theory.

Onwuegbuzie, A.J., Leech, N.L. & Collins, K.M.T. (2012) The qualitative analysis techniques for the review of the literature. *The Qualitative Report*, *17*(56), 1–28, Available at: http://www.nova.edu/ssss/QR/QR17/onwuegbuzie.pdf.
The authors provide a comprehensive consideration of the processes of selection and review as they argue that both of these processes are underrepresented in discussions on literature reviews.

Ridley, D. (2012) *The Literature Review: A Step by Step Guide for Students* (2nd edn). London: SAGE Publications Ltd.
A useful study book and we recommend Chapter 6 which focuses on the structure of a literature review.

Silverman, D. (2013) *Doing Qualitative Research* (4th edn). London: SAGE Publications Ltd.
Please read Chapter 22 as this offers advice on recording your sources but also on constructing your literature review.

10
MANAGING YOUR DATA

THIS CHAPTER SUPPORTS YOUR ABILITY TO

understand the need for effective data management

construct a data management plan

identify and respond to the demands of data ownership

store and dispose of your data securely

CHAPTER OVERVIEW

An important undertaking in any research project is the organisation, storage and tracking of your collected data and this is called data management. This way of working with your data requires the adoption of a set of skills and behaviours that should enable you to work with your data in an appropriate, systematic and consistent manner. To aid you in the development of systematic processes, we provide an overview of the role and function of data management plans.

This chapter therefore, examines a range of strategies for data management that should enable you to work proficiently with the type and quantity of data you may have amassed. These strategies are relevant whether you are working with hard (*paper*) copies or storing your work using various technological devices and formats. As part of our focus on digital forms of storage, we explore the fundamental importance of backing up all of your work.

Underpinning this chapter is the role of data management in enhancing your researcher integrity because being able to show where your data has come from and recording it accurately enable your reader to trace the data you have utilised. This can be a way of enhancing research credibility and increasing confidence in your findings. By the end of this chapter, you should feel you can handle your data in an effective, systematic and secure way.

WHAT IS DATA MANAGEMENT?

Data management is a general term which covers how researchers manage and organise the information used or generated during the research process (see Figure 10.1). At the beginning of your research it is likely your focus will be on collecting data to answer your research question and it may be that thoughts about how you will manage the outcome will not be uppermost in your mind. However, data management is a task that all researchers need to undertake early on in their research. Whilst this can take many forms, the focus is on creating and then implementing a coherent system to organise and manage the data accessed within your research.

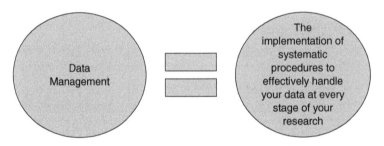

Figure 10.1   A definition of data management

When conducting your qualitative secondary research, you need to consider appropriate management strategies for data storage, security and tracking. Storage and security are particularly central to the success of your research as they enable you to keep your data safe and adhere to ethical and legal principles.

Managing your data is also about tracking it, ensuring that you know where each aspect is located, its relevance to your study and that you are aware of issues relating to data ownership and the intellectual rights of others. This is important as effective data management is also about keeping accurate bibliographic data and ensuring you are keeping track of your references. Thus, effective management of your data is crucial as it supports your ability to effectively complete your research through the systematic organisation of your secondary qualitative data. When done well, your data management skills will highlight your proficiency, present you as a competent researcher, which can provide confidence to others as to the robustness of your results and conclusions. Data management therefore, involves the application of strategies to manage and organise your data from the start to the end of your project.

The term '*data curation*' is frequently used alongside data management as this reflects the whole life span of the research. This recognises the importance of not just managing data from its collection and usage but to its long-term archiving and preservation (Lord et al.

2004). As so much of our data will be stored online in a digital format, the term '*digital cura-tion*' is also used to define the maintenance and preservation of digital research data throughout its lifecycle (DCC 2018). Issues relating to the archiving and long-term storage of data may only be relevant to funded researchers. It is worth considering how this becomes more significant in the light of rapid technological changes should you wish to revisit your research later in your academic career. The benefits of engaging in efficient data management strategies are outlined in Figure 10.2.

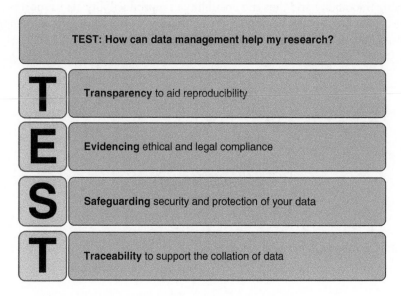

Figure 10.2   The benefits of effective data management

GENERATING A DATA MANAGEMENT PLAN

From the outset, you will need to have a clear plan of how you intend to work with your data. This necessitates your knowing and understanding your data to ensure that your decision making is sound. Your institution or organisation may expect you to create a formal data management plan, as a requirement of your research. This plan needs to cover your intentions during, at the end and sometimes beyond your research. Therefore, data management plans can be useful as they encourage you to think about pivotal issues pertaining to your data early on in your research. This could include how you will handle many of the issues we explored in Chapter 5, pertinent to the use of sensitive data and how you will manage ethical considerations (*anonymisation and processes to ensure confidentiality*). Your data management plan may also need to address legal issues (*not using direct or indirect identifiers*) and how to safeguard your data if you are sharing it (e.g. *with colleagues, peers or at specific research events – i.e. conferences and symposiums*).

Data management plans also have a key role if you are conducting funded research, as these can assist in defining your budget, ensuring you have accounted for aspects such as secure storage and archiving. They also have a very clear function as a tool that when used well can enhance the transparency of your research process as they can show what type of data you will use, how it will be accessed and used. When used alongside the accurate recording of your sources of data, processes such as these aid your research integrity and credibility as you are increasing traceability and thus the possibility of reproducibility. At its most basic, a data management plan is a written document which illustrates your approach to managing your data before, during and after your research (see Figure 10.3).

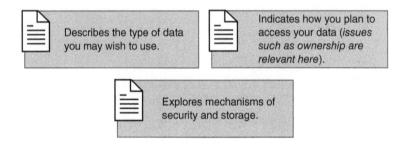

Figure 10.3   The role of a data management plan

What does a data management plan look like?

Many institutions provide templates for data management plans (*see our recommended reading section*) and in most cases they are presented in a question format. Figure 10.4 prompts you to consider key aspects of your data management and ensure you have not omitted any pivotal aspects in your plan.

As we have indicated above, demonstrating effective data management can increase the transparency of your research and therefore, enhance its value and impact. Being able to retrieve and make your data available or accessed by readers on request will aid confidence in both you as a researcher and your research.

To aid your ability to complete a data management plan we offer the following questions and associated prompts (see Figure 10.5). However, we also recommend that you make sure you are aware of your institution's, supervisor's or funding body's expectations as to what you may need to include.

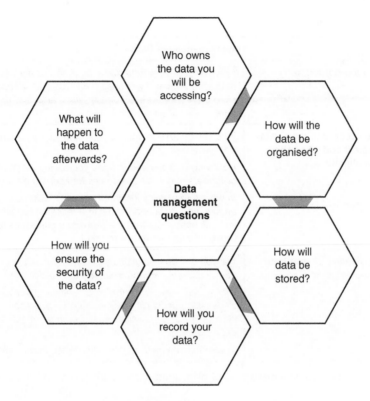

Figure 10.4 Data management plan considerations

Data Management Plan	
Questions	**Considerations**
What type of data will you collect?	*Is the data numerical, textual or graphic?* *Is it personal (e.g. social media, letters or photographs)?*
Are you using data that someone else has produced? **If so, where is it from?**	*Who owns the data? This should lead to a consideration and reflection of data ownership and rights of access.*
How will you store and keep your data secure?	*How will you engage with your data ethically (anonymisation and confidentiality) and legally (not breaching data protection legislation).* *How will you physically store and handle your data?* *If it is in a paper format how will this be secured? If it is digital, is this encrypted and all passwords kept securely?*

(Continued)

Figure 10.5 (Continued)

Data Management Plan	
How will you record the data sources?	*How will you know who owns the data you are using in your research? How will you ensure that the data is recorded and cited correctly? (In accordance with intellectual property rights/rights of ownership.)*
Who may have access to your data during the project and when the project is completed?	*Who will be able to access your data (e.g. your supervisor or peer reviewers)?* *How long do you need to keep your data for? (Your institution or funders may have timescales for keeping data.)* *In what format will your data be stored? (Do you need to archive your data and keep it in a research repository? If so, you will need to access the repository guidelines to check the processes and formats required.)*
How will you dispose of your data once the project is completed?	*Will you use an institutional approach (for example a recommended destruction programme) or shred the information?* *Digital data may be destroyed by deleting, overwriting or degaussing (which is a demagnetizing process to erase a hard drive), or by physically destroying the material (e.g. USBs or DVDs).* *Is your chosen method permanent with no chance of retrieval?*

Figure 10.5 Generating a data management plan: questions and prompts to aid completion

Generating a data management plan is useful if you need to prepare for an interview with an ethics committee. In addition, as we indicated in Chapter 2, even if you do not have to submit a formal data management plan, it can be a useful tool as it encourages you to formalise the procedures you may use within your approach to data. It illustrates your awareness of key issues and will help you engage in research transparency where it would be possible to retrieve your data for review should this be required. Your plan should also cover legal aspects of using data and strategies to be put in place if you use the data. It also enables you as a researcher to know if your research will be subject to possible data access issues. If this is the case, it is best to find out sooner rather than later.

PAUSE FOR THOUGHT

Data management plans

In Chapter 2, we discussed the role of a research proposal which covers many of the key components of qualitative secondary research. We indicated that the section on ethics is often a suitable section to include your approach to data management. However, your institution may require you to submit

> a separate data management plan (see Figure 10.5). Even if you are not required to produce one, creating such a plan can be a very useful strategy to support the progression and advancement of your research.
>
> As always, please refer to your supervisor and your institution's research guidelines to ensure you understand what you need to do.

MANAGING THE COLLECTION OF BIBLIOGRAPHIC DATA

As we stated above, addressing the requirements of data ownership in your research involves respecting the intellectual property rights of the data (see Chapter 5). This requires the '*appropriate recognition of the professional contribution of a dataset's creators and maintainers to its ongoing use*' (Burton et al. 2017: 1732). To achieve this requirement, you should accurately and appropriately record the source of data you are using. This recording is usually in the form of noting down key bibliographic or source details (*e.g. name, date, place of publication*) which are then used to reference the intellectual contribution that other researchers, authors or data producers have made to your research. There are various approaches to referencing and one of the most popular is the Harvard system, also known as 'author-date' style. However, there is no single agreed definitive version of the Harvard system and there are many variations available. You will need to check your institution's or organisation's guidelines or preferences.

All data you employ needs to be recorded in some way to ensure you are managing your data effectively. This recording has a fundamental role to play in your completed research project, as you will need to reference your data to show you are recognising the contribution that others have made to your research. Knowing what needs to be referenced can be problematic; therefore, based on Cottrell's (2013) consideration of referencing, we present, as a minimum the type of input you need to reference:

- **Direct quotation:** This is where the exact words are placed within either quotation marks or are indented to show that the passage of text is not your words.
- **Paraphrased text:** This is where you have read the work of others and have rewritten this in your own words.
- **Key concepts or inspirational thoughts:** This may be where a source (*author or other*) has inspired you or encouraged you to adopt a specific way of thinking.
- **A specific and non-generalised theory, perspective or viewpoint:** This is where you refer to information as facts, figures, ideas or other specialised knowledge that is not in the public domain.
- **Publications:** These can include books, journal articles, web pages, theses, conference reports, policy documents, legal documents and many others.

- **Any images (including video) and audio data:** If you are reproducing the work of others then this should be fully managed and recorded (*and referenced*). This can, as we explored earlier include all forms of images (*graphic and video*), audio data and any pre-existing research data (*e.g. presented in tabular or graphic forms*).

As we move into new ways of thinking about data, we need to consider how this needs to be managed and accurately recorded within our work. We use the term 'reference' but this is also considered as 'citing' and you need to cite all sources used in your research. There are several reasons to ensure that you comply to this requirement:

- **To give credit where credit is due:** Make certain that you give credit to other researchers, authors and data producers by acknowledging their contribution to your research. This shows you have engaged in due diligence and behaved responsibly as an academic. In addition, citing the work of others can validate the arguments you create and enhance the credibility of your research by indicating your selection of quality sources of information.
- **To protect your reputation:** You need to avoid accusations of plagiarism which is, as the University of Oxford (2018) state 'presenting someone else's work or ideas as your own, with or without their consent, by incorporating it into your work without full acknowledgement'. This is considered a serious academic offence by most educational institutions so accessing and knowing your institution's referencing or citation guidelines is essential.
- **To boost transparency:** Citing your sources accurately enables your reader to find and scrutinise these. Being accurate in your citation (*referencing*) of sources does, as we have stated before, aid the transparency of your research. This can increase confidence in you both as an academic and as a researcher.

When accessing and collating a large amount of data sets you may find the use of a reference manager is indispensable. A reference manager is a tool that can be downloaded onto your computer to allow you to record, track, and compile references and bibliographic information. There are different types of referencing tools and software available to you; we do not recommend a specific one. This would depend upon your preference, level of access and choice of device. Data citation is an essential part of your work and here are some examples of software that can support this process:

Endnote: This must be installed onto your computer. You can purchase it or your institution may be able to provide it free of charge. It works with Microsoft Word to automatically format in-text citations and reference lists and create formatted lists of figures and charts. You can also use Endnote as a personal database to gather ownership information from different information sources. There is also a version of Endnote called Endnote Web which can be accessed from any web browser to synchronise your web account with your desktop computer.

Mendeley: This is free for you to download from the web on to your computer through the desktop client, web browser, or through a mobile app. Mendeley automatically captures information required for reference lists and to examine ownership, in a wide variety of referencing formats. It can work best with PDF documents, so if you are primarily using journal articles for your secondary research, this might suit you. Mendeley also incorporates a useful research papers database which contains other users' papers which have been stored in Mendeley.

There are also a number of other free citation managers available such as Zotero. Zotero has a useful DOI/PMID/ISBN searching facility. Other features include online syncing and generation of in-text citations as well as integration with word processing packages such as MS Word. If you are using later versions of MSWord, explore the *Source Manager* feature that provides options for you to manage your references and enables you to automatically generate a bibliography including all of the sources in your work.

PAUSE FOR THOUGHT

Citing your sources

Make sure you know what type of referencing system you need to use. Referencing systems can be regularly updated so it is best to check which version is required. Also, check the following:

- Do you know your institution's or organisation's referencing protocols?
- Do you know the difference between a bibliography and a reference list?

Please access http://epapers. bham.ac.uk/819/2/B016.1_harvard_referencing_guide.pdf to see an example of the Harvard referencing system as used by the University of Birmingham.

STRATEGIES FOR ORGANISING YOUR DATA

The widespread use of technology has moved many researchers away from adopting basic paper-based filing procedures to more high-tech data management strategies. Whilst not exhaustive, Figure 10.6 outlines some examples of data management strategies.

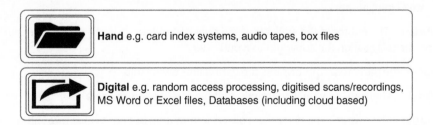

Figure 10.6   Examples of data storage

An effective classification system is required whether you are working with hard 'paper' copies, which need a manual approach to data management or digital versions which require the use of a computer. The adoption of a system that is easy to use, flexible and provides a mechanism for maintaining data tracking and facilitates the collection of key bibliographic details is crucial. This section explores a range of useful strategies, some of which you may be familiar with, that can support the way you manage your work and the data you wish to collect and store.

UNDERSTANDING DATA OWNERSHIP

Inherent within your approach to data management are your responsibilities to those that own the data you may wish to use. This requires you to consider the intellectual property ownership of evidence employed in your research, and acknowledge your sources of data as references or within a bibliography. If you are using photographic images that you access within an image archive (*e.g. Getty Images or British Film Institute*) you will need to explore copyright permissions or issues surrounding fair use.

Irrespective of the type of data you use, recognising and responding to data ownership refers to the need for you to consider the rights of those that own the data (in all its widest forms) that you want to use (see Chapter 5). We have explored in previous chapters that vast amounts of existing data are freely available on the Internet, which by the very nature of the ease of access is often assumed to be free from restrictions on its use. This type of data can be covered by what is known as an 'open data licence', which permits access to and reuse of the information, with few or no restrictions. However, in all cases the original source or author needs to be acknowledged and this requires you to keep precise records of provenance so that the data can be accurately and appropriately referenced. As stated before, always refer to the terms and conditions or terms of use of any website where you access data.

However, finding out who owns the data is not always clear (Loshin 2002). Examples of types of ownership of data can be:

Author – The person creating the information. Authors may also share their ownership; e.g. in the case of joint authors.

Publisher – The author of the work can share their copyright; e.g. in the case of joint authors, or to contractually assign the copyright to a publisher.

Funder – The party that commissions the data claims ownership.

Licenser – Where an individual or organisation buys or licenses the data.

Packager – The owner is the party that collects information but adds value through configuring the data for a specific market.

Compiler – This is the entity (*e.g. a person or company*) that selects and compiles information from different information sources.

Copyright ownership – This is a legal right that grants rights of use and distribution.

Knowing who owns the data you use is important when you engage in your research because you need to know the answers to certain questions before you can begin (see Figure 10.7).

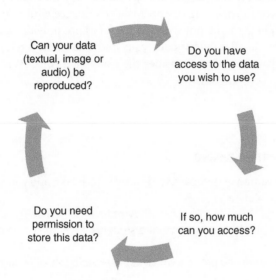

Figure 10.7 Questions to ask about your data

Data indexing

Data indexing is a useful way of capturing key information about your selected data. This process is illustrated in Box 10.1, where you can see how a set of useful headings enables you to gain a comprehensive overview of your selected data. This approach has many benefits as data indexing helps you to:

- **Make clear decisions regarding the importance of this data to your research:** The rating scale may seem like a crude measure but it can aid the selection of your sample and provide evidence of your critical thinking (see Chapter 8).
- **File your data either manually or digitally:** You could add a section which suggests where it should and could be filed. To aid this process, you could use a keyword gained from the data you have read.
- **Save time:** Including a summary and noting any key points will aid your memory if you need to revisit this data.

- **Supports your ability to synthesise:** Knowing the main points and noting any possible concerns and the perspective the author takes, is a productive strategy to employ when you come to write your literature review. It may indicate patterns and themes within your selected data which may enable you to construct a well-informed argument (see Chapter 9).

You can approach this data management strategy in any way that suits your way of working. It can be done using word processing or spreadsheet software with you creating a template. However, manually applied post-it-notes can be useful as not only do they act as a useful and quick memory aid, they can also colour code your information into relevant themes, areas or sections, pertinent to your research. Consider the example in Box 10.1; using a strategy like this may help speed up your analysis.

BOX 10.1   USING DATA INDEXING

As an example, you want to undertake a study on mental health and you identify the following as a useful source of data:

Richardson et al. (2017) A longitudinal study of financial difficulties and mental health in a national sample of British undergraduate students. *Community Mental Health Journal,* *53*(3), 344–352.

You then apply an indexing process which could include the following aspects:

> **Title and author:** *Richardson et al. (2017) A Longitudinal Study of Financial Difficulties and Mental Health in a National Sample of British Undergraduate Students.*
>
> **Summary:** *A longitudinal study of the relationship between mental health and financial concerns.*
>
> **Context and sample:** *454 – 1st & 2nd yr university students (aged 17 – 57 – mean age of 19.9).*
>
> **Most relevant point(s):** *Little relationship of stress to alcohol – those less stressed had greater alcohol reliance. Useful for subjective nature of stress.*
>
> **Drawback(s):** *Lack of representative sample.*
>
> **Rating level (importance):** *4 out of 5.*

File naming and version tracking

It is likely when you write up your work that you will draft and re-draft and, in this process, it is easy to mislay or lose earlier editions. Being able to track your earlier versions will mean you will not lose key data or lose a version you may need to return to. Any versions you make need to be organised and filed in a way that makes sense to you. However, it can be easy to lose data by mis-naming a file. Therefore, to avoid any difficulties apply a system to aid the tracking of your earlier draft versions of your work. This will prevent later difficulties and ensure you are always working on the correct version of your work.

Whilst there are different techniques to adopt (see Figure 10.8) make sure you use a system consistently and that this will enable you to distinguish different versions from one another (*e.g. version 1, v2, v3 etc. or add the time and date*). We recommend that any system you adopt should make sense to you and be easy to employ. Overcomplicated processes will hamper your progress so keep it as clear and as simple as it can be. Figure 10.8 provides some tips and guidance.

Only make new versions for significant changes (small edits can be saved without the need for an updated version).
Try to create memorable but brief file names (*these must make sense to you*).
Use file names to classify the type of files (*version, date order, themes etc*).
Avoid special characters such as ~ ! @ # $ % ^ & * ( ) ` ; <> ? , [ ] { } ' "
Do not use spaces. Some software will not recognise file names with spaces.
Some approaches to file names include: Underscores; e.g. file_name.xxx   Dashes; e.g. file-name.xxx   No separation; e.g. filename.xxx
Work on versions in one place or one folder and save from there. This has more relevance if you have multiple devices but do not have a shared drive (*e.g. OneDrive or iCloud*).
Try not to make file names too long. Long file names do not work well with all types of software.
Include a readme.txt file that explains your naming format along with any abbreviations or codes you have employed.

Figure 10.8   File and tracking strategies

Saving your work: creating a back-up

The importance of making regular back-ups cannot be emphasised enough. There is nothing so down-heartening as realising that the work you have slaved over is now lost, corrupted and possibly beyond use. There are many ways in which your work may be compromised (see Figure 10.9).

Human error: e.g. accidental data deletion or overwrite
Software file corruption: e.g. computer virus
Hardware failure: e.g. a hard drive malfunction or breakdown
Damage or theft: e.g. water damage or being stolen

Figure 10.9   Causes of data loss

The most common cause of data loss is human error and much of this can be eliminated by backing up your work in a systematic way. This means engaging in good research practice and not storing your data or work on just one device, be that on a laptop, a computer hard drive or on an external storage device, as this is risky. Try to develop the practice of saving to two or three places and consider taking sensible precautions such as setting your device to automatically save your work at selected intervals. You may save to a USB, an external hard drive or to the 'cloud'. You could always email your latest version to your own college or personal account. Whatever happens, do not put all your data in just one place!

If using a computer to store your data, it is also recommended that you review your network security and check you have appropriate firewall protection in place and security-related operating systems to avoid viruses, which can also corrupt your data. Your work is too important to lose so make sure you do all you can to safeguard it.

PAUSE FOR THOUGHT

Nothing lasts for ever …

Memory cards and USB drives are not really designed for long-term storage. The data you store may stay valid for up to 10 years (Integral 2018) but the more you use these drives (*i.e. the more you write and delete*) the more quickly the memory in the device will start to degrade. In addition, it is also worth considering that, according to Taylor (2014), about 90 per cent of external hard drives will only last for three years without failure. As for your computer and laptop, the consensus seems to be anywhere from three to six years but this is dependent on the make and you, as the user.

As discussed above, any backups should be made in formats suitable for you to access and use and it is worth discussing any issues or concerns with your institution's IT department who should be able to provide specific/personalised advice and support. If you do lose data seek help immediately; even if it is a hardware or software failure it may be possible to retrieve some of it. If you have your data stolen, then this may need to be reported to your institution or organisation as it could result in a data breach. If this is the case answers to issues such as these may be contained within your institution's data management policy.

Using cloud storage

You might consider using cloud storage to upload your files and folders to an Internet server. There are several cloud storage providers each with their own terms and conditions. We recommend that you study these before using them to store your research data due to possible data protection issues.

You should be aware that there are limits on the use or transfer of data out of or into certain geographical areas. This can have relevance if you are using cloud servers or global data hubs as cloud service providers operate within geographic regions which are policed by different laws and security guidelines (The Law Society 2014).

Cloud-based storage providers such as Google Drive, Dropbox, OneDrive, iCloud or YouSendIt are easy to use, but they are often based overseas. Therefore, it is possible that storing any sensitive data in this way could be in violation of data protection legislation. The UK Data Service (2018) suggests that storing high-risk information (*e.g. files that contain personal or sensitive information, information that is covered by law or that has a very high intellectual property value*) should not be kept in this way. Whilst it may be unlikely that this is the type of data you will access, it is important to be aware of this.

As in all things, there are positives and negatives and it is worth balancing the positives of centralised data and increased ease of access against the negatives of potential data privacy concerns. Be aware of the need for good broadband access and the possibility of having to pay for services and increased storage capacity. Just to add some caution, there is a tendency to consider cloud-based storage as 'safe' but there have been significant issues reported with some crashing and losing data.

Thinking ahead: data preservation

Data preservation is a concern for any researcher who wishes to or has to keep their data. This is mainly because digital technology is developing so quickly that any stored data runs the risk of becoming inaccessible. It may be that future software will not be compatible with current file formats as updated versions of software can alter the formatting of your documents and, depending on the type of data you store, this can be very difficult to resolve. Also, over time, the devices used for storage can become corrupted or damaged. As we have indicated before in this chapter do not be tempted to put all your data in one form of storage and be prepared to upgrade your data as new storage devices and methods become available.

THINKING ABOUT DATA SECURITY

In Chapter 5, we discussed some of the ethical and legal duties placed on researchers to engage in strategies to safeguard data anonymity and confidentiality. In this chapter, we explore this in the context of data security. The level of security you need to adopt will depend on the type of data you want to access. If you are using company business records, traceable social media data or photographs then you will need to keep your data very secure.

Physical security

Physical security focuses on aspects of your environment such as having access to locked cabinets, a lockable desk space or secure cupboards. This physical security should be aimed at keeping all aspects of your research data and your own work safe. This applies to both paper copies and electronic devices (*e.g. computer, laptop or tablet*) and includes ensuring all access codes and passwords are secure. You may feel that the advice offered seems quite basic but it is easy to make simple mistakes which can have devastating long-term consequences.

Digital security

As mentioned before in this chapter, digital data security is essential for all devices being used whether this is a desktop or a portable device (e.g. laptops, tablets and mobile phones). This is also relevant to your external storage devices (e.g. USB, external hard drives). This is important as research from Nissim, Yahalom and Elovici (2017) identified 29 forms of USB focused attacks. These involved infected or malicious attacks gained when using '*free USB charging points*'. The advice they give is to be aware of the potential dangers of any form of free charging. However, as illustrated in Box 10.2, research undertaken by Tischer et al. (2017) found that people will take chances.

Whilst you cannot safeguard your research against every possible loss, you can put in place precautions to prevent access to your data should it be lost or stolen. You can employ methods of encryption; this is the process of encoding data, making it unintelligible and scrambled to others without a key to open it. The need for encryption and security measures are increasing, as more people are falling victim to a whole host of cybercrimes. However, there are ways that you can control access to your files including adopting good security strategies and a common-sense attitude.

BOX 10.2   USERS REALLY DO PLUG IN USB DRIVES THEY FIND

In order to investigate anecdotal evidence that many people, if finding a lost USB will pick it up and plug in into their own computer Tischer et al. (2017) dropped 297 flash drives within a large university campus. The results found that 135 of these were plugged into machines. Whether people were driven by altruistic motives in trying to find the owner or for more self-ish reasons, the user unknowingly opened themselves to attack when they connected the drive, in terms of a physical 'Trojan horse'.

When investigating the reasons for people picking up and connecting the USBs, 68 per cent of users stated that they took no precautions, 16 per cent scanned the drive with their anti-virus software and 8 per cent believed that their operating system or security software would protect them.

The results suggest that if this was an intentional cyber-attack it would be successful and that the average person does not understand the danger of connecting an unknown USB to their computer.

Keeping your data safe is an important part of your research process and Figure 10.10 offers some straightforward, yet effective tips to consider for increasing the security of your data.

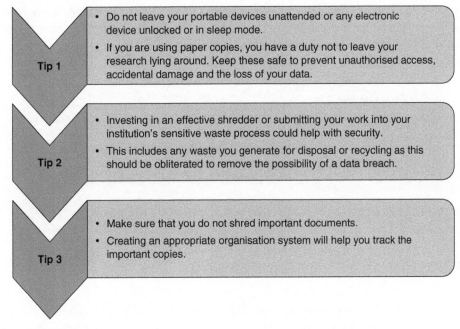

Figure 10.10   Data security tips

PLANNING YOUR DATA DISPOSAL

There will be a point in your research process where you will need to consider data disposal and how your data can be securely destroyed, once it is no longer needed. However, deciding when to dispose of data may depend on your institution or funding body. As there is little consensus as to how long you need to keep your data, if at all. For some institutions, you may have to keep your data for a period of at least six years, whereas for others it may be until after formal assessment by an examination board. Here are two examples of institutional approaches to the retention of data.

- The University of Leicester, UK: 'data must be retained intact for a period of at least six years' (www2.le.ac.uk/offices/researchsupport/integrity/code-of-conduct/5-after-research/5-5-retaining-records-and-research-data).
- The University of Virginia, USA: 'you must keep your research records for at least 5 years and possibly longer' (www.virginia.edu/vpr/irb/sbs/resources_guide_data_retention.html).

After you have completed your research you may need to decide on a date for the disposal of your data. This may require you to consider how you will go about erasing or shredding your data files as this is a vital part of managing your data securely. However, merely deleting files and reformatting a hard drive will not irretrievably destroy the data or prevent future data recovery. Whilst specialised file erasure tools can reduce the risk of recovery to acceptable levels, possibly the only way to guarantee that data is unrecoverable is to physically destroy the media it is stored on. Figure 10.11 illustrates specific approaches to the deletion of data.

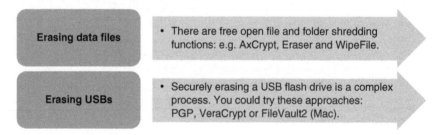

Figure 10.11 Erasing data

REFLECTION AND FURTHER READING

At the beginning of the chapter we set out what you should be able to do when you reached the end of this chapter. To aid your reflection on all we have covered we ask some chapter specific questions. If you are unsure of any of your answers to these questions, please go back to the relevant section to review this aspect.

REFLECTING ON CHAPTER 10

In this chapter we have:

- **Provided a robust rationale for you to engage in strategies for effective data management:** Can you identify three main reasons for the use of data management in your research? Do you know how to create filenames for versions of your work?
- **Provided advice on how to construct a data management plan:** Do you know if you should create a data management plan?
- **Discussed the importance of recognising data ownership:** Do you know what referencing system you should use? Do you know what you should reference in your text? Are you aware of copyright laws?
- **Considered the safe and secure storage of data, including its disposal:** Do you know what type of data you may use? Do you know how this should be stored? Is your computer protected from viruses and theft? Do you have a plan for backing up your work?

WE RECOMMEND FOR FURTHER READING:

Briney, K. (2015) *Data Management for Researchers: Organize, Maintain and Share Your Data for Research Success.* Exeter, UK: Pelagic Publishing.
This is a practical book which offers useful advice on all aspects of document processing and management.

Consortium of European Social Science Data Archives (2017) *Adapt your Data Management Plan.* Available at: www.cessda.eu/content/download/3844/35033/file/20171117DMPQ uestionsCESSDAExpertTourGuide.pdf.
This resource offers a clearly presented list of data management essentials.

Onwuegbuzie, A.J. and Frels, R. (2016) *7 Steps to a Comprehensive Literature Review: A Multi-modal & Cultural Approach.* London: SAGE Publications Ltd.
We recommend that you consider Part Two 'Exploration', and consider Chapter 6, step 3 as this offers an overview of data management strategies such as creating a literature table and the use of computer software.

Stanford Libraries (nd) *Data Management Plans.* Available at: https://library.stanford.edu/ research/data-management-services/data-management-plans.
A well-presented and easy to navigate site from Stanford University that offers a data management planning tool.

(Continued)

(Continued)

Van den Eynden, V., Corti, L., Woollard, M., Bishop, L.& Horton. L. (2011) *Managing and Sharing Data: UK Data Archive.* Available at: www.data-archive.ac.uk/media/2894/managing-sharing.pdf.
This site has a useful section on data formatting and a very clear section on the ethics of consent.

Whyte, A. & Tedds, J. (2011) Making the case for research data management. *DCC Briefing Papers. Edinburgh: Digital Curation Centre.* Available at: www.dcc.ac.uk/resources/briefing-papers.
This is a valuable resource for all aspects of data management and handling.

11
ANALYSING DATA

THIS CHAPTER WILL SUPPORT YOUR ABILITY TO

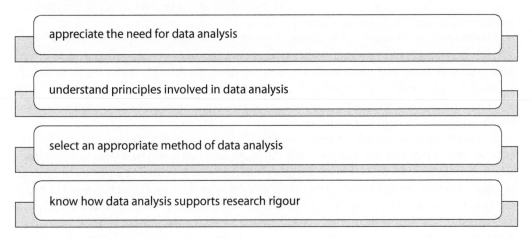

appreciate the need for data analysis

understand principles involved in data analysis

select an appropriate method of data analysis

know how data analysis supports research rigour

CHAPTER OVERVIEW

This chapter sets out to demystify processes of data analysis and it begins with a consideration of the role of theory which, in qualitative analysis, is usually associated with inductive or emergent approaches where theory is generated from your data. We then consider two broad approaches to data analysis. The first is constant comparison which is a cross-data set analysis that generates themes from your data and the second is framework or thematic analysis which is the early identification of themes from a small data sample that can then be applied to the whole data set.

Towards the end of this chapter, we provide an overview of alternative methods of analysis that are appropriate to the analysis of documents within qualitative secondary research. We include methods of discourse and narrative analysis and provide a brief overview of semiotics. We ask you to reflect on how your approach to your analysis can support the confidence that can be had in your research and this chapter concludes with a checklist to help you select a method of analysis suitable to your research question(s) and/or aim(s).

WHY DO I NEED TO ANALYSE MY DATA?

When you analyse data, you are trying to make sense of it and this involves taking your data and turning it into something usable. This requires you to apply processes to your data to facilitate your ability to interpret it. These processes reduce and transform your data into something that enables you to answer your research question. Whilst, you might think that data analysis is something that just happens at the end of your project, it actually begins as soon as you collect your data, as every time you reflect on your data in some way you are engaging in an analytical process (Kvale 1996).

Thinking about analysis needs to begin when you design your research and set your research question(s) and/or aim(s) as the type of data you may want to gather and what you want to do with these shapes the method of analysis used. An example of this would be selecting blogs for your data as you want to explore the construction of personal narratives. This could lead you to consider narrative analysis, whereas exploring advertising imagery may lead you to consider approaches to visual analysis.

One other aspect to consider is how theory will function in your analysis as this could determine the methods of data analysis you select. An example of this would be if you wanted to track specific terminology to see how many times a phrase or word was used in a particular context. You may select discourse analysis to do this as you consider the connection between the social and cultural use of the language and the role of power to be inseparable. In this example, you have already formed some theoretical explanation for what is happening but you need to explore your data to see if this is accurate. If you want to look for this theory in your research then you are applying your theory first as a critical lens through which to view and explain your data. If, however, you want to see what emerges from your analysis and apply theory to explain what is happening then this is an inductive or 'theory after' approach. Therefore, as we examined in Chapters 3 and 4, your approach to data analysis needs to be carefully considered when you design your research as it can guide your choice of data and the way theory may function. Figure 11.1 illustrates the differences in the way you can approach theory in your analysis.

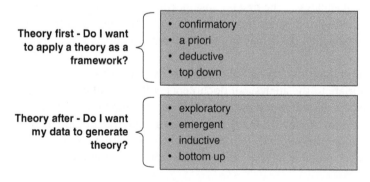

Figure 11.1   Different approaches to the use of theory

As we begin this exploration of qualitative analysis it is worth reiterating that qualitative research is usually considered as a data-driven design which seeks to interpret data (Hammersley 2013). However, as we explore towards the end of this chapter, when we analyse documents as data we may need to adopt a pragmatic approach which accepts that qualitative analysis has to be flexible to meet the needs of the question that is asked and the data it uses.

We begin this chapter by exploring two general approaches to data analysis that are systematic responses that strive for accuracy and clarity. These methods are framework or thematic analysis and constant comparison which are broad-basedmethods designed to make sense of data and reduce and transform it into something meaningful for you to interpret.

ANALYSING DATA USING CONSTANT COMPARISON

Analysis is often presented as a complex and mystical process where meaning just seems to emerge from the data. However, there is no alchemy as analysis is the systematic identification of parts of your data that you identify as being relevant to your research question. Whether you are a qualitative secondary researcher using images or text as data the fundamental principles within analysis are the same. You are trying to get to the heart of your data (Miles & Huberman 1994) by reducing it into something manageable and meaningful. This can be performed through processes of identification (*consistent labelling processes*) and the creation of categories (*theme identification*) through a constant comparison of data. The steps we offer to the constant comparison of your data are easy to follow and it begins with your being reminded of your research question:

- **Refocus:** Refocus on your research question. You should remind yourself of the purpose of your inquiry.
- **Immersion:** Immerse yourself in your data and really get to know it; you have explored the context of its production and checked its quality so here you can focus on the content as being able to answer your research question(s) and/or aim(s). You need to know what it means.
- **Interrogation and identification:** Start to work on your data and interrogate it. This means engaging with your data fully; you can underline it, highlight it but in this process, you are identifying specific events, or instances of something notable appearing and giving these a name (coding). You do this through the process of:

    o **Constant comparison:** This is where you compare all occurences of these instances or events across all sets of data for consistency and accuracy. This may be performed many times as this is where you see patterns and relationships emerging.

- **Creating Categories:** This is where you collate all the notable or specific events that you have identified, named or coded and begin to seek connections between these. This is a process of analytic categorisation as you refine and sort your data leading to the creation of main themes and sub themes. When fully identified, these themes will become your findings.

- **Generating maps/matrices:** You can create maps or matrices to support your management of your data and to enhance your ability to see relationships and connections which can facilitate the interpretation of your findings. You should be able to create a hierachy of concepts or themes.

Refocus on your question(s) and/or aim(s)

Keep in mind your research question as this can help you keep on track and guide your identification or 'coding'. Although data driven means your data should indicate what it contains, it is fair to say very few researchers ever really go into research without some form of concept or theory awareness. Reminding yourself of your question can make the process of meaning making more relevant to you as you make your first tentative steps into your data.

Immersion or familiarisation

Immersing yourself in your data is a process of familiarisation where you get to know as much as you can about all the data you have to analyse. This can be part of the prolonged engagement we explored in Chapter 4 as a strategy to enhance research credibility. Make sure that your reader knows you have spent time understanding your data; record this process clearly in your methodology. Prolonged engagement with your data begins when you consider the context of its production by applying critical appraisal and evaluation to identify the 'what', 'why', 'when', 'where', 'who' and 'how' of its creation.

Data immersion is, as we show in Figure 11.2, a crucial step as it builds the foundation of your analytical focus. By reviewing your data again and again you are seeing if you can identify aspects of interest and note. This can begin as a quick overview to gain holistic oversight and can then evolve into a focused search for repeating events, instances and recognisable units for analysis.

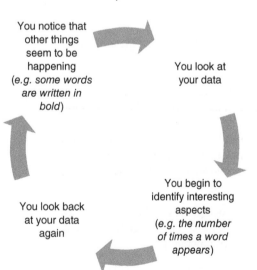

You notice that other things seem to be happening (*e.g. some words are written in bold*)

You look at your data

You begin to identify interesting aspects (*e.g. the number of times a word appears*)

You look back at your data again

Figure 11.2 Immersing yourself in your data

You may repeat the process many times until you feel you have a strong grasp on the type of data you have. Taking time to do this and making notes as you go is important in this early stage of your analytical process. Each word, image or phrase needs to be considered as having the potential to lead to meaningful findings. This is where a coding book, matrix or your research diary can be useful as you can record what is happening in your data.

PAUSE FOR THOUGHT

Using a research diary

To make sure you are being as systematic as you can, we advise that you use a research diary. We introduced the idea of a research diary in Chapter 2 and it can be a useful tool to employ in this part of your research process. Your diary can be used to record your coding schemes, any anomalies that arise and how you responded to these. Keeping accurate records of the labels you apply as codes and the categories you create can support consistency. It can also demonstrate research transparency and research rigour (see Chapter 4). Providing strategies that show how you analysed your data can aid the confidence your reader can have in your results.

Interrogation, identification and constant comparison

We have used the word 'identification' to describe the process of analysis but what you are doing in this process is labelling data as a process of 'coding'. You are identifying something and giving this 'thing' a label. Whilst data immersion helps you gain a big picture of your data, coding is where you break this down to understand components. Being confronted with a large amount of data can be daunting but your role as a researcher is to turn this 'raw' data into something meaningful. This is where you start to work on your data; you interrogate it and engage with it as fully as you can. This can involve aspects of physical interrogation where you underline key parts in your data or highlight important quotations or cut parts of an image up. When you interrogate your data, you can do it in a way that makes sense to you and a little later we offer some suggestions to help you do this.

Your interrogation of your data should identify interesting events, key aspects or specific instances and when found you will need to label these. This is how you convert your 'raw' data into identifiable chunks. Saldaña (2016: 4) provides an eloquent definition of a code as, '*a word or short phrase that symbolically assigns a summative, salient, essence-capturing*

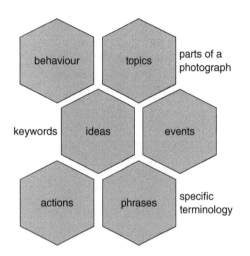

Figure 11.3   Examples of events, instances or behaviour that can be identified in your document

attribute for a portion of language or visual data'. This means that when you code you give something happening or appearing in your data a label that reflects the essence of what you have found. In Figure 11.5 we provide an example of codes applied to text and Figure 11.3 illustrates some of the ways you could identify something in your data. You could find specific terminology used or you could identify a specific form of behaviour such as a laugh or a gesture.

The essential aspect in this approach is in the constant and comparative gaze you take across all sets of data to ensure you are being clear and consistent. This is the 'constant comparison' of this method of analysis. The application of a cross data comparative gaze enables you to make constant judgements and adjustments within and between your data. This process aids the systematic nature of your analytical process as you are ensuring that you can identify each instance of an event, word or image and check that the code applied to this is the same across all forms of data. Cross-checking your codes across multiple forms of existing data makes your findings more comprehensive as it generates key themes (see Box 11.1).

BOX 11. 1   CODING BEAUTY PAGEANT DATA

You want to conduct qualitative secondary research to explore parents' views on beauty pageants. You access open online communities and you come across data such as:

> *'I told her that those little girls are basing their whole self-esteem on just their looks and that she is so much more than a pretty face.'*
> *'Beauty pageants boost self-esteem, they make a girl feel loved and noticed.'*

- You immerse yourself in your data. This alerts you to the frequent use of keywords and phrases in your data.
- You apply codes to these words and phrases as they contain specific language to describe feelings or attitudes. Your codes include 'increased self-esteem', 'parental blame' and 'shaming' and you apply a label consistently to every instance of shame, or parental blame you can find.
- When you have exhausted your data for codes, you review these and you notice patterns. This leads you to sort your data into two main categories or key themes; 'positive views' and 'negative views' and these form your findings.

If you are using multiple sets of data or selecting combined data sets for comparison, constantly comparing your coding and categorisation processes is therefore essential and Figure 11.4 provides some key points to consider when coding.

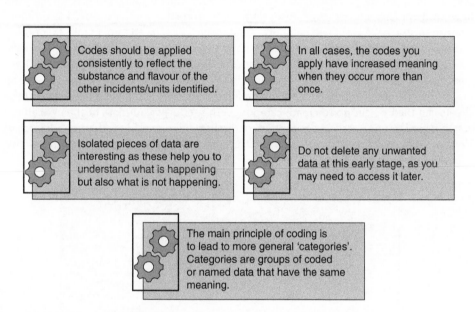

Figure 11.4   Important coding advice

Manual approaches to interrogating and coding your data

The physical manipulation of your data as you interrogate it helps to reinforce its meaning and can encourage you to see patterns and relationships. It can be a creative and enjoyable process because this is where you can physically engage with your data to extract meaning. The processes involved do not have to be high tech, as you can see in the following list of practical strategies:

- You can write on your data: Miles and Huberman (1994) advocate writing in margins and directly on to your text or image. Do not be afraid to make a mess but make sure you have a backup copy of your data just in case!
- Placing or projecting your text or images on a wall to give you fresh perspectives on your data. Sometimes taking a step back from your data can make you see it in a new light. This is a useful strategy if you are using images.
- Cut and stick approaches (see Box 11.2).

BOX 11.2   INTERROGATING YOUR DATA

You can engage with your data by cutting and sticking which may sound basic but is a purposeful approach to your data. First identify your data; in our example, we use data harvested from university prospectuses targeted at students over the age of 21 to promote a return to study. We identified snippets of data which we placed into a table, first noting down where each comment came from. This table was then cut into small strips. Each strip was read and given a notional name and sorted to find instances of similar meaning. These were collated until the data were reduced into five categories as shown in the image. You may need to do this for several pieces of data but the benefit of this method is that these sheets can then be cut up to create categories. This reduces your data further. We advise you to record this process as a photograph or discuss your process in your methodology, so it can be replicated if need be. It is a coding and categorising process that is fully interactive and highly accurate.

- Use sticky notes to label what is happening (see Box 11.3). This enables you to collect all the labels after you have recorded them and physically sort them to create categories. It is a useful shortcut but make sure you take a picture before you move them just in case they get dislodged.

BOX 11.3   MANUAL CODING TECHNIQUES AND PRACTICES

Manual coding lends itself to 'hands on' and creative involvement as you get to know and make sense of your data. It may seem like an arduous task, but it can be a dynamic and organic process (Tesch 1990). Manual coding does not have to be an elaborate process. It can be quite messy as the image below shows. Each one of the sticky labels applied to the text in the image is a unit of something happening. This unit is given a name (code) and when there are similarities and patterns identified in the codes, categories can be created.

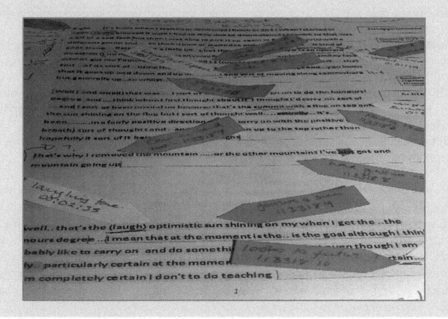

Recording your process

Figure 11.5 shows how you could use a coding table to support your recording and management of your labelling process. It can also aid your memory by reminding you of what is happening in your data as it provides a meaningful context for your coded data.

Data set	Data	Code	Link to category
Prospectus 1 **Narrative 1** **page 15, line 12**	*'I wanted to come to uni to show my children that studying is a good thing.'*	Role modelling	Intrinsic motive?
Prospectus 3 **Narrative 3** **page 3, line 5**	*I work with children who do not think about going to uni. If they know I'm doing it maybe they will want to'.*	Role modelling	Intrinsic motive?

Figure 11.5   An example of a coding table

Using a structured and systematic approach to the recording of your codes is useful because it can do the following:

- **identify the data set:** This helps you know where this information came from in your data set/sets.
- **provide a relevant quotation:** Using quotations or snippets from your data supports your coding decisions, adds transparency to the process and is useful when you are writing up your findings.
- **identify the label applied:** This is the code or label applied. Naming it clearly allows you to check for consistency, shows transparency in the way you defined this code and supports the process of category or theme creation.
- **support category and theme creation:** This is where you group your individual pieces of identified and named data into more substantial and thus, more powerful blocks.

Recording your data in this way supports your ability to see clusters and connections. In addition, keeping a record of your coding processes reflects a systematic and structured approach to the emergence of relationships and your findings. Providing tabular or diagrammatic evidence of your analytical processes can reveal your processes of analysis to others (analytic transparency and audit trail are explored in Chapter 4). The main benefit of such an approach is that by providing evidence of clear and systematic approaches to analysis you can enhance the possibility of your research being replicated and replication is one of the markers of quality that we explored in Chapter 4.

Tips for successful coding

The key to successful coding is to be systematic and consistent and we advise you to record your coding process in some way (*i.e. a diary or matrix*). This is important because you will have to discuss and defend your approach to data analysis in your methodology. Figure 11.6 provides some advice for successful coding.

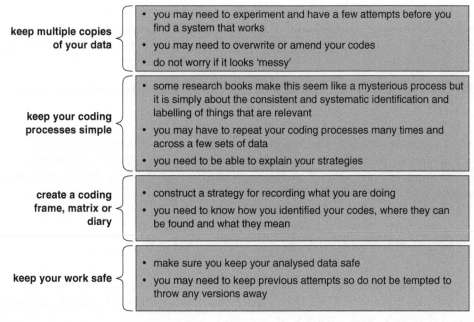

keep multiple copies of your data
- you may need to experiment and have a few attempts before you find a system that works
- you may need to overwrite or amend your codes
- do not worry if it looks 'messy'

keep your coding processes simple
- some research books make this seem like a mysterious process but it is simply about the consistent and systematic identification and labelling of things that are relevant
- you may have to repeat your coding processes many times and across a few sets of data
- you need to be able to explain your strategies

create a coding frame, matrix or diary
- construct a strategy for recording what you are doing
- you need to know how you identified your codes, where they can be found and what they mean

keep your work safe
- make sure you keep your analysed data safe
- you may need to keep previous attempts so do not be tempted to throw any versions away

Figure 11.6   Tips for successful coding

PAUSE FOR THOUGHT

When do I stop labelling or coding?

When do I know I have done enough? This is a question often asked by researchers and the answer is when nothing new emerges from your data. You should make this decision when you are satisfied that the data have been fully explored and interpreted. At this point, you will have inspected your data for completeness (*e.g. when they have nothing new to add*) and it is now redundant (Flick 1998).

Creating categories

After you have coded your data you need to reduce it further to refine the meaning that can be made and this requires you to create categories. Categorisation is where you refine the plentiful and often diverse codes that have been generated into substantial categories. This is an 'iterative' process as you move between your data and the labels or codes you apply trying to group units or instances together.

Just as in your coding process, the categories you create through this process need to be given a label that reflects the nature of the units of data it contains. Miles and Huberman (1994) describe this process as second level coding as it builds on the identification and labelling process (coding):

- Level 1 is labelling or coding;
- Level 2 is categorisation.

Therefore, categorisation is a refining and sorting process where you organise your coded pieces of data to see *which* goes *where* and with *what* and *why*. This is what Patton (2002) defines as seeking convergence and divergence. Convergence is when we look for things that are the same and divergence is when things are different.

Creating maps and matrices

The maps and matrices you create are data management tools that show the analytical processes you have performed. These serve your research by enabling you to visually present your data and show how you arrived at your findings.

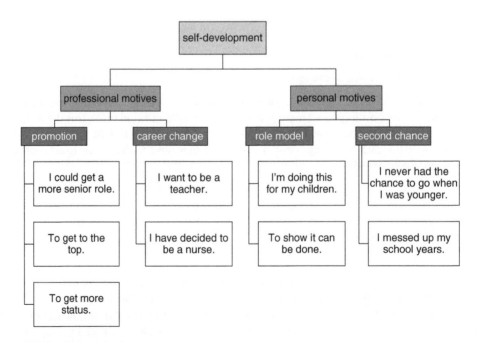

Figure 11.7   A hierarchy tree

This hierarchy tree (see Figure 11.7) illustrates the coding decisions made as individual pieces of data are coded by being given a name or label (*promotion, career change, role model, second chance*; see Box 11.2). It then shows how these first codes were reduced to form two categories (*professional motives, personal motives*). These categories were further reduced to create one key finding (*self-development*). This basic tree diagram can support the writing up of your findings as it traces the development of these enabling you to draw on the data you have coded to act as supporting information to add credibility to your interpretation.

You could present your data within a table as shown in Figure 11.8. It may not have the visual appeal of a tree diagram but is just as useful as it shows your consistent application of codes, how you identified your categories and how these informed your creations of larger more substantive themes.

Category	Professional motives		Personal motives	
code	Promotion	Career change	Role model	Second chance
data	More senior role	Want to be a teacher	Doing it for my children	Never had the chance when I was younger
	Get to the top	Decided to be a nurse	Show it can be done	Messed up school

Figure 11.8   A findings matrix

There are many ways to display your data that show your creation and application of codes. Visual display can add value to your work; artistically, as it can break up the text, but it also demonstrates the transparency of your analytical processes by openly showing your processes of coding and categorisation so judgement can be made on your consistent application of these processes.

ANALYSING DATA USING FRAMEWORK ANALYSIS

A variant on this process of constant comparison is the thematic approach to the analysis of data as presented by Ritchie and Spencer (1994). Like the core processes of constant comparison explored above, the fundamental processes involved are to interrogate and reduce large amounts of data and to provide coherence and structure. This, Ritchie and Spencer (1994) state, involves processes designed to define, categorise, theorise, explain and explore the data as framework or thematic analysis is the generation of themes from data.

When used in a systematic and logical manner, framework (thematic) analysis provides a robust approach and as Nowell et al. (2017) affirm, this approach to analysis can be precise and consistent, as it provides enough detail to enable your reader to determine whether the process undertaken is credible. Therefore, researchers often select this method as it can remove much of the ambiguity and uncertainty that can surround the analytical process. As a coding process, framework (thematic) analysis is flexible, dynamic and iterative and can be used for all forms of data whether this is text or image-based. There are many similarities with constant comparison as, like that approach to data analysis, this method begins with familiarisation with the raw data and the application of cross-data labelling. Figure 11.9 provides an overview of key parts of framework analysis.

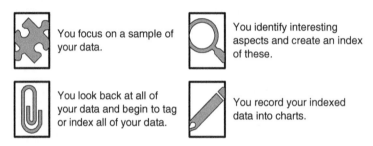

Figure 11.9   An overview of thematic or framework analysis

As in constant comparison, you should begin by refocusing on your research question and as the first step indicates, being focused on the research question(s) and/or aim(s) aids the familiarisation process.

Familiarisation: This is where you begin to identify initial themes or concepts, which is a crucial activity at the start of any analytical process. The difference between constant comparison and framework analysis is that it is not necessary to include the entire data set in this first familiarisation process. Ritchie, Spencer and O'Connor (2003) advocate that you identify a sample of your data with which to create your index or codes. This is the 'framework' created by this approach to analysis. This process helps to reduce the amount of data you have to work with and minimise the time taken. However, deciding whether to take a sample of your data is dependent on the amount of data you have to work with. If you have a limited amount, it may be possible to review it all to identify key aspects and emergent themes.

1a	Role modelling for children
1b	Pay back to society
2a	Increased salary
2b	Promotion at work
3	Career change
4	Second chance
5	Scared and confused

Figure 11.10   Creating an index table

Constructing an index: As you immerse yourself in your data you will begin to identify interesting things happening and, when found, you can create a list or an index of these interesting events. Ritchie, Spencer and O'Connor (2003) use the terminology 'index' rather than 'code' but the process is exactly the same as you are naming parts of your data that appear to have relevance and meaning. This can be seen in Figure 11.10 in the example offered of students returning to study.

Labelling or tagging your data: As you have generated your list of codes or your index you can now go through your data looking for examples of these identified aspects or indexed codes. As Figure 11.11 indicates, you can label (*or tag*) pieces of data according to your identified coded index. The codes or index you have generated provide a focus for your analysis.

Data set	Data	index	Main theme
Prospectus 1 **Narrative 1** **page 15, line 12**	*I wanted to come to uni to show my children that studying is a good thing.*	1a	Role model
Prospectus 2 **Narrative 3** **page 3, line 5**	*I work with children who do not think about going to uni. If they know I'm doing it maybe they will want to.*	1a	Role model
Prospectus 3 **Narrative 2** **page 2, line 4**	*Coming back to study has increased my chance of promotion. I am being offered more challenging things to do and this has boosted my self-esteem no end.*	2b	Increased promotion

Figure 11.11   Recording tagged or indexed data

Sorting the data by theme or concept: The next step is to sort or order the data in some way so that material with similar content or properties is located together. The purpose of sorting the data is to allow you to focus on each subject. Very much like the principles we explored in constant comparison, you are trying to show patterns and connections in your data to identify recurrent themes. To do this, you could create a spreadsheet or a Word table such as this offered in Figure 11.12.

Main themes	**Personal motives**		**Work related**		
Indexes	Role modelling for children	Second chance	Promotion at work	Increased salary	Career change
Data	*I wanted to come to uni to show my children that studying is a good thing.*	*I messed up at school now I have another chance.*	*Coming back to study has increased my chance of promotion. I am being offered more challenging things to do and this has boosted my self-esteem no end.*	*Now I am at uni I had a pay rise.*	*I just wanted to do something different.*

Figure 11.12   Creating main themes

In both framework analysis and constant comparison you are trying to show the systematic processes you took to reduce your data into higher order themes. The more clarity you can bring to this the better, so for this purpose it is worth exploring processes of visual display.

UNDERSTANDING THEORY FIRST APPROACHES

Theory first approaches are not usually associated with qualitative analysis but in qualitative secondary research they can have a role in understanding key elements of the documents you want to analyse. This may be in identifying specific components such as in narrative analysis or content analysis. When you analyse data using a 'theory first' approach you can utilise many of the strategies we explored in constant comparison and specifically, those within framework analysis. The main difference is that the themes you identify will not emerge specifically from your data, as they will be known to you and, thus, they will be applied.

Being pragmatic

If you are unsure of how to analyse your data, you could adopt Creswell's (2009) guidance on the role of theory within coding. This pragmatic approach embraces both deductive and inductive ways of thinking about theory. This is called a 'top down' (theory first) and 'bottom up' (theory after) approach to coding (Crabtree & Miller 1999). Creswell (2009: 187) states that codes can derive from:

- **Topics readers would expect to find from literature and common sense:** This is your conceptual framework based on your reading and your understanding of the world.
- **Codes that were not anticipated:** These are codes that you did not expect to find but offer insight into the problem.
- **Codes that are unusual:** These are codes that stand out as different.
- **Codes that address theoretical perspectives:** These are codes that are based on existing theories or ways of understanding.

Miles and Huberman (1994) state most researchers have some preconceived notions as to what they will find in their data but being too fixed on coding based on established theories and concepts can be detrimental (Maxwell 1996). You may miss interesting things happening in your data that are not identified by your theory or concepts. Therefore, we advise you to consider what you want to know from your data and focus on the need to remain open to emergent concepts and themes and to be flexible in the way you respond to these.

USING COMPUTERS TO ANALYSE DATA

If you prefer or need to use computers as your data set is large, then there are computer assisted qualitative data analysis (CAQDAS) programs available to use. These programs can handle a wide range of data including text, image-based and video and handle substantial amounts. Programs such as NVivo, Atlas.ti, NUD*IST, Transana, HyperRESEARCH and MAXQDA offer significant benefits over manual coding processes such as:

- The ability to create visual representations of data (*e.g. charts, graphs, tables and trees*) that can aid your reader's understanding of your findings.
- The ease of being able to manipulate the categories created and consider alternative ways of approaching your analysis. Although this ease is possible when hand coding, it can be messy and hard to manage. Using a computer can provide a more elegant approach as you can save various versions, showing how you arrived at your findings.
- Removing yourself from the coding process can reduce researcher bias.

If this is a new area to you then there are many websites, YouTube tutorials and other forms of online support (e.g. http://onlineqda.hud.ac.uk/index.php, http://caqdas.soc.surrey.ac.uk/) to guide you. You can also seek advice from your IT department as they may be able to assist you in your selection of software. As a final thought, it is worth appreciating that computers can only do so much of the work; what your findings mean is for you to consider (Gibbs 2014).

Using non-specialist computer programs

You do not have to use a specific data handling package to analyse your data using a computer. There are some tools on your computer that can be used to aid your analysis. For example:

- Digitise your data (*e.g. scan or create documents as a PDF*). This enables you to store it securely, work on it without losing it, and use the interactive functions within PDF readers: explore the editing features that these have to offer.
- Use a word processing package such as MS Word to colour code your data; use the highlighting tools or colour code your text.
- Use the *'find'* feature available in most PDF and word processing packages to count instances of a word or phrase.
- Use the *'review'* feature of a word processing package such as MS Word to add comments to your data (*very useful for applying codes*).
- Excel, Google sheets or Apple Numbers make spreadsheets: using tables in any format is a useful way to record your coding and categorisation process and the development of key themes.

MAKING AN INTERPRETATION

All your analytical processes lead to the presentation of your findings and the discussion and interpretation you undertake. However, these findings need to be interpreted and Coffey and Atkinson (1996) describe this process as transformation, as your coded and categorised data assumes meaning. We explore this in Chapter 13, but it is worth reflecting that the hard work you put in when you analyse your data should lead to robust and significant findings, enabling you to answer your research question(s) and/or aim(s).

EXPLORING DIFFERENT METHODS OF ANALYSIS

There are many different and diverse ways of approaching your analysis. In this section we provide a brief overview of possible and potential methods of analysis that are relevant to the qualitative secondary researcher who uses documents as data. There are very specific approaches such as content analysis which can provide a numerical account of your data as well as approaches specifically supporting the analysis of images. The following section provides a very brief overview of approaches to analysis that have relevance to you as a qualitative secondary researcher.

Discourse analysis

If you want to explore the role and function of discourse, then discourse analysis may be what you need to consider. There are many definitions of discourse and discourse analysis (Phillips & Hardy 2002) but there is basic agreement that when we study discourse, we are considering language as a form of social behaviour (Van Den Berg 2005). In discourse analysis, you will explore units of language such as words and sentences but you will go beyond this. Discourse analysis provides opportunities to explore both form and meaning which means exploring the more abstract and symbolic messages that can convey an understanding of how the social world and social practices are created (Allen 2011) (see Box 11.4).

BOX 11.4   ANALYSING HEADLINES

At a basic level, discourse analysis is an analysis of text, words and significantly, what is happening in between.

You could analyse newspaper headlines over a period of one week to explore a specific event. You may begin by identifying the units for analysis which, as words and grammar, provide a literal meaning. However, discourse analysis enables us to go beyond this and consider the message that is conveyed. This is the symbolic function of the headline.

The headline's meaning goes beyond grammar and needs to be placed into a context that embraces social, cultural and political meanings. We could do this by exploring the font used, the heading's position on the page and the genre of newspaper. When we access online news media we can explore the advertisements that may be placed on the page and not how frequently the headline is updated by following a news stream.

To guide you in your approach to discourse analysis, you could use Fairclough's (1989) three-dimensional framework to support your analysis. This approach to discourse analysis enables you to explore discourse as occurring in three levels (see Figure 11.13).

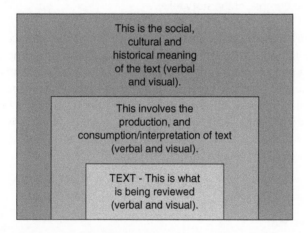

This is the social, cultural and historical meaning of the text (verbal and visual).

This involves the production, and consumption/interpretation of text (verbal and visual).

TEXT - This is what is being reviewed (verbal and visual).

Figure 11.13   Adapted from Fairclough's Three-dimensional model of discourse 1989

Source: Fairclough: *Language and Power* ©1989 Routledge, reproduced by permission of Taylor & Francis Books UK

The aim when using discourse analysis is to understand the '*multiple meanings assigned to text*' (Phillips & Hardy 2002: 74) and Fairclough's model does this by offering a critical exploration of language in social and cultural contexts. An example of the effective use of Fairclough's model would be to explore a piece of legislation and consider it as a document (*its form*), to explore what it means socially and historically (*its discursive practice as a piece of legislation*) and how this document is shaped by the social world and how this document shapes the social world (*social practice – power*). This method of analysis would be suitable for all forms of data, verbal or visual.

Narrative analysis

If you ask a question to understand life stories or how people create personal narratives then you could consider conducting narrative analysis. This is an approach to analysis that helps to understand how people construct and use stories to interpret the world (Bamberg 2012). Narratives are social products which are produced by people in social, historical and cultural locations and they reflect the way people represent themselves and their worlds to themselves and to others.

This approach to analysis systematically identifies how narratives are constructed and what they mean (Bamberg 2012). Therefore, when analysing data, you need to consider that there is a thematic, performative, interactional and structural component of a narrative and each one can be searched for in your data (Riessman 2005). To aid your analysis, you could use the coding and categorisation sequences explored at the beginning of this chapter and identify:

* the 'story' being told;
* how it is told (how the narrative is constructed);
* the intention and purpose of the story teller.

One often underplayed aspect of this form of analysis is the significance of the audience in the function of the narrative (Riessman 1993). This means knowing who is going to read it, in what context and understanding how this influences the narrative that is created. This may have some relevance if you want to explore online forms of data. There may be a performance quality to the narratives created in blogs as the writer may expect their online journal to be read by a wider audience. Alternatively, some people may create narratives unaware of who reads them. Therefore, this method of analysis could be used to explore diverse forms of narrative data such as a personal blog, a diary or letters.

Content analysis

Content analysis straddles the qualitative and quantitative paradigms as there is a strong focus on measurement. In content analysis both the content (*the frequency of words or phrases*) and the context are analysed. This can be performed using computer programs that can automatically scan documents and create an index of the words you hope to find. MAXQDA provides a Key Words in Context tool for this purpose. This method of analysis allows you to turn your document or image from qualitative into quantitative or numerical data.

You can also do this manually by applying codes and seeking patterns and relationships as explored in framework (thematic) analysis. The units for analysis would be clearly defined as you would look for specific words or phrases identified by your conceptual and theoretical frameworks.

You can also undertake a linguistic inquiry and word counts. This can be useful to chart specific word usage as the words people use in their daily lives can reveal important insights into their world. This is based on the belief that documents can reveal *'linguistic fingerprints'* which are created using distinctive vocabulary and word usage (Pennebaker, Mehl, & Niederhoffer 2003: 568). You can count your identified words either manually or using a computer. Your data could be a diary, a set of personal papers or in a sequence of social media posts written by one person. You can also conduct content analysis of images to create *'implicit or explicit classification and quantification'* (van Leeuwen & Jewitt 2001:10).

Content analysis as a quantified approach cannot help you understand the significance or meaning of the frequency of an occurrence. It can only indicate the *what, where, when* but not the *why*.

Visual analysis

You can perform most of the approaches discussed in this chapter on visual data. Each one could lead to a new and unique way of understanding your data so you need to select your approach with a clear understanding of want you want to gain from your data. There is a specific way of exploring images termed 'semiotics' (Chandler 2007). This is where the image is conceived as carrying more information than what it represents. As we show in Figure 11.14, in a semiotic approach to the analysis of images, two levels of possible meaning emerge.

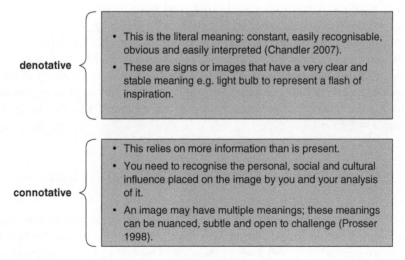

Figure 11.14   Layers of meaning when analysing images

These two layers of meaning can be coded (*named and labelled*) and analysed thematically. It may be that you want to explore the image and its relationship to the viewer or audience (Rose 2001). If this is the case, where the image is found and why it was placed there become significant aspects to consider. You can use images within a field of research called visual ethnography (Pink 2007) where there is an analysis of images linked to specific social or cultural groups to understand their culture.

Grounded theory

Grounded theory is an iterative approach to analysing data based on theory being generated from or grounded in the data. It is, therefore, a data-driven approach to category and theme creation provided by processes of constant comparison (as reviewed earlier in this chapter). However, classic grounded theory is more than an approach to analysis – it is also a research design. Many who undertake this approach to their data do not begin with a literature review or consider the importance of theoretical and conceptual frameworks until after the data has been analysed. There is also no predetermined research problem. As classic grounded theory requires the use of multiple stages of data collection (Corbin & Strauss 2007), this may deter less experienced researchers.

DATA ANALYSIS AND RESEARCH RIGOUR

In Chapter 4, we explored strategies, techniques and processes that could enhance the confidence that you as a researcher and others can have in your research. Making sure you analyse your data in a systematic and consistent way will support research replication and the confidence your reader can have in your findings. Showing how you did this reflects research transparency. How a researcher has arrived at their findings can often be a bit blurred or under communicated. Therefore, we advise you to engage in analytic transparency and be as open and as precise as you can be. Show your hard work and show how you arrived at your findings. Presenting your analysis diligently can aid the credibility of your findings.

ADVICE AND GUIDANCE FOR ANALYSING YOUR DATA

The method of analysis you select should be firmly based on how you need to respond to the research question(s) and/or aim(s) you set. We offer the following advice to guide you in your selection and we support this with a set of questions (see Figure 11.15) designed to further refine your decision:

- **Find a method of analysis that enables you to answer your question as fully as you can:** This sounds basic but make sure you employ a method that lets you find out what you want to find out.
- **Select a method that leads you to reduce your data into something you can understand:** Again, this sounds basic, but make sure you select a method that makes sense as it is easy to be bamboozled by approaches to analysis.
- **Engage in methods of data display that are meaningful to you:** Sometimes methods such as framework analysis can advocate prescriptive approaches to data visualisation that may not suit your way of working. If this is the case, experiment with approaches to data display; this could be the contribution you make to research in your subject.
- **Select a method that facilitates your ability to see what is happening across all of your data sets:** This is important so as to establish the continuity and accuracy of your analysis. If you decide to adopt framework analysis, depending on the amount of data you have you may want to view all of your data and not just a sample.
- **Make sure you employ a consistent application of codes or indexing:** This adds to the accuracy and clarity of your process and to analytic transparency.

You will need to defend your choice of analytic method in your methodology so you need to have this relationship between your question, your data and your method of analysis very clear. Figure 11.15 offers some guidance to support your decision making.

Question	Considerations
What type of data do you want to analyse?	Visual, verbal or object? Is the type of data important; e.g. do you want to analyse your visual data in a specific way?
Do you want to explore the way stories are created and produced?	If yes, then narrative analysis could be the most appropriate method for you to use.
Do you want to explore the use of language (discourse)?	If the answer is yes, it may be advisable to explore the use of discourse analysis to understand the form of a text and its meaning but if you want to know how power works in language then critical discourse analysis may suit your needs
Are you using visual data? If you are, do you want to explore specific features of your data? Do you want to understand your image as more than a picture or photograph?	You could use framework or thematic analysis, content analysis or discourse analysis. However, if you wanted to fully understand the symbolic aspects of your image, you may need to consider the use of semiotics.
Do you want to count the frequency of words or events and see how they are used in context?	If you do, this suggests you may want to employ a method of content analysis. You may want to explore a computer program that can produce KWiC.

(Continued)

Figure 11.15   (Continued)

Question	Considerations
Do you want to see what emerges from your data?	If you do, this suggests you are interested in constant comparison as your findings will emerge as grounded in your data.
Do you want to identify clear and consistent themes in your data?	The answer should be 'yes' and this means that all forms of analysis are possible but the choice depends on your question and what you want to know.
Have you considered the function of theory in your analysis?	As a final thought, consider how theory will function in your analysis; will it be applied as a framework or will it be something that occurs out of your analysis?

Figure 11.15   A checklist for analysis

REFLECTION AND FURTHER READING

At the beginning of the chapter we set out what you should be able to do when you reached the end of this chapter. To aid your reflection on all we have covered we ask some chapter specific questions. If you are unsure of any of your answers to these questions, please go back to the relevant section to review this aspect.

REFLECTING ON CHAPTER 11

In this chapter we have:

- **Clarified the need for data analysis:** Can you name two reasons why data analysis is needed?
- **Provided an overview of underlying principles of analysis:** Do you know what these steps are? How do themes emerge from your data? How will you use theory in your analysis?
- **Offered strategies to support effective data analysis:** How would you record your codes and categories? Could you defend the approach you want to use?
- **Provided an overview of approaches to analysis that may be appropriate within qualitative secondary research:** Do you have a preferred approach to analysis? What should you base your choice on? Could you defend this in your methodology?
- **Explored the role of analysis in supporting aspects of research rigour:** Can you identify a strategy to support research rigour?

WE RECOMMEND FOR FURTHER READING:

Altheide, D. & Schneider, C. (2013) *Qualitative Media Analysis*. London: SAGE Publications Ltd. This is a key text for all those who want to explore qualitative media analysis. We recommend Chapter 3 which sets out the underpinning principles involved in this specialised approach to document analysis.

Bowen, G.A. (2009) Document analysis as a qualitative research method. *Qualitative Research Journal, 9*(2), 27–40.
This article presents a very readable account of the analysis of documents.

Elo, S. & Kyngas, H. (2008) The qualitative content analysis process. *Journal of Advanced Nursing, 62*(1), 107–115.
This article provides a very clear approach to inductive and deductive approaches to content analysis.

Glaser, B.G. & Strauss, A. (1967) *The Discovery of Grounded Theory; Strategies for Qualitative Research.* Chicago: Aldine Publishing Company.
This is the original version of this key text. If you are interested in grounded theory, this is where it all began.

Mason, P. (2005) Visual data in applied qualitative research: Lessons from experience. *Qualitative Research, 5*(3), 325-346.
This article contains a concise overview of visual methods to springboard further exploration.

Miles, M.B., Huberman, M.A. & Saldaña, J. (2013) *Qualitative Data Analysis: A Methods Sourcebook* (3rd edn). California: SAGE Publications, Inc.
This is an updated version of Miles and Huberman's 1994 classic text. This provides an excellent overview of coding, categorisation and theme creation and approaches to research quality.

Saldaña, J. (2012) *The Coding Manual for Qualitative Researchers*. London: SAGE Publications Ltd. This is an extremely useful reference book for anyone who wants to know more about a variety of coding strategies. Section one sets the scene very clearly.

Spencer, L., Ritchie, J. & O'Connor, W. (2003) Analysis: Practices, principles and processes. In J. Ritchie & J. Lewis (eds), *Qualitative Research Practice: A Guide for Social Science Students and Researchers* (pp. 269–293). London: SAGE Publications Ltd.
This chapter and the one that follows (Chapter 11) offer an overview of the principles behind analysis.

12
WORKING WITH NUMBERS

THIS CHAPTER WILL SUPPORT YOUR ABILITY TO

examine the use of numbers in qualitative research

categorise statistics

understand the use of measures of cental tendency

appraise the use of descriptive statistics for numerical data

identify steps in preparing your data for statistical analysis

CHAPTER OVERVIEW

Although this book focuses on the use of qualitative data, there are times when it is not only possible but indeed beneficial to use numbers. Therefore, in this chapter we explore ways that you could use numerical data as a method of analysis within qualitative secondary research. We demonstrate how numbers can play an important role in both illustrating and clarifying your qualitative analyses. To do this, this chapter begins by considering why you may want to use numerical data for qualitative or mixed methods research.

In this chapter, we explore how meaning can be created with numerical data and that even data not immediately recognisable as numerical can be explored easily using statistical methods. This chapter also explains what is meant by statistics, and specifically descriptive statistics, and provides guidance on their role in your data analysis. This includes the application of mathematical measures (*e.g. means and dispersions*) that can help to summarise, interpret and present your data. It will also signpost the possible pitfalls and challenges, within the deployment of descriptive statistics, and so by the end of this chapter you should be able to confidently describe and interpret your data using numbers, through the application of descriptive statistics.

WHY DO I NEED NUMBERS WHEN WORKING WITH QUALITATIVE DATA?

Secondary qualitative research uses forms of data that support the capture of descriptions to enable patterns to be extracted, to form meaning. That said, a qualitative approach to data does not necessarily exclude being able to work with numbers and at times a more quantitative approach to qualitative data can enrich your narrative portrayal and enhance your analysis. In considering the use of numbers in your secondary analysis, we identify that it is possible to work with them in adopting three different approaches:

1. To apply a form of analysis to qualitative data that creates a numerical understanding (*e.g. Content Analysis*).
2. To use qualitative data that has some numerical components (*e.g. scholarly journal articles exploring empirical research*).
3. To employ data that is considered quantitative as it is numerically focused (*e.g. census data, crime statistics*).

As stated, it is possible to see that in most forms of qualitative research, quantitative claims are made. This can be seen when we perform a frequency count and check how much of a 'thing' or instance can be found within the data. When new to this, we often employ statistically orientated language by using terms which include: *many, often, frequently* and *sometimes*. For instance, Morris (2018), when researching the culture of an academy case study, used the following terms to describe the proportions of staff responses from qualitative focus groups and interviews:

* **Overwhelming majority** – approximately 85% of staff;
* **Most** – approximately 75% of staff;
* **Many** – approximately 50% of staff;
* **Some** – approximately 25% of staff;
* **Few** – approximately 15% of staff.

This approach is what led Becker (1970) to coin the term quasi statistics, as this reflects the use of a simple count or percentage in an attempt to add value to the more descriptive results provided by the qualitative data. This is similar to what Sandelowski, Voils and Knafl (2009: 210) identified as '*quantitizing*' qualitative data.

In your qualitative secondary research there may also be the possibility of using mixed approaches for your analysis of mixed types of data (*e.g. using qualitative data that has some numerical component*). This approach crosses the qualitative and quantitative divide (see Chapter 3). Although these may be considered as separate paradigms, it is both possible and at times useful to consider both. This can also offer an alternative way of seeking methodological triangulation and may enhance the credibility and authority of the research findings you produce (see Chapter 4). Additionally, using a blend of non-numeric (*i.e documentary or qualitative*) data and numeric (*quantitative*) data may also provide you with a fuller picture and act as a '*litmus test*' (Linnekin 1987: 920). This is what Chibnik (1999) suggests enables researchers to differentiate between scientifically positioned data and the more humanistically placed descriptive or expressive research.

While quantitative and qualitative data provide different outcomes, they can be gathered from the same data and are often used together to provide a complementary full picture of a population. For example, if data are collected on annual income (*quantitative*), data on occupation (*qualitative*) could also be gathered to reveal more detail on the average annual income for each type of occupation (see Figure 12.1).

Data unit	Numerical question	Quantitative data	Category question	Qualitative data
A person	*How much* do you earn?	£24,000 p.a.	*What* is your occupation?	Gardener
A family firm	*How many* workers are currently employed?	8 employees	*What* type of organisation do you work in?	A family run company

Figure 12.1   Identifying quantitative and qualitative data

HOW DO I BEGIN TO CREATE MEANING FROM NUMBERS?

When endeavouring to create meaning from the numbers, it is possible that the data immersion we explored in Chapter 11 as the first steps within data analysis may provide you with little depth or insight. This is because numbers are not an exact count as they can change depending upon the classifications employed and the measurements (Lewontin & Levin 2000). An example of this can be found in research that seeks to examine changes in food preference and uses the categories for measurement as 'vegetarian' or 'meat-eater'. The reduced range of categories does not allow for the inclusion of categories such as *fruitarian, vegan* and *lacto-vegetarian* which may influence the validity and credibility of the numerical data collated. Not knowing how the data are created therefore impacts on the effectiveness of the interpretation that you can make. Figure 12.2 identifies common examples of quantitative data.

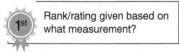

£   Cost: is this net or gross?

%   Percentage: of which proportion?

1st   Rank/rating given based on what measurement?

Figure 12.2   Outlining common examples of quantitative data

Before you begin to consider your approach to numerical analysis, you need to focus on understanding the data set (*qualitative or quantitative*) that you have in front of you. The keywords to use are 'why' and 'how', as you need to understand why and how the data were created. This means taking time to know the answers to certain questions (see Figure 12.3).

Question	Response
What is the data showing?	Get past the headers and examine the evidence.
Is the source reliable?	Are the numbers and evidence consistent?
What is the evidence based on?	Extract arguments and determine the strength of evidence. Can you extract numerical data?
Is there a wide range of relevant contemporary evidence cited?	Examine the reference list.
Where does the data come from?	Determine the sample size, population and location.
What year was the data generated?	Remember that the time frame may impact on the current position due to subsequent policy changes.
How was the data generated?	Can you extract data that you can collate quantitatively?
Are there any ethical concerns?	Identify possible ethical considerations.
Who compiled the data?	Is there any evidence of bias reflected in the numbers?
What are the possible challenges to accepting the data conclusions?	Were the limitations or alternative explanations outlined?
How was the data measured?	Did this involve quantitative analysis or data that we could now count or measure?
What else do I need to know?	Focus on identifying the information that would help you make a more informed decision.
Where can I get more information?	Consider further avenues of support?

Figure 12.3   Questions to ask about your data

Making sense of the figures begins when you start to interrogate them for meaning. This process of meaning making begins with the classification and description of the numbers within your data. These processes when applied in a systematic way enable you to decipher your numerical data's meaning (Diamantopoulos & Schlegelmilch 2002). These processes are similar to qualitative data analysis as you are trying to make sense of your data but, as we are using numbers, we do this via numerical strategies. This sense is achieved by firstly displaying and then interpreting your numerical data in a way that enables you to make clear judgements as to what the numbers actually mean. While you may consider that numbers and the statistical techniques engaged allow the data to speak for themselves, this is only part of the process. You also need to put your findings into context so you can make conclusions based on all the evidence obtained. Therefore, be sure to keep in mind that for the quantitative data to be meaningful it is important to find an appropriate method that supports you to find and explain the meaning in the numbers. Outlined in Figure 12.3 are some questions to consider when you are exploring your data.

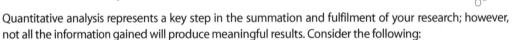

PAUSE FOR THOUGHT

What do numbers really mean?

Quantitative analysis represents a key step in the summation and fulfilment of your research; however, not all the information gained will produce meaningful results. Consider the following:

- How have the data been categorised?
- What influence may this have when '*quantitizing*' your qualitative data?
- What impact may this have on the findings and conclusions of your research?

HOW CAN STATISTICS CREATE MEANING?

One method for creating meaning from numbers is statistics, which comes under the branch of applied mathematics. This approach to numbers is concerned with the study of the probability of events happening based on a collection of known numerical data. The application of statistics enables you to concisely characterise your numerical data. In Figure 12.4 we illustrate what statistics can do within your numerical analysis.

As Figure 12.4 illustrates, statistics can be very useful as they facilitate your attempts to extrapolate mathematical meaning from the data so an interpretation can be made. However, do not worry if the thought of working with numbers fills you with anxiety; you do not need to be a statistician to be able to work effectively with your existing quantitative data (Smith 2011). There are two statistical approaches that are accessible to even novice statisticians which can be very effective when trying to understand numerically orientated data. Figure 12.5 identifies these.

We will focus on descriptive rather than inferential statistics because, when working with pre-existing data that you have not instigated or been involved in, its creation it is more difficult to know for certain that the data you are using are complete. The idea of 'completeness' relates

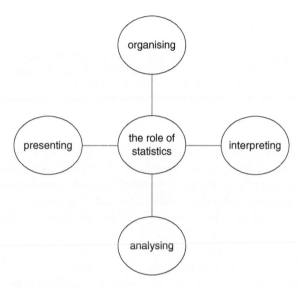

Figure 12.4   The role of statistics

Descriptive statistics

- offers descriptions through numerical calculations, tables or graphs.

Inferential statistics

- uses statistical tests to make judgement about the data, typically used when analysing variables (*these are things that are measured or manipulated in research*).

Figure 12.5   Defining statistical approaches

---

to the transparency of the research and how far your data set outlines all its attributes and specific factors influencing its production. This level of uncertainty is challenging, particularly if you are using inferential statistics as you are trying to reach conclusions and make judgements about the probability level that an observed difference is valid, or due to chance factors. In the end, whilst there is always going to be an element of uncertainty attached to your data, it is your role as a secondary researcher to minimise or acknowledge that uncertainty.

Transparency is therefore key in the statistical production process and will increase the quality of your statistical outcome. Inferential statistics may be used if you choose to conduct a meta-analysis. Due to the nuances and depth involved in this analysis, this book is unable to go into great detail on this technique (*although there are many statistical textbooks which can support you in the task*).

> **Meta-analysis**
>
> • This is a statistical procedure which involves combining data from multiple data sets to explore if the results are statistically significant. In other words, if the results occurred by chance or not.

Figure 12.6 Defining meta-analysis

As a brief overview, a meta-analysis provides a systematic framework for handling and analysing a large number of studies that can aid you in answering your research questions (see Figure 12.6). It is a process of evaluating the decisions and conclusions made within identified data sets and recognising common specific characteristics (*e.g. sample population, date range, data types and research design*). Whilst this process does not need to be overly complicated, it requires organisation and attention to detail and a specific set of inclusion and exclusion criteria for the studies must be defined. Therefore, if you decide to conduct a meta-analysis, you need access to a reasonable body of detailed data. You would then enter the information into a database, and this 'meta-data' is statistically 'meta-analysed' to inferentially test certain hypotheses. An example of a meta-analysis is outlined in Box 12.1.

> **BOX 12.1   THE GREAT DEBATE – GLASS (1978)**
>
> In 1952, Hans J. Eysenck (*who was an influential figure in post-war British psychology*) reasoned that psychotherapy had no significant effect in facilitating the recovery of patients. This prompted a long-lasting debate around the effectiveness of psychotherapy.
>
> To prove Eysenck wrong, Gene V. Glass conducted a meta-analysis to statistically aggregate the findings of 375 psychotherapy outcomes. He examined the duration, type of therapy, age and the IQ of each client. He also noted the therapist's training and background. He applied both descriptive and inferential statistics to the numerical data collated. The results of this led Glass to conclude that psychotherapy did work.
>
> Since this time there have been thousands of investigations exploring psychotherapy and the debate continues to this day. For example, Dragioti et al. (2017) conducted a meta-analysis of 173 pertinent studies and 247 previously conducted meta-analyses on the outcomes of psychotherapy to assess the credibility of the evidence presented. They reported that whilst almost 80 per cent of meta-analyses supported the use of psychotherapy, they argued that only a few meta-analyses provided objective and convincing evidence.

There are many types of meta-analysis you may wish to consider; however, to perform a confident meta-analysis, it is critical to have a full understanding of the information provided and explicit data to access, in order to apply your statistical test. You need to be able to compare and measure like with like and this is where the difficulties and weakness of meta-analysis often lie. Research aims may look similar but researchers may employ quite different methods and samples in their investigations. Even Glass (1976: 351) commented it could be akin to '*mixing apples and oranges*', meaning you are not comparing like for like. However, whilst pooling data through meta-analysis can create problems, meta-analysis can be useful in determining if scientific findings are consistent and generalisable (Biondi-Zoccai et al. 2011).

DESCRIPTIVE STATISTICS

Descriptive statistics is a technique for simply describing what the data shows and, as such, it can be an effective way to reduce substantial amounts of data into a simpler summary. To illustrate how you can utilise descriptive statistics to create meaning in your research, we explore these measures in Figure 12.7.

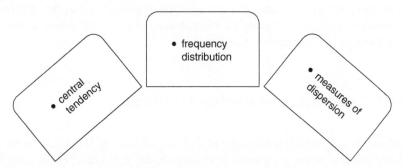

Figure 12.7   Statistical measures within descriptive statistics

These tools as shown in Figure 12.7 support your ability to see patterns and relationships in your qualitative data through quantitative analysis. However, before we do this, it is important to note that as a form of analysis, descriptive statistics not only offers opportunities to present your data in visually appealing ways that add clarity but it can also provide visual impact. As discussed in Chapter 13, we propose that time is spent considering forms of data display and representation as it is an essential part of your research project. It indicates your problem-solving capabilities and it communicates the points you want to make with increased efficiency (Larkin & Simon 1987). Such an approach creates a précis of the research findings which can be statistical, graphical and text based.

PAUSE FOR THOUGHT

Descriptive statistics

Descriptive statistics are used to describe what is going on in your data and can help you to manage and present relevant features of your data more thoroughly and convincingly.

- The presentation of your data can be offered in a variety of formats (*charts, tables, diagrams*) but you always need to use words to place your understanding of your data into a meaningful context (see Chapter 13).

Descriptive statistics can support you in communicating clearly and simply what the data indicates, thus facilitating a straightforward analysis which gives clarity and meaning, leading to a more concise, relevant and persuasive summary.

Although you may feel apprehensive when using quantitative forms of analysis, it is worth knowing that many descriptive strategies can be applied using basic arithmetic techniques. This makes them well within the grasp of most researchers. The following section explores the measures used within descriptive statistics.

Strategy 1 – measures of central tendency

Central tendency is a numerical measurement that pinpoints a single value as being typical of an entire distribution of scores (Gravetter & Wallnau 2000). It is a descriptive statistical strategy because it supports your ability to describe or present a set of data in a simplified and succinct way. It is a frequently employed statistical measure that can both identify and describe the central position, or 'average' within a group of data.

As illustrated (see Figure 12.8) there are two types of positional average; the median and the mode:

- **Median:** This is the average value in which half the values are less than the median and half the values are greater than the median.
- **Mode:** This is the second positional average and shows a higher frequency in the series.

There is one statistical average and this is called the mean:

- **Mean:** This is obtained by adding all the items of the series and dividing this total by the number of items.

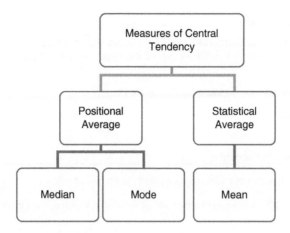

Figure 12.8 Measures of central tendency

Whilst the general concept of 'average' can be ambiguous, through measures of central tendency we can access statistical averages using these measurements of the *mean, median* and *mode*. Figure 12.9 provides examples of these measures so you can see what they look like in practice. You should see that the mean, median and mode are calculated using different strategies and often result in different average values. It is therefore important to understand what these statistical measures of average tell us about the original data, in order to decide which measure of 'average' (*or most typical*) is the most appropriate and useful to describe a data set.

In Figure 12.9, we have calculated three forms of 'average' measures that represent the typical value within a distribution of data. However, using these three measures we were able to create two different numbers: 13 and 14. As secondary researchers, the differences demonstrate some of the difficulties faced with the deployment of measures of central tendency as you could potentially end up with three different figures all pertaining to measure the 'average'. Therefore, the selection of the appropriate 'average' is important, as the inappropriate selection could result in bias and confusion as we illustrate in Box 12.2.

BOX 12.2 WHEN AVERAGES ARE LESS THAN 'AVERAGE'

President George W. Bush of the USA used measures of central tendency in a potentially misleading way. He told the American people that he had countersigned a bill resulting in an 'average' tax reduction of $1,089. In fact, President Bush was referring to the mean rather than the median. This figure ended up being misrepresentative, since the massive cuts were actually given to a small amount of extremely wealthy American tax payers, which skewed the data. This made the $1,089 average tax reduction a disingenuous figure, since the vast majority of American tax payers did not benefit from a tax reduction (Robinson & Scherlen 2007).

MEAN	The average

- The mean is calculated by adding up the total figures of the research data and then dividing the total by the individual number of data. This provides a summary of the distribution via a single number.

- $0 + 20 + 9 + 14 + 14 + 30 + 4 = 91$ We divide 91 by 7 = 13.

- **Therefore the mean is 13.**

MODE	The most common

- The mode is the number that appears most frequently in the set of data.

- $0 + 20 + 9 + 14 + 14 + 30 + 4$ We can see that 14 appears twice which is once more than any other measurement.

- **Therefore the mode is 14.**

MEDIAN	The middle value

- The median is the middle value in a set of data. By arranging all of the scores from smallest to largest we can identify the middle score in the distribution. It is the score at which 50% of the data falls below and 50% of the data fall above.

- $0 + 4 + 9 + 14 + 14 + 20 + 30$. By listing the data in numerical order we can then locate the value in the middle of the list.

- **Therefore the median is 14.**

Figure 12.9   Calculating the average percentage

Which 'average' should I use?

Mean

Whilst being a straightforward measure, one problem with the mean is that it is sensitive to extreme values. For example, consider the following set of data: **3, 6, 9, 12 and 12,000**. The total of the five numbers adds up to 12,030. The 'average' or mean (12,030 divided by 5) is calculated to 2,406. The figure created is an 'arithmetic' mean which does not provide anything useful regarding the concentration of the individual numbers. Therefore, the arithmetic average is not the best measure to use with data sets containing a few extreme values.

Median

It is easy to find the *median* as we do not need to conduct any calculations. To arrive at the median, we arrange the data scores in numerical order, from highest to lowest, or smallest to largest; we then identify the middle value, which is the *median*. If there is an even number of observations, the median is the average sum of the two middle values. The median is useful, as unlike the mean, very large or very small values do not unduly impact on the outcome value. However, this method can take a long time to calculate, particularly for a large data set.

Mode

The mode can be easily identified as it is the value that occurs most frequently in the data. Although, some data sets do not have a mode because each value occurs only once. The mode is also the only measure of central tendency that can be used for data measured in a nominal scale. Nominal scale data is information collected under categories rather than numerically and as a result there can be more than one mode or no mode at all.

PAUSE FOR THOUGHT

Final thought

Measures of Central Tendency enable us to condense our data into a single value and make comparisons; however, keep in mind:

- No one 'average' can be regarded as the best;
- Each average has its own usefulness and drawbacks;
- An appropriate selection of an average depends on the specific requirements of the data.

Strategy 2 – frequency distribution

Frequency distributions are tables, graphs or any visual display that can be used to organise and present frequency counts. It is done in this way so that the information can be interpreted more easily. Therefore, a frequency table is a simple way to display the number of occurrences of a particular value or characteristic. It is a common way to describe a single variable (such as age or status) and numbers, as frequencies can also be presented as percentages. Figure 12.10 is an example of a frequency distribution table and the numbers in the list represent a frequency distribution.

Frequency	Percentage	Decimal	Fraction
25 out of 100	25%	0.25	1/4
50 out of 100	50%	0.50	1/2
75 out of 100	75%	0.75	3/4

Figure 12.10   Frequency distribution table 1

Depending on the variable, the numerical data values may be represented in the distribution. In Figure 12.11 we used data that indicate how many school assistants are both employed and taking Foundation Degree level study (Morris 2009). Firstly, the values were grouped into categories before calculating percentages.

Area	Number of school assistants employed	Number of school assistants taking degrees	Percentage of school assistants taking degrees
A	86	7	8.14%
B	71	9	12.68%
C	175	28	16%
D	183	27	14.75%

Figure 12.11   Frequency distribution table 2

Percentages can be employed in research analysis by allowing different sample totals or amounts to be easily compared. The example offered in Figure 12.10 illustrates this as the number of school assistants taking Foundation Degrees in key areas can be compared with each other. To further explore the data, Morris (2009) demonstrates in Figure 12.12 how Excel can enable a large amount of data to be organised and presented clearly helping the analysis.

Q1: Type of School Establishment		Q2: No. Of TA (ft - pt)		Q3: Number Taking Degree level study	
No. and Type of Establishment		ft	pt		Percentage
1	Primary	12	10	5	22.73
2	Primary	3	8	1	9
3	Primary	0	13	0	0
4	Nursery & Primary	5	0	1	20
5	Primary	5	3	2	25
6	Primary	2	10	2	16.66
7	Primary	0	4	0	0
8	Primary	18	2	2	10
9	Secondary	5	2	1	14.28
10	Primary	5	4	0	0
11	Secondary	4	10	1	7.14
12	Nursery	4	3	2	28.57
13	Primary	6	0	0	0
14	Primary	11	3	2	14.28
15	Secondary	16	0	5	31.25

Q1: Type of School Establishment		Q2: No. Of TA (ft - pt)		Q3: Number Taking Degree level study	
No. and Type of Establishment		ft	pt		Percentage
16	Secondary	8	2	0	0
17	Secondary	4	2	1	16.66
18	First School	1	0	0	0
19	Primary	0	18	1	5.55
20	Primary	2	4	2	33.33
21	Secondary	12	0	3	25
22	Secondary	7	6	0	0

Figure 12.12   Working with Excel

Excel can be a powerful tool to employ and is fairly easy to learn. Through Excel's ability to organise your data where you can select their simple statistical and plotting functions, you may gain further insight into your data. However, when using Excel ensure that you enter your data accurately and in a consistent format as this is critical for the success of your research analysis (see https://support.office.com/en-us/article/create-a-worksheet-in-excel-94b00f50-5896-479c-b0c5-ff74603b35a3). Should you need additional guidance, there are many informative texts (see further reading) and informative YouTube videos that explain how to work with Excel.

Strategy 3 – measures of dispersion

As well as measures of central tendency and frequency distribution, when analysing quantitative data, you can also identify the dispersion (*also known as the distribution spread*) of the data. The dispersion of values can be especially useful to your interpretation of your data because the dispersion, or variation, is what we would want to explain. Common examples of measures of statistical dispersion are variance and standard deviation. These represent the spread of the values which indicate how the data are distributed in relation to the average. Most data scores, for example IQ scores, when plotted on a graph would reflect a 'normal distribution curve' (see Figure 12.13). This is where most values would be in the middle or 'the average', due to having an IQ score of 100, with a few having either very high or low IQ scores, falling either side of the average.

You can also measure the distribution or spread of scores via the range or variability of the quantitative data, known as the dispersion. For instance, the lowest IQ measured at 55 and the highest 145 offers a variance of 90. The measure of the spread also enables you to examine how the data has been represented and whether an examination of an average may be beneficial. One example is if the spread of values is too large then an average may not be a useful representation of the data, since a large spread may indicate significant differences between values or scores.

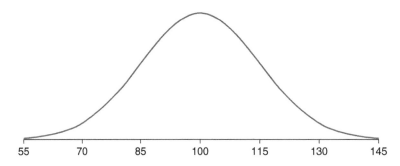

Figure 12.13 An example of a normal distribution graph

For instance, if we come back to our IQ example and imagine we conducted research to sample 10 participants' IQs, however this time our IQ highest measure is extended from 145 to 190 due to a very intelligent participant (*a top estimate IQ for Einstein*). This may alter the 100 average and skew our results, since the top score has now been substantially increased.

HOW DO I USE DESCRIPTIVE STATISTICS IN MY RESEARCH?

Having discussed the strategies for employing descriptive statistics, we will now demonstrate how you could apply this approach to your existing secondary data set. Figure 12.14 provides a five-step approach.

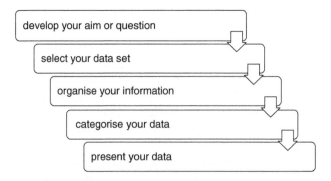

Figure 12.14 Five steps to descriptive statistical analysis

To guide you through this process we will work through a response to the following aim:

AIM: To investigate the impact of providing laptops to all school children.

Step 1: Develop your research question

The first part of this process is to develop your research question, for example 'Would laptops have an impact on the creativity of school children? or 'Would the attainment of school children increase if they were provided with laptops?'

To answer these questions, we could review secondary data sources: both national and international. As previously identified in this chapter, we can gain useful quantitative data from both quantitative and qualitative information. This can be through distinct, or separate quantitative or qualitative studies, or combined through mixed methods (*using both quantitative and qualitative data*) research. You would therefore need to consider what type of data you are going to need and their usefulness depends upon many factors.

Step 2: Select and evaluate your data set

The second step is to consider the relevance, credibility and robustness of the evidence. You will need to interrogate your sources to ensure you have a relevant sample(s). During your secondary data evaluation process, you need to understand and familiarise yourself with the original research. Ensure that you understand the *why*, *what*, *when* and *how* of data production (see Chapters 6 and 8). This is crucial, since you cannot effectively evaluate anything without having the full picture to support your judgement. One of the main things you need to consider at this point is 'What are my deal breakers for final inclusion?' This is where you assess your data for its suitability and we provide an example of this in Figure 12.15, where we review the data within Morris (2011) 'Digital Bridge or Digital Divide? A Case Study Review of the Implementation of the Computers for Pupils Programme'.

Deal breaker: should I include the research in my investigation?	
Question	**Response**
What is the data showing?	A case study of the implementation of the 'Computers for Pupils Programme' which provided laptops to school children.
Is the source reliable?	The data has been triangulated between investigations of both pupils and students.
What is the evidence based on?	An examination of a cohort of students and teachers in a Birmingham secondary school in the United Kingdom.
Is there a wide range of relevant contemporary evidence cited?	35 references with most dating from post 2002.
Where does the data come from?	46 pupils and four ICT teachers.

(Continued)

Figure 12.15 (Continued)

Deal breaker: should I include the research in my investigation?	
What year was the data generated?	The data was gathered in 2010 and published in 2011.
How was the data generated?	A questionnaire to pupils which includes open and closed responses and a semi-structured group interview for the teachers.
Are there any ethical concerns?	The responses and the school are anonymised.
Who compiled the data?	The data from students is only from a small Year 9 cohort in one school in Birmingham, UK.
What are the possible challenges to accepting the data conclusions?	Due to the small size of the cohort it is deemed problematic in making generalisations to the broader population.
How was the data measured?	The open and closed responses from the questionnaire and the semi structured nature of the group interview, offer data for both qualitative and quantitative analysis.
What else do I need to know?	The questionnaire and responses are included in the appendix, which offers access to most of the dataset.
Where can I get more information?	The paper has been cited seven times and this may provide an avenue to access further research.

Figure 12.15 Questioning your data

Step 3: Organise your data

Having evaluated your data sources, the third step is to prepare the data for analysis. This needs you to take a systematic and standardised approach, meaning you need to be methodical and consistent in your organisation of the data set. For instance, you might transfer all your data into a single electronic folder. When you have extracted and identified all the relevant bits of information or variables of interest, it is helpful to keep renamed copies and/or establish a new data file. This will ensure that you do not lose valuable steps while you are organising and rearranging the data for analysis.

Step 4: Categorise your data: select the statistical method for analysing your data e.g. frequency

The fourth step is to begin the process of categorising your data so you can compare a response or data set, in preparation for statistical analysis. Continuing our examination of the journal paper by Morris (2011), Figure 12.16 provides an example of how qualitative methods have been employed to explore participant experiences of a programme designed to provide laptops to pupils in a Birmingham secondary school. The data below represents the responses from a small part of the research, where an open-ended question asked participants if there was anything else they would like to mention about the programme. The data was qualitative in that it listed a series of responses to the question; however, we can convert their views into quantitative data which can then be interpreted with statistical procedures. In the case of this data set we must decide how we are going to categorise the 21 responses (25 students chose not to respond to the question). For instance, we could easily categorise them into positive, neutral, or negative experiences in order to answer our research question.

Is there anything else you would like to mention about the laptop or Computers for Pupils programme?

1. *"My laptop no longer works, the screen don't come on"* – **negative**

2. *"The charger stops working after about six months so be prepared"* – **negative**

3. *"The laptop is really slow and you only run 2 programs before the laptop froze, or give the laptop more memory"* – **negative**

4. *"It's too slow"* – **negative**

5. *"The laptop is slow even after I deleted most of the programs/files. I use it rarely"* – **negative**

6. *"The laptop isn't very fast; it has low memory and the battery dies out really fast, and it sometimes cuts out even when the battery is full of energy, it is very slow"* – **negative**

7. *"My laptop is slower after I have deleted files off my laptop"* – **negative**

8. *"The screen is very small there should be a bigger laptop and why install a webcam bet lots of parents don't agree with that!"* – **negative**

9. *"The laptop is too small, too slow, it has no CD/DVD drive, memory is too small and everything takes longer then it really does"* – **negative**

10. *"Please will you be able to give me a CD/DVD drive and I hope you will make it faster with the latest software"* – **negative**

11. *"The laptop charger does not work and the laptop keeps crashing it would help if we were allowed to bring the laptop in school so they can fix it"* – **negative**

12. *"My laptop screen is broke"* – **negative**

13. *"I would like a sound recorder and editor with a picture editor"* – **negative**

14. *It is very slow it needs to go faster"* – **negative**

15. *"Yes, it hasn't got a lot of memory"* – **negative**

16. *"No thank you"* – **neutral**

17. *"The computers run too slow"* – **negative**

18. *"To have music software e.g. Cubase, Paintshop Pro"* – **negative**

19. *"I don't know"* – **neutral**

20. *"I don't know"* – **neutral**

21. *"It has got a virus and faults with the software"* – **negative**

Figure 12.16 Laptop questionnaire responses

Frequency Table		
Category	Number	Percentage
Positive Comments	0	0.0%
Neutral Comments	3	14.3%
Negative Comments	18	85.7%

Figure 12.17 Laptop questionnaire responses by category frequency

Next, when calculating the final quantitative data, you will need to consider if the measure you have applied (*e.g. measures of central tendency*) is the most appropriate for ensuring clarity and analysing the data effectively. In the case of this rudimentary example, a frequency distribution will enable the frequency of results under each category to be simply displayed, along with their associated percentages (see Figure 12.17).

Step 5: Present your data

In your fifth and final step, it is now relatively easy to analyse your quantitative data. This can be undertaken using Excel as you can apply a table style, create PivotTables and quickly insert totals. You can then use these tables to quickly create different types of charts and graphs. For instance, below we have displayed a simple bar chart which has been produced in Excel. Following an analysis of all available data sets, we would then be free to begin the finding and conclusion sections of the research now aided by our appropriate statistical analysis and neatly presented data (see Figure 12.18).

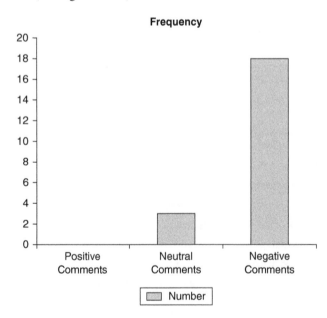

Figure 12.18 Frequency bar chart of laptop comments by category

For the example we used, we could conclude that laptops should not be provided to school children since there have been a high proportion of negative comments. Although this data does not consider the impact on the 25 students that chose not to leave a comment. We would therefore need to establish whether this was due to having a positive experience with the laptops and, in reality, we would need a much larger data set in order to reach a possible conclusion, as well as first establishing the criteria for appraising the success of the laptop deployment and use, for children.

REFLECTION AND FURTHER READING

At the beginning of the chapter we set out what you should be able to do when you reached the end of this chapter. To aid your reflection on all we have covered we ask some chapter specific questions. If you are unsure of any of your answers to these questions, please go back to the relevant section to review this aspect.

REFLECTING ON CHAPTER 12

In this chapter we have:

- **Examined the use of numerical (*quantitative*) data in your research:** How confident do you feel about working with numbers?
- **Outlined forms of statistical analysis:** Can you explain the different forms of statistical analysis? Do you know which one would add benefit to your analysis?
- **Identified examples of descriptive statistics:** Which ones would be particularly useful to your research? Which ones do you feel confident to construct?
- **Summarised steps in the organisation of the data to support your numerical analysis:** Could you apply these five steps in your analysis?

WE RECOMMEND FOR FURTHER READING:

Brase, C.H. & Brase, C.P. (2016) *Understanding Basic Statistics* (7th edn). Boston, USA: Cengage Learning.
This useful book provides practical guidance and clearly outlines the links between statistics and the real world. Techniques of Microsoft Excel, MINITAB, and SPSS are covered.

(Continued)

(Continued)

Johnston, M.P. (2014) Secondary data analysis: A method of which the time has come. *Qualitative and Quantitative Methods in Libraries*, *3*, 619–626. Available at: www.qqml.net/papers/September_2014_Issue/336QQML_Journal_2014_Johnston_Sept_619-626.pdf
In this paper, secondary data analysis is presented as a viable process when approached in a systematic way.

Salkind, N. (2016) *Statistics for People Who (Think They) Hate Statistics* (4th edn). Thousand Oaks, CA: SAGE Publications, Inc.
This will be useful to those who are new to numerical approaches to analysis. It provides a thorough but user-friendly guide.

Seale, C. (2017) Preparing data for statistical analysis. In C. Seale (ed.), *Researching Society and Culture* (4th edn) (pp. 337–349). London: SAGE Publications Ltd.
Seale's chapter provides an accessible account of statistical approaches to data analysis.

13

PRESENTING YOUR FINDINGS AND FORMING CONCLUSIONS

THIS CHAPTER SUPPORTS YOUR ABILITY TO

reflect on your findings

present your findings clearly and logically

explain limitations and create recommendations for future research

construct your conclusion

appreciate the need for effective communication

CHAPTER OVERVIEW

This chapter explores the presentation of your findings. These findings have arisen from your process of analysis and this chapter explores the essential and critical process of presenting what you have discovered in a clear and coherent manner. We discuss how you make meaning involving your critical reflection of these findings which involves creating a linkage between your theoretical and/or conceptual framework and the sources of data you selected as robust and credible in your literature review. Additionally, in this chapter, we outline the way data can be employed as quotations and presented as images within your findings section to add clarity and support to the points you raise. Presenting your findings clearly and effectively can enhance their meaning and enable your reader to fully comprehend all you have accomplished.

This chapter examines how you can present your conclusions not only as a reflection on your project but also as a contribution to knowledge of your subject. We encourage you to be open about what your research has or has not achieved and to identify any significant factors that may have influenced your findings. Finally, towards the end of the chapter we focus on an often-undervalued (but crucial) aspect which is the generation of meaningful and useful recommendations for future research.

WHAT HAPPENS AFTER YOUR ANALYSIS?

After your analysis you begin the presentation of your findings but, as we emphasise, it is impossible to provide an absolute and definitive template for precisely how things need to be done. This is partly because institutions, funding agencies and some subject disciplines have individualised and highly specialised approaches to how your whole project needs to be presented. We also refrain from doing this because your research is unique to you. Therefore, before you begin to write up this important section, we advise you to check if there is a specific approach you may be required to adopt. You should know what is expected of you and how much autonomy you may have before you approach this concluding section.

What we do provide in this chapter is a practical grounding in some of the main aspects you need to consider when presenting your findings. This should encourage you to have the confidence to consider this part of your research process as a celebration of what you have achieved and showcase your capability for research.

WHAT IS A FINDINGS SECTION?

In this section of your research you set out what your analysis has or has not revealed and you will identify your main or substantive findings. As we explore a little later, there are different ways to approach this part of your inquiry. You may have to report your findings and present these as a discrete chapter or section summarising each one or you may have to provide a more integrated chapter. At some point you will have to show what your findings mean both to you and to the field or discipline your research topic is within. This is where you interpret and discuss your research results and thus demonstrate your understanding of what they mean.

This understanding should not exist in isolation as you need to provide a meaningful context for what you have found. This means that within your report, study or project you will have to discuss the relevance, significance and meaning of your findings. This discussion is a synthesised interpretation where you orchestrate links to existing literature as confirmatory and informative (see Chapter 9), forge connections to your theoretical or conceptual frameworks (see Chapter 3) and address your research aim(s) and question(s) (see Chapter 2).

As you begin this, you need to feel assured there are no absolute rules and you can only do your best to communicate what the data reveal within the purpose or context of the study. Therefore, when you need to approach the meaning making process of your research it would be useful to reflect on Patton's (2002: 480) definition:

> Interpretation means attaching significance to what was found, making sense of findings, offering explanations, drawing conclusions, extrapolating lessons, making inferences, considering meanings, and otherwise imposing order on an unruly but surely patterned world.

Presenting the story of your findings is a key part of any research study so take time to consider how you can communicate the significance of your research and your effectiveness in answering your research question(s) and aim(s). Your findings need to include relevant details to explain what you have found (see Figure 13.1).

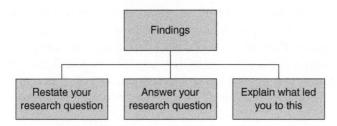

Figure 13.1   What to include in your findings section

Reflecting on your findings

When you are sure you know how to continue with this part of your inquiry, the first thing we recommend is that you stand back and reflect. This may be easier said than done as when you get to this point of your research process you may feel very tired and desperate to submit your work. However, consider this as an additional meaning making process as analysis is ongoing and presenting your findings offers you further opportunities to make connections and patterns, and explore relationships.

Take time to think about your results and to consider how you want to go about communicating these findings in a meaningful and accessible way. Golden-Biddle and Locke (2007: 6) describe this as deciding on your *'theorized storyline'* or the development of a 'plot' which sets out the narrative or structure you want this section on your research findings to have. This can be a demanding part of your research process, but it can also

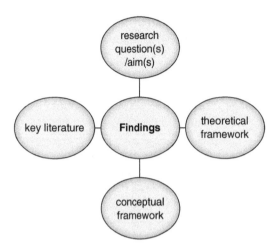

Figure 13.2   Key factors to consider when selecting your key findings for discussion

be one of the most enjoyable as this is where you show what you are made of as a researcher, as an academic and as a writer. This is because in this section you bring the threads of your research together and showcase your academic knowledge and skills. Therefore, taking time to reflect should help you clarify your thoughts and support the creation of the story you need to tell.

Your findings represent a crucial aspect of your research and where, in most marking, grading or assessment schemes, the highest marks are awarded. This is mainly because this section is where you demonstrate your ability to synthesise, integrate and generally to contribute to existing knowledge (see Figure 13.2). Your findings section is therefore, the pinnacle of your research project as it is the reward for all your hard work and conscientious effort. Consider the investment you made in devising your aim, clarifying your research questions, collecting and analysing your data and then see this section as where this investment pays off.

As you begin this process, please consider the wise words of Becker (1986) who firmly believes that the first thing to recognise when organising and presenting your material is that your results are as individual as your research and therefore there is **NO** one right way.

PAUSE FOR THOUGHT

There is NO one right way!

It is more than likely that you will have to follow some form of presentation guidelines. However, these may only be guidelines and the lack of certainty they provide may have the potential to cause apprehension. To gain some control, be guided by the following:

- Discuss your concerns with your supervisor or tutor after reading your guidelines.
- Explore how others have approached this task. Your institution may have an archive or repository of past theses or research projects available for you to review. However, do not be tempted to copy what has been done. Your research is like you; it is highly individual and how another person approaches their findings may not suit your question or your research approach.
- Discuss your approach with your colleagues or peers.

Preparing your findings for interpretation and discussion

In the creation of your storyline, you need to consider which findings are going to help tell your story. When preparing your results for discussion, reflect on the phrase offered by Golden-Biddle and Locke (2007) and remember this section as your '*theorized storyline*'. This is where you make links to your theory and start to develop a theoretical argument to account for your findings and to put your results into some sort of context (see Figure 13.2). The sources you employed to significant effect in your literature review will aid you in this task.

As we explored in Chapter 11, qualitative analysis turns your data into findings but you may need to consider the substantive significance of these (Patton 2002). It is more than likely that your research may have identified more findings than you have word count to include. This is where you need to apply a clear and critical gaze to identify your key findings and include those that have particular significance. This could be because they have greater frequency or reflect a stronger theoretical link. This narrowing down of your findings may be facilitated by the creation of a table or matrix which provides a visualisation of your results (see Figure 13.3). Engaging in such a critical and evaluative process before you start writing will direct your focus and encourage you to have confidence as you begin writing about your findings. Whilst a process like this can take time, we encourage you to adopt this strategy as it will save you time later when you write up your research findings.

Finding	Link to aim/question	Link to key concepts	Link to theoretical perspective	Links to existing literature
Students offer professional reasons for their return to study	Responds to student motives	Motives – gender	ERG theory – sense of growth	Links to Reay (2003) – aspirational narrative

Figure 13.3 A justification matrix

WRITING YOUR FINDINGS SECTION

We have encouraged you to think of your findings section as a place where you can tell the story of your research and, like all good stories, it needs to make sense and be enjoyable to read. By enjoyable, we mean it has fluency, clarity and accuracy in what it presents. Above all else, it should be written in such a way that your reader should not have to work too hard to understand your results. You should provide all the evidence needed to make sense of what you have uncovered through your research. Providing a credible interpretation of your findings so the links, patterns and connections you make are explicit and accessible to your reader is essential. Remember that your reader is making judgements about your work so you need to ensure that you provide evidence of the claims you are making. We explore this later, but it is worth considering how you will use quotations, images and graphical data display as a means of support.

However, your findings are more than a story; they are an academic or scholarly contribution to the field of knowledge that exists on your subject. Therefore, you need to consider how you will present your findings and justify and evaluate these in such a way as to reflect an academic and critical consideration. This includes being open by revealing all your findings, even those that do not match or address the questions you started with (Robson 2002).

Presenting your findings

As we discussed earlier, we cannot provide an absolute version of how to structure your findings section. This is because there are diverse ways of completing this process. You can see this if you open a *how to write your research* textbook or venture online to explore web pages that offer advice on theses or dissertation writing. If you do, you may experience a deluge of advice, leaving you faced with a barrage of competing approaches. If you persevere with your search and decide to access the web pages of specific institutions, you will see that most request highly specified approaches that are dependent on individual disciplines and academic schools. In general, there seems to be little or no consensus as to a specific way of completing this section. This is something Thomas (2009: 227) discusses when he reviews the many ways findings can be presented. We explore these different strategies next (see Figure 13.4).

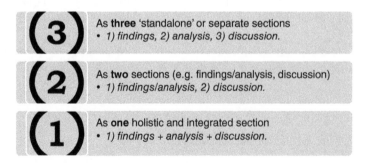

Figure 13.4 Three ways to present your findings, analysis and discussion

There are strengths in all the possible approaches you may need or choose to take. If you have some choice, consider the following to aid your selection:

- A *stand-alone* or *two-sectioned* approach enables you to focus on each section in depth.
- An *integrated* approach where you are combining all the key parts affords you an opportunity to weave these into your discussion, reflecting a more holistic dialogue.

We approach the writing up of findings as an integrated section that includes analytical aspects and a discussion of the results the research has generated. We do this because we feel it reflects the qualitative paradigm we explored in Chapter 3, which suggests that data should be explored in as real a manner as possible (Robson 2002). Additionally, we argue that linking your findings and analysis to the aspects explored in Figure 13.1 leads to enhanced contextualisation and thus, increased meaning.

If you do have to provide a stand-alone approach, then we have included an example of a very concise summary of the findings as an illustration of how this can be performed (see Box 13.1). The summary is based on a secondary analysis of 30 empirical studies conducted across eight different countries (Australia, Brazil, Canada, New Zealand, Norway, Singapore, United States and the United Kingdom) by Kourgiantakis, Saint-Jacques and Tremblay (2013) between 1998 and 2013. They wanted to examine the effects of problem gambling on families. This research involved asking additional questions (*e.g. What is the impact of problem gambling on families and what is the role of families in problem gambling treatment?*) that had not been asked of the original data set to provide an alternative perspective on the topics without having to intrude further into vulnerable populations. In Box 13.1 is our brief and concise summary of the research conducted by Kourgiantakis et al. (2013) which addresses the question '*What is the impact of problem gambling on families?*'

BOX 13.1   PROBLEM GAMBLING AND FAMILIES: A SYSTEMATIC REVIEW, BY KOURGIANTAKIS ET AL.(2013)

Question: *'What is the impact of problem gambling on families'*: Interpretation of key arguments and findings

1. Children

   Whilst only three of the studies contained child-only samples, many of the studies included children in their research. The results indicate that children of problem gamblers were likely to display emotional and behavioural difficulties. They highlighted that loss is a major factor in their lives. This is in terms of lack of attention, stability, or parental absence of their caregivers thrusting them into a role full of responsibilities. These difficulties are also reflected by adults with parents of problem gamblers which impact on their own adult relationships.

   (Continued)

(Continued)

2. Relationships

The results indicated that spouses are vulnerable to the negative consequences effects of gambling problems and experienced strains not only on their financial security, but their physical, emotional and mental states due to the high levels of stress associated with trying to maintain family stability. However, it was noted that most of the studies investigated female partners rather than males.

3. Lack of recognition

It was found that there is a lack of awareness from family members on recognising problem gamblers. This can exacerbate the difficulties and results found that only 3 to 5 per cent of problem gamblers seek help. However, adopting coping strategies can buffer some of the more adverse effects on family members.

The results gained have important implications for practitioners to develop and extend procedures and support. However, it is recognised that when analysing the findings there may be cultural differences influencing the validity of the results. Also, some of the studies did not include details on the specific criteria of the family member. These factors may reflect a lack of consistency and confusion within the findings, but to address challenges the researchers believed that clear definitions were provided to confidently make comparisons and similar results were found across all 30 studies, indicating reliability.

Although it is impossible to provide you with a definitive template as to how to present your findings, here are two possible ways that you could approach the construction of this section. Either approach will add clarity to the 'storyline' you are trying to create.

- **Under thematic headings:** Your identification of key findings should lead you to know which findings have most significance and those that have less (see Chapter 11).
- **Under your research questions:** Depending on the number of aims or questions you have created, it is possible to discuss your findings and analysis under each as identified. This means you will need to classify your themes to match each aim or question and this can be undertaken using a matrix (see Figure 13.3).

It is worth reiterating that themes, categories, concepts or theories do not just 'emerge' from your data; your role as the researcher needs to 'make it so' (Sandelowski 1995: 371).

PAUSE FOR THOUGHT

Exploring the functions of your word processing program to aid the presentation of your findings

The use of headings can be a simple and effective way to signpost the significance of topics and themes identified in your findings. These can be ranked and ordered to reflect their importance and used to subdivide the story of your research.

If you are familiar with the 'heading' functions in Word, please use these as, when viewed in the navigation pane, these show the story of your discussion as you write it. If you are less familiar with Word, we suggest you access support either through your institution or via YouTube to assist you further.

Exploring your findings

When you have decided on the structure of your section, you need to consider what your findings mean. Patton (2002: 467) offers the following question prompts which can be used to aid this process. They can be applied to your findings to justify and explore how they may relate to what is already known on your subject. You will also need to evaluate your findings and challenge the claims you make and their overall credibility. It is worth reflecting that if you do not challenge your findings, then it is very likely someone else will. Based on these questions we recommend that you ask yourself the questions outlined in Figure 13.5 which will aid this justification and evaluation process.

1. How solid, consistent and coherent are your findings?
Ask yourself: Did I engage in triangulation processes? If I did, how can these processes be related to the credibility and consistency of my findings? Do my findings make sense in relation to the question(s) I asked and/or the aim(s) I set?
2. To what extent and in what ways do your findings increase and deepen your understanding of the focus of inquiry?
Ask yourself: Do my findings add to existing knowledge and if they do, in what way?
3. To what extent are your findings consistent with the existing body of knowledge?
Ask yourself: Do they support or confirm what is already known about the focus on my inquiry? Do they provide any challenge to existing views or theory?
4. To what extent are your findings useful?
Ask yourself: Do my findings contribute to theory building? Do they inform practice, policy or procedure in any way?

Figure 13.5   Asking questions of your findings (based on Patton 2002)

Within your findings, it is likely that you have a few if not more outcomes that strengthen accepted or current thinking. It may be that you have identified a new way of thinking about your subject or located a gap in current knowledge. Whatever your findings reveal, your task is to explain *what* you identified, and *how* and *why* these matter as you want to give your findings meaning and relevance. You can also consider the following as part of this process of justification and evaluation (see Figure 13.6).

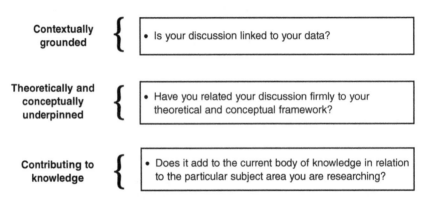

Figure 13.6   Justifying your research findings

- **Contextually grounded:** Your findings need to be linked in some way to the data you have analysed. Taking your findings away from your data creates a vacuum which the reader cannot fill. Contextually grounding your findings aids understanding of the meanings that emerge. This can be through the use of quotes and data visualisation strategies and techniques can be employed to provide a context for your findings and to act as supporting evidence for any knowledge claims made. This will help your readers understand your results more clearly through demonstrating the integration of a set of associations and relationships between and among the various concepts you formulate.
- **Theoretically and conceptually underpinned:** Your theoretical and conceptual frameworks need to be evident within your discussion of your findings section. This may be because you applied a theoretical perspective as a deductive approach to analysis (see Chapter 11) and your findings are thus very theoretically focused. You should be able to make convincing links to your conceptual framework by your reference to existing literature (see Chapter 3). Justifying the findings in relation to your aim(s) and question(s) and making the links to your conceptual framework indicates your knowledge of how these relate. Making connections to these aspects of your research process brings the research full circle and supports claims for research coherence as emphasised throughout this book (see Chapter 4).
- **Contributing to knowledge:** This is where, through your justification of your findings and by your integration of the aspects of the research, you indicate how your findings add to

existing knowledge. You may have identified key agreements or tensions or you may have identified a critical gap which your findings have exposed. Perhaps your theoretical perspective was so unusual that it has located a new way of thinking about a key issue. Your work may not provide anything ground-breaking but your results will have relevance to the subject area you have explored. Sometimes it is what you did not expect to find that can add to knowledge and this is important as it can often be the start of other people's research journeys or a new path for your own.

PAUSE FOR THOUGHT

The role of theory and supporting evidence

When you present your findings, you are showing what you have found out following your analysis but you need to interpret these to say what they mean. Stating your findings as a list or summary will not enable your reader to understand your findings as an answer to your question. Therefore, you need to draw upon your theory and literature. In Chapter 3 we explored theory as something already known, such as a named theory and as concepts that you and your reading bring to the research. This is where they come into good use. They act as confirmation of your findings or as support for alternative reasons for your findings. This is where you bring all that critical appraisal, evaluation and synthesis together. This is where you make sense of your inquiry

---

Evaluating your findings

After the analysis of your data, the next task is to construct an effective explanation of your findings. The first question asked by Patton (2002; see Figure 13.5) '*How solid, consistent and coherent are your findings?*' challenges you to respond to issues pertaining to credibility, confirmability and whether you answered your research question. All research requires you to provide some explanation as to whether your results were anticipated or unexpected. Therefore, during the discussion of your findings you need to evaluate the influence of any limitations or qualifications offered on your findings. These may be factors related to the type of data used, the age of the data, how you sampled it, or even how you used it. It is also related to your influence on the data. As we explored in Chapters 3 and 4, who we are as researchers can leak into the research we produce.

When evaluating your findings also explore thoroughly any differences between anticipated and actual results. Any discrepancies will need to be fully explored and so will the possible significance in relation to your overall research (Swales and Feak 2004) (see Figure 13.7).

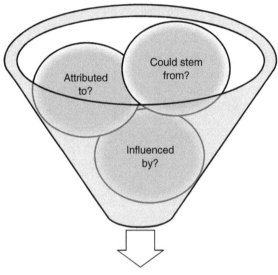

**Explaining the difference between
anticipated and actual results**

Figure 13.7   Evaluating research findings

Evaluating your findings allows your reader to appreciate the limitations of your research but it also highlights your researcher integrity. In Chapters 3 and 4, we explored the role of research transparency and strategies that could secure rigour to support the quality of your research. Therefore, being transparent places you as a researcher with integrity. Please consider the additional advice on research rigour we provide next.

Reflecting on your own influence on the data: We explored this as *reflexivity* in Chapter 3, as a self-critical reflection of how who you are as a researcher may influence your results through the choices and decisions you make. As Golden-Biddle and Locke (2007: 64) state, '*the person of the researcher is seen as firmly embedded in any inquiry effort*'.

Acknowledging any known or perceived weaknesses or limitations in your research: You need to acknowledge any deficiencies or probable shortcomings in your research in order to convince your readers of your research credibility. This might mean identifying key issues such as not gaining access to the data you required or losing your data in some way. It might mean identifying an issue in the way you analysed your data. Whatever the concern may be, it is best to identify any anomalies. This will enable you to state why your findings were different from expectations, and in what way.

Evaluating your findings also means being clear about the exciting and interesting things that may have emerged from your data. Communicate these claims clearly because the goal of research is to produce research that adds to knowledge and contributes to the research field, and you should want people to know your contribution. Therefore, try not to focus on the possible flaws and factors that may have negatively influenced your results; state what you achieved:

- Emphasise the strengths of your data analysis and what worked well.
- State very clearly if you identified something new or were able to see something from an unfamiliar perspective.
- Demonstrate that you have engaged with your literature in an academic and scholarly way or applied a unique theoretical perspective.
- Showcase your engagement in your particular field or discipline.

The discussion and presentation of your findings is not just a rehash or summary of the results from your analysis. At this stage, you need to demonstrate original thinking in relation to your findings. The discussion you provide should be an active construction and representation that reflects the insight you have gained. It should, '*strike a balance between descriptive, explanatory and interpretative evidence*' (Richie and Lewis 2003: 289) and provide a space where you and your personality shine through. The Figure 13.8 exemplifies effective and ineffective approaches to the presentation of your findings.

In an effective presentation:	In an ineffective presentation:
✓ **It is easy to understand the significance of your findings. Your reader follows your flow and the arguments you make.** ✓ **Your findings link clearly to your theoretical and conceptual framework. Your reader can make sense of your research journey and see your work as a coherent whole.** ✓ **You reflect on and link back to your aim(s) and questions(s). This makes reading this section easier as there is a meaningful context offered.** ✓ **You create a convincing and persuasive 'story' about what your data means. You do not describe but you provide a clear narrative of your findings weaving in theory, concepts and making links to your explored literature.** **When done well, confidence will flow from your research.**	✗ It is hard to see the importance of any of your findings. ✗ You do not link to theory or concepts; instead you provide a list of what emerges. ✗ This does not enable the story of your research to flow. Your reader must do all the work and join it together. ✗ You do not make any links to your research question(s) or aim(s) so it is impossible to understand the relevance of this section. ✗ You present a set of descriptive comments. **A findings section like this will not enhance your research study – it undermines its potential.**

Figure 13.8   Comparing effective and ineffective discussions of findings

COMMUNICATING YOUR FINDINGS EFFECTIVELY

To make sure you are persuasive in your discussion of your findings, be aware of the language you use. In Chapter 9, we discussed the need for you to write with a particular reader in mind and as you do, try to match this reader's expectations of your work (*e.g. your peers, your tutor,*

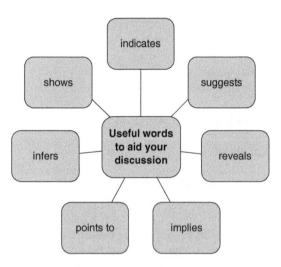

Figure 13.9   Using verbs to support your discussion

your marker or wider audience). Writing for a specific or imagined reader or audience can influence the style and the tone of your language.

In a piece of academic research, the style of writing needed for the presentation is important. Clear and well-constructed text provides accessibility but it also enables you to demonstrate your level of understanding through your critical consideration of your findings. Presenting your findings reflecting a clear, reasoned and plausible argument can convincingly demonstrate your own capabilities and reflect your level of ownership of your research.

One way to achieve effective communication is in the precision of your language and this precision is essential when discussing the conclusions that are beginning to form. We often hear or read in headlines that researchers have 'proved' something. But the word 'prove' is too absolute as it means that something has been demonstrated beyond any doubt. The word *prove* could make your reader suspicious. Whilst you may have carried out robust and compelling research, it is highly unlikely that it will be immune to any of the factors that could have influenced the credibility of the results. Using statements which include the verbs 'proves', 'establishes', or 'confirms' can suggest a lack of awareness of these factors. Therefore, we advise you to use words that reflect elements of judicious review, and in this, you demonstrate your cognisance of influencing factors and thus, research integrity. Examples of verbs to support your discussion are outlined in Figure 13.9.

Consider how the words applied in italics (*in the bullet points below*) suggest a tentative link rather than absolute causation:

- It is likely that reducing sugar in prepared food *may* lower the risk of type two diabetes.
- Reducing sugar intake *appears* to lower the risk of type two diabetes.
- Results of this research suggest that reducing sugar intake *could* cut the risk of type two diabetes.
- Reducing sugar intake *contributes* to lowering your risk of type two diabetes.

PAUSE FOR THOUGHT

Consider the function of verbs in your work

Frels, Onwuegbuzie and Slate (2010; xxii; *see recommended reading*) provide a typology of verbs within scholarly writing and present these as three major categories: statements, cognition, and knowledge and action. When verbs represent knowledge or action these refer to '*the presumption of truth or finding evidence for truth either by coming-to-know or by some type of action'.* Therefore, they have relevance when you discuss your findings and form conclusions as the verb you use indicates your relationship to knowledge. Frels, Onwuegbuzie and Slate (2010: xxii) provide the following categorisation:

- procedural verbs (*e.g., conducted, analysed*);
- visual verbs (*e.g., displayed, confirmed*);
- evidence-based/data-driven verbs (*e.g., tested, embarked*);
- creation verbs (*e.g., engendered, generated*);
- direct object verbs (*e.g., sampled, developed*).

The verb *find* is useful in academic contexts to describe the way knowledge is gained but because it is so useful, the past tense of this verb *found* is frequently overused. A thesaurus can be useful in suggesting alternative words.

DATA DISPLAY AND VISUALISATION

Data display and visualisation have a role within the presentation of your research as they connect your analysis and discussion to your original data. When we consider data display and visualisation we refer to the display or use of any form of data in a manner that aids the meaning, coherence and relevance of the findings you present.

Using quotations or examples of text within your findings

As a qualitative secondary researcher, it may be necessary to include excerpts or sections of the data you have used for your analysis. This can add strength and credibility to the discussion you provide through amplifying the meaning of your findings. Through employing selective and representative direct quotations, where appropriate, they can clarify and emphasise your key themes.

Here are some useful things to consider:

Use direct quotations: This can allow your reader to understand the findings of the analysis, and to enable them to judge the credibility of the claims you make. When done well, the use of *'rich and vivid exemplary quotations'* (Chenail 1995) can add a meaningful context to the findings you present.

Include just enough text in the excerpt or quoted segment: This is so that your reader will understand its meaning, but do not include so much that there is extraneous or non-relevant material inserted.

Present text consistently: If you are using an excerpt from a known text you need to present this consistently, so the text can be identified. It is worth including any other relevant information that can enable the reader to appreciate the strength of the relationship between the quotation offered and the finding it is linked to.

Present text appropriately: Demarcate the quoted text so it is possible for your reader to realise these are *not* your words. There are many ways to do this; e.g. use bold, italics, indent or use single or double quotation marks. Reference appropriately and include information that identifies the data quoted but be mindful of the need not to disclose any information that can be traced to a specific person, as with all data, this needs to be anonymised and coded.

Keep in mind that the use of quotations should not take the place of your analysis or discussion of the findings. Weaving these into the findings can add support to all the points explored to aid your justification of, and the significance of, your findings.

Using images, tables and diagrams

In Chapter 11, we explored how the processes of coding and categorisation led to the creation of themes. We discussed how presenting this diagrammatically, or in a table format, could help you see links, patterns and connections. Visual displays are *'an organized, compressed assembly of information that permits conclusion drawing and action'* (Miles & Huberman 1994: 11). However, just as with the use of direct quotations we explored above, you still need to adopt a judicious approach to their use within your findings section. Rather than just being decorative, they need to add value to the process of meaning making because, as Kirk (2016: 21) attests, data visualisation is *'about facilitating understanding'*.

Keep in mind that the main goal of any diagram or visual display of information is to help communicate quickly, clearly and efficiently. Images, diagrams and tables can be used very effectively to make the work visually more appealing, but it is best to consider, as Eisner (1997: 8) states, that visual presentation should be part of *'illuminating rather than obscuring the message'*. Typically, however, visual information can help with making it more memorable; other benefits of effective visual display are outlined in Figure 13.10.

When presenting your findings, you may use tables or figures and whilst they should be able to be interpreted without supporting text, you still need to contextualise these into your discussion to show how these images advance your argument (Silverman 2013). The data hierarchies and frameworks we discussed in Chapter 11 and charts shown in Chapter 12 would be useful to insert as they would communicate the steps taken in your analysis and

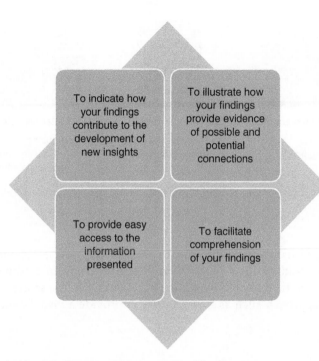

To indicate how your findings contribute to the development of new insights

To illustrate how your findings provide evidence of possible and potential connections

To provide easy access to the information presented

To facilitate comprehension of your findings

Figure 13.10   Defining the benefits of effective visual display

indicate how the main findings were generated. In addition, a word chart such as the one we present in Figure 13.11 provides an eye-catching approach to communicating key findings. This would be useful if you were generating keywords in context or wanted to show recurrent themes that emerge from your data.

Many computer programs, as we explored in Chapters 11 and 12, will generate data visualisations. They can provide maps and networks showing relationships and connections within your data. However, there are also tools available within most word processing packages and it is worth exploring what your preferred program has to offer. We provide a few ideas to stimulate your thinking as word-based data can be presented in many ways. Consider the suggestions in Figure 13.12, based on findings generated through research that explored social housing policy in the UK.

You could use a program such as MS Word and the SmartArt features it provides to communicate

Findings are:

Assertions

Conclusions

*Discoveries*DECLARATIONS

Judgements Proclamations **Verdicts**

Figure 13.11   Word chart

Figure 13.12 Visual display of an example of qualitative secondary research exploring social housing policy in the UK

your findings in a visually appealing way. In the example offered in Figure 13.13, we have presented key findings as a list to begin the discussion of findings. This would provide your reader with an overview adding accessibility to the section they are about to read. Using an approach such as this would also provide a visual conclusion to your findings section.

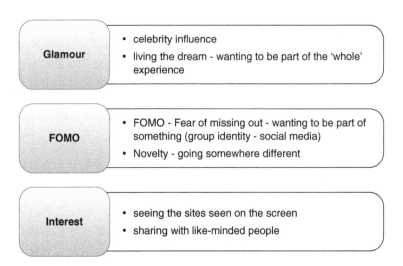

Figure 13.13 Presenting findings as a list to begin a discussion

There are lots of ways of presenting your findings, but we reiterate that these must add value to the points you are making. Visual displays when used effectively can provide specific points of interest as they break down large chunks of text. Therefore, we encourage you to explore and be creative in the way you present your findings but make sure they are relevant, communicate meaning and used in context.

Using appendices

You may have relevant but non-essential information that you want to include as you feel that it will help the reader understand your results. If this is the case, then you should consider adding an appendix. The appendix is useful for placing further evidence of your results, but you need to consider carefully what information goes there rather than in the body of the chapter. Use appendices wisely as too many suggest poor judgement and, consider the following advice provided in Figure 13.14.

Appendices are not usually included in the word count, but be guided by your institution and organisation.	Make reference in the main text or footnote of your work that material is located in a specific appendix.	Use letters or numbers when referring to the different appendices; e.g. Appendix A, the next Appendix B.	The appendix goes after your reference list or bibliography.

Figure 13.14   Tips for using an appendix

WRITING YOUR CONCLUSION

Your conclusion offers you the chance to leave a lasting impression on your audience and impress your reader with the knowledge you have generated. Therefore, your concluding section needs to summarise your findings and reiterate the main results of your research. This is where you emphasise what has been learnt, what it has achieved and how your research represents a contribution to knowledge.

Your conclusion requires you to question your findings and consider different interpretations. Only conclusions that are justifiably drawn from the findings should be made and this is not the place to introduce new material. Keep in mind that the purpose of your research is to critically consider all possible explanations. These include any limitations of your research design as well as the implications of your findings.

Identifying your research limitations

All studies have limitations but being able to recognise these and admit to them is a sign of a good researcher. These limitations can be anything that influenced the interpretation of the findings or impacted on the ability to generalise (Price & Murnan 2004). An example of a limitation would be if your sample was lacking in some way and this led you to limit the scale of your analysis. It may be tempting just to leave it there but offer reasons as to why you believe the data was unavailable and use this as an opportunity to describe the need for future research. There are many benefits of identifying your research limitations, some of which are outlined in Figure 13.15.

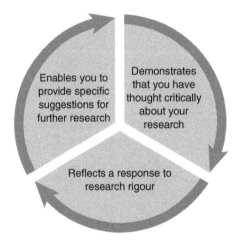

Figure 13.15 The benefits of identifying your research limitations

The limitations of your research are not a deal breaker and admitting to issues and concerns that influenced your research shows a commitment to research transparency and robust endeavour. No research is without some sort of limitations or compromises, therefore, to demonstrate you are a convincing and sound researcher check that you:

- describe each limitation and explain why it exists;
- explain why each limitation could not be overcome;
- assess the impact of each limitation in relation to your aim.

WRITING YOUR RECOMMENDATIONS

Your recommendations need to put forward specific suggestions and/or solutions. Therefore, you should include a short section on any suggestions, limitations and/or recommendations that you could offer based on your experience and knowledge gained from conducting your research. It is not enough to simply recommend that action needs to take place; you need to be specific. This attention to detail will ensure that each recommendation you provide is feasible and fully focused on your findings.

We advise you to consider three categories of recommendation (see Figure 13.16) as a framework for this part of your research process. Such an approach adds structure and focus to a section in the research process that can be overlooked or treated as an afterthought.

These recommendations might come from unexpected findings or from the non-answering of your research question or not fully meeting your aim.

Do not see any of this as a failing in your research; it may be that the data did not provide all the answers you required. If this was the case then suggest why and provide a research strategy that could be used to explore such aspects in future; use this as a recommendation.

Recommendations play a role in the continuity of research and support the development of knowledge and research practice. They also indicate as we have emphasised before, research transparency increasing the confidence level in the robustness of your findings. Writing recommendations can seem like a chore at the end of your research but remember what we said before, always finish leaving a good and lasting impression. Figure 13.16 offers suggested categories of recommendations that you might be able to adopt.

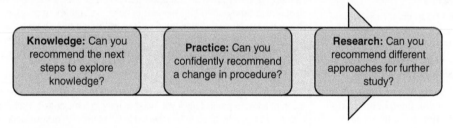

Figure 13.16   Creating recommendations

FINAL CONSIDERATIONS

Whilst not an exhaustive checklist, in Figure 13.17 we have provided a few key considerations for you to reflect on when you are completing the presentation of your findings.

Ask yourself ...	Consider ...
Have I included an introductory paragraph or section that will provide a context for understanding my results? **Have I restated my question or aim, enabling my reader to make sense of my results?**	Always have the notion of a specific reader in mind. This will encourage you to write in a way that enables you to 'tell' the story of your research. Including a paragraph or section that reacquaints the reader with your research problem. This stops them from having to go back to where this was stated in your research. Make it easy for your reader to know what is happening, how and why and, if you have multiple sections in your presentation, signpost them.
Have I included visual elements in an appropriate way? **Am I demonstrating my academic skills effectively?**	It can be tempting to provide long sections of narrative text but it is possible to include a range of visual or diagrammatic information. Being able to create a diagram from your data illustrates key skills of synthesis and concision. But do not overdo this as you also need to show you can construct persuasive text.

(Continued)

Figure 13.17   (Continued)

Ask yourself ...	Consider ...
Have I been systematic in the way I have presented my findings? **Have I adopted a clear and logical approach to my organisation?**	Making sure you have adopted or are using a clear and logical approach is essential. Communicate in a manner that is accessible to your reader. Consider if you are using headings effectively and in a standardised way. Are you signposting what is significant or not? Your reader should not have to work to hard so make it as easy as possible for them.
Have I included so much information in my work that it is now cluttered and confusing?	As explored earlier, focus on those findings that relate to the problem you set yourself. Other findings can be attached in an appendix or used to signpost further research possibilities in your recommendations section.
Have I concluded each section effectively? **Have I been clear in what I wanted to achieve in this section?** **Have I synthesised my results to add further clarity?**	Highlight the most important findings you want your readers to remember. Depending on the approach taken to your presentation section, you may need to provide a concluding statement or section at the end of each section included. It is worth doing this as you are trying to provide a reading path through your research that enables your reader to follow what you are presenting without getting lost.
Am I going to use appendices and if I am, have I signposted where these are in my text (cross referenced)? **Have I checked that these are relevant?**	As explored above appendices can play an important part in your presentation of findings particularly if you need to refer to a major text. Therefore, it is possible this may need to be inserted in full at the end of your work. However, make sure you have a clear rationale for this and that any appendices used are cross referenced so they are easy to find. Your reader (marker) may get too frustrated if they have to work too hard to find these.

Figure 13.17   A checklist to support the presentation of your findings

The writing up of your findings can be an interesting and satisfying task in your research. This is because every researcher needs to communicate their findings and discuss them in a way that readers will understand the impact made in terms of contribution to existing knowledge. Make it clear what you have found out. Even if you suspect that what you have found is trivial, your findings have a role in contributing to the relevant knowledge base, thus providing you with the opportunity to communicate the contribution that all your hard work has made.

PAUSE FOR THOUGHT

Consider your reader

Presenting your findings as comprehensively as they deserve is challenging. However, your presentation of your findings should not be a detective story where your reader needs to work out for themselves what your findings mean. Ensure you make your points explicit to your reader. You can begin by introducing the chapter or section to signpost your approach.

REFLECTION AND FURTHER READING

At the beginning of the chapter we set out what you should be able to do when you reached the end of this chapter. To aid your reflection on all we have covered we ask some chapter specific questions. If you are unsure of any of your answers to these questions, please go back to the relevant section to review this aspect.

REFLECTING ON CHAPTER 13

In this chapter we have:

- **Explained the importance of reflecting on your findings:** Why should you reflect on your findings before you write?
- **Demonstrated how you can present your findings clearly and logically:** How will you present your findings? What role does theory play? Why would you use quotations in your findings?
- **Explored the creation of meaningful and relevant recommendations:** Can you identify three ways to consider your recommendation?
- **Discussed the need for open disclosure of any research limitations:** Why should you disclose any factors that influenced your research?
- **Offered guidance on the construction of your conclusion:** What role does your conclusion play in your research project?
- **Presented techniques and strategies to support effective communication:** How should you write your conclusion?

WE RECOMMEND FOR FURTHER READING:

Bloomberg, L.D. & Volpe, M. (2018) *Completing Your Qualitative Dissertation: A Roadmap from Beginning to End* (4th edn). Thousand Oaks, CA: SAGE Publications, Inc.
We recommend Chapter 9 'Analyzing Data and Interpreting Findings'.

Kirk, A. (2016) *Data Visualisation*. London: SAGE Publications Ltd.
This is an excellent key text for anyone interested in the visual presentation of data. It is an accessible read and offers a wealth of creative and effective data visualisation solutions.

(Continued)

(Continued)

Merriam, S.B. & Tisdell, E.J. (2016) *Qualitative Research: A Guide to Design and Implementation* (4th edn). San Francisco, CA: Jossey-Bass.
This is an accessible and clearly written book and we recommend Chapter 10 which focuses on writing up qualitative research.

Miles, M.B., Huberman, A.M. & Saldaña, J. (2014) *Qualitative Data Analysis: A Methods Sourcebook* (3rd edn). Thousand Oaks, CA: Sage Publications Inc.
We recommend two chapters within Part 3, Chapter 11, Drawing and Verifying Conclusions and Chapter 12, Writing About Qualitative Research.

White, C., Woodfield, K., Ritchie, J. & Ormston, R. (2013) Writing up qualitative research. In J. Ritchie, J. Lewis, C. McNaughton Nicholls & R. Ormston (eds), *Qualitative Research Practice: A Guide for Social Science Students and Researchers* (2nd edn) (pp. 367–396). London, UK: Sage Publications Ltd.
This is one of many useful chapters within this updated edition.

14

BEING A QUALITATIVE SECONDARY RESEARCHER

explore what it means to be a qualitative secondary researcher

reflect on the skills you have developed

check if your research is ready for submission

know how and where to disseminate your research

CHAPTER OVERVIEW

Every chapter in this book so far has explained and guided you in the construction of your qualitative secondary research. In this, the final chapter, we explore what you have achieved and the skills you may have developed. In doing so, the chapter emphasises the benefits in stepping back to reflect on the processes involved to explore the impact of the experience. This is so you can fully appreciate the skills that you have or will have developed during your research. One key feature of this chapter is the provision of a checklist to focus you on pivotal aspects of the research process and we ask a range of questions to check that your research project is ready for submission.

This chapter concludes with guidance on a range of possible next steps or options for disseminating your findings and getting your results out to those that may want to read or act upon what you have found out. This is an important consideration as whilst you may have completed your research as part of the requirement for an academic programme, rather than the findings gathering dust, you may find that many people would be really interested to read what you have found out.

WHAT MAKES A 'GOOD' QUALITATIVE SECONDARY RESEARCHER?

A 'good' qualitative secondary researcher is curious, resilient and passionate about wanting to know something in depth and detail. They undertake their research in a systematic way, focused on producing credible findings and as they complete their project, they learn new skills and new ways of knowing that will support them as they move into the next stage of their academic and professional life.

This chapter comes at the end of this book as a celebration of what you have achieved. As you undertook this journey you developed skills and attributes or enhanced the ones you began with. You will have changed because all experiences lead to forms of change. Therefore, knowing how you have changed can be a powerful way of making sense of your research process and can help you use the skills you have developed to increased advantage.

In this concluding chapter, we explore some of the skills and attributes you may have developed and enhanced and demonstrate how these skills can spur you into a whole new career. This requires you to reflect on the process, the importance of which we explore next.

WHY SHOULD I REFLECT ON MY RESEARCH PROJECT?

As you complete your research, it is an opportune time to reflect on what you have achieved and how you have achieved this. Reflection can take many forms as you focus on different aspects of an experience. It could be on you and how you approached your study, it could be on the study itself and it could be on what you want to do next as a consequence of your experiences. We will cover these aspects in this chapter and encourage you to see reflection as an important part of your research process as it not only encourages insight but can also promote further learning. In this way, we can use reflection to develop ourselves and our capabilities as we move from one stage to another; reflection therefore, plays a crucial role in your self-development. Leaders in theories of reflection such as Dewey (1933) link reflection and learning and present this as a meaning making process that leads to changes in learning behaviour and attitudes. Therefore, reflection is crucial in both developing yourself as a researcher and in the production of robust research.

When we reflect, we do so to make meaning of the experiences we have undergone. For example, you could try to make connections from your research and from relationships among the elements of the experience gained. Rolfe et al.'s (2001) reflective model can also be a useful strategy to assist this process as it is based upon three simple questions: 'What? So what? Now what?' These prompts can encourage broader insights into the research process and keep your reflection focused.

What? Report what happened, objectively, without any judgement or interpretation.

So, what? What did you learn from the experience? What difference did it make?

Now what? How will you think or act in the future as a result?

We explore reflection in two ways: first, as reflection on your research project as we provide a checklist to ensure you are ready to submit your work; and second, as reflection on you as the person who has created and achieved this project. Achieving the completion of a research project is something to feel very proud of. Also, you will have added to what is known about your subject in many ways. Therefore, at the end of this chapter we explore ways you can disseminate and present of your findings and make sure your contribution is acknowledged. We begin, as we show in Figure 14.1, by asking you to reflect on your research project.

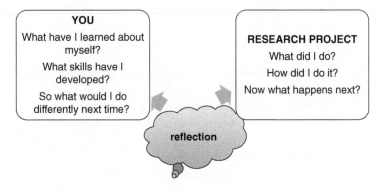

Figure 14.1   Reflecting on your research process

Reflecting on your work

Reflection is not just thinking and wondering what you did, it is an interpretive process where you make sense of the experience of completing your research project. We advise you to think of it as the final part of your project and something you need to do before you submit your work. It is making sure you have done all you can to achieve the task you were set. Engaging in this type of reflective practice should help to improve the quality of your submission. At the beginning of this book we recommended that you factor in some extra time or reflection time as this enables you to stand back and adopt a less subjective and more objective appraisal of what you have achieved.

Therefore, we offer a checklist to guide you in this reflection process. We have isolated key parts of your research process and ask questions to prompt and extend your thinking. However, as we have emphasised throughout this book, we cannot offer a template for your submission as you will need to refer to your institution's guidelines or research handbook. We reiterate and advise most firmly that you should refer to particular institution guidelines to ensure the specific discipline or own organisational requirements are met to ensure accuracy of the format of your submission. This helps prevent wasted time, effort and/or lost marks and helps you produce work that meets all the requirements set. Please refer to this but bear in mind the questions we have outlined in the checklist provided (see Figure 14.2) as you do.

Key sections and questions	Clarifying questions as guidance
Knowing the timeframe for completing your research	• Do you know key dates for submission? • Prepare a timeline. • Put this up somewhere noticeable.
Question and aim	• Have you created clear and focused question(s) and/or aim(s)? • Are these communicated in the text in sections (e.g. *introduction*, *literature review* and *findings*) to provide your reader with an understanding of the focus of your inquiry?
Abstract	• Do you need to include one? • If you do, have you summarised what you did, why you did it, how you did it and your findings?
Rationale	• Have you provided a persuasive and informed rationale? • Have you made your reader 'care' about your research?
Ethics	• Do you need to make any of the data in your research anonymous? (*Data protection*) • Have you checked ownership and if you need any permissions to use the data? • Did you need to consider issues of informed consent? • Have you considered your research behaviour as being part of your role as an ethical researcher? (*Accurate referencing, open and transparent*)
Literature review	• Have you referenced accurately? • Is the section logically constructed? • Do your headings make sense? • Have you provided a concluding paragraph drawing your main points together? • Have you fully focused on your research question? • Are these included in this section to focus your reader? • Did you provide divergent perspectives? • Have you indicated changes and debates in current thinking? • Is this critically written? • Have you synthesised your sources? • Did you use a narrative hook?
Methodology	• Have you described the actions taken to investigate your research problem? • Did you state why and how your research will be carried out? • Have you defended your decision making?

Key sections and questions	Clarifying questions as guidance
	• Have you included enough information necessary for your reader to understand your research?
	• Have you written this in the past tense to show it is something you did?
	• Have you made sure that you have included your approach to ethics; sampling and data selection (*critical appraisal*); identified and defended your choice of research strategy, discussed your theoretical framework and your methods of analysis?
Analysis	• Have you included an introduction to the analysis to your research?
	• Did you explain how you created meaning?
	• Have you shown how your analysis was performed?
	• Did you create maps or matrices? Are these included as diagrams or inserted in the appendix as evidence of your approach?
	• Is your analysis section written in such a way that your reader could follow your processes?
Findings	• Have you included your research question(s) and/or aim(s) to refocus your reader?
	• Have you written a summary using key findings from your research to support your major points?
	• Have you used your literature to confirm or dispute your findings?
	• Is this used in a persuasive and authoritative way?
	• Have you discussed results that may not fit in with your research question and explained why this might be the case?
	• Have you presented this section in a logical and clear way?
	• Are your illustrations clearly labelled?
	• Is all the information included readable?
	• Have you related to the information in your text?
Conclusions	• Have you set out clearly what you can conclude, providing a detailed summary about what you have learned and the contribution that your research has made?
	• Did you weigh up the evidence and explore any findings that do not 'fit' your answer?
	• What new questions have been raised?
Limitations	• Did you identify any factors that may have influenced the validity of your findings?
	• Have you highlighted possible weakness?
Recommendations	• Are your recommendations meaningful and relevant? Have you indicated:
	o What would you do differently?
	o What would be the next steps?
	• Are there any gaps that need to be addressed?

(Continued)

Figure 14.2 (Continued)

Key sections and questions	Clarifying questions as guidance
References	• Have you recorded all your source information accurately (*using your required referencing system*)? • Have you correctly cited all your sources?
Checking for accuracy	• Have you proofread and edited your work? • Have you checked you have not exceeded the word limit? • Did you ask a friend to be your critical friend to read your work through?
Appendix	• Have you checked that you are only including information, that whilst not essential, can defend your analysis or corroborates your conclusions in any way? • Do you need to include a data management plan? • Have you included the correct details of the appendix to the relevant page number(s)?
Tables of contents/ Glossary	• Do you need to include a table of contents? If yes, is this accurately presented? (*Pages are recorded accurately next to the correct topic*) • Have you listed your chapter or section titles ensuring these reflect what appears in your work? • If you have to include a glossary, have you checked you have include all key terms fully and accurately? • Have you listed these in alphabetical order?
Have you checked you know how to submit the work?	• Are you fully aware of the presentation and submission requirements or guidelines? (*You may be asked to sign a form to confirm that the work you submit is in accordance with your institution's or organisation's regulations*)

Figure 14.2 Checklist for your research project completion

USING A COMPLETION CHECKLIST

Checklists can be useful tools to use before, during and after the completion of your research project as they keep you focused on what you have to achieve and how it needs to be achieved. So even though this is provided in this final part of this book, it does not mean it can only be used at the end.

What happens if things do not go to plan?

We have referred to instances and events that can make a research study go awry and this can happen in spite of all your careful planning and preparation. As you come to the end of your research process we encourage you to discuss any last-minute concerns you may have about your work with your supervisor. In Chapter 13 when we discussed the presentation of your findings and conclusions we stated that sometimes you can use these experiences as learning pointers for others so you can record your limitations of concerns and use any issues as a possible recommendation point.

Being a good researcher is about being honest and we have discussed the need for transparent research as a process to promote credibility. If things did not go to plan, please be open. If you have any issues, please make sure you take advantage of any help available to you and act on any feedback given. Please do not suffer in silence. Keep in mind that your research is an opportunity to demonstrate your ability to investigate and report your findings. If you feel that you were unable to answer every or even any question you had on your topic the important skill to demonstrate is to be able to reflect on why this occurred. That is the true sign of a skilled researcher.

Reflecting on your skills development

As we discussed at the beginning, we do not just want you to reflect on your work but also on yourself as a person who has completed their project. In some institutions you may be required to submit a reflective statement about your research process and if you do, we advise you to use models of reflection to guide your thinking process. Models of reflection are useful because, as Dewey (1933) emphasises, reflection is more than mere thought, it is a sequence of thinking processes that lead to a consequence or a *'proper'* outcome (Dewey 1933: 2–3). This outcome should result in your development, increased self-insight and ideas for a plan of future action. Therefore, reflection is an *'active'* and *'persistent'* process (Dewey 1933: 5) that leads to new ways of knowing.

There are many models that you can use to prompt your process of reflection and we offer Gibbs' (1988) approach where you ask yourself a set of sequentially ordered questions to help you understand your experience. Taking a sequential approach is something Dewey proposed as driving consequences or changes in thinking and behaviour. This is because the action you take in the final stage will feed back into the first stage of your next experience. For you this might be employment or future research, beginning the process again. However, reflection, although a valuable process, can be a difficult and at times challenging process. This is because reflection requires you to be honest in all you have or have not achieved.

Gibbs' sequential approach involves six steps: you can use an approach like this to explore the whole project or to focus on a specific event that occurred whilst you were completing it. The focus here is on you and your response to your research experience.

Description: *What happened?* This is where you provide an overview of your project experiences or a specific event: did something happen that you need to understand in more depth?

Feelings: *What did you think and feel about it?* This could focus on the whole project or on one key event. Knowing what, why and how you feel about something is a step towards knowing what it means to you and thus, enables you to learn from it.

Evaluation: *What were the positives and negatives?* It can be customary to only focus on the negative aspects here but good experiences need to be understood so we can replicate them. We tend to focus on negative experiences as learning points but good ones direct our learning as much as anything else.

Analysis: *What sense can you make of it?* This is where you begin to interpret the experience. You may need to focus on a specific part to really understand a key event of your research as a whole. This is where you start to make connections and link this experience to others you may have.

Conclusion: *What else could you have done?* When we start to think of alternative ways of thinking about an experience we are already learning from it and devising new ways of thinking and behaving.

Action Plan: *What will you do next time?* This is where you clearly state these new ways of thinking. This is what Dewey (1933) would consider the consequences of your experience as it shapes an outcome. This is where you plan to move forward.

Consequently, Gibbs' (1988) way of thinking about reflection and the sequential form it can take can be a powerful tool to help us understand who we are and who we want to be. The next section explores some of the skills that we hope, when you reflect, you will acknowledge you have developed. As we discussed in Chapter 2, some of these skills you will have had when you started, some may have been advanced and some may have been developed during your research process. Only you can know how and in what way you have developed and therefore, reflection is a highly individual process that is bound up in honest self-appraisal.

Your research skills

When you conduct research, you need to utilise a wide range of skills. These range from the relatively basic (*the ability to look something up*) to the more complex (*analysing your data*). Some of these skills you will already be proficient at, but others may take time to develop as you gain more experience as your research progresses. The important thing to remember is that like anything else something new takes time and effort. However, through being engaged in research, your skills will develop as you progress through the particular stages and challenges (*e.g., problem solving, communication and analytical thinking;* Brew 2012). The acronym TAPE (see Figure 14.3) illustrates how the research process supports your development as a researcher.

Higher level thinking skills

When you were researching you will have been exposed to situations where you have to employ higher level thinking skills. In Chapter 9, we explored this when we discussed the

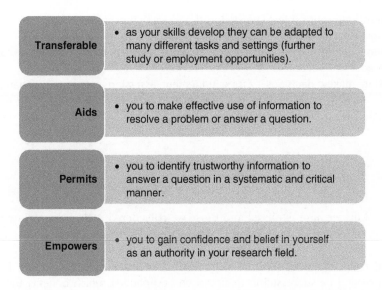

Transferable
- as your skills develop they can be adapted to many different tasks and settings (further study or employment opportunities).

Aids
- you to make effective use of information to resolve a problem or answer a question.

Permits
- you to identify trustworthy information to answer a question in a systematic and critical manner.

Empowers
- you to gain confidence and belief in yourself as an authority in your research field.

Figure 14.3   TAPE: exploring the skills and attitudes you may develop from your research

skills needed to complete your literature review but now we refer to the updated taxonomy of skills identified by Anderson et al. (2001). This classification reflects a more active form of thinking with the application of action words.

- **Creating:** You are generating new information
- **Evaluating:** You are making judgement based on criteria
- **Analysing:** You are reviewing dissecting material
- **Applying:** You are implementing to a new context or practice
- **Understanding:** You are determining meaning
- **Remembering:** You are able to recall knowledge

These skills demonstrate capacities within the research project and they can be translated into key activities and understanding. Remembering is the most fundamental process as it underpins all you do. No one expects you to be able to remember everything but you need to have the capacity to retain information in order to learn. Sometimes we need support mechanisms to do this effectively, especially when there is too much to handle. For this reason, we provided strategies to aid remembering in the data management and literature recording processes we explored in earlier chapters (Chapters 10 and 9). Using Anderson et al.'s (2001) revised taxonomy based on Bloom et al. (1956) we link the skills they identify to your research process and we begin with understanding as a lower skill and end with creating as a higher skill as this is where you have created knowledge that can now add to what is known about your subject:

- **understanding:** your subject knowledge, the research processes;
- **applying:** research skills in context;
- **analysing:** identifying key components of your research topic, creating a conceptual framework;
- **evaluating:** making decisions, passing judgement, assessing and appraising data;
- **creating:** making sense of your data, generating your findings and adding to existing knowledge.

Skills for employability

Many of the skills we have explored and those we considered within the acronym TAPE are skills that can support your employability. These are the skills that Yorke (2003: 8) defines as:

> skills, understandings and personal attributes – that make individuals more likely to gain employment and be successful in their chosen occupations, which benefits themselves, the workforce, the community and the economy.

There is a move away from employers seeing a graduate's achievements as only related to their subject discipline towards the recognition of the contribution of the skills gained through conducting research. The acquisition of these skills gained through conducting your research will promote the cluster of skills associated with increasing your employability (Bandaranaike & Willison 2015). These competencies are called transferable skills, as they represent capabilities that can be applied to many workplace contexts and industries, making them particularly attractive attributes for employers.

The top 10 skills that contribute towards employability are outlined together with questions for you to reflect on. This list is adapted from: Top ten skills for employability (TARGETjobs 2018).

1. **Commercial awareness (or business acumen):** Did you conduct research relevant to your workplace?
2. **Communication:** Was your research write-up clear, focused and relevant to the reader?
3. **Teamwork:** Did your research require you to liaise with others?
4. **Negotiation and persuasion:** Consider the rationale for your research; were you able to persuade others convincingly as to why your research was required?
5. **Problem solving:** Did you demonstrate a logical and analytical approach to solving any problems or issues in your research?
6. **Leadership:** This refers to potential to motivate or lead others as well as delegating tasks, setting deadlines and leading by example. Did you demonstrate any leadership qualities?
7. **Organisation:** How effectively were you able to prioritise work and meet deadlines?
8. **Perseverance and motivation:** How did you manage the challenges that may have arisen during your research?

9. **Ability to work under pressure:** Did you experience any stress during your research and, if so, how were you able to manage this?

10. **Confidence:** How much confidence do you have in your research findings?

Reflecting on the list of the Top ten skills for employability, consider which you have gained during your research; these could be more relevant and useful than you initially think. Therefore, when you are applying for employment, consider the skills you have developed and how these can be useful to include in your Curriculum Vitae (CV). Be explicit about the skills you gained during your research. When applying for jobs, whether on the application form or at interview, you may be asked to outline or discuss examples of when you managed a project, solved a problem or demonstrated initiative. If your research topic is particularly relevant to your chosen career, this also provides a talking point at interview to illustrate how really interested and committed you are to that area.

Research processes as character building

Character is a broad concept but it relates to attributes or dispositions that you may have or have developed when you started and ended your research process. In Chapter 2, we considered this in relation to the work of Carol Dweck (2006) and her work on mindsets, especially the development of growth mindsets rather than fixed ways of engaging in the world. Cultivating more of a growth mindset leads people to take on challenges they can learn from and they can find more effective ways to improve, to persevere when they experience setbacks and failure. As you near the end of your research project we hope you have developed a growth mindset that accepts ambiguity, accepts learning from failure and sees this as an opportunity to develop. We hope you were able to learn from the feedback that was offered during your project and use this to enhance your learning. Adopting a growth mindset is strongly linked to notions of resilience, self-belief and self-efficacy, and resilience is a character trait linked to success (Bharathiar 2008). Finally, when we discuss character, we hope that you will also have retained that most essential of all of life skills and traits ... a good sense of humour!

Skills for living in data rich societies

One of the key principles of our approach to qualitative secondary research has been the need to know what data (*information*) comprises and how to evaluate and appraise its quality and function in your research project. As a secondary researcher selecting the 'right' type of data for your research is based on your ability to make informed decisions about your data. Living in an information rich society requires skills of critical appraisal and evaluation to know if data are authentic, meaningful and credible. The examples of fake news we explored earlier in

Chapter 6, should illustrate the need to go beyond a surface understanding of what is presented as fact to explore how and why data are produced. Therefore, some of the skills we hope you have developed are those relating to the ability to make effective judgements and decisions about data, as being media and information literate in such a data rich world becomes a necessity. Being media and information literate means you make informed choices because you understand how and why information is produced. Possessing these literacies enhances your ability to analyse and critically evaluate both content and means of production to comprehend as fully as possible the way information is created and communicated.

WHAT HAVE I LEARNT AS A QUALITATIVE SECONDARY RESEARCHER?

You will have learnt many things by the time you complete your project and we have explored some of these under processes of reflection and evaluating your work. What you have learnt and what this means will be individual to you but we hope you have learnt a lot about yourself and the process of research. In this section we consider some of the wider skills you may have developed. We will begin by considering what we hoped you have achieved which is a sense of achievement.

Sense of achievement

Coming to the end of any project is something to celebrate and it is an achievement. As Thomas Carlyle is acknowledged as saying '*Nothing builds self-esteem and self-confidence like accomplishment*', and this saying points to the role of achievement as a motivating force to move forward. Whatever you choose to do post research project, it is important to accept that this achievement is yours to own.

Making decisions

Developing an identity as a secondary researcher requires you to reflect not only on the process of undertaking research, but the process of becoming a researcher. In your day-to-day life, it is more than likely that you will have investigated and explored information around you (*e.g. the particular options on your mobile phone deal or reviews and costs of a weekend away*). As you have completed your project and as you look back on your journey, an advantage of being a researcher is that you have been '*engaged in the conception or creation of new knowledge, products, processes, methods and systems, and in the management of the projects concerned*' (European Commission 2005: 15). Integral to this is the decision-making tasks you undertake. As we show in Box 14.1, being able to make decisions requires you to be able to collect as much information as you can to make informed or 'right' decisions.

BOX 14.1 COCA-COLA MARKETING DISASTER

In 1985, the Coca-Cola Company due to failing market share decided to change the formula of Coca-Cola. Blind taste tests conducted in thirteen US cities involving over 190,000 participants found that over half of those tested preferred the new Coke over the original flavour. Coca-Cola therefore, confidently introduced the new version and removed the original formula from sale.

Despite their research, indicating that the new recipe would likely be a popular choice, withdrawing the original turned out to be a costly mistake and they suffered a huge backlash from their customers. The main problem was that Coca-Cola only considered opinions and perceptions of taste as the deciding factor in consumer buying behaviour. Other hugely relevant variables such as the emotional connection consumers had with the original version and what the brand represented to them, were not considered.

(www.coca-colacompany.com/stories/coke-lore-new-coke)

Truth is arbitrary

Hopefully you have realised that truth is an arbitrary construct which depends on whose version it is and why. It is useful to note that all research, whether carried out by those relatively inexperienced or those more expert, is also open to some kind of interpretation and understanding based on the perspective or positioning of the researcher. Therefore, as you complete your research project you should have the skills to enable you to work within this ambiguity and see it for what it is. This is part of living in an uncertain world where you need your skills of critical judgement to make sense.

Becoming an expert

One of the key developments you will have made in yourself may be something you are less likely to admit and this is your claim to be the expert of your research. At the end of your project, no one will know your research as well as you do; you will know how it is constructed and how it is written and you will know how your findings were generated and what these now mean to knowledge in your subject area. You are now adding to the field of knowledge and can claim to be an expert on your research. It may surprise you how many people might be interested in reading what you have found. As a consequence of sharing, new opportunities may open up to you.

Learn from experts

In considering qualitative secondary research you will have been exposed to ways of thinking from leaders in your field. You will have used their knowledge to add to yours. This is a process of standing on the shoulders of giants but remember you can take this learning further. When you research you are also adding to what is known and so your work has a place in your knowledge area or domain. This is why you should consider sharing it.

HOW CAN I DISSEMINATE MY RESEARCH?

People may want to know about your findings and you may want to share them so, in this section, we consider how you can disseminate your findings. You may have to do this as a condition of your study and this is where you should discuss with your supervisor how to best do this. You may consider that your research is too small or not relevant enough for larger sharing platforms. However, think about this carefully. There is a rise in student publications where 'novice' or undergraduate students can publish their work but there are also, as we explored in Chapters 6 and 7, a wealth of professional, vocational, subject or domain specific academic journals. There are also other avenues to support the dissemination of your research and these include conferences, some of which are specifically for undergraduate and graduate work (Spronken-Smith et al. 2008).

Publication of your work can add to the authenticity of your research experience and support the growth of your academic knowledge and profile. In the right journal it can epitomise the highest level of possibilities for dissemination. However, what you do, how you do this and if you want to do this, has to be an individual decision but in Figure 14.6 we offer four effective ways to disseminate your research.

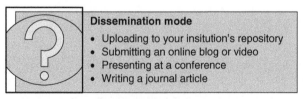

Dissemination mode
- Uploading to your insitution's repository
- Submitting an online blog or video
- Presenting at a conference
- Writing a journal article

Figure 14.4 Disseminating your research findings

An institutional repository

The Internet has altered opportunities for communication, both formal and informal. One major area of change is in scholarly communication of research and many higher educational institutions provide services including a data repository for the storage and sharing of data (Gragin et al. 2010). There are different types of repositories including:

- **Discipline/subject based repositories:** these are not restricted to any one particular institution for their input; they can also be local, national or international.
- **Institutional repository:** this provides an accessible digital storage place to facilitate dissemination and promote research outputs.

The main difference among the different repositories is the content they collect and manage. Subject based repositories can be either commercial or non-commercial set up by community members and adopted by the wider community. Foster and Gibbons (2005) offer a definition of an institutional digital repository which they state is '*an electronic system that captures, preserves, and provides access to the digital work products of a community*'.

Whilst an institutional repository as a research storage facility is growing in popularity due to the recognition of its convenience in disseminating ideas and supporting collaboration, Sarker, Davis and Tiropanis (2018: 3) recognise the provision could improve channels of dissemination further and that there is the '*need to make it accessible to industries or funding bodies for commercialisation of research to contribute to the social economy*'. However, the data services offered by institutional repositories vary with the resources of the particular university or organisation and you will need to check what is available at your institution.

Creating or submitting a blog

A 'blog' is the shortening of 'weblog' which is an online website where you can write text posts and upload images and have them published. Whilst they have evolved over time, most blogs have a range of functions that enable your reader to engage with the information you present. Blogging has rapidly become a popular way to communicate information and this can include your research findings. Figure 14.7 illustrates possible sites where you can post your research.

Which one you choose is up to you and as technology advances so do the programs available for use, so it is best to explore what is on offer and check that it meets your needs. Please check the terms of service and check you

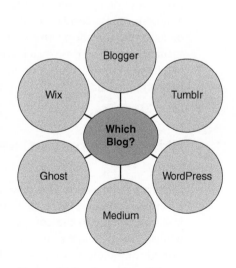

Figure 14.5   Examples of Blogs

retain rights to your intellectual property. Also, reflect on some of the issues we considered in Chapter 5 relating to the ethics of posting information online and consider how you would feel if a researcher used your work for their research.

Presenting at a conference

During your academic career or in the workplace, it is likely that you have been required to give some sort of presentation. After you have completed your research project it seems a shame not to expand these experiences and explore as many ways as possible to disseminate your findings. Whilst presenting at a conference is not a common occurrence for most students, they can provide invaluable opportunities to share your work and network with other students and professionals.

There are several different kinds of conferences, your own institution or organisation might host yearly conferences or you can access them through your own particular subject field or discipline. Many conferences are very student friendly and provide opportunities for both undergraduate and graduate students to engage in their events. Here are two examples:

- **The British Conference of Undergraduate Research:** promotes the dissemination of undergraduate research in all disciplines (for further information access www.bcur.org/).
- **The International Conference of Undergraduate Research:** provides an annual event which showcases the work of undergraduate researchers from any discipline or area (for further information access www.icurportal.com).

When attending a conference for the first time many opt to present a poster rather than give a more formal presentation. Poster sessions involve presenting a summary of your research on a poster. This means that you would talk for less time as your poster usually includes the main points. This gives you a less daunting way in to conferences to disseminate your research and its significance whilst providing you with an opportunity to practise your presenting and networking skills.

Writing a journal article

There are many reasons for disseminating your research in a journal. First, it may seem such a waste to leave new research on the shelf, especially as you have put so much hard work into it. Secondly, due to the competitiveness of the job market in and out of academia, getting published will enhance any curriculum vitae. Finally, there might be a professional compulsion to communicate your research as you want to make a contribution and move knowledge on or contribute to a change in practice (McGrail, Rickard & Jones 2006).

If you decide you want to publish in a journal, read some carefully in your particular field of study. Ask your institution's librarian for advice and check that your research is within the scope of the journal that you want to send your article to. Always follow the submission requirements. If you submit your work and receive a rejection or a revise and resubmit response, please do not get disheartened and give up. It is not unusual for even experienced researchers to be turned down many times before acceptance. Like us, when you do receive an email from the journal editor telling you that your peer-reviewed article is accepted, you will feel a sense of accomplishment and perhaps a thirst for more!

Future possibilities

Did you conduct research because it was a requirement of an academic course, for your workplace or just because you like it? Whatever the reasons, you may still need to think about your next steps, for example higher level study or your career path. As outlined previously the skills developed during your research can help as a springboard to your future success. Researchers are required in many areas of employment including, local and central government, private business and charities.

Whether you wish to conduct further research or not, employers look for and value strong transferable skills that you will have developed during your research project. Contact your institution careers department or research jobs online.

Figure 14.6   What will you do next?

REFLECTION AND FURTHER READING

At the beginning of the chapter we set out what you should be able to do when you reached the end of this chapter. To aid your reflection on all we have covered we ask some chapter specific questions. If you are unsure of any of your answers to these questions, please go back to the relevant section to review this aspect.

REFLECTING ON CHAPTER 14

In this chapter we have:

- **Examined the need to address particular institutional or organisational research submission guidelines:** Do you know the stipulations and submission requirements of your particular institutional or organisation?
- **Explored what it means to be a qualitative secondary researcher:** What qualities do you think contribute to your being a successful researcher?
- **Reflected on the research skills that you have developed:** Which of your skills do you think are particularly useful when conducting research? Which skills do you still need to develop further?
- **Investigated ways to disseminate your research:** Would you like to disseminate your research to the wider community? Which dissemination strategies appeal to you?
- **Considered how your research may add to your employability:** What skills would you emphasise on your CV?
- **Considered future research opportunities:** Do you know what will be your next steps?

WE RECOMMEND FOR FUTURE READING:

Belcher, W.L. (2016) *Writing Your Journal Article in Twelve Weeks: A Guide to Academic Publishing Success*. Princeton, NJ: Sage.
This is a valuable and detailed resource for those looking to produce an article from their qualitative research.

Moon, J.A. (1999) *Learning Journals: A Handbook for Academics, Students and Professional Development*. London: Kogan Page.
This key text provides guidance and advice on the processes of reflection.

Williams, L. (2012) *Ready Made CVs: Winning CVs and Cover Letters for Every Type of Job* (5th edn). London: KoganPage.
This book provides practical support to enable you to develop and present a CV to make that vital good first impression. It also guides you through getting that important first job as well as guiding those who have had a career break.

A GLOSSARY OF KEY TERMINOLOGY

Abstract: A brief summary of a larger piece of your research that includes, for example, *what* you did, *why* and *how* the results were gained.

Aim: The researcher's state of intent (*e.g. to explore changes in attitudes towards cannabis use*).

Analysis: A break-down and review of research information collected to gain better understanding.

Appendix: The section after the main text containing supplementary materials.

Archive: Stored public or private records or documents which can be examined as research data.

Artefacts: Artefacts are representations that are used to facilitate the understanding of a group's or individual's beliefs, values, and/or behaviours. In this book, the term is used to describe physical objects.

Audit trail: This is the process of documenting all of the relevant steps taken during research.

Author: The person who has created the information, music or artwork.

Bar chart: A graph that illustrates the data in the form of categories (*e.g. behaviours observed*).

Bias: Bias can occur either intentionally or unintentionally and reflects any inclination to deviate from the truth (*e.g. in data collection, data analysis and interpretation*).

Bibliography: This is a list of all of the sources used (*whether referenced or not*) in the process of researching your work (*including e.g. authors' last names, date of publication, publisher*). It is usually presented in alphabetical order.

Boolean operator: This facilitates a search for two concepts in combination with each other. An example of its use is in the use of the term "AND" in between keywords which will narrow your search. Alternatively, using the Boolean operator "OR" leads to your search being widened.

Central Tendency: A measure that defines the typical or average characteristic; the three main measures of central tendency are 'mean', 'median' and 'mode'.

Citation: This provides the relevant information on the sources used, the use of which would be necessary to find that source again (*e.g. author, title of the work and date of publication*).

Citation chaining: Using an existing source (*e.g. journal article*) as a starting point for finding more useful resources. By using the reference list of sources already accessed, you search backwards and forwards for materials that are cited and also sources that cite your existing original resource.

Cloud: This is a remote database where digital data can be stored across multiple servers (*and locations*) and is typically owned and managed by a hosting company.

Coding: A process of classifying data for analysis. Coding helps researchers find similar patterns and connections across their data.

Coding system: A coding system is created during data analysis. It is a list of the categories created when the researcher is coding.

Concept: A general idea of a phenomenon that can represent an object or idea.

Concept mapping: This is a visual tool that illustrates how abstract ideas are related to help understand how one concept can be related to other concepts.

Conclusion: This recaps the main findings and provides a summary reiterating the most important evidence supporting those findings.

Confidentiality: The requirement to keep some types of information private or anonymous.

Consistency: If we assess information on different occasions and gain similar results, then the assessment could be said to be consistent.

Constant comparison: This is a method for analysing data that involves checking your coding processes across all possible data sets. It is often associated with grounded theory but is used as a basis for qualitative approaches to analysis.

Content Analysis: A method for organising narrative qualitative data into identified themes and concepts.

Copyright: A right that gives creators the right to permit (*or not permit*) what happens to their creations. It prohibits unauthorised use, copying, or any alteration of information. Copyright laws include a fair use exemption which allows limited uses for non-commercial purposes.

Creative Commons licences: Creative Commons is a non-profit organisation that provides public copyright licences that enable the free distribution of otherwise copyrighted work.

Credibility: The confidence that the research was conducted in a robust manner.

Data: This is the term used to describe information created or collected from a range of sources. It is used within qualitative secondary research to add insight into people, phenomena, ideas or events.

Data analysis: The process by which data are organised and subjected to a systematic analysis either manually or electronically to identify patterns in research data. Data analysis is an umbrella term that refers to many forms of analysis such as content analysis, thematic analysis and visual analysis.

Data collection: The process of gathering and recording data when undertaking a research project.

Data curation: *Digital curation* is the long-term management and preservation of *digital* data.

Data indexing: This is a data management process as you can use an index to help find and sort records faster.

Data management: Practices and policies related to the supervision of information in relation to their archiving, analysing, interpreting, sharing and publishing.

Data Protection: The protection of the collection, storage, use and dissemination of personal data.

Data reduction: This involves the appraisal of data and generally results in a reduced data set.

Database: This is a collection of articles from a selected list of sources such as journals, magazines, and/or newspapers. They can contain hundreds of thousands of articles and allow you to search through several journals at once.

Deduction: The process of reasoning from the more general to the more specific; for example, beginning with a theory that can be tested.

Demographics: This is the categorisation of participants using categories such as their age, education, ethnicity, and gender.

Dependability: This relates to the accuracy of the findings and the degree to which the findings are supported by the data collected.

Descriptive Statistics: Basic statistics used to describe, illustrate and summarise data through the use of graphs and measures of the dispersion of data which is presented, such as variance or range.

Diary (research diary): This is a document recording a researcher's activities and considerations during their research. When used, it can form part of an audit trail (*see Audit trail*).

Digital security: This is an umbrella term used to include the tools you can apply to protect your identity, research data and technology in the online and mobile world (*e.g. anti-virus software, web services, biometrics*).

Discourse: Communication in the form of language that can be verbal, in the form of words and speech, or non-verbal in attitude or gestures.

Discourse analysis: This is a general term for the approaches to the analysis of language use or semiotic events.

Documents: These are sources of evidence in a wide variety of forms that provide information which can be used as data.

Employability: This represents a set of skills and attributes that contribute towards gaining positive employment.

Endnote: This is a software program which enables the storing and organising of citation information in conjunction with word processor software (*e.g. Microsoft Word, Apple Pages, OpenOffice*) to insert citations and create bibliographies.

Epistemology: A way of understanding how we know what we know.

Ethical codes of conduct: These are written guidelines of ethical practice usually provided by an institution, profession or organising body to define a researcher's conduct in a research study.

Ethics: The moral principles or rules of conduct which are laid down in the codes of conduct produced by professional bodies or individual countries for the protection of participants in research.

Exclusion criteria: The set of distinguishing principles which result in being excluded in the study (*e.g. date, location, population, etc.*).

Familiarisation (*see immersion*): The process during which the researcher immerses themselves into their research to fully understand the information, key ideas and recurrent themes.

Findings: These are the outcomes of a research project.

Framework analysis (*see thematic analysis*): This approach to analysis is also termed thematic analysis as it seeks to distinguish possible similarities and differences, before attempting to explore relationships in the data.

Gatekeeper: A person whose permission or approval is necessary to gain access to a research site or setting.

Generalisability: The extent to which research findings and conclusions within a research study can be applied to the wider population.

Grounded theory: The development of theory from the inductive analysis of data. This approach is generally used in qualitative research in which the data are analysed to extrapolate a theory to explain the phenomenon under investigation.

Growth mindset: This is the belief that the mindset that drives our actions and abilities can be developed through positive thinking, dedication and hard work.

Harvard referencing style: This is a generic form that uses the author's surname, first name, year of publication, title (*italicised or underlined*), publisher and place of publication.

Helsinki Declaration: Ethical guidelines for conducting medical research involving human participants adopted by the World Medical Association.

Identifiers (direct): These are variables that indicate linkable details of individuals or units (*e.g. names, addresses, driver's licence numbers, etc.*).

Identifiers (indirect): These are variables (*e.g. pieces of personal information*) that can be problematic as they may be used together or in conjunction with other information to identify individual respondents (*e.g. area of residence, level of education, occupation, income etc.*).

Immersion (*see familiarisation*): This is where the objective is to get to know the data well and be familiar with and understand the particular specific aspects.

Inclusion criteria: The set of distinguishing principles that studies must meet to be included in the research review (*e.g. date, location, population etc.*).

Inductive: Works from the specific to the more general whereby patterns are identified which are then extrapolated to create general conclusions or a general theory.

Inferential statistics: Mathematical strategies to analysing data using statistical tests that allow the researcher to make inferences about whether the results are significant or not.

Informed consent: The practice of participants in research making an informed decision to participate in research.

Insider researcher: Research undertaken by those that possess intimate knowledge and characteristics of the specific research sample (*e.g. cultural, biological and occupational*).

Intellectual property: A legal term that refers to literature, artistic works, discoveries and inventions.

Intellectual Property Rights: Intellectual property rights give creators, companies or owners of a work certain controls over its use. Some of the rights require registration (*e.g. patents*) while others occur routinely upon the work's creation (*e.g. copyright*).

Interpretation: A fundamental part of the analysis of data that requires understanding based on corroboration and extrapolation to bring out the meaning.

Interpretivist: The interpretivist approach assumes the researcher plays a subjective role in their research and accepts some personal involvement in the research and in the drawing of conclusions.

Keyword: A word which summarises the major concept and is often used when searching.

Library catalogue: Bibliographic details of items in a library.

Literature review: An evaluative report of information related to your selected area of study which provides contextualisation and critical appraisal.

Matrix: A spreadsheet or table that contains numerous cells into which summarised data are entered by codes (columns) and cases (rows).

Mendeley: This is a freely available reference manager, which works particularly well with PDFs to enable you to gather and organise references, upload documents and generate citations and bibliographies.

Meta-Analysis: A statistical technique that combines and analyses data across multiple studies.

Methodology: This is the approach adopted when conducting research (*e.g. the paradigm, theoretical model and techniques applied*).

Narrative Analysis: This is a form of qualitative content analysis which views narratives as interpretive devices of the social products produced in specific contexts (*e.g. cultural, social, historical and setting*).

Normal Curve: A graphical representation of a mathematically defined curve that is bell-shaped in which the mean, median and mode are all in the same interval.

Nuremberg Code: The first international set of standards to guide the ethical behaviour of researchers. It was written because of the findings of the Nuremberg Council during the war crimes tribunals in 1947.

Objectivity: Level of impartiality whereby there is a presumption of lack of individual influence, bias and prejudice during the research process.

Open access: The online availability of academic work which is free of charge to access and read.

Open data: This refers to data that can be freely used.

Ontology: The set of beliefs about the nature of reality, existence and knowledge.

Paradigms: These are conceptual frameworks or views of the world that shape the way a researcher will conduct their research. They may be reflected by their beliefs about ontology (*what is reality*) and epistemology (*what is knowledge*).

Peer review: This involves peer experts within a discipline evaluating submitted work, for example reviewing journal articles for publication. This provides a sense of authority and confidence.

Philosophy: Our philosophical positions represent the foundations of the fundamental beliefs and analysis which we apply to concepts or practices.

Pie chart: This is a descriptive statistic which illustrates in a graphical form a circle that is divided into sectors representing a proportion of the whole.

Plagiarism: This involves the act of intentionally or unintentionally misrepresenting someone else's work as one's own.

Population: All members of the group, case or class of subjects under study.

Positionality: Positionality is a concept which accepts that a researcher's personal characteristics (*e.g. race, gender, age and sexuality*), values, beliefs and views influence how they see the world and thus the research they create.

Positivism: Positivism is an approach to research reflecting the philosophical notion that the only sure way to reveal the truth is through application of objective scientific means. This assumes the researcher is objective with no personal influence on the collection or interpretation of data.

Pragmatism: Encompasses the use of both qualitative and quantitative research. It is not based on a particular fixed view of what 'reality' is but focuses on choosing techniques that best meet the research purposes.

Primary research: The collection of new or original data using a range of researcher designed and defined tools. Primary research generates data that do not yet exist.

Qualitative research: Collects data that are non-numerical to find out more in-depth information about an issue, type of person or behaviours.

Qualitative secondary research: A systematic approach to the use of existing textual or image-based data to provide ways of understanding that may be additional to or different from the data's original purpose (see the definition in Chapter 1).

Quantitative research: Collects data that is numerical and can be 'counted' as it involves the measurement of quantities or amounts and often involves statistical analysis.

Random sampling: A procedure for ensuring that the sample drawn from a population has an equal chance of being selected for inclusion in the sample.

Range: The distance between the lowest and the highest value in a set of scores.

Rationale: The explanation as to why a research study needs to take place, why it is important and what purpose it serves.

Recommendations: These are suggestions as to the best course of action that can be taken in light of the research findings.

Reference list: A list of all sources of information that have been used to support the research study (*e.g. authors' last names, date of publication, publisher – see Harvard referencing*). It is usually presented in alphabetical order.

Reflexivity: Being '*reflexive*' means that you are critically thinking about your role and influence in the research process.

Reliability: This relates to the consistency or dependency of a measure or a research outcome (*e.g. the degree to which the results of a research are consistent with the results of similar studies*).

Repository: A storehouse or collection of files, often hosted by a third-party such as an academic institution, to collect and store the intellectual output such as research material and electronic e-theses.

Representative sample: A sample that includes typical individuals from all subgroups of the targeted population.

Research: The systematic process of finding and analysing information for the purpose of answering a question(s) or to provide a solution.

Research design: The research design is the way the researcher formulates the problem and designs a project to address the aim of the research.

Research objectives: These are the specific steps which guide the activities of the research in order to achieve the research aim.

Research proposal: The proposal outlines concisely the proposed strategies in relation to a researcher's selected research method, research design, sample and timings.

Research quality: This is the use of strategies and procedures to ensure that the conducted research has rigour. Research quality ensures that research is robust, conforms to ethical standards and is open for scrutiny.

Research question(s): The question(s) that the research is designed to answer (*e.g. the question(s) you ask guide and shape the research process*).

Rigour: The degree to which the research has been carried out conscientiously and accurately to recognise and minimise the factors which could have influenced the results. This is strongly associated with the creation of research quality and the terms are used interchangeably in this book.

Sample: The population or units researched in a study.

Sample bias: Occurs when the sample collected represents only certain members of the population, rather than representing the whole of the population at large.

Search engine: A software program or script available through the Internet that allows you to search a website, catalogue, or the Internet.

Secondary analysis: *This is a specific approach to the use of existing data* that was collected for the purposes of a prior research study.

Secondary research: This is a research approach that uses data that already exists in a variety of forms.

Semiotics: The analysis of visual material such as signs, text or visual sources to extract meaning.

Scanning: This is speed reading through a text to find specific information (*e.g names or numbers*).

Skim reading: This is reading through a text quickly to get the general sense of the meaning.

Snowballing: This is a sampling technique whereby in secondary research an existing source is used to gain the next source thus growing like a rolling snowball.

Standard deviation: A measure of the variability or spread of scores.

Standardised procedures: Every step of the research is conducted in exactly the same way.

Subjectivity: How a person's thoughts, experiences, or attitudes influence the research.

Supervisors: These are usually appointed by a researcher's institution or organisation to assist in the planning and carrying out of research to ensure those they supervise are aware of the required standards or obligations.

Systematic: Carried out according to or reflecting an orderly methodical system.

Systematic sample: Where the sample is chosen via a specific strategy (*e.g. every 50th research paper in a list*).

Thematic (*framework*) analysis: A method for analysing qualitative data by identifying topics, areas or patterns of meaning.

Theoretical framework: The application of theories to structure and support the research both at the launching point and throughout the investigation.

Theory: A system of interconnected ideas based on known principles that condenses and organises our knowledge. Theory provides a tentative explanation of phenomena which is never proven but represents the most logical explanation based on currently available evidence.

Transferability: The degree to which the results of the research can be generalised or applied to other contexts or settings.

Transparency: This is the strategies taken by researchers to ensure that their research reflects openness and accountability.

Triangulation: The process of using multiple techniques or sources in your research process (*e.g. when gathering data, using multiple researchers, analysts, and/or multiple theoretical perspectives*).

Validity: The degree to which a study accurately reflects or assesses the specific concept that the researcher is attempting to measure.

REFERENCES

Ahmad, R., Komlodi, A., Wang, J. & Hercegfl, K. (2010) The Impact of User Experience Levels on Web Credibility Judgments. *ASIS&T '10 Proceedings of the 73rd ASIS&T Annual Meeting on Navigating Streams in an Information Ecosystem, 47/6*. Available at: https://onlinelibrary.wiley.com/doi/epdf/10.1002/meet.14504701180 (accessed 05/05/18).

Al Ani, M., Al Subhi, L. & Bose, S. (2016) Consumption of fruits and vegetables among adolescents: A multi-national comparison of eleven countries in the Eastern Mediterranean Region. *British Journal of Nutrition, 116*(10), 1799–1806.

Al-Lela, O.Q.B., Bahari, M.B., Al-Abbassi, M.G., Salih, R.M.M., Elkalmi, R.M. & Shazia Q Jamshed (2014) Are parents' knowledge and practice regarding immunization related to pediatrics' immunization compliance? A mixed method study, *Pediatrics, 14*(29).

Allen, A. (2011) Foucault and the politics of ourselves. *History of the Human Sciences, 24*(4), 43–59. DOI: 10.1177/0952695111411623

American Educational Research Association (AERA 2011) *Code of Ethics American Educational Research Association Approved by the AERA Council February 2011*. Available at: www.aera.net/Portals/38/docs/About_AERA/CodeOfEthics(1).pdf (accessed 10/08/18).

Anderson, L.W., Krathwohl, D.R., Airasian, P.W., Cruikshank, K.A., Mayer, R.E., Pintrich, P.R., Raths, J. & Wittrock, M.C. (2001) *A Taxonomy for Learning, Teaching, and Assessing: A Revision of Bloom's Taxonomy of Educational Objectives*. New York: Pearson, Allyn & Bacon.

Andrews, L., Higgins, A., Andrews, M.W. & Lalor, J.G. (2012) Classic grounded theory to analyze secondary data: Reality and reflections. *Grounded Theory Review, 1*(11), 1–13.

Archer, J. (2000) Sex differences in aggression between heterosexual partners: A meta-analytic review. *Psychological Bulletin, 126*, 651–680.

Association of Internet Researchers (AoIR) (2012) *Ethical Decision-Making and Internet Research: Recommendations from the AoIR Ethics Working Committee (Version 2.0)*. Available at: https://aoir.org/reports/ethics2.pdf (accessed 12/08/18).

Atkinson, P. & Coffey, A. (2011) Analysing documentary realities. In D. Silverman (ed.) *Qualitative Research* (3rd edn). London: SAGE Publications Ltd.

Bamberg, M. (2012) Narrative analysis. In H. Cooper, P.M. Camic, D.L. Long, A.T. Panter, D. Rindskopf & K.J. Sher (eds), *APA Handbook of Research Methods in Psychology, Vol. 2. Research Designs: Quantitative, Qualitative, Neuropsychological, and Biological* (pp. 85–102). Washington, DC, US: American Psychological Association.

Bandaranaike, S. & Willison. J. (2015) Building capacity for work-readiness: Bridging the cognitive and affective domains. *Asia-Pacific Journal of Cooperative Education, 16*(3), 223–233.

Bandura, A. (1977a) Self-Efficacy: Toward a unifying theory of behavioral change. *Psychological Review, 84*(2), 191–215.

Bandura, A. (1977b) *Social Learning Theory.* Englewood Cliffs, NJ: Prentice Hall.

Bandura, A. (1997) *Self-Efficacy: The Exercise of Control.* New York: W.H. Freeman.

Barbacariua, C.L. (2014) Parents' refusal to vaccinate their children: An increasing social phenomenon which threatens public health. *Procedia – Social and Behavioral Sciences, 149,* 84–91.

Barlow, C. (2016) Documents as 'risky' sources of data: A reflection on social and emotional positioning – a research note. *International Journal of Social Research Methodology, 19*(3), 377–384.

Baverstock, A. (2016) Is peer review still the content industry's upper house? *Learned Publishing, 29*(1), 65–68.

BBC News (2018) *Children's word of the year revealed.* Available at: www.bbc.co.uk/news/uk-44372686 (accessed 23/06/18).

Bean, S.J. (2011) Emerging and continuing trends in vaccine opposition website content. *Vaccine, 29*(10), 1874–1880.

Becker, H. (1970) *Sociological Work – Method and Substance.* Chicago, IL: Alan Lane/The Chicago Press.

Becker, H.A. (1986) *Writing for Social Scientists: How to Start and Finish your Thesis, Book or Article.* Chicago, IL: The Chicago Press.

Bell, J. (2005) *Doing your Research Project: A Guide for First-time Researchers in Education, Health and Social Science* (4th edn). Maidenhead, Berkshire: Open University Press.

Beyrer, C. & Kass, N.E. (2002) Human rights, politics, and reviews of research ethics. *The Lancet, 360*(9328), 246–251.

Bhandari, M. (2018) Social media cues and news site name: What do they mean for online news perception? *Newspaper Research Journal, 39*(2), 169–179. Available at: https://doi.org/10.1177/0739532918775699.

Bharathiar, N. (2008) The resilient individual: A personality analysis. *Journal of the Indian Academy of Applied Psychology, 34,* Special Issue, 110–118.

Biondi-Zoccai, G., Lotrionte, M., Landoni, G. & Modena, M.G. (2011) The rough guide to systematic reviews and meta-analyses. *HSR Proceedings in Intensive Care & Cardiovascular Anesthesia, 3*(3), 161–173.

Bishop, L. (2007) A reflexive account of reusing qualitative data: Beyond primary/secondary dualism, *Sociological Research Online, 12*(3). Available at: www.socresonline.org.uk/12/3/2.html. Doi:10.5153/sro.1553.

Blaxter, L., Hughes, C. & Tight, M. (2010) *How to Research* (4th edn). Berkshire: Open University Press.

Blaxter, M. (2004) Mothers & Daughters: Accounts of health in the grandmother generation, 1945–1978 [computer file]. Colchester, Essex: UK Data Archive [distributor], July. SN: 4943.

Bloom, B.S., Engelhart, M.D., Furst, E.J., Hill, W.H. & Krathwohl, D.R. (1956) *Taxonomy of Educational Objectives, Handbook I: The Cognitive Domain.* New York: David McKay Co Inc.

Bohannon, J. (2013) Who's afraid of peer review? *Science, 342*(6154), 60–65. DOI: 10.1126/science.342.6154.60.

Booth, W C., Colomb, G.C. & Williams, J.M. (2008) *The Craft of Research* (3rd edn). Chicago, IL: The University of Chicago Press.

Boud, D. & Falchikov, N. (2007) Developing assessment for informing judgement. In D. Boud & N. Falchikov (eds), *Rethinking Assessment for Higher Education: Learning for the Longer Term* (pp. 181–197). London: Routledge.

Breen, L.J. (2007) The researcher 'in the middle': Negotiating the insider/outsider dichotomy. *The Australian Community Psychologist, 19*(1), 163–174.

Brew, A. (2012) Teaching and research: New relationships and their implications for inquiry-based teaching and learning in higher education. *Higher Education Research & Development, 31*(1), 101–114.

Brine, J. & Waller, R. (2004) Working-class women on an Access course: Risk, opportunity and (re)constructing identities. *Gender and Education, 16*(1), 97–113. DOI: 10.1080/0954025032000170363.

British Conference of Undergraduate Research (nd) www.bcur.org/ (accessed 16/08/18).

British Educational Research Association (2018) *Ethical Guidelines for Educational* (4th edn). Available at: www.bera.ac.uk/researchers-resources/publications/ethical-guidelines-for-educational-research-2018 (accessed 15/08/18).

Brunson, E.K. (2013) The impact of social networks on parents' vaccination decisions. *Pediatrics. 131*(5), e1397–404. DOI: 10.1542/peds.2012-2452.

Bryman, A. (2008) *Social Research Methods* (2nd edn). New York: Oxford University Press.

Bryman, A. (2012) *Social Research Methods* (4th edn). Oxford: Oxford University Press.

Budapest Open Access Initiative (2002) *Budapest Open Access Initiative.* Available at: www.budapestopenaccessinitiative.org/read (accessed 20/08/18).

Burns, N. & Grove, S.K. (2003) *The Practice of Nursing Research: Conduct, Critique and Utilization* (3rd edn). Toronto: WB Saunders.

Burton, P.R., Banner, N., Elliot, M.J., Knoppers, B.M. & Banks, J. (2017) Policies and strategies to facilitate secondary use of research data in the health sciences. *International Journal of Epidemiology, 46*(6), 1729–1733. Available at: http://doi.org/10.1093/ije/dyx195.

Cadwalladr, C. & Graham-Harrison, E. (2018) Facebook and Cambridge Analytica face mounting pressure over data scandal. Available at: www.theguardian.com/news/2018/mar/18/cambridge-analytica-and-facebook-accused-of-misleading-mps-over-data-breach (accessed 14/06/18).

Cameron, S. & Price, D. (2009) *Business Research Methods: A Practical Approach*. London, UK: CIPD.

Carusi, A. & Jirotka, M. (2009) From data archive to ethical labyrinth. *Qualitative Research, 9*(3), 285–298.

Cercone, J.L., Beach, S.R.H. & Arias, I. (2005) Gender symmetry in dating intimate partner violence: Does similar behaviour imply similar constructs? *Violence and Victims, 20*(2), 207–218.

Chandler, D. (2007) *Semiotics: The Basics*. Abingdon, Oxon: Routledge.

Chenail, R.J. (1995) Presenting qualitative data. *The Qualitative Report, 2*(3), 1–9. Available at: https://nsuworks.nova.edu/tqr/vol2/iss3/5.

Cheng, H.G. & Phillips, M.R. (2014) Secondary analysis of existing data: Opportunities & implementation. *Shanghai Arch Psychiatry, 26*(6), 371–375.

Chibnik, M. (1999) Quantification and statistics in six anthropology journals. *Field Methods, 11*, 146–157.

Clough, P. & Nutbrown, C. (2012) *A Student's Guide to Methodology* (3rd edn). London: SAGE. Publications Ltd.

Coca-Cola (2012) *The Real Story of New Coke*. Available at: www.coca-colacompany.com/stories/coke-lore-new-coke (accessed 03/07/18).

Coffey, A. & Atkinson, P. (1996) *Making Sense of Qualitative Data: Complementary Research Strategies*. Thousand Oaks, CA: SAGE Publications, Inc.

Collins, K.M.T., Onwuegbuzie, A.J. & Jiao, Q.G. (2007) A mixed methods investigation of mixed methods sampling designs in social and health science research. *Journal of Mixed Methods Research, 1*(3), 267–294.

Collins, V.E. & Carmody, D.C. (2011) Deadly love: Images of dating violence in the 'Twilight Saga'. *Affilia: Journal of Women and Social Work, 26*(4), 382–394. DOI: 10.1177/0886109911428425.

Conn, V.S. & Rantz, M.J. (2003) Research methods: Managing primary study quality in meta-analyses. *Researching in Nursing and Health, 26*(4), 322–333.

Cooper, G. & Meadows, R. (2016) Conceptualising social life. In N. Gilbert & P. Stoneham (eds), *Researching Social Life* (4th edn). London: SAGE Publications Ltd.

Corbin, J. & Strauss, A. (2007) *Basics of Qualitative Research: Techniques and Procedures for Developing Grounded Theory* (3rd edn). Thousand Oaks, CA: SAGE Publications, Inc.

Corti, L. & Thompson, P. (1995) Archiving qualitative research data. *Social Research Update* (10), Department of Sociology, University of Surrey. Available at: www.soc.surrey.ac.uk/sru/SRU2SRU102.html (accessed 11/10/17).

Corti, L., Van den Eynden, V., Bishop, L. & Wollard, M. (2014) *Managing and Sharing Research Data: A Guide to Good Practice*. London: SAGE Publications Ltd.

Cottrell, S. (2005) *Critical Thinking Skills*. Basingstoke: Palgrave Macmillan.

Cottrell, S. (2013) *The Study Skills Handbook* (4th edn). Basingstoke: Palgrave Macmillan.

Coughlan, M., Cronin, P. & Ryan, F. (2007) Step-by-step guide to critiquing research. Part 1: Quantitative research. *British Journal of Nursing, 16*(11), 658–663.

Crabtree, B.F. & Miller, W.L. (1999) *Doing Qualitative Research*, Thousand Oaks, CA: SAGE Publications Inc.

Creswell, J.W. (1998) *Qualitative Inquiry and Research Design Choosing Among Five Traditions.* Thousand Oaks, CA: Sage Publications.

Creswell, J.W. (2009) *Research Design: Qualitative, Quantitative, and Mixed Methods Approaches* (3rd edn). Thousand Oaks, CA: SAGE Publications Inc.

Daniel, J. (2012) *Sampling Essentials: Practical Guidelines for Making Sampling Choices.* London: SAGE Publications Ltd.

Data Protection Act 1998. Available at: www.legislation.gov.uk/ukpga/1998/29/contents (accessed 12/08/18).

Da-Silva, E.R., Coelho, L.B.N., de Campos, T.R.M., Carelli, A., de Miranda, G.S., de Souza dos Santos, E.L., Silva, T.B.N.R. & da Silva dos Passos, M.I. (2014) Marvel and DC Characters Inspired by Arachnids. *The Comics Grid: Journal of Comics Scholarship*, 4(1), Art. 11. DOI: http://doi.org/10.5334/cg.aw.

Davies, B., Browne, J., Gannon, S., Honan, E., Laws, C., Müller-Rockstroh, B. & Petersen, E.B. (2004) The ambivalent practices of reflexivity. *Qualitative Inquiry*, 10(3), 360–389.

DCC (2018) *What is Digital Curation?* Available at: www.dcc.ac.uk/digital-curation/what-digital-curation (accessed 19/08/18).

Denscombe, M. (2007) *The Good Research Guide: For Small-scale Social Research Projects* (3rd edn). Maidenhead: Open University Press.

Denscombe, M. (2010) *The Good Research Guide: For Small-scale Social Research Rrojects* (4th edn). Berkshire: Open University Press.

Denzin, N.K. (1978) *The Research Act: A Theoretical Introduction to Sociological Methods.* New York: McGraw-Hill.

Denzin, N.K. (2009) The elephant in the living room: or extending the conversation about the politics of evidence. *Qualitative Research*, 9(2), 139–160. DOI: 10.1177/1468794108098034.

Denzin, N.K. & Lincoln, Y.S. (2005) *The SAGE Handbook of Qualitative Research.* Thousand Oaks, CA: SAGE Publications Inc.

Department for Work and Pensions (DWP 2014) *The Use of Social Media for Research and Analysis: A Feasibility Study.* Available at: www.gov.uk/government/organisations/department-for-work-pensions/about/research#research-publications (accessed 02/03/18).

Department of Health. (2001) *Healthy Lives, Healthy People: A call to action on obesity in England.* Available at: www.gov.uk/government/publications/healthy-lives-healthy-people-a-call-to-action-on-obesity-in-england (accessed 02/02/17).

De Simone, C. (2007) Applications of concept mapping. *College Teaching*, 55(1), 33–36.

Dewey, J. (1933) *How We Think: A Restatement of the Relation of Reflective Thinking to the Educative Process* (2nd edn). Boston, MA: D.C. Heath & Co Publishers.

Diamantopoulos, A. & Schlegelmilch, B.B. (2002) *Taking the Fear out of Data Analysis: A Step-by-Step Approach.* London: Thompson.

DLA Piper (2017) *DATA PROTECTION LAWS OF THE WORLD Full Handbook.* Available at: www.dlapiperdataprotection.com (accessed 23/05/18).

Doolan, D.M. & Froelicher, E.S. (2009) Using an existing data set to answer new research questions: A methodological review. *Research and Theory for Nursing Practice: An International Journal*, 23(3), 203–215.

Dragioti, E., Karathanos, V., Gerdle, B. & Evangelou, E. (2017) Does psychotherapy work? An umbrella review of meta-analyses of randomized controlled trials, *Acta Psychiatrica Scandinavica, 136*(3), 236–246. DOI: 10.1111/acps.12713.

Duffy, B. (2005) The analysis of documentary evidence. In J. Bell *Doing your Research Project: A Guide for First-time Researchers in Education, Health and Social Science* (4th edn) (pp. 122–136). Maidenhead, Berkshire: Open University Press.

Dweck, C.S. (2006) *Mindset: The New Psychology of Success*. New York, US: Random House.

Economic and Social Research Council (ESRC) *The Research Ethics Guidebook: A Resource for Social Scientists*. Available at: www.ethicsguidebook.ac.uk/Consent-72 (accessed 12/07/18).

Eisner, E.W. (1997) The promise and perils of alternative forms of data representation. *Educational Researcher, 26*(6), 4–10.

Elliott, D. (2015) Secondary data analysis. In F.K. Stage & K. Manning (eds), *Research in the College Context: Approaches and Methods* (2nd edn) (pp.175–184). New York, NY: Routledge.

European Commission (2005) *The European Charter for Researchers. The Code of Conduct for the Recruitment of Researchers*. Available at: www.euraxess.at/sites/default/files/am-509774cee_en_e4.pdf (accessed 23/08/18).

Eynon, R., Fry, J. & Schroeder, R. (2008) The ethics of internet research. In N.G. Fielding, R.M. Lee & G. Blank (eds), *The SAGE Handbook of Online Research Methods* (pp. 23–41). London: SAGE Publications Ltd.

Facebook (2018) *Data Policy*. Available at: https://en-gb.facebook.com/about/privacy (accessed 15/08/18).

Fairclough, N. (1989) *Language and Power*. London: Longman.

Fairclough, N. (1992) *Discourse and Social Change*. Cambridge: Polity Press.

Flick, U. (1998) *An Introduction to Qualitative Research*. London: SAGE Publications Ltd.

Foster, N.F. & Gibbons, S. (2005) Understanding faculty to improve content recruitment for institutional repositories. *D-Lib Magazine [online], 11*(1). Available at: www.dlib.org/dlib/january05/foster/01foster.html (accessed 02/07/18).

Fox, A., Gardner, G. & Osborne, S. (2015) A theoretical framework to support research of health service innovation, *Australian Health Review, 39*(1), 70–75.

Frels, R., Onwuegbuzie, A. & Slate, J. (2010) Editorial: A Typology of Verbs for Scholarly Writing. *Research in the Schools, 17*(1), pp. xx–xxxi.

Geertz, C. (1973) *The Interpretation of Cultures: Selected Essays*. New York: Basic Books.

Gibbs, G. (1988) *Learning by Doing: A Guide to Teaching and Learning Methods*. Oxford: Oxford Further Education Unit.

Gibbs, G. (2014) Using software in qualitative analysis. In U. Flick (ed.) *The SAGE Handbook of Qualitative Data Analysis* (pp. 277–294). London: SAGE Publications Ltd.

Gillies, V. & Edwards, R. (2005) Secondary analysis in exploring family and social change: Addressing the issue of context. *Forum Qualitative Sozialforschung: Qualitative Social Research Forum, 6*(1), Art. 44. Available at: www.qualitative-research.net/fqs-texte/1-05/05.

Glaser, B.G. (1963) Retreading research materials: The use of secondary data analysis by the independent researcher. *American Behavioural Science, 6*(10), 11–14.

Glaser, B.G. & Strauss, A.L. (1967) *The Discovery of Grounded Theory: Strategies for Qualitative Research*. Chicago, IL: Aldine Publishing.

Glass, G.V. (1976) Primary, secondary, and meta-analysis of research. *Educational Researcher, 5*, 3–8.

Glass, G.V (1978) Integrating findings: The meta-analysis of research. *Review of Research in Education, 5*, 351–379.

Golden-Biddle, K. & Locke, K. (2007) *Composing Qualitative Research* (2nd edn). Thousand Oaks, CA: SAGE Publications Inc.

Goldman, K.D. & Schmalz, K.J. (2004) The matrix method of literature reviews. *Health Promotion Practice, 5*(1), 5–7.

Gragin, M., Palmer, C.L., Carlson, J.R. & Witt, M. (2010) Data sharing, small science and institutional repositories. *Philosophical Transactions of the Royal Society, 368*(1926), 4023–4038. DOI: 10.1098/rsta.2010.0165.

Gravetter, F.J. & Wallnau, L.B. (2000) *Statistics for the Behavioural Sciences*. Stanford, CA: Thomson Learning Inc.

Gray, B. (2009) *'New Moon' shatters opening day record. Box Office Mojo*. Available at: www.boxofficemojo.com/news/?id=2626 (accessed 17/05/18).

Grbich C. (1999) *Qualitative Research in Health*. London: Sage Publications.

Guba, E.G. (1981) Criteria for assessing the trustworthiness of naturalistic inquiries. *Educational Technology Research and Development, 29*(2), 75–91.

Guba, E.G. & Lincoln, Y.S. (1994) Competing paradigms in qualitative research. In N.K. Denzin & Y.S. Lincoln (eds), *Handbook of Qualitative Research* (pp. 105–117). Thousand Oaks, CA: SAGE Publications Inc.

Guba, E.G. & Lincoln, Y.S. (1998) Competing paradigms in qualitative research. In N.K. Denzin & Y.S. Lincoln (eds), *The Landscape of Qualitative Research: Theories and Issues* (pp. 195–220). Thousand Oaks, CA: SAGE Publications Inc.

Hammersley, M. (2013) *What is Qualitative Research?* London: Bloomsbury.

Hand, M. (2016) Visuality in social media: Researching images, circulations and practices. In L. Sloan & A. Quan-Haase (2016) *The SAGE Handbook of Social Media Research Methods* (pp. 215–231). London: SAGE Publications Ltd.

Hardy, C. & Phillips, N. (1999) No joking matter: Discursive struggle in the Canadian refugee system. *Organization Studies, 20*(1), 1–24.

Hart, C. (1998) *Doing a Literature Review*. London: SAGE Publications Ltd.

Heaton, J. (1998) Secondary Analysis of Qualitative Data, *Social Research Update 22*. Guildford, University of Surrey Institute of Social Research. Available at: http://sru.soc.surrey.ac.uk/SRU22.html (accessed 22/08/18).

Heaton, J. (2004) *Reworking Qualitative Data*. London: Sage.

Held, V. (2006) *The Ethics of Care: Personal, Political, and Global*. New York: Oxford University Press, Inc.

Hellawell, D. (2006) Inside-out: Analysis of the insider-outsider concept as a heuristic device to develop reflexivity in students doing qualitative research. *Teaching in Higher Education, 11*(4), 483–494. DOI:10.1080/13562510600874292.

Hill, A. & Spittlehouse, C. (2003) What is critical appraisal? *Evidence-Based Medicine*, 3(2): 1–8. Available at: http://citeseerx.ist.psu.edu/viewdoc/download?doi=10.1.1.524.2610&rep=rep1&type=pdf (accessed 02/01/17).

Hilton, S., Hunt, K. & Petticrew, M. (2007) MMR: marginalised, misrepresented and rejected? Autism: a focus group study. *Archives of Disease in Childhood*, 92(4), 322–327.

Hinds, P.S., Vogel, R.J. & Clarke-Steffen, L. (1997) The possibilities & pitfalls of doing a secondary analysis of a qualitative dataset. *Qualitative Health Research*, 7(3), 408–424.

Hodder, I. (1994) The interpretation of documents and material culture. In N. Denzin & Y.S. Lincoln (eds), *Handbook of Qualitative Research* (pp. 393–402). Thousand Oaks, CA: SAGE Publications Inc.

House of Commons, Digital, Culture, Media and Sport Committee (2018) *Disinformation and 'fake news': Interim Report: Fifth Report of Session 2017–19*. Available at: https://publications.parliament.uk/pa/cm201719/cmselect/cmcumeds/363/363.pdf (accessed 13/07/18).

Imenda, S. (2014) Is there a conceptual difference between theoretical and conceptual frameworks? *Journal of Social Sciences*, 38(2), 185–95.

Integral (2018) *USB – How long will data stay valid for on a USB drive?* Available at: www.integralmemory.com/faq/how-long-will-data-stay-valid-usb-drive (accessed 12/06/18).

International Conference of Undergraduate Research (ICUR) (nd) *Two days. Eight Countries. Five Continents*. Available at: www.icurportal.com/ (accessed 20/08/18).

Israel, M. & Hay, I. (2006) *Research Ethics for Social Scientists*. London: SAGE Publications Ltd.

Joosten, T. (2017) Social media: Blogs, microblogs, and Twitter. In M. Allen (ed.), *The SAGE Encyclopedia of Communication Research Methods* (pp. 1631–1633). Thousand Oaks, CA: SAGE Publications Inc.

Kelly, M. (2010) The role of theory in qualitative health research, *Family Practice*, 27(3), 285–290.

Kennedy, H., Elgesem, D. & Miguel, C. (2017) On fairness: User perspectives on social media data mining. *Convergence: The International Journal of Research into New Media Technologies*, 23(3), 270–288. Available at: https://doi.org/10.1177/1354856515592507

Kirk, A. (2016) *Data Visualisation: A Handbook for Data Driven Design*. London: SAGE Publications Ltd.

Klopper, R., Lubbe, S. & Rugbeer, H. (2007) The matrix method of literature review. *Alternation*, 14(1), 262–276.

Kourgiantakis, T., Saint-Jacques, M.-C. & Tremblay, J. (2013) Problem gambling and families: A systematic review. *Journal of Social Work Practice in the Addictions*, 13, 353–372.

Kress, G. (2003) *Literacy in the New Media Age*. London: RoutledgeFalmer.

Kuan Hon, W., Millard, C. & Walden, I. (2011) The problem of 'personal data' in cloud computing: What information is regulated? – the cloud of unknowing. *International Data Privacy Law*, 1(4), 211–228.

Kuhn T.S. (1970) *The Structure of Scientific Revolutions* (2nd edn). Chicago, IL: University of Chicago Press.

Kvale, S. (1996) *InterViews: An Introduction to Qualitative Research Interviewing*. Thousand Oaks, CA: SAGE Publications Inc.

Kwek, D. & Kogut, G. (2015) Knowledge of prior work and soundness of project: A review of the research on secondary analysis of research data. *Technical Report, Office of Education Research*. Singapore: National Institute of Education.

Labaree, R. (2018) *Organizing Your Social Sciences Research Paper: 6. The Methodology*. Available at: http://libguides.usc.edu/writingguide/methodology (accessed 19/08/18).

LaCour, M. & Green, D.P. (2014) When contact changes minds: An experiment on transmission of support for gay equality. *Science, 346*(6215), 1366–1369. DOI: 10.1126/science.1256151.

Larkin, J.H. & Simon, H.A. (1987) Why a diagram is (sometimes) worth ten thousand words. *Cognitive Science, 11*, 65–99. DOI:10.1111/j.1551-6708.1987.tb00863.

Lather, P. (1991) *Getting Smart: Feminist Research and Pedagogy With/in the Postmodern*. London: Routledge.

Lave, J. & Wenger, E. (1991) *Situated Learning: Legitimate Peripheral Participation*. Cambridge: Cambridge University Press.

Lee, R.M. (1993) *Researching Sensitive Topics*. Thousand Oaks, CA: SAGE Publications Inc.

Leong, S., Mishra, N., Sadikov, E. & Zhang, Li. (2012) Domain bias in web search. *WSDM'12*. Available at: www.microsoft.com/en-us/research/wp-content/uploads/2012/02/domain-bias.pdf (accessed 10/11/17).

Levy, G. (2010) *Hitler's Diaries*. Available at: http://content.time.com/time/specials/packages/article/0,28804,1931133_1931132_1931123,00.html (accessed 23/04/18).

Lewis, I. & Munn, P. (1987) *So You Want to Do Research*. Edinburgh: The Scottish Council for Research in Education.

Lewontin. R. & Levin, R. (2000) Let the numbers speak. *International Journal of Health Services, 30*(4), 873–877. Available at: https://doi.org/10.2190/0D66-KFBJ-VYVH-9A8J.

Lin, Y.H.K. (2016) Collecting qualitative data. In I. Palaiologou, D. Needham & T. Male (eds), *Doing Research in Education Theory and Practice* (pp. 156–177). London: SAGE Publications Ltd.

Lincoln, Y.S. & Guba, E.G. (1985) *Naturalistic Inquiry*. Newbury Park, CA: SAGE Publications Inc.

Linnekin, J. (1987) Categorize, cannibalize? Humanistic quantification in anthropological research. *American Anthropologist, 89*, 920–926.

Lord, P., Macdonald, A., Lyon, L. & Giaretta, D. (2004) From data deluge to data curation. In *Proceedings of the UK e-Science All Hands Meeting*, 2004. Available at: www.ukoln.ac.uk/ukoln/staff/e.j.lyon/150.pdf (accessed 03/07/18).

Loshin, D. (2002) *Knowledge Integrity: Data Ownership*. Available at: www.datawarehouse.com/article/?articleid=3052 (accessed 02/08/18).

Lusher, A. (2018) *The Hitler Diaries: How Hoax Documents Became the Most Infamous Fake News Ever*. Available at: www.independent.co.uk/news/uk/home-news/hitler-diaries-anniversary-sunday-times-extracts-hoax-fake-news-germany-a8337286.html (accessed 18/07/18).

Maslow, A.H. (1943) A theory of human motivation. *Psychological Review, 50*(4), 370–396.

Maslow, A.H. (1954) *Motivation and Personality*. New York: Harper.

Mauthner, N.S. (2012) 'Accounting for our part of the entangled webs we weave': Ethical and moral issues in digital data sharing. In T. Miller, M. Mauthner, M. Birch & J. Jessop (eds), *Ethics in Qualitative Research* (2nd edn). London: SAGE Publications Ltd.

Mauthner, N.S., Parry, O. & Backett-Milburn, K. (1998) The data are out there, or are they? Implications for archiving and revisiting qualitative data. *Sociology, 32*(4), 733–737.

Maxwell, J.A. (1996) *Qualitative Research Design: An Interactive Approach.* Thousand Oaks, CA: SAGE Publications Inc.

May, T. (1997) *Social Research: Issues, Methods and Process.* Buckingham: Open University Press.

Mays, N. & Pope, C. (2000) Assessing quality in qualitative research. *BMJ: British Medical Journal, 320*(7226), 50–52.

McCarthy, S. (2013) The European Copyright Directive and Combinatorial Explosion. *European Journal of Current Legal Issues, 19*(2). Available at: http://webjcli.org/article/view/245/317 (accessed 18/08/18).

McGrail, M.R., Rickard, C.M. & Jones, R. (2006) Publish or perish: A systematic review of interventions to increase academic publication rates. *Higher Education Research & Development, 25*(1), 19–35.

Merriam, S.B. (1988) *Case Study Research in Education: A Qualitative Approach.* San Francisco, CA: Jossey-Bass.

Merriam, S.B. (2009) *Qualitative Research: A Guide to Design and Implementation.* San Francisco, CA: John Wiley & Sons.

Merriam, S.B. & Tisdell, E.J. (2016) *Qualitative Research: A Guide to Design and Implementation* (4th edn). San Francisco, CA: John Wiley & Sons.

Merton, R.K. (1967) *On Theoretical Sociology: Five Essays, Old and New.* New York: Free Press.

Mezirow, J. (1978) Education for perspective transformation: Women's re-entry programs in community colleges, *New York: Teachers College, Columbia University.* Available at: http://pocketknowledge.tc.columbia.edu/home.php/viewfile/download/177564 (accessed 19/08/18).

Mezirow, J. (1991) *Transformative Dimensions of Adult Learning.* San Francisco, CA: Jossey-Bass.

Miles, M. & Huberman, A. (1994) *Qualitative Data Analysis.* Thousand Oaks, CA: SAGE Publications Inc.

Morris, J.P. (2011) Digital bridge or digital divide? A case study review of the implementation of the 'Computers for Pupils Programme' in a Birmingham Secondary School. *Journal of Information Technology Education, 10,* 17–31.

Morris, J.P. (2018) Is this the culture of academies? Utilising the cultural web to investigate the organisational culture of an academy case study. *Educational Management Administration & Leadership,* 1–22. Available at: https://doi.org/10.1177/1741143218788580.

Morris, T.M. (2009) *An Investigation into the Provision and Impact of Foundation Degrees for Teaching Assistants.* A thesis submitted to The University of Birmingham for the degree of Doctor of Philosophy. Available at: http://etheses.bham.ac.uk/633/1/Morris10PhD_A1b.pdf.

Morse, J.M. (1991) Approaches to qualitative-quantitative methodological triangulation. *Nursing Research*, *40*(2), 120–123.

Morse, J.M. (2003) Principles of mixed methods and multimethod design. In A. Tashakkori & C. Teddlie (eds), *Handbook of Mixed Methods in Social & Behavioral Research* (pp. 189–208). Thousand Oaks, CA: SAGE Publications Inc.

Morse, J.M., Barrett, M., Mayan, M., Olson, K. & Speirs, J. (2002) Verification strategies for establishing reliability and validity in qualitative research. *International Journal of Qualitative Methods*, *1*(2), 13–22.

National Institutes of Health (nd) *The Nuremberg Code*. Available at: https://search.nih.gov/search?utf8=%E2%9C%93&affiliate=nih&query=Nuremberg+&commit=Search (accessed 12/08/18).

Needham, D. (2016) Constructing the hypotheses/creating the research question(s). In I. Palaiologou, D. Needham & T. Male (eds), *Doing Research in Education Theory and Practice* (pp. 59–80). London: SAGE Publications Ltd.

Neuman, W.L. (1997) *Social Research Methods: Qualitative and Quantitative Approaches* (3rd edn). Boston: Allyn & Bacon.

Nickerson, A.J. & Sloan, T.W. (2002) Data reduction techniques and hypothesis testing for analysis of benchmarking data. *International Journal of Production Research*, *37*(8), 1717–1741.

Nielsen, J. & Pernice, K. (2010) *Eyetracking Web Usability*. California: New Riders.

Nissim, N., Yahalom, R. & Elovici, Y. (2017) USB-based attacks. *Computers & Security*, *70*, 675–688. Available at: https://doi.org/10.1016/j.cose.2017.08.002.

Norris, N. (1997) Error, bias and validity in qualitative research. *Educational Action Research*, *5*(1), 172–176.

Norum, K.E. (2008) Artifacts as Data. In L.N. Given (ed.), *The SAGE Encyclopedia of Qualitative Research Methods Volumes 1 & 2* (pp 25–26). Thousand Oaks, CA: SAGE Publications Inc.

Nowell, L.S., Norris, J.M., White, D. & Moules, N. (2017) Thematic analysis: Striving to meet the trustworthiness criteria. *International Journal of Qualitative Methods*, *16*(1). Available at: https://doi.org/10.1177/1609406917733847.

O'Leary, Z. (2004) *The Essential Guide to Doing Research*. London: SAGE Publications Ltd.

Onwuegbuzie, A.J. & Frels, R. (2016) *7 Steps to a Comprehensive Literature Review: A Multimodal & Cultural Approach*. London: SAGE Publications Ltd.

Onwuegbuzie, A. J.& Leech, N.L. (2005) On becoming a pragmatic researcher: The importance of combining quantitative and qualitative research methodologies. *International Journal of Social Research Methodology*, *8*(5), 375–387. DOI: 10.1080/13645570500402447.

Open Data Handbook (nd) *The Open Data Handbook*. Available at: https://opendatahandbook.org/guide/en/introduction/ (accessed 18/08/18).

Parry, O. & Mauthner, N.S. (2004) Whose data are they anyway? Practical, legal and ethical issues in archiving qualitative research data. *Sociology*, *38*(1), 139–152.

Patton, M.Q. (2002) *Qualitative Research and Evaluation Methods* (3rd edn). Thousand Oaks, CA: SAGE Publication Inc.

Passerini, L. (2012) Expert voices. In S.E. Baker & R. Edwards (eds), How many qualitative interviews is enough (pp. 32–33). *National Centre for Research Methods Review Discussion Paper*. Available at: http://eprints.ncrm.ac.uk/2273 (accessed 25/01/17).

Payne, G. & Payne, J. (2004) *Key Concepts in Social Research*. London: SAGE Publications Ltd.

Penketh, C. & Goddard, G. (2008) Students in transition: Mature women students moving from Foundation Degree to Honours Level 6. *Research in Post-Compulsory Education*, *13*(3), 315–327.

Pennebaker, J.W., Mehl, M.R. & Niederhoffer, K.G. (2003) Psychological aspects of natural language use: Our words, our selves. *Annual Review of Psychology*, *54*, 547–577.

Perry, G. (2001) *Aspects of Myself*. Available at: www.tate.org.uk/art/artworks/perry-aspects-of-myself-t07904 (accessed 20/07/18).

Phillips, N. & Hardy, C. (2002) *Discourse Analysis: Investigating Processes of Social Construction*. Thousand Oaks, CA: SAGE Publications Inc.

Pink, S. (2007) *Doing Visual Ethnography* (2nd edn). London: SAGE Publications Ltd.

Polit, D.F., Beck, C.T. & Hungler, B.P. (2001) *Essentials of Nursing Research: Methods, Appraisal and Utilization* (5th edn). Philadelphia: Lippincott Williams & Wilkins.

Price, J.H. & Murnan, J. (2004) Research limitations and the necessity of reporting them. *American Journal of Health Education*, *35*(2), 66–67. Available at: https://doi.org/10.1080/19325037.2004.10603611.

Prosser, J. (1998) *Image-based Research: A Sourcebook for Qualitative Researchers*. London: Falmer Press.

Punch, K. (2013) *Introduction to Social Research: Quantitative & Qualitative Approaches* (3rd edn). London: SAGE Publications Ltd.

QDR (Qualitative Data Repository) (2017) About the Qualitative Data Repository. Available at: https://qdr.syr.edu/about (accessed 16/08/18).

Rambo, N. (2015) *Research Data Management: Roles for Libraries, 19*. Available at: https://doi.org/https://doi.org/10.18665/sr.274643 (accessed 12/11/17).

Randolph, J.J. (2009) A guide to writing the dissertation literature review. *Practical Assessment, Research & Evaluation*, *14*(13), 1–13.

Reay, D. (2003) A risky business? Mature working-class women students and access to higher education. *Gender and Education*, *15*(3), 301–317.

Richardson, T., Elliott, P.A., Roberts, R. & Jansen, M. (2017) A longitudinal study of financial difficulties and mental health in a national sample of British undergraduate students. *Community Mental Health Journal*, *53*(3), 344–352.

Riessman, C.K. (1993) Narrative analysis. *Qualitative Research Methods*, Series, No. 30. Newbury Park, CA: SAGE Publication Inc.

Riessman, C.K. (2005) Narrative analysis. In N. Kelly, C. Horrocks, K. Milnes, B. Roberts & D. Robinson (eds), *Narrative, Memory & Everyday Life* (pp. 1–7). Huddersfield: University of Huddersfield. Available at: http://eprints.hud.ac.uk/id/eprint/4920/ (accessed 17/08/18).

Ritchie, J. & Lewis, J. (2003) Generalising from qualitative research . In J. Ritchie & J. Lewis (eds), *Qualitative Research Practice* (pp. 263–286). London: SAGE Publications Ltd.

Ritchie, J. & Spencer, L. (1994) Qualitative data analysis for applied policy research. In A. Bryman & R.G. Burgess (eds), *Analyzing Qualitative Data* (pp.173–194). London: Routledge.

Ritchie, J., Spencer, L. & O'Connor, W. (2003) Carrying out qualitative analysis. In J. Ritchie & J. Lewis (eds), *Qualitative Research Practice* (pp. 219–262). London: SAGE Publications Ltd.

Robinson, M. & Scherlen, R. (2007) *Lies, Damned Lies and Drug War Statistics: A Critical Analysis of Claims Made by the Office of National Drug Control Policy*. Albany, NY: State University of New York Press.

Robson, C. (2002) *Real World Research: A Resource for Social Scientists & Practitioner Researchers* (2nd edn). Oxford: Blackwell.

Rolfe, G., Freshwater, D. & Jasper, M. (2001) *Critical Reflection for Nursing and the Helping Professions: A User's Guide*. Basingstoke: Palgrave Macmillan.

Rose, G. (2001) *Visual Methodologies: An Introduction to the Interpretation of Visual Materials*. London: SAGE Publications Ltd.

Saldaña, J. (2016) *The Coding Manual for Qualitative Researchers* (3rd edn). Thousand Oaks, CA: SAGE Publications Inc.

Sandelowski, M. (1995) Focus on qualitative methods. Qualitative analysis: what it is and how to begin. *Research in Nursing and Health*, *18*, 371–375.

Sandelowski, M., Voils, C.I. & Knafl, G. (2009) On quantitizing. *Journal of Mixed Methods Research*, *3*(3), 208–222. DOI: 10.1177/1558689809334210.

Sarker, F., Davis, H. & Tiropanis, T. (2018) *The Role of Institutional Repositories in Addressing Higher Education Challenges Learning Societies Lab, School of Electronics & Computer Science*. Available at: https://eprints.soton.ac.uk/271694/1/The_Role_of_Institutional_Repositories_in_addressing_Higher_Education_Challenges.pdf (accessed 31/06/18).

Saunders, M., Lewis, P. & Thornhill, A. (2009) *Research Methods for Business Students* (5th edn). Harlow, Essex: Pearson Education Ltd.

Scott, J. (1990) *A Matter of Record: Documentary Sources in Social Research*. Cambridge: Polity Press.

Seale, C. (1999) *The Quality of Qualitative Research*. London: SAGE Publications Ltd.

Seale, C. & Silverman, D. (1997) Ensuring rigor in qualitative research. *The European Journal of Public Health*, *7*, 379–384.

Sheriff, M.Q., Hendrix, K.S., Downs, S.M., Sturm, L.A., Zimet, G.D. & Finnell, S.M.E. (2012) The role of herd immunity in parents' decision to vaccinate children: A systematic review. *Pediatrics*, *130*(3), 522–530.

Silverman, C. & Alexander, L. (2018) *How Teens in The Balkans are Duping Trump Supporters with Fake News*. Available at: www.buzzfeednews.com/article/craigsilverman/how-macedonia-became-a-global-hub-for-pro-trump-misinfo#.kf5W5Lx0qJ (accessed 20/07/18).

Silverman, D. (2013) *Doing Qualitative Research* (4th edn). London: SAGE Publications Ltd.

Smith, A.K., Ayanian, J.Z. & Covinsky, K.E. (2011) Conducting high-value secondary dataset analysis: An introductory guide and resources. *Journal of General Internal Medicine*, *26*(8), 920–929.

Smith, E. (2011) *Using Numeric Secondary Data in Education Research*. Available at: www.bera.ac.uk/resources/using-numeric-secondary-data-education-research (accessed 02/01/18).

Smith, L.E., Amlot, R., Weinman J., Yiend, J. & Rubin G.J. (2017) A systematic review of factors affecting vaccine uptake in young children. *Vaccine, 35*(45), 6059–6069.

Snee, H. (2012) Youth research in Web 2.0: A case study in blog analysis. In S. Heath & C. Walker (eds), *Innovations in Youth Research*. Basingstoke: Palgrave Macmillan.

Soloman, D.J. (2007) The role of peer review for scholarly journals in the information age. *Journal of Electronic Publishing, 10*(1). Available at: http://dx.doi.org/10.3998/3336451.0010.107.

Spronken-Smith, R., Bullard, J., Ray, W., Roberts, C. & Keiffer, A. (2008) Where might sand dunes be on Mars? Engaging students through inquiry-based learning in geography. *Journal of Geography in Higher Education, 32*(1), 71–86.

Sque, M., Long, T. & Payne, S. (2003) Organ & tissue donation: Exploring the needs of families. Final report for the British Organ Donor Society. [*Final report of a three-year study commissioned by the British Organ Donor Society, funded by the Community Fund,* February 2003; cited 2017 Jan 21]. Available at: http://body.orpheusweb.c.uk/Report.html (accessed 27/11/17).

Stake, R.E. (2005) Qualitative case studies. In N.K. Denzin & Y.S Lincoln (eds), *The SAGE Handbook of Qualitative Research* (3rd edn) (pp. 443–466). Thousand Oaks, CA: SAGE Publications Inc.

Stewart, D.W. & Kamins, M.A. (1993) *Secondary Research: Information Sources and Methods.* Newbury Park, CA: SAGE Publications Inc.

Straus, M.A. (2004) Prevalence of violence against dating partners by male and female university students worldwide. *Violence Against Women, 10*(7), 790–811.

Strauss, A.L. & Corbin, J.M. (1990) *Basics of Qualitative Research: Grounded Theory Procedures & Techniques.* Newbury Park, CA: SAGE Publications Inc.

Swales, J.M. & Feak, C.B. (2004) *Academic Writing for Graduate Students* (2nd edn). Ann Arbor, MI: University of Michigan Press.

Swan, S.C., Gambone, L.J., Caldwell, J.E., Sullivan, T. P. & Snow, D.L. (2008) Violence victim. A review of research on women's use of violence with male intimate partners. *Violence and Victims, 23*(3), 301–314.

TARGETjobs (nd) *What are the top 10 skills that'll get you a job when you graduate?* Available at: https://targetjobs.co.uk/careers-advice/career-planning/273051-the-top-10-skills-thatll-get-you-a-job-when-you-graduate (accessed 18/08/18).

Tashakkori, A. & Creswell, J.W. (2007) Editorial: Exploring the nature of research questions in mixed methods research. *Journal of Mixed Methods Research, 1*(3), 207–211. DOI: 10.1177/1558689807302814.

Taylor, B. (2014) *Behind the Spec Sheet.* Available at: www.pcworld.com/article/2451774/cloud-storage-vs-external-hard-drives-which-really-offers-the-best-bang-for-your-buck.html (accessed 23/06/18).

Tesch, R. (1990) *Qualitative Research: Analysis Types and Software Tools.* New York: Falmer Press.

The Law Society (2014) *Cloud Computing.* Available at: http://www.lawsociety.org.uk/support-services/advice/practice-notes/cloud-computing/ (accessed 20/08/18).

Thomas, G. (2009) *How to do Your Research Project.* London: SAGE Publications Ltd.

Thomas, G. (2011) The meanings of theory. *British Educational Research Association*. Available at: www.bera.ac.uk/researchers-resources/publications/meanings-of-theory.

Thompson, P. (1975) *The Edwardians: The Remaking of British Society*. London: Routledge.

Thomsen, T.U. & Hansen, T. (2015) Perceptions that matter: perceptual antecedents and moderators of healthy food consumption. *International Journal of Consumer Studies, 39*, 109–116.

Tischer, M., Durumeric, Z., Bursztein, E. & Bailey, M. (2017) The danger of USB drives. *IEEE Security & Privacy, 15*(2), 62–69. DOI:10.1109/MSP.2017.41.

UK Copyright Service (2017) *Fact sheet P-27: Using the work of others*. Available at: www.copyrightservice.co.uk/copyright/p27_work_of_others (accessed 19/08/18).

UK Data Service (2018) *Data Security*. Available at: www.ukdataservice.ac.uk/manage-data/store/security (accessed 19/07/18).

Universities UK (2012) *Oversight of Security-sensitive Research Material in UK Universities*. Available at: www.universitiesuk.ac.uk/policy-and-analysis/reports/Pages/oversight-of-security-sensitive-research-material-in-uk-universities.aspx (accessed 19/08/18).

University of Birmingham (nd) *Preparing and Quoting References using the Harvard System*. Available at: http://epapers.bham.ac.uk/819/2/B016.1_harvard_referencing_guide.pdf (accessed 20/08/18).

University of Oxford (2018) *Referencing*. Available at: www.ox.ac.uk/students/academic/guidance/skills/referencing?wssl=1 (accessed 12/08/18).

Van den Berg, H. (2005) Reanalyzing qualitative interviews from different angles: The risk of de-contextualization and other problems of sharing qualitative data. *Forum Qualitative Sozialforschung / Forum: Qualitative Social Research, 6*(1). Available at: www.qualitative-research.net/index.php/fqs/article/view/499/1074 (accessed 12/06/18).

Van Leeuwen. T. & Jewitt, C. (2001) *Handbook of Visual Analysis*. London: SAGE Publications Ltd.

Vosoughi, S., Roy, D. & Aral, S. (2018) The spread of true and false news online. *Science, 359*(6380), 1146–1151. DOI:10.1126/science.aap9559.

Wakefield, A.J., Anthony, A., Linnell, J., Casson, D.M., Malik, M., Berelowitz, M., Dhillon, A.P., Thomson, M.A., Harvey, P., Valentine, A., Davies, S.E., & Walker-Smith, J.A. (1998) RETRACTED: Ileal-lymphoid-nodular hyperplasia, non-specific colitis, and pervasive developmental disorder in children, *Early Report: THE LANCET, 351*(9103), 637–641. Available at: https://doi.org/10.1016/S0140-6736(97)11096-0.

Wallace, M. & Wray, A. (2011) *Critical Reading & Writing for Postgraduates* (2nd edn). London: SAGE Publications Ltd.

Wang, R.Y., & Strong, D.M. (1996) Beyond accuracy: What data quality means to data consumers. *Journal of Management Information Systems, 12*(4), 5–34.

Wellington, J. (2000) *Educational Research: Contemporary Issues and Practical Approaches*. London: Continuum.

Wenger, E. (1998) *Communities of Practice: Learning, Meaning, and Identity*. Cambridge, UK: Cambridge University Press.

Wilson, K., Barakat, M., Vohra, S., Ritvo, P. & Boon, H. (2008) Parental views on pediatric vaccination: The impact of competing advocacy coalitions. *Public Understanding of Science*, *17*(2), 231–243.

WMAGA (World Medical Association General Assembly) (1964) *Declaration of Helsinki. WMA General Assembly, Helsinki*. Available at: www.wma.net/policies-post/wma-declaration-of-helsinki-ethical-principles-for-medical-research-involving-human-subjects/ (accessed 19/08/18).

Wolcott, H.F. (1994) *Transforming Qualitative Data: Description, Analysis, and Interpretation*. Thousand Oaks, CA: Sage Publications, Inc.

World Intellectual Property Organisation (WIPO) *Berne Convention for the Protection of Literary and Artistic Works*. Available at: www.wipo.int/treaties/en/ip/berne/ (accessed 14/07/18).

Xiao-Bai, L. & Varghese, J. (2008) Adaptive data reduction for large-scale transaction data. *European Journal of Operational Research*, *188*(3), 910–924. DOI:10.1016/j.ejor.2007.08.008

Yorke, M. (2003) *Employability in Higher Education: What It Is – What It Is Not*. Available at: www.ed.ac.uk/files/atoms/files/hea-learning-employability_series_one.pdf (accessed 16/08/19).

Yue, Y., Patel, R. & Roehrig, H. (2010) Beyond position bias: Examining result attractiveness as a source of presentation bias in clickthrough data. *WWW '10 Proceedings of the 19th international conference on World wide web*. DOI:10.1145/1772690.1772793.

INDEX

abstract 304
academic sources of data 126–127, 156–158
   academic books 28, 42, 87, 126
   journal articles 29, 42, 82, 105, 123, 126, 127;
     see also open access
   scholarly articles 18, 126, 128, 136, 145, 149, 157, 173,
     189, 190, 194, 257
aims 45, 48, 50, 284
American Educational Research Association (AERA)
   107, 108
analysis *see* qualitative and quantitative data analysis
analytic transparency 90, 91, 93–94, 240, 243, 252, 253
Anderson, L.W. 309
anonymisation 41, 106, 115, 118; *see also* ethical
   principles
anonymity 95, 103–106, 118, 226; *see also* anonymisation
appendices 295, 298
archives 154, 156, 160
artefacts as sources of data 19, 126, 138–139, 145, 174
Association of Internet Researchers (AoIR) 105
attitude development 302, 309
audience 132, 173, 206, 250, 252, 290
audit trail 90, 93, 94, 185, 193; *see also* research quality
authenticity of data 23, 81, 105, 126, 127, 130,
   131, 135, 137, 138, 139, 146, 168–169, 174,
   175, 185, 193; *see also* Scott's criteria for
   document quality

Barlow, C. 19
bias 71, 72, 91, 136–137
   confirmation 43, 73, 195
   media 131, 169
   researcher 72, 184, 195, 247
   sampling 180–181
   selection 73
   website 152
bibliographic details 217, 218, 219; *see also* references

Bishop, L. 128–129, 120
Bloom, B.S. 196, 309
Bohannon, J. 127
bookmarks 150
British Education Research Association
   (BERA) 107

Carmody, D.C. 133, 134
CARS Checklist 173–174
categorisation *see* constant comparison, creating
   categories
charts *see* data display, charts
citation chaining *see* daisy chaining
citations *see* references
classifying data 18, 19–20, 21, 125, 126, 177, 193
   as advertent 20, 125
   as inadvertent 20, 125
   for literature review 21, 123–124, 177, 193–194
   non-numeric 258
   numeric 162, 250, 256
   see also qualitative data
cloud storage 114, 225
codes of conduct, 81,100, 101, 102, 104, 106,
   107, 109–11
coding *see* constant comparison, coding processes
coding advice 237, 241
coding scheme 235
coding table 240
coherence 27, 45, 80, 90, 244, 287, 292
Collins, K.M.T. 184
Collins, V.E. 133, 134
completeness *see* constant comparison, completeness
   (of coding)
computer analysis 247, 274
computer protection 224–225
concept mapping 39
concepts, 57, 58–59, 63–65

conceptual framework, 42, 50, 63–64, 66, 70, 73, 192, 193, 246, 279, 286

conclusions *see* writing conclusions

confidentiality 81, 95, 103–106, 108, 118, 146, 213, 226; *see also* ethical principles

confirmability 90, 92, 93–94,175, 185, 287; *see also* research quality

consistency 45, 80, 90, 208, 234, 235, 237, 241, 285

Consortium of European Social Science Data Archives (CESSDA) 156

constant comparison 233–243
   coding processes 233, 234, 235, 237, 238, 240, 240–241, 242, 246, 247
   completeness (of coding) 178, 241, 261
   creating categories (categorisation) 233, 234, 237, 239, 241-242, 243
   hierarchy tree 242–243, 247
   identification (of codes) 233, 234, 235, 241, 242
   immersion 84, 91, 123, 233, 234–235; *see also* familiarisation
   interrogation 233, 235–236
   labelling 233, 235, 241, 242
   manual coding 238–239
   theme creation 234, 236, 240, 243
   see also qualitative analysis

constructs 66, 74; *see also* concepts

content analysis *see* qualitative analysis, content analysis

copyright 115–116, 118, 124, 139, 161, 220–221; *see also* intellectual property

Cottrell, S. 204, 217

creating a back-up 223–224

Creative Commons 116, 162

credibility 15, 16, 23, 32, 81, 123, 126, 127, 133, 135, 136, 137, 139, 158, 168, 169, 171, 173, 174, 175, 190, 258, 271
   of data *see* Scott's criteria for document quality
   of findings *see* findings, credibility of
   of research 26, 69, 71, 72, 83, 86, 90, 91–92, 93, 97, 117, 166, 178, 185, 234

Creswell, J.W. 246

critical appraisal and evaluation 44, 73, 90, 92, 123, 127, 133, 138, 154, 173–175, 177, 190, 234, 311; *see also* data quality

critical evaluation 170, 185, 194

critical reading 190, 196, 202

critical thinking 16, 31–32, 44, 53, 92, 173, 204, 221

critical writing 190, 196, 202

daisy chaining 150

Da-Silva, E.R. 129

data curation 212–213

data, definition of 18

data display 207, 243, 253, 275, 282, 291–294
   charts 219, 244, 247, 264, 274, 207, 243, 275, 291–294
   diagrams 206, 264, 292–293
   maps 85, 190, 234, 242, 292, 305
   matrix (matrices) 83, 191, 201, 235, 241, 243, 281, 285
   quotations 291–292

data disposal 227, 228

data distortion 166, 169, 175

data driven *see* theory, data driven

data indexing 156, 221–222

data loss 223–225

data management 53, 196, 212–213, 219

Data Management Plan 51, 52, 114, 213–217, 306

data ownership 22, 117, 212, 215, 217, 220–221, 304

data preservation 225

data privacy 105

data protection legislation 106, 108, 114–115, 118, 119; *see also* cloud storage

data quality 92, 166, 167–178, 185, 195; *see also* sampling

data reduction 129, 149, 167, 170–178, 184; *see also* sampling

data search strategies 147–151

data security 226–227

data selection 21, 123, 145, 177; *see also* data quality; sampling

data sharing 108, 128

data storage 23, 156, 160

data transparency 90, 92

deductive approach to theory *see* theory, deductive approach to

demonstrating subject knowledge 81, 123, 190, 196, 310

Denscombe, M. 178

dependability 26, 90, 91, 92, 93–94, 167, 185; *see also* research quality

descriptive statistics 260, 263–275
   frequency distribution 263, 267–269
   mean 266
   measures of central tendency 263, 264
   measures of dispersion 263, 269–270
   median 266–267
   mode 266, 267
   positional average 265
   statistical average 265
   see also quantitative analysis

Dewey, J. 302, 307, 308

diagrams *see* data display, diagrams

digital data store 156

discourse analysis *see* qualitative analysis, discourse analysis

dissemination of your research 314–317
institutional repositories 315
journal article writing 314, 316–317
presenting at conferences 316
writing blogs 315–316
document, definition of 18–19, 122–123
Dweck, C. 311

Educational Resource Information Center (ERIC) 158
employability 16, 310–311; *see also* skill development
encryption 215, 226
epistemology *see* research positions, epistemology
ethical criticism 199–200
ethical principles 100–108
ethics 25, 51, 37, 81, 89, 99–118, 124, 137,
213–214, 216, 304
being an ethical researcher 100, 116–117
changing field of 110
data gatekeepers 117
definition of 100
ethical issues 104, 110–113
ethical searching 146
ethics checklist 117–118
using existing research data 108
see also data protection legislation
ethics committees 37, 113, 216
Excel 40, 180, 219, 247, 269, 268, 274; *see also* data display
existing research as sources of data 128, 156

Facebook 104, 106–107, 159
Fairclough, N. 133, 249
Fairclough's Model of Discourse 249
fair use 116, 139, 162
fake news 130–131, 135, 154
familiarisation 91, 234, 244; *see also* constant comparison,
immersion
file naming 223
finding sources of data 154–163
academic 157–158
personal 158
popular culture 161
public 159–161
quantitative data 162
research 156
visual/artefact 162
see also search engine strategies
findings 74, 277–297
communication of 289–291
construction of 282–287
credibility of 15, 89, 90, 91, 93, 171, 175, 243,
252, 258, 285, 287, 290, 291
evaluation of 288–289

exploration of 285–286
interpretation of 123, 234, 248, 260, 269,
278–279, 281–282
reflecting on 279–280
researcher influence on 71–72, 141
role of theory in 58, 59, 60, 65, 67, 74
writing up 281–282
findings checklist 297–298
framework analysis 243–246
familiarisation 244
indexing 244–245, 253
labelling (tagging/tags) 245
theme creation 244, 245, 246
see also qualitative analysis
Frels, R. 290–291
frequency distribution *see* descriptive statistics, frequency
distribution

Gantt charts 40
generalisability 81, 92, 166, 179, 185; *see also*
research quality
Gibbs, G. 307, 308
Glass, G.V. 262, 263
Goldilocks test 49
Goldman, K.D. 190
Google scholar 158
Green, D.P. 111
grounded theory *see* qualitative analysis, grounded theory
Guba, E.G, 90

Hart, C. 200
hierarchy tree *see* constant comparison, hierarchy tree
hot topics *see* sensitive topics
Huberman, A. 237, 242

identification, of codes *see* constant comparison,
identification (of codes)
identifiers, direct and indirect 104
immersion *see* constant comparison, immersion
impact factor 127, 157, 172; *see also* data quality
inclusion/exclusion criteria 92, 165–166, 167, 175–176;
see also data quality
index creation 244
indexing *see* framework analysis, indexing
inductive approach to theory *see* theory, inductive
approach to
inferential statistics *see* quantitative analysis,
inferential statistics
informed consent 81, 106–108, 109, 113, 118, 137, 146,
304; *see also* ethical principles
informed judgement 40, 44, 166, 167, 172;
see also data quality

insider research 72, 117
intellectual property 115–116, 118, 217–218,
    220, 315–316; *see also* copyright
internet research 105
interpretivist *see* research paradigms, interpretivist
interrogating data *see* constant comparison, interrogation

Johnson, W. 110–111
justification matrix 281

key words 148
Key Words in Context *see* qualitative analysis,
    Key Words in Context
knowing the context of data production 21, 23, 24, 31–32,
    81, 94, 125, 126, 128, 136, 154, 167, 174, 234
knowing your data 170–171
knowledge contribution, to subject/discipline 166, 189,
    253, 278, 280, 282, 288–289, 295, 298
knowledge distortion 71, 137, 171, 172
Kourgiantakis, T. 283

labelling *see* constant comparison, labelling
LaCour, M. 111
libraries 116, 147, 154, 161
Lincoln, Y.S. 90
literature review 51, 64, 74, 188–209
    argument signposting 204–205
    beginning your review190–191
    construction of 197–199
    creating authority 204
    creating a narrative hook 199
    definition of 17–18, 189
    effective use of verbs 205–206
    engaging in ethical criticism 199–200
    literature matrix 191
    literature review checklist 208–209
    paragraph starters 203
    questions to support synthesis 203
    reading for 41
    researcher influence on 195–196
    selecting sources for 21, 123–124, 126, 145,
        177, 185, 192–195
    synthesis 200–203
    synthesis matrix 201

manual coding *see* constant comparison, manual coding
maps and matrices *see* data display, maps; data display,
    matrix (matrices)
mean *see* descriptive statistics, mean
meaning, of data 16, 21, 23, 70, 81, 123, 126, 139, 141,
    144, 168, 170, 175, 185, 194; *see also* Scott's criteria
    for document quality

measures of central tendency *see* descriptive statistics,
    measures of central tendency
measures of dispersion *see* descriptive statistics,
    measures of dispersion
median *see* descriptive statistics, median
Merriam, S.B. 20, 126
methodology 74, 77–96
    creating a research 'recipe' 24, 74, 89, 95
    data analysis and 88–89, 234, 238, 240, 253, 304
    definition of 79
    main components of 78–89
    research positions and 60, 62, 63, 80
    research proposal and 51
    research strategies and 82–87
    writing up 94–96
metrics 127, 158, 172, 176; *see also* data quality
Miles, M. 237, 242
mind mapping 39
mindset 53–54, 311
mixed use of data 87–88, 257, 271
mode *see* descriptive statistics, mode
museums *see* visual sources of data, museums

narrative analysis *see* qualitative analysis,
    narrative analysis
native advertising 132, 153
neutral *see* neutrality
neutrality 71, 91, 94
non-random sampling *see* sampling,
    non-probability sampling
normal distribution *see* quantitative analysis,
    normal distribution
Nuremberg code 101

objectives 45, 49, 51
objectivity *see* research positions, objectivity
online collections *see* visual sources of data,
    online collections
online security 162–163
ontology *see* research positions, ontology
open access 115, 157–158

Patton, M.Q. 285
peer review 112, 127, 157, 169
personal achievement 312
personal sources of data 134–135, 158
    diaries 20, 92, 134, 135, 158, 169, 251
    micro blogs 134, 158
    specialist archives 158
    weblogs 22, 84, 105, 108–109, 124, 134, 135,
        158, 169, 250
Phillips, N. 130

plagiarism 218
planning strategies 37–40
popular culture sources of data 129–134, 161
    cartoons 129
    comics 129
    digital collections 161
    ebooks and digital libraries 161
    fiction books 133–134
    magazines 133
    news media 19, 92, 130–133, 167, 248–249
positional average *see* descriptive statistics,
    positional average
positivist *see* research paradigms, positivist
pragmatist *see* research paradigms, pragmatist
primary research 14, 15, 16
private data 106
project completion checklist 304–306
prolonged engagement 90, 91, 234
protection from harm 102–103, 105
public domain 104, 107, 116, 117, 146, 162, 217
public sources of data 135–137, 159–160
    intergovernmental agencies 159–160
    national archives 161
    non-governmental agencies 160
    open data 136, 159

qualitative analysis 25, 58, 70, 74, 81, 82,
    88, 123, 141, 231–254, 257
    analysis advice and checklist 252–254
    constant comparison 233–243
    content analysis 87, 250–251
    discourse analysis 87, 248–249
    framework (thematic) analysis 243–246
    grounded theory 183, 252
    Key Words in Context 250
    narrative analysis 250
    pragmatic approach to 246
    role of theory in 232, 246
    semiotics 133, 141, 251–252
    visual analysis 251
qualitative data 14, 18–19, 52, 61, 78, 87, 105, 122–123
    definition 14, 87, 122–123
    documents as 18–19, 121–141, 155
    types of 18–19, 105, 122
    see also classifying data
Qualitative Data Repository (QDR) 156
Qualitative Secondary Research (QSR) 13–33
    benefits of 16–18
    criticisms of 15
    definition of 14, 16
    QSR overview 24–26
    rationale to undertake 27–32

quantitative analysis 256–275; *see also*
    descriptive statistics
    categorising data 268, 272–273
    descriptive statistics 260, 263–275
    evaluating data 271–272
    gaining meaning from numbers 258–260
    immersion 259
    inferential statistics 261, 262
    knowing your data 259
    meta-analysis 262–263
    normal distribution 270
    organising data 272
    quasi statistics 258
    presenting data 274
    values 264, 266, 267, 268, 269
    working with numbers 26, 257
quantitative data 85, 86, 87, 93, 162, 183, 256–260
quasi statistics *see* quantitative analysis, quasi statistics
quotations *see* data display, quotations

random sampling *see* sampling, probability sampling
rationale 36–37, 51, 74, 197, 304
re3data.org 158
reading, importance of 23, 41, 45–46, 63, 74, 145
reading loops 42
reading online 44, 132
reading strategies 42–43
recommendations *see* writing recommendations
reference managers 218–219
references 116, 118, 124, 220, 295
referencing *see* references
referencing systems 219
reflection 41, 93, 288, 302–303, 307–308; *see also*
    research diary
reflexivity 63, 71–74, 90, 94, 141, 172, 288
replicability *see* replication
replication 93, 118, 166, 185, 240, 252; *see also*
    research quality
repository 216, 315
representativeness of data 23, 73, 81, 92, 95, 123,135, 140,
    168, 169, 175; *see also* Scott's criteria for
    document quality
reputational harm 117, 118, 146
research aims 45, 48, 50, 284
research confidence 87, 90, 94, 171, 212, 252, 297
research context 51, 127, 198
research design 24–26, 33, 63, 78–79; *see also*
    methodology
research diary 40–41, 73, 90; *see also* reflection
research limitations, 295–296
research motivation 36
research paradigms 60–62; *see also* theory

interpretivist 61
positivist 60
pragmatist 61–62
research positions 25, 60–63, 95; *see also* theory
epistemology 60
objectivity 60–61, 71, 93
ontology 60–61, 62
pragmatism 61–61
subjectivity 60–61, 71
research proposal 37, 51, 216
research quality 25, 26, 63, 73, 89–98, 117,
166, 185, 194
data analysis and 252
four criteria of 90–94
research questions 22, 45–50
being specific 50
effective questions 47, 50
Goldilocks test 49
types of questions 46
worthwhile research 47
research statement 47
research strategies 26, 79, 82–88, 139–140; *see also*
methodology
research transparency 72, 94, 97, 167, 171, 193,
213, 218, 235, 261, 288, 296, 297
researcher influence 16, 25, 58–59, 60–62, 71–73, 80,
93, 94, 100, 141, 181, 195–196, 288; *see also* bias,
researcher; reflexivity
researcher values 59, 67, 71, 72
rigour 15, 26, 62, 88, 89, 91, 117, 166, 175, 185, 235,
252, 288; *see also* research quality
Ritchie, J. 243, 244

safe searching 153–154
sampling 25, 78, 81, 89, 90, 92, 95, 123, 141,
165–186, 305
cluster 182
combined sampling strategies 184–185
non-probability sampling 181–183
opportunity 182
probability sampling 179–181
purposeful 182
quota 182
research quality and 185
sample size 183–184
sampling frame 183
snowball 182
stratified 182
systematic 182
see also data quality; data reduction
scanning *see* reading strategies
Schmalz, K.J. 190

Scott's criteria for document quality 15, 21, 23, 81, 123,
146, 168, 170, 175, 185
search engine strategies 150–151
secondary analysis 29, 129
self-management strategies 40
semantic scholar 158
semiotics *see* qualitative analysis, semiotics
sensitive data 102, 103, 104, 106, 107, 114, 124, 225
sensitive topics 17, 30–31, 49, 50, 124–125, 163
skill development 16, 52–54, 307–311
academic skills 52, 53, 209, 280, 297
becoming an expert 313–314
communication skills 16
critical thinking skills 16, 17, 31–32, 196
higher level thinking skills 196, 308–310
media and information literacy skills 16, 147, 312
research skills 48, 52, 54, 309–310
search skills 17, 147, 193
understanding 'truth' 313
skimming *see* reading strategies
Snee, H. 108, 135
snowball sampling 182, 183
snowball searches 149
social media data 22, 104–105, 134–135
sources of data 125–139; *see also* academic sources of
data; artefacts as sources of data; existing research
as sources of data; personal sources of data; popular
culture sources of data; public sources of data; visual
sources of data
Spencer, L. 243
spreadsheet *see* Excel
statistical average *see* descriptive statistics,
statistical average
statistics *see* quantitative analysis
subjectivity *see* research positions, subjectivity
summarise *see* reading strategies

thematic analysis *see* framework analysis
theoretical framework 21, 24, 66, 80, 195, 280
theory 25, 56, 57–74, 80, 82
applying a critical lens to 67
applying 'theory after' 70, 74, 232, 246
applying 'theory first' 70, 74, 232, 246
data analysis and 70, 232–233, 234, 246, 250, 254
data driven 70, 233, 234, 235
deconstructing theory 59
deductive approach to 70, 232, 246
defining 25, 58–59
inductive approach to 70, 232, 246
interdisciplinary approach to 69
findings and 281, 286, 287, 289
literature review and 59, 189

middle-range theory 67–68
role of 65
types of 65–68
working with multiple theories 69
see also research paradigms;
    research positions
theory of knowledge 25, 60, 62, 63
thick description 90, 93, 94, 95
time management strategies 40
Tischer, M. 226, 227
Tisdell, E.J. 20, 126
traceability of sources 159, 212, 213, 214
tracking data 212, 220
transferability 16, 81, 83, 85, 86, 87, 90, 92–93, 166, 185;
    see also research quality
transferable skills 310, 317
triangulation 62, 69, 86, 87, 90, 91–92, 94, 258
    analyst triangulation 91
    methodological triangulation 62, 86, 87, 90, 92, 258
    theoretical triangulation 69, 91–92
    triangulation of sources 70, 91
trustworthiness 21, 72, 89, 93, 97, 122, 141, 167, 194
    of data 122, 167
    of findings 21, 72
    of research 89, 92, 93, 97, 141, 194
Twitter 21, 107, 130, 134, 158, 159, 169
types of data 18–19, 28; *see also* qualitative data;
    sources of data

UK Data Archive 156
UK Data Service 148, 225

value free 61, 94
variables 64, 181, 184, 261, 273
vases, as data 139; *see also* artefacts as sources of data
version tracking 223
visual analysis 251–251
visual ethnography 252
visual sources of data 126, 137–138, 162, 251
    checklist for evaluating visual data 138
    images and photographs 137
    museums 22, 154
    online collections 162
visualisation, of data 253, 281, 286, 291–292;
    see also data display
Vosoughi, S. 130

Wakefield, A.J. 112
website credibility 151–153, 154
world view *see* research positions
writing about theory and concepts 73–74
writing a literature review 197–209
writing a methodology *see* methodology, writing up
writing conclusions 212, 260, 290, 295–296
writing findings *see* findings, writing up
writing for a specific audience 206, 290
writing recommendations 74, 97, 296–297, 298